Reframing Europe's Future

The global financial crisis which erupted in 2008 had an astounding yet varied impact on the European Union (EU), with some countries benefiting from the crisis while others suffered. Today many more and varied voices articulate increasing frustration, dissatisfaction, distrust and cynicism with the current state of affairs in Europe.

This book addresses the challenges and failures of the European construction today from an interdisciplinary perspective. It seeks to identify the deeper, structural causes of the failure of the European project by investigating a variety of aspects, placing Europe in a historical perspective and interpreting its trajectory in a global context. In doing so it argues that the EU, the unfinished European polity, the single European market, and the set of supranational institutions, are not sustainable in their present forms.

This text will be of key interest to students and practitioners of international relations, economics, European studies, democracy and contemporary European and global challenges.

Jody Jensen is the Director of International Relations at the Institute of Social and European Studies and Senior Research Fellow at the Institute of Political Sciences at the Hungarian Academy of Sciences.

Ferenc Miszlivetz is Academic Programme Director at the Institute for Global and European Integration Studies at Corvinus University in Budapest, Scientific Advisor of the Institute for Political Sciences at the Hungarian Academy of Science and President of the board of ISES Foundation.

Routledge advances in European politics

1. **Russian Messianism**
   Third Rome, revolution,
   Communism and after
   Peter J.S. Duncan

2. **European Integration and the Postmodern Condition**
   Governance, democracy, identity
   Peter van Ham

3. **Nationalism in Italian Politics**
   The stories of the Northern League, 1980–2000
   Damian Tambini

4. **International Intervention in the Balkans since 1995**
   Edited by Peter Siani-Davies

5. **Widening the European Union**
   The politics of institutional change and reform
   Edited by Bernard Steunenberg

6. **Institutional Challenges in the European Union**
   Edited by Madeleine Hosli, Adrian van Deemen and Mika Widgrén

7. **Europe Unbound**
   Enlarging and reshaping the boundaries of the European Union
   Edited by Jan Zielonka

8. **Ethnic Cleansing in the Balkans**
   Nationalism and the destruction of tradition
   Cathie Carmichael

9. **Democracy and Enlargement in Post-Communist Europe**
   The democratisation of the general public in fifteen Central and Eastern European countries, 1991–1998
   Christian W. Haerpfer

10. **Private Sector Involvement in the Euro**
    The power of ideas
    Stefan Collignon and Daniela Schwarzer

11. **Europe**
    A Nietzschean perspective
    Stefan Elbe

12. **European Union and E-Voting**
    Addressing the European Parliament's internet voting challenge
    Edited by Alexander H. Trechsel and Fernando Mendez

13. **European Union Council Presidencies**
    A comparative perspective
    Edited by Ole Elgström

14 **European Governance and Supranational Institutions**
Making states comply
Jonas Tallberg

15 **European Union, NATO and Russia**
Martin Smith and Graham Timmins

16 **Business, The State and Economic Policy**
The case of Italy
G. Grant Amyot

17 **Europeanization and Transnational States**
Comparing Nordic central governments
Bengt Jacobsson, Per Lægreid and Ove K. Pedersen

18 **European Union Enlargement**
A comparative history
Edited by Wolfram Kaiser and Jürgen Elvert

19 **Gibraltar**
British or Spanish?
Peter Gold

20 **Gendering Spanish Democracy**
Monica Threlfall, Christine Cousins and Celia Valiente

21 **European Union Negotiations**
Processes, networks and negotiations
Edited by Ole Elgström and Christer Jönsson

22 **Evaluating Euro-Mediterranean Relations**
Stephen C. Calleya

23 **The Changing Face of European Identity**
A seven-nation study of (supra) national attachments
Edited by Richard Robyn

24 **Governing Europe**
Discourse, governmentality and European integration
William Walters and Jens Henrik Haahr

25 **Territory and Terror**
Conflicting nationalisms in the Basque country
Jan Mansvelt Beck

26 **Multilateralism, German Foreign Policy and Central Europe**
Claus Hofhansel

27 **Popular Protest in East Germany**
Gareth Dale

28 **Germany's Foreign Policy Towards Poland and the Czech Republic**
Ostpolitik revisited
Karl Cordell and Stefan Wolff

29 **Kosovo**
The politics of identity and space
Denisa Kostovicova

30 **The Politics of European Union Enlargement**
Theoretical approaches
Edited by Frank Schimmelfennig and Ulrich Sedelmeier

31 **Europeanizing Social Democracy?**
The rise of the party of European socialists
Simon Lightfoot

32 **Conflict and Change in EU Budgetary Politics**
Johannes Lindner

33 **Gibraltar, Identity and Empire**
E.G. Archer

34 **Governance Stories**
Mark Bevir and R.A.W. Rhodes

35 **Britain and the Balkans**
1991 until the present
Carole Hodge

36 **The Eastern Enlargement of the European Union**
John O'Brennan

37 **Values and Principles in European Union Foreign Policy**
Edited by Sonia Lucarelli and Ian Manners

38 **European Union and the Making of a Wider Northern Europe**
Pami Aalto

39 **Democracy in the European Union**
Towards the emergence of a public sphere
Edited by Liana Giorgi, Ingmar Von Homeyer and Wayne Parsons

40 **European Union Peacebuilding and Policing**
Michael Merlingen with Rasa Ostrauskaite

41 **The Conservative Party and European Integration since 1945**
At the heart of Europe?
N.J. Crowson

42 **E-Government in Europe**
Re-booting the state
Edited by Paul G. Nixon and Vassiliki N. Koutrakou

43 **EU Foreign and Interior Policies**
Cross-pillar politics and the social construction of sovereignty
Stephan Stetter

44 **Policy Transfer in European Union Governance**
Regulating the utilities
Simon Bulmer, David Dolowitz, Peter Humphreys and Stephen Padgett

45 **The Europeanization of National Political Parties**
Power and organizational adaptation
Edited by Thomas Poguntke, Nicholas Aylott, Elisabeth Carter, Robert Ladrech and Kurt Richard Luther

46 **Citizenship in Nordic Welfare States**
Dynamics of choice, duties and participation in a changing Europe
Edited by Bjørn Hvinden and Håkan Johansson

47 **National Parliaments within the Enlarged European Union**
From victims of integration to competitive actors?
Edited by John O'Brennan and Tapio Raunio

48 **Britain, Ireland and Northern Ireland since 1980**
The totality of relationships
Eamonn O'Kane

49 **The EU and the European Security Strategy**
Forging a global Europe
Edited by Sven Biscop and Jan Joel Andersson

50 **European Security and Defence Policy**
An implementation perspective
Edited by Michael Merlingen and Rasa Ostrauskaitė

51 **Women and British Party Politics**
Descriptive, substantive and symbolic representation
Sarah Childs

52 **The Selection of Ministers in Europe**
Hiring and firing
Edited by Keith Dowding and Patrick Dumont

53 **Energy Security**
Europe's new foreign policy challenge
Richard Youngs

54 **Institutional Challenges in Post-Constitutional Europe**
Governing change
Edited by Catherine Moury and Luís de Sousa

55 **The Struggle for the European Constitution**
A past and future history
Michael O'Neill

56 **Transnational Labour Solidarity**
Mechanisms of commitment to cooperation within the European Trade Union Movement
Katarzyna Gajewska

57 **The Illusion of Accountability in the European Union**
Edited by Sverker Gustavsson, Christer Karlsson, and Thomas Persson

58 **The European Union and Global Social Change**
A critical geopolitical-economic analysis
József Böröcz

59 **Citizenship and Collective Identity in Europe**
Ireneusz Pawel Karolewski

60 **EU Enlargement and Socialization**
Turkey and Cyprus
Stefan Engert

61 **The Politics of EU Accession**
Turkish challenges and Central European experiences
Edited by Lucie Tunkrová and Pavel Šaradín

62 **The Political History of European Integration**
The hypocrisy of democracy-through-market
Hagen Schulz-Forberg and Bo Stråth

63 **The Spatialities of Europeanization**
Power, governance and territory in Europe
Alun Jones and Julian Clark

64 **European Union Sanctions and Foreign Policy**
When and why do they work?
Clara Portela

65 **The EU's Role in World Politics**
A retreat from liberal internationalism
Richard Youngs

66 **Social Democracy and European Integration**
The politics of preference formation
Edited by Dionyssis Dimitrakopoulos

67 **The EU Presence in International Organizations**
Edited by Spyros Blavoukos and Dimitris Bourantonis

68 **Sustainability in European Environmental Policy**
Challenge of governance and knowledge
Edited by Rob Atkinson, Georgios Terizakis and Karsten Zimmermann

69 **Fifty Years of EU-Turkey Relations**
A Sisyphean story
Edited by Armagan Emre Çakir

70 **Europeanization and Foreign Policy**
State diversity in Finland and Britain
Juha Jokela

71 **EU Foreign Policy and Post-Soviet Conflicts**
Stealth intervention
Nicu Popescu

72 **Switzerland in Europe**
Continuity and change in the Swiss political economy
Edited by Christine Trampusch and André Mach

73 **The Political Economy of Noncompliance**
Adjusting to the single European Market
Scott Nicholas Siegel

74 **National and European Foreign Policy**
Towards Europeanization
Edited by Reuben Wong and Christopher Hill

75 **The European Union Diplomatic Service**
Ideas, preferences and identities
Caterina Carta

76 **Poland within the European Union**
New awkward partner or new heart of Europe?
Aleks Szczerbiak

77 **A Political Theory of Identity in European Integration**
Memory and policies
Catherine Guisan

78 **EU Foreign Policy and the Europeanization of Neutral States**
Comparing Irish and Austrian foreign policy
Nicole Alecu de Flers

79 **Party System Change in Western Europe**
Gemma Loomes

80 **The Second Tier of Local Government in Europe**
Provinces, counties, départements and landkreise in comparison
Hubert Heinelt and Xavier Bertrana Horta

81 **Learning from the EU Constitutional Treaty**
Democratic constitutionalism beyond the nation-state
Ben Crum

82 **Human Rights and Democracy in EU Foreign Policy**
The cases of Ukraine and Egypt
Rosa Balfour

83 **Europeanization, Integration and Identity**
A social constructivist fusion perspective on Norway
Gamze Tanil

84 **The Impact of European Integration on Political Parties**
Beyond the permissive consensus
Dimitri Almeida

85 **Civic Resources and the Future of the European Union**
Victoria Kaina and Ireneusz Pawel Karolewski

86 **The Europeanization of National Foreign Policies towards Latin America**
Lorena Ruano

87 **The EU and Multilateral Security Governance**
Sonia Lucarelli, Luk Van Langenhove and Jan Wouters

88 **Security Challenges in the Euro-Med Area in the 21st Century**
Mare Nostrum
Stephen Calleya

89 **Society and Democracy in Europe**
Oscar W. Gabriel and Silke Keil

90 **European Union Public Health Policy**
Regional and global trends
Edited by Scott L. Greer and Paulette Kurzer

91 **The New Member States and the European Union**
Foreign policy and Europeanization
Edited by Michael Baun and Dan Marek

92 **The Politics of Ratification of EU Treaties**
Carlos Closa

93 **Europeanization and New Member States**
A comparative social network analysis
Flavia Jurje

94 **National Perspectives on Russia**
European foreign policy in the making
Maxine David, Jackie Gower and Hiski Haukkala

95 **Institutional Legacies of Communism**
Change and continuities in minority protection
Edited by Karl Cordell, Timofey Agarin and Alexander Osipov

96 **Sustainable Development and Governance in Europe**
The evolution of the discourse on sustainability
Edited by Pamela M. Barnes and Thomas C. Hoerber

97 **Social Networks and Public Support for the European Union**
Elizabeth Radziszewski

98 **The EU's Democracy Promotion and the Mediterranean Neighbours**
Orientation, ownership and dialogue in Jordan and Turkey
Ann-Kristin Jonasson

99 **New Democracies in Crisis?**
A comparative constitutional study of the Czech Republic, Hungary, Poland, Romania and Slovakia
Paul Blokker

100 **Party Attitudes Towards the EU in the Member States**
Parties for Europe, parties against Europe
Nicolò Conti

101 **The European Union and Occupied Palestinian Territories**
State-building without a state
Dimitris Bouris

102 **Portugal in the European Union**
Assessing twenty-five years of integration experience
Laura C. Ferreira-Pereira

103 **Governance and European Civil Society**
Governmentality, discourse and NGOs
Acar Kutay

104 **The EU, Migration and the Politics of Administrative Detention**
Edited by Michela Ceccorulli and Nicola Labanca

105 **Political Representation in the European Union**
Democracy in a time of crisis
Edited by Sandra Kröger

106 **New Approaches to EU Foreign Policy**
Edited by Maciej Wilga and Ireneusz Pawel Karolewski

107 **Democracy, Law and Religious Pluralism in Europe**
Secularism and post-secularism
Edited by Ferran Requejo and Camil Ungureanu

108 **Contemporary Spanish Foreign Policy**
Edited by David Garcia and Ramon Pacheco Pardo

109 **Reframing Europe's Future**
Challenges and failures of the European construction
Edited by Jody Jensen and Ferenc Miszlivetz

Reframing Europe's Future
Challenges and failures of the European construction

Edited by Jody Jensen and Ferenc Miszlivetz

LONDON AND NEW YORK

First published 2015
by Routledge
2 Park Square, Milton Park, Abingdon, Oxfordshire OX14 4RN

and by Routledge
711 Third Avenue, New York, NY 10017

First issued in paperback 2016

Routledge is an imprint of the Taylor & Francis Group, an informa business

© 2015 Jody Jensen and Ferenc Miszlivetz

The right of Jody Jensen and Ferenc Miszlivetz to be identified as the authors of the editorial matter, and of the authors for their individual chapters, has been asserted in accordance with sections 77 and 78 of the Copyright, Designs and Patents Act 1988.

All rights reserved. No part of this book may be reprinted or reproduced or utilised in any form or by any electronic, mechanical, or other means, now known or hereafter invented, including photocopying and recording, or in any information storage or retrieval system, without permission in writing from the publishers.

Trademark notice: Product or corporate names may be trademarks or registered trademarks, and are used only for identification and explanation without intent to infringe.

British Library Cataloguing in Publication Data
A catalogue record for this book is available from the British Library

Library of Congress Cataloging in Publication Data
Reframing Europe's future : challenges and failures of the European construction / edited by Jody Jensen and Ferenc Miszlivetz.
   pages cm. – (Routledge advances in European politics)
   Includes bibliographical references and index.
   1. European Union. 2. European Union countries–Politics and government–21st century. 3. European Union countries–Economic conditions–21st century. I. Jensen, Jody. II. Miszlivetz, Ferenc.
   JN30.R446 2014
   341.242'2–dc23   2014012393

ISBN 13: 978-1-138-23822-0 (pbk)
ISBN 13: 978-1-138-77988-4 (hbk)

Typeset in Times New Roman
by Wearset Ltd, Boldon, Tyne and Wear

Contents

List of figures	xiv
List of tables	xvi
Notes on contributors	xvii
Introduction	1
JODY JENSEN AND FERENC MISZLIVETZ	

PART I
Landscape during crisis: reframing interpretations and expectations   5

1   **Europe: an epistemological crisis**   7
GYÖRGY SCHÖPFLIN

2   **Geopolitical scenarios for European integration: the decades to come**   19
JÓZSEF BÖRÖCZ

3   **Like a phoenix from the ashes: looking for a constitutional moment in crisis**   35
DORIS WYDRA AND SONJA PUNTSCHER RIEKMANN

4   **Disruption or consolidation? Ideological orthodoxies and heresies**   53
JODY JENSEN

PART II
Economic, financial and monetary aspects of the EU crisis 71

5 The cost of fiscal disunion in Europe and the new model of fiscal federalism 73
GUIDO MONTANI

6 From democratic dissatisfaction to financial crisis 93
DÓRA GYŐRFFY

7 The origin and characteristics of the Euro crisis and solutions 115
TIBOR PALÁNKAI

PART III
Landscape in the 'peripheries': inside and outside the EU 137

8 Anatomy of the Euro-crisis 139
ANNAMARIA ARTNER

9 Does austerity prevail over democracy? Two bad models: Italy and Greece 152
FEDERICO RAMPINI

10 Yugoslav and EU decline: the dynamics of dissolution and sovereignty reframed 160
STEFANO BIANCHINI

PART IV
Citizenship and democracy in Europe 179

11 The crisis of the Euro, the crisis of the European Union and the crisis of democracy in Europe 181
PHILIPPE C. SCHMITTER

12 The life and death of democracies 189
STUART HOLLAND

13 Freedom, citizenship, culture and the changing role of the intellectual class: a European perspective 207
STEVE AUSTEN

PART V
**The future of Europe: navigating between national
sovereignty and democratic cosmopolitanism** 221

14 **The EU and the quest for political union** 223
JAAP HOEKSMA

15 **Europe between two worlds** 237
ELEMÉR HANKISS

16 **The post-Euromaidan future for Europe** 249
FERENC MISZLIVETZ

Index 260

Figures

2.1	Trajectories in global economic weight: the EU and its main competitors, 1950–2008	22
2.2	Growth projections under Scenario 0: EU membership unchanged. Forward projection by fifty years, based on 1951–2008 patterns	27
2.3	Growth projections under Scenario 2: *North-Atlantica* and its competitors. Forward projection by fifty years, based on 1951–2008 patterns	29
2.4	Growth projections under Scenario 3: *Northern Eurasia* and its competitors. Forward projection by fifty years, based on 1951–2008 patterns	31
4.1	Confidence in the global economy, global cooperation and global governance	54
4.2	Predictions of greatest disruptions over the next 12 months	54
6.1	Trust and satisfaction in the EU, 2004–2011	94
6.2	Satisfaction with democracy and fiscal balance in the EU-12, 1998–2007	99
6.3	Satisfaction with democracy in the CEE-10, 2002–2007	99
6.4	Public debt in the CEE-10, 2002–2007 (% of GDP)	100
6.5	Credit to private sector in the CEE-10, 2002–2008 (% of GDP)	101
6.6	Public and private debt in the CEE-10, 2007/2008	101
6.7	Public and private debt in the CEE-8, 2007/2008	102
6.8	Trust in public institutions in Hungary, 2006	104
8.1	Harmonized index of consumer prices, January 1996–September 2012 (1996=100)	143
8.2	Balance of non-EU27 trade, 1999–2011 (millions of Euro)	144
8.3	Balance of trade with EU27, 1999–2011 (millions of Euro)	145
8.4	Trade balance with Germany, 1999–2011 (millions of Euro)	146
8.5	Current account, balance of income, 1991–2011 (millions of Euro)	147
8.6	Balance of payments: current and capital account, 1991–2011 (millions of Euro)	147

8.7 Increase of the consolidated foreign claims of the French and
    German banks together in the PIIGS between June 2004 and
    March 2008 (percent)   148
8.8 Change in share of national GDP/cap to Euro12 average,
    1995–2007 (percentage point)   149
8.9 Standard deviation of GDP/cap in the Eurozone 12, 1995–2011
    (Euro per inhabitant)   150

Tables

2.1	Rank, global economic weight (share in gross world product) and top-down cumulative weight of the top fifteen political units in the world, 2008	21
15.1	Historical turning points	240
15.2	Changing rules of behaviour	241
15.3	The transition from modernity to post-modernity	242

Contributors

Annamaria Artner is an economist and a Senior Research Fellow at the Institute of World Economics at the Hungarian Academy of Sciences, and Professor at King Sigismund College. Her recent research fields are crisis, employment, the Eurozone, Ireland, Greece and Brazil.

Steve Austen is a permanent fellow at the Felix Meritis Foundation in Amsterdam. He is a columnist for *MM Nieuws* and a board member of the European House for Culture in Brussels. He is also a Senator in the European Cultural Parliament and a member of the initiative 'A Soul for Europe'.

Stefano Bianchini is Professor of East European Politics and History at the University of Bologna and the Director of the Interdisciplinary Master in East European Studies. He is the Scientific Co-director of the European Regional Master in Democracy and Human Rights at the Universities of Sarajevo and Bologna, the Director of the Institute for Studies on East Central and Balkan Europe at the University of Bologna and Vice President of the Association for Studies of Nationalities based at the Harriman Institute, Columbia University, New York.

József Böröcz is Professor of Sociology at Rutgers, the State University of New Jersey and a Research Professor of International Studies at the Péter Pázmány Catholic University. Recently, he was a Visiting Senior Fellow at the Center for the Humanities at the University of Leipzig. Some of his research interests include: comparative macrosociology, international development and its discourses, global structures, geopolitics and political economy, state socialism and emergence of supra state regional public authority in Europe.

Dóra Győrffy is an Associate Professor at the Péter Pázmány Catholic University in Hungary. Her research concerns the political economy of fiscal reforms, European monetary integration and financial globalisation.

Elemér Hankiss is a renowned scholar and Senior Researcher at the Institute of Sociology and Institute of Political Sciences at the Hungarian Academy of Sciences. He has written extensively on the values system in Hungary and Central Europe, as well as on global civilisation. His concept of *Second*

Society has been much cited in East European Studies. He has been a professor at Stanford University, the Bruges and Florence University Institutes as well as the Central European University.

Jaap Hoeksma is a philosopher of law, the Director of Euroknow and creator of the board game 'Eurocracy'. He initiated an international conference on the place of the EU in international law that was held at the Peace Palace in The Hague in June 2011. He has written a series of blogs on the Westphalian system of international relations for the website of the Peace Palace Library. In the run-up to the elections for the European Parliament in 2014, Mr Hoeksma is conducting the EU Democracy Tour, which is to result in the presentation of the first ever *Citizens' Definition of the European Union*.

Stuart Holland has been a British Labour politician and academic. He is an advisor to the EU's Economic and Social Committee. He has published widely on post Keynesian economic theory, globalisation, European integration and public policy and teaches at the Faculty of Economics of the University of Coimbra, Portugal.

Jody Jensen is a Senior Research Fellow at the Institute of Political Sciences at the Hungarian Academy of Sciences. She is also the Director of International Relations at the Institute for Social and European Studies (ISES). Her major research fields include global governance, transformation of the nation state, governing global markets and global civil society.

Ferenc Miszlivetz is a Jean Monnet Professor and a Senior Research Leader at the Institute of Political Science Institute at the Hungarian Academy of Sciences. He is the Director of the Institute for Social and European Studies, a Jean Monnet European Centre of Excellence. He holds a UNESCO Chair in Cultural Heritage Management and Sustainability. His major works are on the European construction, transformation and integration in East and Central Europe, and civil society.

Guido Montani teaches International Political Economy at the Faculty of Economics at the University of Pavia. He was General Secretary and President of the European Federalist Movement in Italy and is Vice President of the Union of European Federalists. His major fields of research and publication include: economic integration, globalisation and financial crisis.

Tibor Palánkai is a University Professor at the Corvinus University of Budapest where he was rector and an award-winning economist. He is a member of the Hungarian Academy of Sciences. His main areas of research are European economic integration and international division of labour.

Sonja Puntscher Riekmann is Professor of Political Theory with a focus on European Policy, and the Director of the Salzburg Centre of European Union Studies, a Jean Monnet Centre of Excellence. She has been a full member of the Austrian Academy of Sciences since 2006.

Federico Rampini is *la Repubblica*'s New York Bureau Chief. Previously, he served as a columnist and correspondent for *la Repubblica* in Beijing, where he inaugurated the publication's China bureau. As a special envoy, he travels frequently to India, Japan and Southeast Asia.

Philippe C. Schmitter is an Emeritus Professor of the Department of Political and Social Sciences at the European University Institute. He has published widely on comparative politics, European and Latin America regional integration, transitions from authoritarian rule and democratisation processes, and the intermediation of class, sectoral and professional interests. More recently, he has been examining the possibilities for post-liberal democracy in North America and Europe. He has won many international awards for his scholarly contributions to political science.

György Schöpflin is a member of the European Parliament from Hungary. He is formerly a Jean Monnet Professor of Politics at the University College London.

Doris Wydra is a Senior Scientist and Executive Director of the Salzburg Centre of European Union Studies (SCEUS) at the University of Salzburg. She is in charge of the management of the European Union Studies programme and teaches and researches on the European Union and integration studies.

Introduction

Jody Jensen and Ferenc Miszlivetz

Many fundamental questions have emerged since the global financial crisis began. These include how we want to live on this planet and how we want to live with each other. Questions have been raised about our present trajectory, examining the premise on which the present system is built. It is clear from the protests of people and from the 'appalled' and 'outraged' academics that something big has to change. No change simply means we will fail; therefore, change must come.

Whereas earlier crises of European integration have been endogenous in nature, the crisis which erupted in 2008 was exogenously determined by the crisis in the US. This has become a cumulative crisis in the EU as well, meaning that some countries have benefited more from the crisis whereas others have suffered. This has broken down into a clear North–South divide that has reinforced traditional stereotypes and undermined further any notions of European solidarity. In addition, one set of key actors, the epistemic community of economists and politicians, are for the first time at a near loss as to how to confront the current challenges. In previous crises, there was always a pro-integration bias to proposed solutions on which consensus was based; today that is far from clear as more and varied voices articulate increasing frustration, dissatisfaction, distrust and cynicism with the current state of affairs in Europe.

Social scientists – for good reasons – have been criticized for their failure to anticipate or foresee the fundamental economic, political and social upheavals of the past decades, or the outbreak of the global financial and debt crisis. What analysis does exist has not sufficiently addressed the relationship between globalization and democracy, governance and globalization, globalization and civic participation and engagement. Along with politicians and their experts, they were unprepared for the waves of democratic aspirations and spontaneous mass demonstrations for change of the past years from the Middle East via the US and Europe to Turkey and most recently Ukraine. The waves of protests and unrest across the regions of Mediterranean and Eastern Europe or the emergence of Occupy! movements in western countries did not fit the conventional mental frame of analysts. Caught in the logic of 'unlimited' capitalist development and the archaic nation state paradigm, political and social science analysis has remained largely confined and reduced to options within the boundaries of the nation state.

Some social scientists, including authors in this volume, promote the idea that the project of European construction has always accelerated because of periods of crisis. This assumes that crises are positive catalysts for wider and deeper integration. But since 2008 many people are now questioning whether crisis is necessarily always a good motivator for European integration. Some of the underlying questions addressed in this volume are what differentiates this crisis from previous crises, and what the present malaise reveals about the deeper, structural and systemic challenges Europe faces today. This requires, among other things, placing Europe and the European Union in a broader global context of fast-paced and powerful changes for markets, states and societies. At the same time, the distinguishing features of the present prolonged and interdependent crises must be extracted.

This volume attempts to outline what got us into crisis and also, more importantly, informs us about our options. Many of the papers included in this volume were presented at an international workshop and conference in Budapest entitled: 'Europe in the World: Crises and Responses: Navigating Europe's Future' in November 2012 sponsored by the Institute for Social and European Studies and the Péter Pázmány Catholic University. The conference participation included not only academics but figures from public life from the east and west. Other selections were solicited from public intellectuals who are daily engaged with the challenges Europe is facing. Therefore, the volume attempts to provide a balance between academic papers and insights from distinguished practitioners. This was done consciously to present a volume that is more accessible to the general public as well as to the academic community. It also presents a unique perspective from Central and Eastern Europe, new member states and EU peripheries, regarding the crisis, its perception, responses and its implications for this part of Europe that has not been adequately addressed before. This makes the volume distinct from other works on the crisis to date.

The volume tries to challenge current assumptions and notions of the free market system we know, as well as the discourse and frames through which the crisis has been viewed and analysed. The volume is inherently interdisciplinary and each section reflects a wide range of interdependent fields and approaches. The first part (Landscape during crisis: interpretations and expectations) begins with the underlying, epistemological causes of the crisis in Europe (Schöpflin) and places European developments in a global context (Böröcz, Jensen). Lessons from the historical evolution of the American republic could provide insight to current European deadlock (Wydra, Puntscher Riekmann).

Important and distinguishing aspects of the financial and monetary crisis and prospective solutions are outlined in Part II (Economic, financial and monetary aspects of the EU crisis), which delves deeper into the economic and financial costs and failures of the present monetary crisis (Montani, Győrffy, Palánkai). In this part, the presentation of both general and specifically East and Central European perspectives are in evidence, as well as proposals for reform.

The third part (Landscape in the 'peripheries') delivers a unique and important view of the crisis from the EU and European peripheries and provides more evidence of the profound regional effects of the financial crisis. Many have suggested that the financial and debt crisis with subsequent EU austerity policies is exacerbating divisions in Europe. A general approach (Artner) is presented along with two other related examples and lessons of crises and failures (Rampini, Bianchini).

One of the most serious implications of the crisis is faced in Part IV (Citizenship and democracy in Europe). The financial crisis has posed new and serious threats and challenges to the way politics functions at the EU and the nation state levels. The question is raised about the sustainability of the European construction in the present structure of EU governance (Schmitter). The present crisis is also put into the historical context and philosophical roots of democracy (Holland). There is an illuminating debate about freedom and democracy and the necessity of increased citizen participation in finding methods and means to address imbalances in the economic and political systems by validating European citizenship as a viable alternative to regressive, nationalistic tendencies that have (re)surfaced as another reaction to crisis (Austen).

Part V (The future of Europe: navigating between national sovereignty and democratic cosmopolitanism) places current European challenges in a broader cultural and historical framework, situating Europe today in terms of values and beliefs (Hankiss), and providing new proposals for moving forward (Hoeksma). The concluding essay addresses the possibilities and potential for Europe's future in a redefined geographic (global), political (national, multilevel, regional) and active, citizen-based context with the construction of a new social contract (Miszlivetz).

The wide international contributions from many fields and perspectives provide new and thought-provoking ways of looking at global, regional and national challenges. What the contributions have in common is a commitment to changing the current order while endorsing a more balanced multi-stakeholder (states, markets and society) approach to problem-solving. This means inquiring into the deeper levels and structures of the present crisis, on the values and mindsets underneath the surface, in order to find more equitable, just and sustainable solutions. The volume is designed for concerned citizens as well as for academics and practitioners. It provides a broad, interdisciplinary and accessible description and analyses of the complex and interdependent crises Europe and the world confront today.

Part I
Landscape during crisis
Reframing interpretations and expectations

1 Europe

An epistemological crisis

György Schöpflin

What we are looking at is far more than an economic crisis and far more than a crisis of European integration, even if much of the analysis chooses to explore it from this perspective. While the perspective is valid in itself, it has the consequence of hiding other processes – political, cultural, sociological – that affect the crisis and, by ignoring them, we make the solution of the crisis less likely. In short, deep changes are taking place in Europe and some of these are partly accelerated by the economic crisis, which has exposed the fragility of Western material well-being. It is in this sense that the word 'crisis' is appropriate – social realities are increasingly out of alignment with institutions and elite thinking.

The crisis has also brought into question the reliability of both state and market as the central organising principle of Western democracy. After 1945, a great deal of trust was invested in the state as rational redistributor and allocator, as well as the ultimate source of rationality. By the late 1970s, this was being questioned and the dysfunctions of the state were to be eliminated by the market. The market, therefore, was seen as the supreme source of rationality. Note here that, whereas the state is and must be a political category, the market is understood as free of politics and is a primarily economic process, albeit culture, psychology and other factors are now recognised as forming a part of market behaviour. The elevation of the market to paramount significance ignored, however, the political implications of the shift that effectively amounted to abandoning politics and political inputs into the central processes of society. Democracy was thereby reduced to something narrower, almost to being a spectator with few legitimate points to make. At the same time, the functioning of the market was naturalised and to some extent sacralised. The supreme rationality of the market ruled and was above and beyond questioning; those who did raise objections were dismissed as 'irrational' or as 'dinosaurs' or 'reactionaries'.

What is strongly suggested is that it is not sufficient to see the crisis as either an economic or a political or even a sociological one, even if all these spheres are out of alignment with how they are widely understood, but crucially that Europe is in the grip of an epistemological crisis, above all where the elites are concerned. In summary, an epistemological crisis can be diagnosed when the assumptions and discourses of a particular normativity, of a plausibility structure sustained by an elite, are out of alignment with the way in which other elites construct the world and, vitally, the social support enjoyed by the counter-elite is real and cogent. Hence those inside the liberal consensus repeatedly find themselves in contradictions that they do not, indeed cannot, recognise and when the evidence of their contradictory position is presented to them, they wave it away or ignore it.

In this instance, the cognitive world constructed by the liberal consensus cannot adequately fathom the qualities of the decorrelation and dealignment that Europe is in, a world where political elites pursue normative goals that do not correspond to, let alone respond to, the aspirations of society. The rising inequality, fear of economic deterioration and the inter-generational crisis may be the most central here. Indeed, even the term 'society' may be a misnomer, given the fragmentation of power. All of which should make it clear that those inside the consensus cannot grasp adequately why things have gone wrong and, consequently, still prescribe policies that either do nothing (at most little) or exacerbate the crisis.

The explanation that can help to clarify this state of affairs is that the liberal consensus may well have started out life as relatively open. The proposition that the 'best of left and right' traditions would generate a set of norms that would suit the conditions in Europe after the collapse of communism was persuasive and certainly helped to give the left a new lease on life by ending its suspicion of the market, as well as burying its long-standing penchant for nationalisation. What was less predictable was that in a relatively short period of time, a decade and a half, the consensus would evolve into an ideology and that, in turn, acquired the qualities of an identity. Identities do, of course, change over time, but in this instance, there was precious little incentive for change, especially as the neo-conservative embrace of market fundamentalism, that markets solve everything, coincided with the left's pro-market turn. The two – neo-liberalism and the consensus – imperceptibly merged their different approaches, not least because the left had abandoned its traditional critical stance towards the market, which then gave market-mindedness a near monopoly; certainly it was a hegemony that Gramsci would have recognised.

The principal characteristics of epistemological closure, as argued, is that those inside the box are persuaded of the correctness of their views, do not admit alternatives, regard those who emerge with counter-arguments as tiresome and certainly not as worthy adversaries. Perhaps most significantly in the current context is their propensity to grow more and more introverted and conservative (in the sense of rejecting innovation and even change). In other words, closure appears to be dynamic.

It follows that those so affected will tend to interpret events, change, processes, phenomena according to their epistemological criteria and this generally means that there is an ever greater distance between what the sociological reality happens to be and what those inside the closure think it is. There is, then, a cognitive gap.

What is notable about the liberal consensus is the constant proclamation of its openness, its commitment to diversity, to multiculturalism, to innovation and to a strong, normative concept of a single humanity. In reality, liberal consensus is increasingly nothing of the kind where openness is concerned. As it condenses its discourses, it correspondingly closes itself off from the ideas, process or inputs that might challenge or undermine its cherished ideology. Hence what we are looking at in sociological reality is not a commitment to openness etc., but to a targeted openness and so on. The consensus is open to some, but far from all; indeed intuitively I have the sense that it is less open now than it was a decade ago, but these things are hard to prove. This propensity to target specific objectives, to privilege some social groups over others, demonstrates that the universalism of the consensus is not as universal – driven by the vision of a single humanity – as it would like to claim.

A particular and rather successful instrument wielded by the protagonists of the consensus is 'politically correct' language. Clearly an aspect of insisting on morality over politics, and the association with Marxist–Leninist usage is quite deliberate, allows the consensus to silence discordant and dissenting voices without having to put forward an argument. It is taken to be self-evident and that's it. This does not, of course, mean that those holding these views stop thinking them; it's just that they are silenced. There is a more than ghostly similarity here to communism – both are reflections of monistic thought-worlds. The politically noteworthy difference is that there is no vanguard party to act as enforcer, although social pressure can be just as effective, if not more so. But like all hegemonies, these thought-worlds tend to harden and carry within them the seeds of their own weaknesses. They tend to be anti-innovative, above all because they are inclined to see themselves as an end state ('end of history'). If only the champions of political correctness were to read Bakhtin, they would know that sooner or later tightly defined systems become vulnerable to challenge from outside. We are some way from the challenge for the time being, however. What we have instead is a revitalisation of the universalist moral legislation dissected by Bauman. From the perspective of democracy as the exercise of power by the consent of the governed, two old-new problems arise. One is who has the right to define PolKorr, indeed the entirety of the liberal consensus, how can significant swathes of opinion simply be excluded (as 'populist' or 'xenophobic' or whatever) from the democratic debate? The other is that of the *quis custodiet*, who has oversight of the liberal elite to prevent the excesses? What we are looking at is, indeed, an elite construct, which – whether we approve or not – is cultural and not open to debate with a range of alternative views. Here it is worth adding that no plausibility structure lives for ever and the more tightly it is constructed, the more it moves towards monology (Bakhtin again), the more it lays itself open to a dramatic collapse.

Possibly the most damaging aspect of this is the readiness to shout 'racism' whenever one of the groups favoured by the liberal consensus comes in for criticism. There is a twofold problem here – the simultaneous denial and acceptance of collective representation and the transmission of the verbal weapon to the affected group that whatever happens to them is the result of 'racism' (the racism of the majority), with the result that the group in question acquires a greatly simplified concept of causation, and one in which it has no responsibility, or agency for which responsibility is assumed. One response to this is radicalisation.

The liberal consensus has not, I would suggest, reached the stage of Mary Douglas's enclave culture which erects a 'wall of virtue' around itself and rigidly excludes everything that does not conform. Bakhtin's monology also resembles this. What can be said, however, is that some adherents of the consensus are tending in the enclave direction. The characteristics of this particular closure are broadly structured by a commitment to human rights, democracy, the support of immigrant minorities and the LGBT community, gender equality and, to a rather more muted extent, the disabled. In all these cases, the definition of the category is entirely in the hands of those inside the closure and, in acting as a reality-defining agency, they are active in seeking to impose their reality definitions on others. Because these categories are part of a monistic system, its members can readily ignore precedents, parallels or inconsistencies that might undermine the closure. In truth, this closure is political, so that political interests and power will override external inputs that might threaten the solidity of the closure.

This can happen even when the exercise of this power goes counter to the purported values of the system – the commitment to openness is maybe the one abused most flagrantly, seeing that a closure by definition is antagonistic to new ideas, external inputs, different logics and, indeed, to alterity. In brief, the proclaimed principles and ideals of the closure, despite the assumptions to the contrary, are not universal, but are targeted at whatever suits the political aims of the members of the closure. And it goes without saying, or should, that the selection criteria of what is targeted are firmly under the control of the insiders.

There are further consequences resulting from the crisis. Liberalism, being a lineal descendant of the universalist aspirations of the European Enlightenment, always did have trouble with collective identities. In the Enlightenment scheme of things, these were destined to fade away as a transcendental universe of reason – one that invariably resembled the assumptions of those putting these ideas forward – would triumph over petty particularities. Nothing of the kind happened, of course, and even in the heyday of Enlightenment thought, there were counter-arguments and proposals put forward to challenge these assumptions, Herder's being the most obvious, for which he has been excoriated as a proto-fascist ever since. The entire history of modern nations (which are completely different from states, whatever current English usage ordains) refutes the assumption, but then those in the grip of a transcendental normativity seldom bother with evidence that undermines one's case.

If we fast-forward to the 1990s, the consensus imperceptibly took another step, this time about collectivities. Its protagonists, influenced no doubt by the 'end of history' argument, concluded that, hurray, finally these tiresome collective identities were finished and the dawn or mid-morning of universalism had arrived. This coincided with the unipolar moment, that brief decade when the US appeared to be in possession of the agenda of the world. The consensus simply integrated the 'ought' into the 'is', that collective identities should fade and, actually, they had faded. The shift from referring to states as nations simply mirrored this, consciously or not.

This shift can clearly be seen as a move into unreality, something that is generally evident when a sizeable number of people confuse the *sein* and the *sollen*, the *is* and the *ought*. In effect, and this is a further reason why it is proper to refer to an epistemological crisis, the reality that collective identities were alive and well just could not be decoded by the categories available to the consensus. Matters grew worse when it emerged that these collective identities were not only prospering, but that they were able to go on generating political and cultural power. In the context of the EU, the rise of intergovernmentalism and the nation state interest were clear enough. Outside Europe, as with China, for example, the consensus had little to say other than make disapproving noises. In a way, the inability of liberalism to find an answer to nationhood and other identity collectives is its greatest weakness, one that it cannot acknowledge, even if there is a perfectly respectable national liberal alternative around. Yes, but that throws universalism out the window and that is unacceptable, because that would force the consensus to acknowledge that the project of turning the rest of the world into etiolated imitations of the West had failed, failed in spades as a matter of fact.

In this perspective, the West's love of moral legislation for the rest of the world lives on as an aspect of the consensus. This is encountering increasing resistance and refuses to accept this resistance. This is yet another facet of the crisis. Universalism and the moral legislation are imposed within Europe as well, of course, and here the resistance is dismissed as populism, a word that currently means 'something that I don't like' (and can't fathom as to why it attracts a growing number of votes). Much the same problem is posed by religion, above all the slow realisation that, outside Europe, religion remains a powerful force and inside, religiousness – including believing without belonging – may be on the increase.

What follows from this is that liberalism, as currently understood, tends to see these collective identities as deviant or, the worst-case scenario, as proto-fascist or even crypto-fascist. Note that the term 'fascist' has nothing to do with historical fascism à la Mussolini, but has become a generic word of condemnation in the liberal vocabulary. This is precisely because it has been torn from its historical roots; it can be applied freely to any phenomenon or process that the user dislikes.

Another aspect of the epistemological crisis can be found in the strikingly contradictory view of the state in the assumptions of liberal universalism. As liberals, they are hostile to etatism and believe that individual interactions are sufficient to ensure whatever it is that liberal universalism wants to ensure – life, the universe and everything. In their moral legislative role, on the other hand, the same reality-defining agency looks to the state to enforce moral regulation. An incontrovertible example is the way in which legal instruments are used to punish Holocaust denial and anything that can be squeezed into the category of hate speech – a category that is necessarily subjective and flexible. It also has the advantage that it can be made retroactive and thereby rewrite the past.

On the other hand, the sections of society that do not identify with this universalising morality try to find refuge elsewhere. They can do this in a variety of ways, the most obvious of which is the opportunity structure provided by democracy – to vote for another party, one that does not espouse moralising. The universalists respond by labelling them 'populist' and endow populism with all the qualities of darkness that they can muster – notably that they are intolerant, racist, xenophobic and so on. What this labelling rather misses, however, is the linkage between populist and people, that by demonising the populists, they also, not all that indirectly, demonise the people. And that raises very interesting questions about the kind of democracy that the universalists favour, one without people, presumably, because people have the pesky habit of harbouring aspirations at variance with those of the universalising elites.

Anti-politics

This raises the problem of anti-politics. Anti-politics is, in brief, about creating a political world in which there is no further conflict, because the overwhelming majority agree on the basic principles of what is 'good', i.e. the moral content of the elite belief system has been integrated by society. Both the criteria of deciding what is good and their application have come together in a kind of unity. Because notionally there is such wide-ranging agreement, there are no serious problems with the elite-led quality of this idealised system. Note that here too that the *sein* and the *sollen* are seriously confused. Anti-politics, however, mixes the ideals of the few with the aspirations of the many, but being elite-led despises the latter, hence the charges of populism.

At the institutional level, left and right seem to be in broad agreement on this, many decisions – as we shall see – are outsourced to legal, to technocratic, to bureaucratic decision making, to NGOs, and to the market. In all of these areas of power, conflict is either concealed or it is settled opaquely or it is declared non-conflictual, thereby adding to the spaces of depoliticisation. From the liberal elite's perspective, in real rather than rhetorical terms, this is advantageous because it allows the liberal ethos to reign and rule unchallenged – it is unchallenged because the possible modes of challenge have been marginalised.

In political reality, because this system of thought does not enjoy hegemony, let alone monopoly, it is imposed with strong discursivity by an elite that sees itself as a Leninist vanguard, albeit it has no Cheka to back it up, even if it would vigorously reject the analogy. But the evidence, if not compelling, is at least thought-provoking. The entire edifice of the PolKorr imposes a language and a form of thinking that cannot, and may not, be deconstructed. Attempts to do so are ignored or shouted down and those who adopt this line of argument are in effect expelled from the general conversation. The outcome is that the range of political action is curtailed, just as it was under communism. Of course there are substantial differences, there are no Gulags, no all-pervasive secret police, secret courts, even if surveillance is intensifying all the time. Still, where the analogy holds is in the depoliticisation. Under communism, the party had a monopoly of political decision making. In the realm of the liberal consensus, there are indeed inputs from a wide variety of sources, but the fundamentals of the system are taboo and thus placed beyond questioning. To anyone who knows the contours of late communism, there are enough similarities for this to be alarming.

So the question can be put in this way, can one have politics without conflict? Yes, if we are in the grip of myths of social harmony, that we have nearly reached a conflict-free unity. The very different reality is a nuisance, but can be overcome with a little effort. This, it would appear, is the underlying normativity of the liberal consensus.

The state

All states are not alike, they never were, and the same is true for polities and political systems. This is important, because it means that there is no political monoculture as yet, so that alternatives can be found and used as counter-examples. The liberal consensus prefers to look the other way when these counter-examples are cited or to treat them as temporary anomalies. Real alternatives are not permissible, they cannot be in a thought-world governed by a single mode of discourse, the moral monism so feared by Isaiah Berlin among others.

Yet what the liberal consensus appears unable to notice is that it is under challenge not only from those who would argue that democracy cannot be reduced to a single ordering principle – the particular hegemonic variant of liberalism now current – but also from those who are either indifferent to democracy or hostile to it. These latter forces are weakening the state in ways that are recognised at the empirical level, but are seldom seen as a part of the crisis of the state. We can begin from the narrative of the Weberian state, that the state controls the monopoly of violence within its frontiers, that there is a uniform distribution of authority and that the state is the ultimate source of rationality.

Globalisation, however, has begun to erode this model of the state, meaning that it is less effective in taxing, listing and controlling the population than previously. In effect, growing numbers are escaping the purview of the state as refugees, migrants, neo-nomads, including high-status migrants; tax nomads, tax shelters are reducing the income of the state and cyberspace is eroding the role of the state as a source of rationality. What we are seeing is a process where high-status economic actors have moved beyond the control of even high-capacity Western states, mimicking the low-status nomads and migrants who are doing likewise. The irony is that the ideology of liberal consensus, with its privileging the freedom of the market, helps to sustain this environment. To the liberals may be added the libertarians who regard the state as a form of theft, a phenomenon admittedly more common in the US than in Europe.

James C. Scott (2009) in his *The Art of Not Being Governed* identifies a social and political process to the effect that sections of the population heavily burdened by the exactions of the state would move beyond its reach. His area of investigation is, broadly, the hill country between Nagaland and western China, but his insight can be applied to contemporary conditions (of which he may or may not approve). Whereas historically it was primarily people who moved to escape the state, and this was as true of Europe and Russia as of Southeast Asia, with globalisation this has been the behaviour of capital.

What is noteworthy about this worldwide process of capital escaping the control of the taxing and supervising state is that it fits neatly into all the assumptions of interest maximisation and rationality. It is entirely rational for a corporation to establish a tax regime that ensures that it does not pay tax on the profits that it generated in a high or medium tax jurisdiction when there are others with very low or even zero tax rates, i.e. offshore tax shelters. This may be hard on the state and its citizens, but as long as it is legal, the corporation does not have to worry. The market is king and all issues of ethics are subordinate to interest maximisation.

Several points are worth making here. First, there is the grand historical irony that it was Marx and the communists who proclaimed the withering away of the state, yet it is capitalism – some call it vulture capitalism – that is doing the real damage. Second, those who remove their (vast) legal profits from the control of the democratic state are no different structurally from the Russian and other former Soviet oligarchs who are doing likewise. The difference lies in how the money was acquired in the first place, by more or less legal activities in Western democracies and by blatant asset stripping in the former Soviet Union. Third, the money-making industry sees to it that there is next no trickle down. At best, there are jobs in the finance and ancillary industries that become not wholly unlike Russian-style asset stripping, except that it is legal though hideously complex. In real terms, it steadily siphons off the assets of those not in the finance industry, like the savings of the middle classes. Fourth, in a peculiar kind of way the process described here mimics civil society or, to be more accurate, brings into being semi-civil and uncivil society. It is semi-civil, because it is legal or at least at the margins of legality or it can be regarded as uncivil because it cares nothing for the rest of society.

This market, then, generated autonomous capital that has acquired considerable political power that it uses to ensure that states do not impose regulations that would curtail its activities. All sites of power do something analogous, but what makes this different is that bases of this power are already beyond the limits of the state and are based on weak states that lack the capacity to supervise them. Short of reimposing colonial rule, something that liberalism and capital would do everything to prevent anyway, there is very little that the affected democratic states can do. The issue raises interesting questions about state sovereignty and whether it can be sustained in its present form. The process points towards another factor. The protagonists of the market argue their case in economic terms, but what we have seen in the last two decades is that economic power will generally be converted into political power in order to secure the reproduction of the system that gave rise to this new-found political power in the first place. It should be added that capital does continue to engage with the state, and does so from a significantly more powerful position than in the past.

The primary aim of this engagement is, as argued, that regulation on the free movement of capital and the autonomy of the sector should be as light as possible. To this end, those in the sector have developed a discourse and established the ancillary support system – lobbies, PR firms, accountants, financial advisors – to deploy the discursivity and to provide it with legitimacy. Overcoming the activities of regulators, finding loopholes and so on, is a key dimension of this. Given the rewards, the sector has been able to cream off a sizeable section of the talented and is regularly able to outfox the state. The state, broadly speaking, has been unable to meet this challenge to its power and equally importantly to its capacity and effectiveness. The reality is that the actions of the capital sector erode, if not actually undermine, citizenship by creating massive disparities. This threatens democracy itself. The rise of so-called populist parties is one of the consequences, as we have seen.

At the same time, the state is still the ultimate guarantor of legality and the legal system, of property, and of contracts. It sustains a legal system that is necessary for the continued functioning of the system. This creates a striking tension between the two, that capital disdains the state, but uses it for its purposes and blackmails it by the too-big-to-fail argument. This contradiction too is a part of the epistemological crisis that the liberal consensus must deal with, because society suffers as a result through its disempowerment.

This dissection of the role of capital should be seen in the overall context of the argument that Europe is grappling with an epistemological crisis. The activity of capital has created patterns that gravely weaken the equality of citizenship, including civic solidarity and trust, without which citizenship is worth little. On the other hand, the hegemonic discourses mask this sociological and political reality. The intellectual toolkit of the liberal consensus cannot deal with this and analogous phenomena. Interestingly, the somewhat tepid revival of curiosity about Marx and his analysis of capitalism has yet to produce anything that might represent a breakthrough in thinking. And the European Left, which feels itself at home in the embrace of the liberal consensus, abandoned its belief in Marxism far too recently to be comfortable with it again, quite apart from the intellectual failure, as well as much else, represented by the collapse of communism.

The return of evil

There is another dimension to this crisis that seldom receives much attention. The liberalism that we have today has basically abandoned its Enlightenment foundations in an unexpected fashion. Enlightenment rationality might have taken over great bundles of assumptions from Christianity – the central one being that history has a purpose, human betterment, and linearity – but in one crucial respect it also innovated. The banishing of evil also meant the abandonment of absolutes other than reason itself, but that was always too varied and contingent to function effectively as an absolute. This created a two centuries long space for liberalism to stand for tolerance and progress, implying that history has no end.

This abjuring of absolutes and denial of evil – evil cannot coexist with a faith in human improvement – was quietly abandoned in the early 1990s. And it was certainly tacit, even if the response to Fukuyama's essay made a good deal of noise. There were several steps in this process. First, there was the collapse of communism, which eventually (a rather short eventually) left social democracy dangling, with nowhere to go. The second was the helplessness of Western Europe when it came to dealing with the aftermath of communism. Dazzled by the peaceful transition almost everywhere, it had no answers to the collapse of Yugoslavia and, such was my personal experience, was not ready to listen to arguments that might have prevented the mass killing. The implication is that, when confronted with what appeared inexplicable, how could the former Yugoslavs not respond to universal liberalism? The answer was 'ancient hatreds' or 'irrationality' or 'ethnic entrepreneurs', all of them with the presence of evil discernibly visible behind them. No one formulated it in these terms at the time; after all, to have done so would have meant confronting the West's own haplessness.

The third step was the similarly silent proclamation of the Holocaust as absolute evil. This proved to be a major step. It rehabilitated evil as an accepted category in European thought and, at the same time, provided a firm answer to the challenge of post-modernity, that everything is text, that we do not have even rationality as a definitive and hard system by which to orientate our lives. If there is evil, obviously, then universal reason has failed; and if there is absolute evil, then logically there must also be lesser evil.

Liberalism took on these categories of thought, again more tacitly than anything else, and this reception proved to be something of a liberation from the dilemma enunciated by Isaiah Berlin, the problem of incommensurability of some values. It achieved this by allowing liberalism to target certain values as positive and others as negative, not actually declaring them 'evil', but the underlying assumption set was there. It also made liberal universalism more focused and allowed West Europeans to acknowledge their colonial pasts, with profuse apologies, but to side-step the problem of unequal power relations whether as between the West and 'the rest' or, equally, as between European states and cultures. The danger of moral monism that this shift represented was not noticed or was ignored or dismissed, even though – as Isaiah Berlin made amply clear – it was precisely this moral monism that was responsible for Soviet totalitarianism.

The bounded universalism of the consensus further creates opportunities to deal with the difficulty that social democracy could never solve – the flourishing of collective identities that are a constant impediment to universalism. In sum, Western democratic collectivities are declared to be 'post-national', therefore, their cultural particularities are benign, maybe folkloric, whereas the Central Europeans (and this is where we came in with Yugoslavia) are suspect, far more so than the West Europeans. Thus when a political movement (Scotland, Catalonia) seeks state independence, this is disliked, but not condemned in the terms reserved for the Central Europeans. There is no consistency in this. The sociological reality that a discursively constructed identity that cannot be categorised as anything other than ethnic lives on in France or England or anywhere else in Western Europe is simply screened out.

Finally, the 'hard' quality of the new evil made the liberal consensus much more operational than before. The superimposition of morality over politics was a further advantage, because it gave the consensus the method for ignoring tiresome issues like popular sovereignty and, the old dilemma, what happens when a political community opts for illiberalism, as it is currently doing in statistically (and politically) significant numbers.

Thus the operationability of the consensus paradoxically produced a bounded universalism. Certain groups had the backing of the quietly redefined liberalism, like some minorities (immigrants, Roma, LGBT), but not others (historic and linguistic minorities, the losers of globalisation). The social exclusion of some was condemned, but that of others, like the traditional manual working class, could be ignored. Most interestingly, the slow decline of the economic security of the middle classes, coupled with the emergence of the super-rich and their ability to shift policies to their advantage, could be ignored.

The reality of this redistributive injustice seemingly troubled the consensus not at all. The new liberalism has opted for freedom over equality, ignores the tension that was at the heart of the left in the 1945–1991 era, and is not concerned with consequences; conceivably this may have been an implicit reaction (an overreaction?) to the extreme unfreedom practised by communism and a sensibility that it was this that made the utopian project of the left impossible. The proposition that there could be an equality of freedom plays no role in this kind of thinking and that the ideal goal of 'progressive' thought is to strive to maintain an equilibrium between the two is likewise absent. The outcome, the staggering inequalities and consequent limitations on freedom, has yet to be confronted. The consensus remains unimpressed, though it is now beginning to be aware of the political implications of redistributive injustice as the vote for those dismissed as 'populists' has begun to rise throughout Europe.

The present inequalities are being reproduced and, given current assumptions, this cannot even be perceived adequately. Furthermore, the new global structures make it impossible, or at least uniquely difficult, to find a way out. In summary, European modernity assumed that growth would persist and thereby secure permanent upward mobility and/or a steady incremental access to materials goods that would be passed on from one generation to the next. This assumption has come apart, sizeable sections of society are, at best, level pegging, but more likely facing a shrinking disposable income, a decline in their capital accumulation – social, cultural as well as material – and they are no longer able to transmit this to the next generation. In a word, progress is over; perhaps the word 'progress' should be underlined here. If this proposition is even halfway accurate, and *ceteris paribus* this seems plausible, then all the major European political assumptions about a linear development towards a better future are best discarded. Radically new thinking is needed, but this is seldom available or, if it is offered, it is ignored.

Bibliography

Berlin, Isaiah (1998) 'Value Pluralism', Available: www.cs.utexas.edu/~vl/notes/berlin.html.

Fukuyama, Francis (2012) 'The Future of History: Can Liberal Democracy Survive the Decline of the Middle Class?', *Foreign Affairs*, January/February.

Krastev, Ivan (2010) 'A Retired Power', *The American Interest*, July/August.

Malik, Kenan (2000) 'Let Them Die', *Prospect*, November.

Mouffe, Chantal (2005) 'The "End of Politics" and the Challenge of Right-wing Populism', in Panizza, Francisco (ed.) *Populism and the Mirror of Democracy*, London: Verso.

Mulgan, Geoff (2007) 'Mary Douglas Remembered', *Prospect*, no. 135, June.

Savoie, Donald J. (2010) *Power: Where Is It?*, Montreal: McGill-Queen's University Press.

Schöpflin, George (2012) *Politics, Illusions, Fallacies*, Tallinn: Tallinn University Press.

Scott, James C. (1998) *Seeing like a State: How Certain Schemes to Improve the Human Condition Have Failed*, New Haven: Yale University Press.

Scott, James C. (2009) *The Art of Not Being Governed*, New Haven: Yale University Press.

Taleb, Nassim Nicholas (2007) *The Black Swan: The Impact of the Highly Improbable*, London: Penguin.

Townsend, Mark (2011) 'Searchlight Poll Finds Huge Support For Far Right "If They Gave Up Violence"', *The Guardian*, 27 February.

Urry, John (2003) *Global Complexity*, Cambridge: Polity.

2 Geopolitical scenarios for European integration
The decades to come

József Böröcz

In this chapter, I undertake two tasks. First, I summarize my position regarding the question of just what the European Union is, via a *longue-durée*, geopolitical reading of the history of the emergence of the capitalist world-system as a global fact and the role of west European actors (states, capital and citizenries) in that process. Second, I outline three alternative scenarios for the near future of west European integration as it attempts, I argue, to maintain, or perhaps even increase, its global economic weight in the face of significant historical difficulties and external competition.

I have observed a series of lacunae in three distinct scholarly literatures. First, doing research on the transformation of the eastern half of Europe and in northern Eurasia after state socialism, I noticed that analysis of the astounding power of foreign corporations in taking over the productive capacities, as well as the deep involvement of the European Union and its most powerful member states, in the crafting of a political, legal, discursive, cultural and emotional environment conducive to such an externally led transformation in eastern Europe, was almost entirely absent from scholarly writing about the transformation.

Second, the abundant literature on the EU seems to sidestep what appeared to be, from the perspective of the global historical sociology of power and authority, the most fundamental question at hand: namely, just what is the EU? With most scholarship on the EU focused internally – treating their object almost exclusively as an amalgam of its member states – a workable theory of the external form, relations and effects of the EU seemed to be noticeably absent from the extant literature. Mahua Sarkar and I co-authored and published a study (Böröcz and Sarkar 2005) on these twin subjects, arguing that the EU's success was a fundamentally relational phenomenon. It had to do with the EU's ability to manage an intricate network of geopolitical actors – mainly states and intergovernmental organizations of great global sway – that had significant executive capacities. The EU was a remarkably interesting political animal that managed effectively to externalize the task of the enforcement of its legal output.

If we examine that network-based strategy of distributed enforcement – a geopolitical arrangement that is, we argue, unique to the EU – we find that it is rooted in the distinctively central role the states of Western Europe (today, without any exception, members of the EU) had played in the specific history of the four-and-a-half centuries of global 'governance' before the emergence of the EU, commonly known as colonialism. Attention to that historical rootedness brought me to a third lacuna: the absence of a specific link between the history of colonialism on the one hand and the EU, leading to a somewhat imprecise and flattened conceptualization of 'Europe', a key operative concept in postcolonial and anticolonial theory.

The dismantling of the colonial system involved the drastic reorganization of global governance. From a tightly hierarchical network structure with west European powers at its center, the post-independence period saw a shift to European regionalism (Polanyi 1945, Polanyi-Levitt 2004). In response to the triple challenge of the impossibility of war among west European societies, the precipitous loss of colonial power (and the resulting reduction in the effective control over global resources by west European actors) and the appearance of state socialism as a regional threat on their eastern borders, west European societies reinvented the idea of a pan-Europe.

The resulting supra-state public authority, the European Union, cannot be considered over its six-decades-long history as a state because it lacks, and explicitly excludes, the possibility of the construction of an executive apparatus of its own below 'Brussels'. Hence the EU is a historically new, and unique, supra-state public authority, one that even has a few vaguely quasi-democratic features, although clearly not fully comparable to any liberal-democratic state in terms of its political system, especially because of its deficiencies in providing formal avenues for accountability.

With its budget under 1 percent of the total GDP (and decreasing), the 'EU-as-a-state' would be an astonishing outlier among the world's states, whose budgets account for between 10.4 percent and 156.4 percent of their gross domestic products, with a mean of 35.1 percent and a median of 33.3 percent (Heritage Foundation 2013).[1] This is especially so if we were to contrast the EU to its twenty-seven member states where the range in terms of state spending as percentages of the GDP is 34.6 to 56.1 percent, with a mean of 46.3 percent and a median of 48.4 percent (Heritage Foundation 2013).[2]

The EU can only be described as a weakling in the company of states with, on average, forty-six times less redistributive power than its member states. As a result, the European Union has drastically less of an economic capacity to act independently than its members. As such, this supra-state political entity can be seen as a real-life embodiment of a neoliberal dream of a quasi-state. That quasi-state supra-state, however, has a set of powerful geopolitical interests in the implementation of its legal regulations, something that it does by subcontracting it to its member states, and the pursuance of its overall hegemony in the global system. A key ingredient of that subcontracted assurance of hegemony is the total economic sway of the states that constitute the EU. Economic weight is, hence, an immediate and absolutely pressing concern for the European Union. I argue that, to a very large extent, pursuit of global economic weight explains the EU's behavior in the global realm.

Pursuit of global economic weight

Global economic weight can perhaps be best understood as a geopolitical equivalent of market share, one of the most coveted dimensions of growth by for-profit corporations. Empirically, I define it as the share of the GDP (or any other estimate of economic performance) of a given public authority as percentage of the total gross world product. In attempting to apprehend it empirically, I rely on the widely used Geary-Khamis Purchasing Power Parity estimates produced by British economic historian Angus Maddison.[3] *Ceteris paribus*, the greater share of the global economic output occurs within the borders of any public authority, the greater the geopolitical sway of that public authority vis-à-vis all other actors. Of course, specific aspects of geopolitical relations might make other dimensions – e.g., population size and composition, access to natural resources or navigable avenues of transport, military capacity, degrees and forms of social mobilization, access to specific technologies, distribution of income among other public authorities, etc. – more vital, so we ought not to think of global economic weight as the only significant dimension of geopolitics in every context. Nevertheless, it serves my overall analytical purposes for two reasons: economic capacity does underlie many other aspects of geopolitical capacity in a very powerful way, and estimates of economic output are among the more readily available conventional measures for the world's states.

Table 2.1 lists the world's top fifteen political units with the greatest economic weight as of 2008; Figure 2.1 depicts nearly six decades in the trajectories of the top six. Two things should be very clear from these displays. First, the world has an economically very uneven political structure: the six heaviest economic actors comprise 69 percent and the top fifteen account for 83 percent

Table 2.1 Rank, global economic weight (share in gross world product) and top-down cumulative weight of the top fifteen political units in the world, 2008 (computed from Maddison 2010)

Rank	Global economic weight in 2008	Unit	Cumulative weight (top-down)
1	18.6	USA	18.6
2	18	EU	36.7
3	17.5	China	54.1
4	6.7	India	60.8
5	5.7	Japan	66.5
6	2.5	Russia	69.0
7	2.5	Brazil	71.5
8	2.0	Indonesia	73.5
9	1.9	South Korea	75.4
10	1.7	Mexico	77.1
11	1.6	Canada	78.7
12	1.2	Turkey	79.9
13	1.1	Thailand	81.1
14	1.0	Australia	82.1
15	0.9	Taiwan	83.0

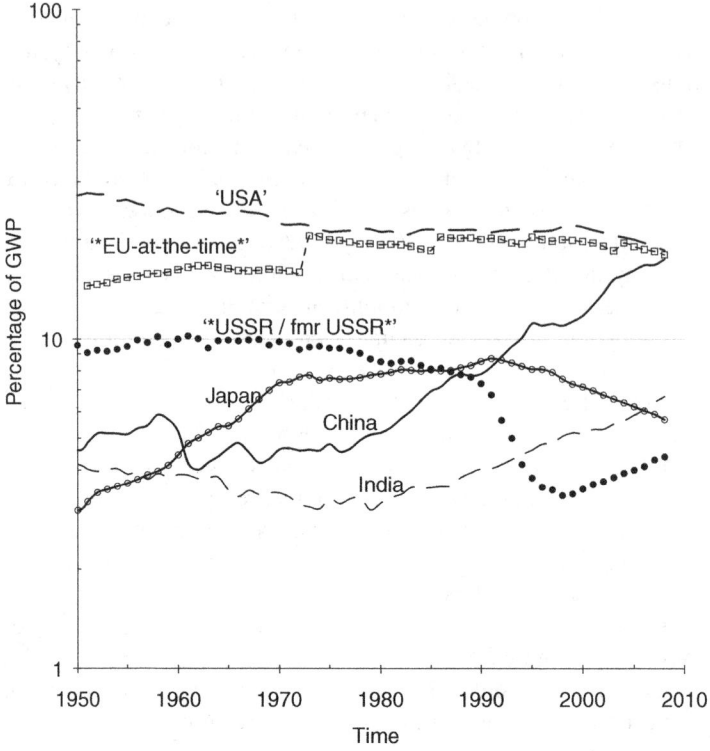

Figure 2.1 Trajectories in global economic weight: the EU and its main competitors, 1950–2008 (computed from Maddison 2010).

of the total economic output of the 144 polities that appear in Maddison's data sets.

Clearly, as Figure 2.1 indicates, second, the EU was a great initial success[4] in terms of lending global sway to its chronically weight-impaired member states. In its first year of existence, it already stood at 14.9 percent of the gross world product, a level never achieved by any single west European state during the two millennia covered in Angus Maddison's data. This put the new unit of west European integration considerably above not only the USSR, but also all other single global actors except the United States. In the early 1970s, the EU experienced a considerable gain in global economic weight, surpassing the 20 percent mark in 1973. Since then, it has fluctuated between 18.5 percent and 20 percent, with a perceptible downturn during the last years of the first decade of the twenty-first century. This palpable recent decline constitutes a deep structural problem that underlies the much-discussed current economic crisis of the EU. In the context of the world as a whole, the EU's trajectory over the last thirty-five years or so has been remarkably parallel with the United States, whose global economic weight declined from 22.9 percent to 19.1 percent between 1973 and 2008.

There is, of course, more to the story. A closer look at the curve representing the EU in Figure 2.1 reveals that the time covered in this graph (1951 to 2008) consists of several distinct periods, marking the economic history of the EU with a rather peculiar pattern. The pattern we see is that of intervals of considerable consistency separated from one another by clear breaks. Two things are to be noted here. First, those breaks coincide with the enlargements of the EU, starting with the 1973 accession of Denmark, Ireland and the UK, and proceeding through the admission of Greece (1981), Portugal and Spain (1986), Austria, Finland and Sweden (1995), the 'Big Bang' accession of eight erstwhile state socialist states plus Cyprus and Malta (2004) and, most recently, the entry of Bulgaria and Romania (2007).

Equally striking, the periods between accessions are marked, almost without exception, by a tendency of steady decline in the EU's global economic weight. In fact, as it turns out, the EU's global economic weight increased marginally (from 14.49 percent to 16.7 percent) during the first thirteen years of its existence. Since then, of the remaining twenty-nine non-accession pairs of years, we have only seen five[5] when the EU registered an increase in its global economic weight. The magnitudes of these non-accession increases are minuscule in comparison to the gains in economic weight that have occurred through enlargement. Since 1995, the accessions (resulting in the addition of altogether twelve new member states) have not even compensated for the losses of global economic weight that had occurred during the immediately preceding period. As a result, with its 18.05 percent share in the gross world product in 2008, the EU stood almost 2.5 percent below its peak position of 20.54 percent (estimated by Maddison to have occurred in 1973). Put simply, the EU shows a very clear and recurrent tendency of losing the economic component of its geopolitical sway in the world, and compensates for such losses by periodic enlargements. From a strictly geopolitical economic point of view, enlargements are a necessity for the EU to maintain the global economic weight it needs in order to be able to continue with its success in influencing patterns in global flows of value as well as the rules of global economic and other geopolitical conduct.

The graph also shows quite clearly the gradual decline of the USSR from the early 1970s to the end of the 1980s, followed by a precipitous decline associated with the collapse of the institutional structures of state socialism (Böröcz 2012), as well as the dramatic upswing of China and the less steep, nonetheless robust, upturn of India. Put differently, the latest time point for which Maddison's data offer estimates marks a historic event: the global economic weight of the People's Republic of China (in 2008, 17.48 percent of the world economy) has, for all intents and purposes, 'caught up' with the levels of the EU and the USA. This is as clear a marker of a new era in the global geopolitics of economic relations as it gets. The essence of this new historic situation of the early twenty-first century is that, for the first time since the late nineteenth century, no single western actor is in a position of unchallenged economic dominance in the world.

It should be noted that, despite the clear tendency of a decline, these figures mark a considerable degree of global privilege: In 2008, when the EU had control over more than 18 percent of the gross world product, it did so with about 7 percent of the world's population.

Global dominance and the geopolitics of alternative futures

Imagine, for a moment, that a state were to adopt a strategy of global weight gain similar to what the EU has implemented during the past almost-six decades: increase (or regain) its global economic weight through a series of highly regularized processes whereby it incorporates other states. Given the prominence of the Westphalian logic in international relations as it is practiced in the interstate system today, such a strategy would clearly be only imaginable by reliance on (or at least the credible threat of) the use of military force. Either way, any state that would pursue such a policy would likely have already had to face severe international sanctions of all kinds, if not counter-violence. It is a fascinating commentary on the power of the innovative, non-state public authority structure that the EU has managed to institute that it can proceed with this strategy without appreciable acrimony; in fact, the immediate political problem it has faced, for at last two decades, has been the rush of would-be member states positioning themselves for potential membership.

This regularity might also offer a hint concerning the much-debated end point, geopolitical limit, or, as in EU jargon, 'finality', of the EU's expansion. Joschka Fischer, former Foreign Minister of Germany, thematized the problem of 'finality' in a now-famous speech at Humboldt University, in the context of a call for resolute action on 'Eastern Enlargement', as follows:

> [The EU] was never exclusive [...] but always open to other European states, and so it should remain until finality has been achieved. [...] For fifty years the division of Europe cut right through Germany and Berlin, and, on the eastern side of the Wall and barbed wire, an indispensable part of Europe, without which European integration could never be completed, waited for its chance to take part in the European unification process. That chance came with the end of the division of Europe and Germany in 1989/90.
>
> (Fischer 2000)

Translating Fischer's points into the language of global geopolitical analysis, the EU has 'never [been] an exclusive' organization and it has a pan-European mandate. Therefore, the EU must proceed with 'Eastern Enlargement'. That was the order of the day at the turn of the millennium.

The question of the EU's 'finality' emerges in a radically different way today. Based on the materials presented above, the idea of maintaining and, if possible, increasing the European Union's global economic weight appears as a key geopolitical objective for the institutions that constitute the center of power in the European Union.

In abstracto, two interconnected, yet analytically separable, processes can produce the outcome of maintaining/increasing the EU's global economic weight. First, with the help of a dose of wishful thinking, it is possible to imagine that the EU could, at some point in the future, make a sudden shift to an economic trajectory of high growth, i.e., an experience of economic expansion that is higher than the expansion of the world economy as a whole. Given the grave inequalities in living standards, infrastructure, production capacity, productivity, quality of life, etc. within the existing European Union, arguably there is much room for such growth. This would imply a series of Gerschenkronian 'fits and starts', especially in the poorer parts of the EU. The trouble is that, given the near-catastrophic initial declines into which the former state socialist economies were allowed to sink during the fifteen to twenty year period elapsed between the end of state socialism and their admission to full membership in the EU, it is not possible, even as much as a generation after the collapse of state socialism in eastern Europe, to identify any piece of empirical evidence to show that this indeed is happening (Böröcz 2012). Given that the societies in the eastern half of the continent have never during the history of modern capitalism been fully 'on par' with Western Europe, it would require an unusually large dose of optimism to expect it to happen in the near future.

As suggested above, greater-than-global-average growth in Western Europe happened in only five of the twenty-nine non-accession pairs-of-years between 1964 and 2008. Even in the first thirteen years of its existence, i.e., during the growth years of 1951 to 1963, the EU's share in the world economy increased from 14.49 to 16.7 percent of the world mean. During the same time period, Japan's share in the gross world product increased by 1.63 times. South Korea and Singapore redoubled their global economic weight between 1965 and 1977, and 1967 and 1979, respectively, and continued with an approximately 1.68 to 1.7 times growth pattern thereafter. In other words, the growth of the EU's share in the GWP during its initial growth years (1.15 times over thirteen years) hardly qualifies as spectacular if compared to the most successful Asian nation states in the 1950s, 1960s and 1970s. In the most recent data years (1996 to 2008), the People's Republic of China's share in the gross world product increased 1.59 times, and Vietnam (1.43 times) and India (1.39 times) are not lagging far behind. All of those examples – and the most recent ones of course include the two most populous states of the world – register considerably steeper rates of growth than the EU has ever seen.

Assuming that humankind will avoid a new world war, in the absence of a catastrophic collapse of any non-European actors, and short of a non-linear event sending the EU on some burst of economic growth (such as the discovery of a new technology which the current EU is uniquely qualified to base its growth on, or the invention of a socio-political mechanism that could spur the productivity of the aging societies of Europe that have seen a drastic reduction of total labor time), the EU's current situation hardly warrants the expectation of an economic burst from Western Europe.

Absent such non-linear events, the European Union is left with only one possible tool to maintain its relative economic weight in the world economy:

continuation of its policy of strategic enlargements. This stratagem is made possible by the EU's distinctive structure as a non-state quasi-state in a context where most of its competitors are conventional states. In other words, the idea of maintaining/increasing global economic weight by way of strategic enlargements is unique to the EU. It is also a technique that the EU has used throughout its existence, with moderate success. It went from 14.5 percent to around 20 percent of the world economy over the course of its fifty-some year history included in the data.

The question is where to turn for possible enlargement targets, and how to manage such processes. I will examine three possible scenarios with respect to the first problem. Where will enlargement turn next, and where will it stop?

Scenario 0: business as usual

We can think of 'business as usual' as a comparative baseline for the three alternative scenarios to be examined more closely. Scenario 0 would imply that the EU freezes its membership at its current twenty-eight.

To examine the implications of a no-further-enlargement strategy, Figure 2.2 extends the story included in Figure 2.1 into the future. It performs a simple thought experiment: Based on the patterns observed between 1950 and 2008, it projects[6] the curve of each of the six actors included in Figure 2.1, by fifty years, forward, into the future. As with all thought experiments, the results ought to be taken with an enormous grain of salt but, as we shall see, a number of striking deductions offer themselves from this exercise. First, it is clear that the curve that represents the European Union in a global context is turning sharply downward in a very short time.[7] This suggests that the EU's current trends lead to a marked decline in terms of its global economic weight.

Whether the loss of the current global economic weight is a catastrophic event or not is a matter of evaluation. It can be argued that, should the given trends continue, the EU's share in the gross world product would not drop below its current population share of 7.2 percent (Eurostat 2012) until around 2055, i.e., the EU's population would enjoy a greater share of the global product than its population share for another forty-some years.[8] Depending on where, in which part of the world outside of Western Europe, and under what conditions, real growth would occur, this could point in the direction of a more just global distribution of income (Böröcz 2005, Milanovic 2006, Commers et al. 2008), especially given that global state-to-state inequality has shown a tendency to increase over time (Milanovic 2003, Figure 3), especially in global economic weight, and the fact that a considerable part of that increase is due to the very formation of the EU as a singular entity (Böröcz 2009, Figures 4.10–4.15). Given the well-nigh complete absence of a critical political conversation about the EU's relative privilege in the world and its possible disappearance over time, it is reasonable to surmise, however, that this trend would find relatively little by way of political support in the European Union today.

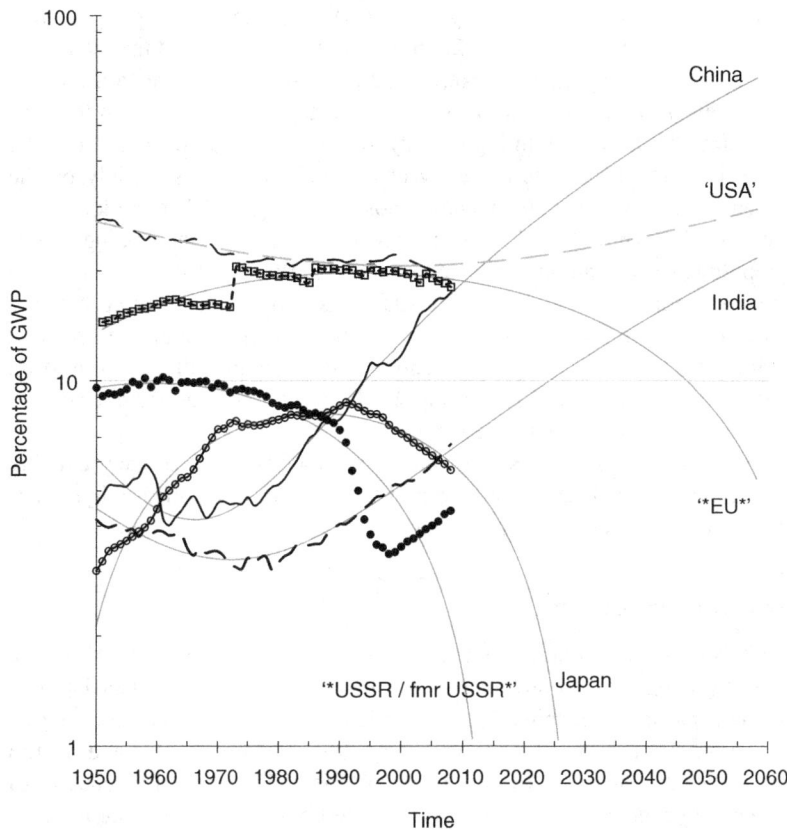

Figure 2.2 Growth projections under Scenario 0: EU membership unchanged. Forward projection by fifty years, based on 1951–2008 patterns (computed from Maddison 2010).

Scenario 1: already planned enlargements

According to the relevant website of its Directorate General for Enlargement as of the writing of this study in early February 2013, in addition to the European Union's latest accession of Croatia, five other 'candidate countries' (the Former Yugoslav Republic of Macedonia, Iceland, Montenegro, Serbia and Turkey; European Commission 2013) are involved in negotiation concerning membership. The Directorate General also mentions three additional states – Albania, Bosnia and Herzegovina, and Kosovo – under the legally non-binding category of 'potential candidates', defined as *'promised the prospect of joining when they are ready'* (European Commission 2013).

For the thought experiment of Scenario 1, let's use the (very generous) assumption that all nine of those enlargements will take place at lightning speed.

Should that happen, the EU's share in the gross world product would increase, computed at 2008 levels, from 18.05 percent to 19.51 percent, i.e., approximately to the point where the USA stood in 2006. Based on this figure, in the interest of parsimony, we can safely skip the exercise of performing the projection into the future: A brief glance at the upward-pointing curve of China, and even to some extent the United States (both in Figure 2.2) should be enough to suggest that the anticipated increase due to the currently considered expansions, mainly on the Balkan Peninsula and in west Asia, cannot possibly bring the EU to a global economic weight that would be relevant to a conversation about the sharing of relative geopolitical power among the heaviest actors in the world-system.

To recap, neither the freezing of the EU at its current membership, nor the swift execution of its already planned enlargements will produce the effect of maintaining or increasing the global geopolitical hegemony of west European states, capital and populations, something that all three sets of actors have grown used to over the course of the last few centuries.

The remaining two scenarios step out of the bounds of the already existing political arrangements. They consider possible enlargements in clearly hypothetical terms. They represent two alternative logics.

Scenario 2: North-Atlantica

A second scenario would consider the prospect of the creation of a supra-state institution by entering into an 'ever closer union' with the European Union's largest export partner, the United States. The United States played a decisive role in the creation (Böröcz 2009), and has always been a close military and overall strategic ally of the European Union. In spite of the national security concerns of the last twelve years or so, visa-free travel in the USA has been gradually introduced for all Schengen citizens. On the eve of the re-election of Barack Obama as President of the United States, politicians of key EU member states called for the establishment of a Trans-Atlantic free trade zone (Suffragio 2012, *Wall Street Journal* 2012), and on February 12, 2013, the President announced that negotiations will begin within a few months (*Global Post* 2013). Extrapolating from this development, it is possible, for the sake of a thought experiment, to ask the question: What impact would this have on the global structural position of west European states, capital and citizens?

Figure 2.3 presents results of the relevant calculations in a visual form. It creates a fictitious entity, *North-Atlantica*, by adding the global economic weights of the three NAFTA member states to those of the EU, and computes the trajectories of this imaginary entity fifty years into the future.

As Figure 2.3 indicates, this merger would create a gigantic actor on the world scene. Had it been in existence in 1973, *North-Atlantica* would have comprised a staggering 46.3 percent of humankind's total economic output and, even in the relatively decline year of 2008, it would have a share of just over 40 percent of the gross world product. To put this in perspective, Maddison's *longue-durée* data suggest that never in the last two millennia of human history

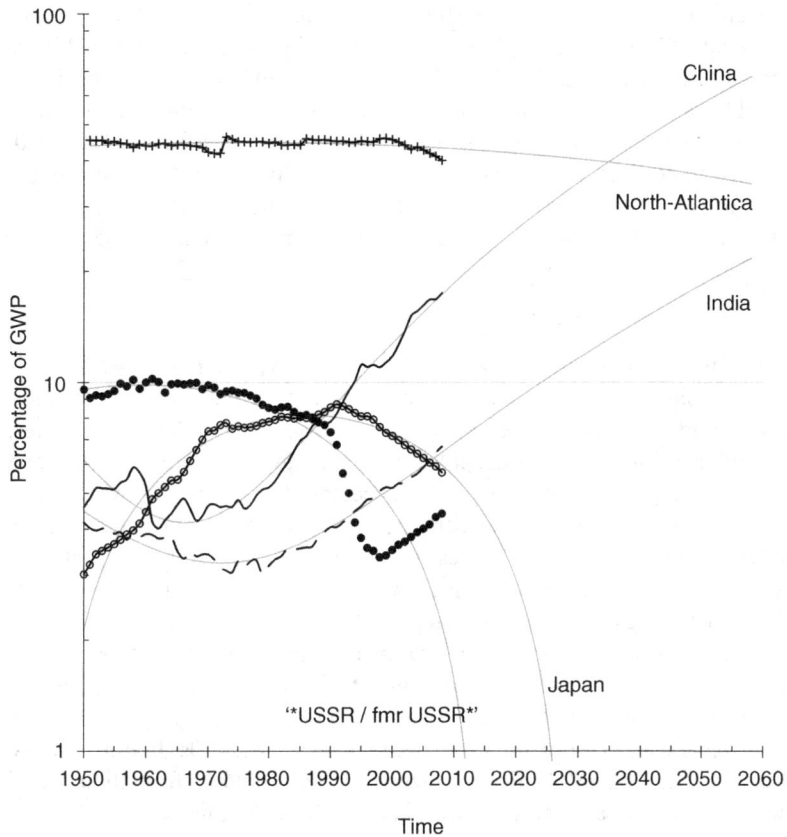

Figure 2.3 Growth projections under Scenario 2: *North-Atlantica* and its competitors. Forward projection by fifty years, based on 1951–2008 patterns (computed from Maddison 2010).

has there been a single entity with such an economic weight; the world record holder is China in 1820 with just under one-third of all the world's output.

Clearly, the formation of the North Atlantic Free Trade Agreement is not imminent. Nor is a free trade agreement the same as the EU (remember that, for the latter, it took approximately two human generations to evolve into the quasi-constitutional polity that it is today). There are of course an enormous number of practical, not to mention moral and political, issues, difficulties, stumbling blocks and pitfalls. Clearly, a single political entity that comprises 40 percent of the economic power of humankind with less than 12 percent of its population would constitute a gigantic structural problem, likely an insurmountable challenge for peaceful global governance. It is also clear that such a geopolitical merger would elicit as-yet unpredictable reactions from all actors, within as well as outside of *North-Atlantica*.

The point of this exercise was to examine the effects of this scenario on the global position of Western Europe (or, to be more precise, in this case, of *North-Atlantica*) in terms of global economic weight. The message of Figure 2.3 in this regard is absolutely clear: This merger would create a political unit that would have the economic means to dominate the world – but no longer than for another two and a half decades or so. The graph suggests that around 2040, the projected trend lines for *North-Atlantica* and China would intersect again. The creation of *North-Atlantica* might postpone the manifestation of the resulting deep structural conflict by another generation, but would not solve it.

Scenario 3: Northern Eurasia

A third possible approach to the issue of global shares would consider the possibility of a fusion of the European Union with its immediate eastern neighbor, and most important source of energy, the Commonwealth of Independent States. This set includes two large and geopolitically consequential states – Russia and Ukraine – and a group of much smaller successor states, many of which have been engaged in local geopolitical conflicts with each other, but ones that are indispensable for Europe partly because of their energy and raw materials resources, partly due to their location between the current EU and those states with significant energy and raw materials.

The results, shown in Figure 2.4, are by and large similar to those of the previous test, only with a different time line. *Northern Eurasia* would indeed create a relatively large entity, but the curve representing the projection for its future intersects with that of China some time in the early 2020s. In other words, *Northern Eurasia* would decline in a mere ten years, and its formation would postpone the geopolitical conflict with China only by a short time.

Conclusions

The above analysis says emphatically nothing about the political viability, even the remote possibility, of any of the above scenarios. This aspect of the near future requires much more and careful work that cannot be undertaken here. Hence, I will make one brief comment in this regard. Thinking about the Scenarios 2 and 3 definitely invokes two distinct notions of what is possible. The NAFTA area is comprised of three states, all of which are the products of remarkably similar patterns of state formation: white west European settler colonialism, subjugation of native populations, severance of the west European colonial tie, continued influx of European populations and a recognizably west-European-oriented political, intellectual and moral posture. The most powerful of the three states, the United States, has played an extremely pronounced role in both the defeat of the Nazi 'Europa-Projekt' and the establishment of the post-World War II order, with the Marshall Plan, the formation of NATO and the creeping establishment of the European Union as the three pillars of that post-war order. In contrast, the eastern ally in the defeat of Nazism, and

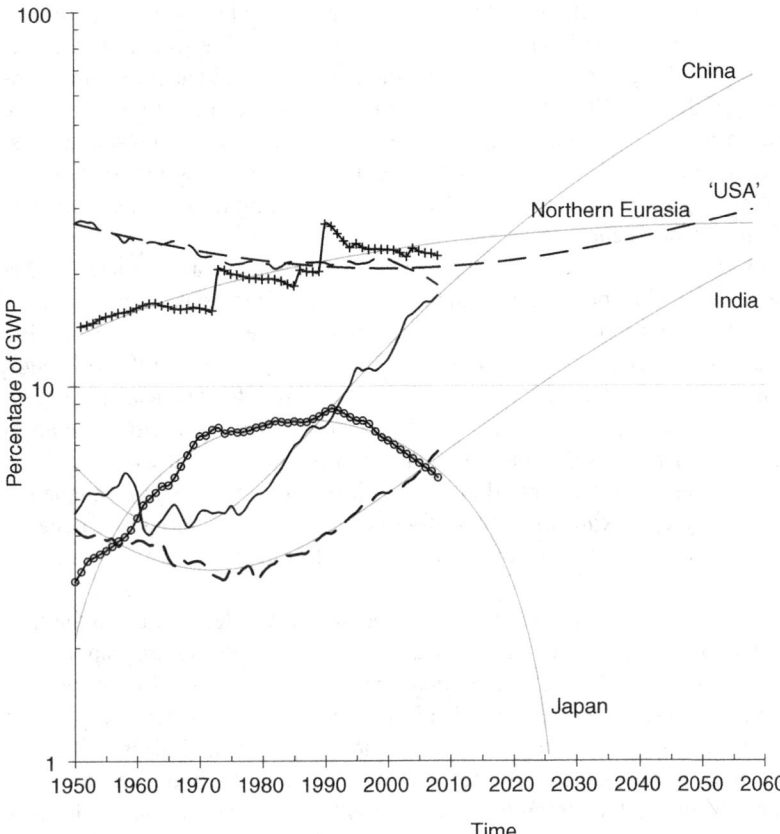

Figure 2.4 Growth projections under Scenario 3: *Northern Eurasia* and its competitors. Forward projection by fifty years, based on 1951–2008 patterns (computed from Maddison 2010).

incidentally, the one that bore by far the greatest human and economic cost in that victory, the USSR, continues to be widely regarded through historical lenses as a menace that has recently been subjugated, to a large extent, by the use of military threat, as well as overall political, economic, cultural and moral hostility. The extreme dependence of Western Europe on the United States for military and overall geopolitical-strategic defense is widely known but it does not constitute a problem to be reckoned with; the extreme dependence of Western Europe on the post-Soviet CIS for energy, raw materials and labor is widely discussed as a problem. As pioneering work by Kees van der Pijl (1984, 1998) and other members of the Amsterdam group on political economy indicates, the long-term geostrategic cooperation and dependency, the pattern of oscillating shifts between investment flows from Western Europe to North America and the other way round, the intense technological interchange across the Atlantic and a deep cultural understanding of a vague sense of 'Europeanness' has led to the emergence of an amalgam Atlantic Ruling Class, with specific global geopolitical interests that point beyond either national, or even North American or west European scales. Nothing even remotely comparable could be said about the relationship between the post-Soviet capitalist ruling classes of northern Eurasia and the west European (or, as we have argued: Atlantic) bourgeoisie. As a result, at least in the realm of ruling class formation, there exist significant tangible social structural facts that point in the direction that Scenario 2 might be a bit more feasible to implement than Scenario 3.

Finally, as with all thought experiments, we should always remember that they serve a specific purpose and that they can be dangerously misleading if taken out of their proper context. The purpose of this exercise was examining three alternative scenarios strictly in terms of one dimension, the relative weight of the political units that the current EU could, possibly, given a number of extraordinarily strong assumptions, form by extending the possibility of enlargement to strategically chosen partners. The results indicate that even the most 'successful' scenario – the formation of *North-Atlantica* – would postpone the decline only by approximately twenty-five years or so. Two and a half decades is an extremely short period when it comes to the formation of large geopolitical units.

Put differently, none of the three scenarios offer a viable solution to the task of maintaining the geopolitical privileges enjoyed by the states, capital and citizens that constitute key stakeholders in European integration. What appeared, for two centuries or so, as the iron rule of the geopolitical character of capitalism – that 'western' actors, institutions, organizations, interests and ideas will dominate the entire globe, determine the rules of conduct and choose the terms of acceptable behavior for the entire system – will have to change in a relatively short time. It appears that the most important task is preparing humankind – and, perhaps most of all, European constituencies – for the inevitable changes that will beset the world as a result of this transformation.

Notes

1 Because of the outliers, the global standard deviation is 15.1, and the coefficient of variation is 0.430.
2 The EU-wide standard deviation is 6.07 and the EU-wide coefficient of variation is a mere 0.13. In other words, the EU-wide variation in the relative size of state budgets is more than three times tighter than for the world as a whole, grouped around a mean that is approximately 15 percent higher than the world average.
3 The conversion into percentages of the gross world product has a methodological advantage as well. It eliminates comparability problems over time.
4 Two entities are marked by *asterisks* in this graph, signaling that the figures represented in them are, at least partly, products of computations on my part. The *European Union* is an artificial entity I created by summing the GDP estimates of its members at the time. Figures for the *USSR* are results of computations in the post-1990 period. (Both totals have, like all other figures in this paper, been further converted to percentages of gross world product for the given year.)

5 1968–1969, 1978–1979, 1988–1989, 1990–1991 and 1997–1998.
6 The projections are second-order polynomial regression lines, calculated on the basis of the 1950–2008 patterns. (In the case of the EU, created in 1951, the 1951–2008 patterns are used.)
7 Argument can be made that the downward turn of the EU's curve is an artifact of the statistical pattern for the regression line, chosen arbitrarily. The nature of the EU's global shares data is such, however, that neither the third-, nor even the fourth-order polynomial regression produces an upward-turning projection. Moreover, the pattern of even the fifth-order polynomial – an absurdly strong assumption, allowing five sign changes in the direction of the EU's growth pattern – shows a line that turns upward and 'catches up' with China no sooner than in the 2040s, i.e., at least approximately one generation from now.
8 To be noted is that the 7.2 percent figure for the EU's share in world population is the current estimate, and it is bound to continue dropping, so that the EU's per capita GDP will not sink to the world average even by 2055.

Bibliography

Böröcz, József (2005) 'Redistributing Global Inequality: A Thought Experiment', *Economic and Political Weekly*, February 26.
Böröcz, József (2009) *The European Union and Global Social Change*, London and New York: Routledge.
Böröcz, József (2012) 'Notes on the Geopolitical Economy of Post-State-Socialism', in Solinger, Dorothy J. and Bandelj, Nina Bandelj (eds.) *Socialism Vanquished/Socialism Challenged (1989–2011)*, New York: Oxford University Press, 2012, pp. 103–124.
Böröcz, József and Mahua Sarkar (2005) 'What Is the EU?', *International Sociology*, June, pp. 153–173.
Commers, M.S. Ronald, Vandekerckhove, Wim and Verlinden, Ann (eds.) (2008) *Ethics in an Era of Globalization*, Aldershot, UK: Ashgate.
European Commission (2013) 'European Enlargement, Current Status', Available: http://ec.europa.eu/enlargement/countries/check-current-status/index_en.htm.
Eurostat (2012) 'European Population Compared with World Population', Available: http://epp.eurostat.ec.europa.eu/statistics_explained/index.php/European_population_compared_with_world_population.
Fischer, Joschka (2000) 'From Confederacy to Federation: Thoughts on the Finality of European Integration', Speech at the Humboldt University in Berlin, May 12, Available: http://goo.gl/wfTJd.
Global Post (2013) 'Obama Calls for Free Trade Pact with the European Union', February 13, Available: www.globalpost.com/dispatch/news/thomson-reuters/130213/update-1-obama-calls-us-free-trade-pact-european-union.
Heritage Foundation (2013) '2013 Index of Economic Freedom', February 8, Available: www.heritage.org/index/explore?view=by-variables.
Holman, Otto and Kees van der Pijl (1996) 'The Capitalist Class in the European Union', in Kourvetaris, George A. and Moschonas, Andreas (eds.) *Impact of European Integration. Political, Sociological and Economic Changes*, Westport, CT: Praeger, pp. 55–74.
Maddison, Angus (2010) *Statistics on World Population, GDP and Per Capita GDP, 1–2008*, Available: www.ggdc.net/MADDISON/Historical_Statistics/horizontal-file_02-2010.xls.
Milanovic, Branko (2003) 'The Two Faces of Globalization: Against Globalization as We Know It', *World Development*, vol. 31, no. 4, pp. 667–683.

Milanovic, Branko (2006) 'Global Income Inequality: A Review', *Global Economics*, vol. 7, no. 1, January–March, pp. 131–157.

van der Pijl, Kees (1984) *The Making of an Atlantic Ruling Class*, London: Verso.

van der Pijl, Kees (1989) 'Ruling Classes, Hegemony, and the State System: Theoretical and Historical Considerations', *International Journal of Political Economy*, Fall, pp. 7–35.

Polanyi, Karl (1945) 'Universal Capitalism or Regional Planning', *The London Quarterly of World Affairs*, January, pp. 1–6.

Polanyi-Levitt, Kari (2004) 'Development and Regionalism: Karl Polanyi's Ideas and the Contemporary World-System Transformation', Inaugural Lecture at the Conference on the Transformation of the World-System: Insights from the Work of Karl Polanyi, Budapest: Hungarian Academy of Sciences, November 5–6, Available: www.karipolanyilevitt.com/wp-content/uploads/2011/01/budapest-address-Kari-Polanyi.pdf.

Suffragio (2012) 'Andrew Moravcsik, Brookings Panel Explore US-EU Relations in Obama's Second Term', Available: http://suffragio.org/2012/11/09/andrew-moravcsik-brookings-panel-explore-us-eu-relations-in-obamas-second-term/.

van der Pijl, Kees (1984) *The Making of an Atlantic Ruling Class*, London: Verso.

van der Pijl, Kees (1998) *Transnational Classes and International Relations*, London: Routledge.

Wall Street Journal (2012) 'EU Leaders Press Obama on Economy, Security', Available: http://online.wsj.com/article/SB10001424127887323894704578104543325069724.html.

3 Like a phoenix from the ashes
Looking for a constitutional moment in crisis

Doris Wydra and Sonja Puntscher Riekmann

Introduction

In 1997, an article in the *Economist* (1997) entitled 'Goodbye, Federal Europe?' stated that even the Germans, Europe's most fervent supporters of a European federation, were fading in their support. The Maastricht treaty did not bring about further European unification; a monetary union had been created without an accompanying political union. Whereas monetary policy was highly centralized, economic, fiscal and social policy remained de-centralized in spite of treaty provisions calling for coordination. Warnings about the fallacy that a political union facilitating convergence of these policies would as a corollary to monetary union somehow emerge over time were not taken seriously, whereas the possibly detrimental implications of a union not being an optimal currency area were shunned. Moreover, institutional arrangements fostering joint decision traps as theorized by Scharpf (1994) already in the early 1990s were not considered as hindrances to efficient decision-making, but rather as instances of the typical muddling through that had nevertheless taken European integration quite far.

When in 2000 Joschka Fischer in his famous Humboldt speech evoked the vision of a European federation, reactions were at best ambivalent. The constitutional treaty did not introduce the far-reaching changes in the constitutional framework of the Union, as demanded by Fischer – the creation of a two-chamber parliament and a European government with a directly elected president – and failed in two referenda and was then, by removing all references to a state-like structure, transferred into the Reform Treaty. In 2009, the crisis hit Europe and, although originally constructed as a genuinely American crisis for which Europe would have to bear the global aftershocks of economic recession, the ensuing debt crisis dramatically cast into the limelight the legal and institutional inadequacies of the European project. Sovereignty reflexes, lacking rule compliance, political considerations trumping agreed-upon regulation and a European population no longer supporting further integration make finding an easy way out increasingly difficult. Can the European Union survive this 'stress-test' or is the crisis testing the limits of the European states to integrate? For those supporting European integration, the answer was, according to German Chancellor Merkel, 'We need more Europe, not less'. Therefore, there was no alternative to taking measures to guarantee the Euro.

In the end, what does more Europe mean? Do we witness this crisis finally culminating in the constitutional moment of an 'ever closer Union'? In their Manifest for Europe, Daniel Cohn-Bendit and Guy Verhofstadt come to the conclusion that a common currency is incompatible with separate nation states. It either results in the foundation of a federal state and a postnational Europe or the European currency is doomed to vanish (Cohn-Bendit and Verhofstadt 2012: 13). In an interview with *Die Zeit* (2012: the article entitled 'A crazy vision of Europe'), Cohn-Bendit characterized this 'end of the nation state' as a revolutionary process. Although critically commented and skeptically challenged, the idea of a federal Europe is again on the agenda. *The Financial Times*, discussing the federal plans of Angela Merkel (*Financial Times* 2012) and Jose Manuel Barroso in a CNN interview, said that a federation in Europe was unavoidable if the common currency was to survive (Barroso 2012b).

In the current crisis, European politics is more than ever defined by mixed-motive situations (Scharpf 1994: 30) where cooperation is hampered by the conundrum of rational-egoistic stances and the need to find a common solution. The question posed to the Union's actors is a very old one: How to build a community of heterogeneous members in which a common interest is pursued. Generally, as Scharpf put it, community building occurs in view of common threat and commonly perceived vulnerability. Indeed, the fall of the Euro as the most ambitious project of the Union in the last two decades poses such threat.

In this vein, even if circumstances and situational logics diverge, a comparison with other integration processes that have come to such crossroads may be instructive. Since the first aspirations of the European Union to create a monetary union and, even more so, since this Eurozone tumbled into the debt crisis, the fiscal federalism of the United States served as a reference point and model for comparison. From the beginning, especially the American academia was rather skeptical about the possibilities of the Euro to be a real success story, mainly referring to the theory of optimum currency areas (OCA), a theory that, building on the work of Mundell, was especially prominent in the US from the 1970s. Its basic argument is that only regions with high labor mobility should have a unique currency (Mundell 1961; Sala-i-Martin and Sachs 1991: 2). The main conclusion was that the European Union was much less an OCA than was the US and, above all, it lacked the necessary institutions and processes to overcome the problems related to this. Putting the comparison with the United States' evolution towards fiscal federalism at the center, it has to be stressed that this too was a highly contested process that underwent highs and lows, with outcomes that were far from predictable. It was about institutional integration as much as about redistributive bargaining. It was about a conflict of state representation and representation of social interests (Weiler 1982; Scharpf 1994: 42).

This article proceeds in the following way: first we have to answer the question of how a constitutional moment can be characterized. How to recognize a constitutional moment when confronted with it. In the next step, a closer look has to be taken at what Bruce Ackerman (1991) has defined as the constitutional moments of US history. Can this be compared to the European experience, and most importantly, can US federalism, especially fiscal federalism, serve as a learning example for the European Union? Returning to the European Union, we have to confront the question of whether federalism can be the answer to Europe's constitutional crisis and how this will change the Union (and overcome its shortcomings). How can we assess mechanisms (the ESM, the Six-Pack, the Fiscal Compact and the Commission's Blueprint for a deep and genuine economic and monetary union) in the perspective of a revolutionary, constitutional moment for the EU? What are the odds that this crisis provides the EU with the chance to rise like a phoenix from the ashes and build a stronger, effective, prosperous and democratically legitimate federation?

What is a constitutional moment?

That the European Union is living through its harshest crisis is evident. For three years now, Greece has been constantly at the brink of default. Youth unemployment is at record heights in Spain. In Italy, first governed by an unelected '*governo tecnico*' to gain control of the immense state debts, the populist five-star movement of Beppo Grillo and Berlusconi left the country without much perspective to form a stable government after recent elections. The chance that the UK might leave the Union after a referendum, probably to take place in 2017, is not all that remote. In Germany, the Bundesrat vetoed the fiscal compact. In Austria, several constitutional complaints against the European Stability Mechanism have been filed. Increasing concerns are voiced by several EU member states about the state of Hungarian democracy under Prime Minister Orban. And while the European crisis seems to deepen, there is at least the hope that, in finding ways to stand up to the challenges, the European Union will reach a constitutional moment, creating a Union which is able to overcome national interests for common goals, to gain the support of its citizens, to reach out for further members without fear of overstretching and secure prosperity in global competition.

The crisis of the Union is a constitutional crisis. Bestor (1964: 328) defines a constitution as:

> the aggregate in all matters of laws, traditions, and understandings – in other words, the complex of institutions and procedures – by which a nation brings to political and legal decision the substantive conflicts engendered by changes in all the varied aspects of its societal life.

Although this sentence was written from an American perspective and the Union does not qualify as a nation, this is valid for the EU as well. If this legal complex is no longer able to manage conflict, does not allow for adequate response in a situation that demands a response, or its structure is inadequate and resolving a crisis is only possible by breaking the rules, we witness a constitutional crisis. At such moments, the constitutional system itself is tested and a failure of the constitution to perform its central functions is likely (Whittington 2002: 2099). Whittington further distinguishes between a crisis of constitutional operation and a crisis of constitutional fidelity. While the first aspect refers to cases where 'following of the correct constitutional procedures leads to multiple conflicting endpoints' and that represent a failure of the constitution to perform its central functions, the second aspect relates to situations where actors are no longer willing to abide by existing constitutional arrangements and call into question the provisions, values and legitimacy of the constitutional set-up (Whittington 2002: 2111). Often both forms of crisis interconnect and we can recognize this in the current European crisis.

Clearly, when the default of Greece became a very real threat to the Eurozone as such, the Treaty of Lisbon – although set up to silence the demands for recurring treaty reforms for a long time – did not readily provide the Eurozone members with procedures they just had to follow to overcome the problem. The ensuing discussions around a possible 'bailout' and whether Article 122 or Article 125 TFEU (Treaty on the Functioning of the European Union) had to be applied to the situation give ample evidence for this. Finally, the treaty had to be amended by a simplified revision procedure (Article 136 TFEU) to allow for the establishment of the European Stability Mechanism. To strengthen fiscal discipline even a new international treaty had to be set up outside the EU Treaty framework (Treaty on Stability, Coordination and Governance in the Economic and Monetary Union), as it was clear from the outset that there were member states (UK, Czech Republic) not willing to participate in this stricter austerity imposing regime. This leads us to the second aspect of the crisis. It is probably, first and foremost, a crisis of fidelity. First, member states did not take their own rules seriously and implemented them inconsistently. On quite a number of occasions, politics trumped rule observance. Greece was allowed to join the Eurozone because of the optimism that it could reach the criteria within the following years and because political reasons outweighed economic concerns. When France and Germany violated the Stability and Growth Pact, it was a political decision taken in the Council not to go ahead with the deficit procedure. And the crisis worsened the lack of trust, not only in the instruments, but between member states. As Commission President Barroso highlighted in his speech on the state of the Union in September 2012:

> Time and again, we have allowed doubts to spread. Doubts over whether some countries are really ready to reform and regain competitiveness. Doubts over whether other countries are really willing to stand by each other so that the Euro and the European project are irreversible.

The cleavage between 'donor' and 'debtor' countries is becoming more pronounced.

As Bellamy and Castiglione (1997a: 610) state: 'Constitutional politics takes place when some crisis manages to unite the people and leads them to transcend their own particular interests and consider the common good.' So crisis sparks constitutional moments. Bruce Ackerman (1991), in his seminal work *We the People! Transformations*, characterized constitutional moments as brief and rare constitutional episodes, which can clearly be set apart from 'ordinary' politics (although the possibility to always clearly distinguish between these two forms of politics is doubted by Castiglione and Bellamy 2004). The constitutional moment is marked by discontinuity and by transformation (Walker 2004: 368), and according to Ackerman it is up to the citizens to make their own clear (and sovereign) voice heard in decisive moments of politics (Ackerman 1991).

As Walker (2004: 369) stresses, Ackerman's scheme was conceived for historical explanatory purposes, and in the following we will compare constitutional moments of US history with European experience. Although the main focus looks to whether there is a chance for a constitutional moment for Europe in this current crisis, the question may still be put forward: whether the European Union already has had its share of constitutional moments.

Usually, the legal framework of the European Union is not thought of as a full-fledged constitution, rather as a constitution in the making. This is also expressed by the term 'constitutionalization', referring to the process by which the European Court of Justice has developed the primacy of EU law over national laws (de Burca 2004: 558), creating rights and obligations of the individual and providing efficient instruments for implementation. To qualify as a constitutional moment, 'ordinary' politics before and after should be very different (Walker 2004: 369). Two such moments can probably be found in the history of the European Union so far: the founding of the European Coal and Steel Community, setting up a political order based on the interdependence of the economies of the participating states and vesting it with a unique institutional design; second, the Treaty of Maastricht, establishing citizenship, a common foreign and security policy and the European Monetary Union. Why not also qualify the Constitutional Treaty as a constitutional moment (as according to Ackerman also failures may become constitutional moments)? Of course the convention method for changing the EU primary law was revolutionary, but still cannot be regarded as broad public mobilization. Although institutional changes were introduced into the legal framework, the parliament strengthened, the pillar structure removed, it more or less carried further a process already started with the Treaty of Maastricht. The adoption of the EU Charter on Fundamental Rights as part of EU primary law could also probably speak for a deeper transformation. Still, the Charter mainly codified the status quo that had been established in the decades before by the ECJ. So while Ackerman identified three constitutional moments in the 200-year history of the United States, the (very much younger) European Union is still waiting for the decisive moment that might lead us out of the crisis. The next section will therefore take a cursory glance at the US constitutional moments, to see if this in any way relates to current European experiences, but also to see whether we can learn anything from the US example.

What can we learn from the US?

In the US case, the decisive steps towards federal Union were put in place by the First (1774) and Second Continental Congress (1775), leading to the enactment of the Constitution in 1789. Nationalists like Washington, Hamilton and Madison regarded federalism mainly as a means to create a consolidated government and to reduce the powers of the single states, although Madison, Jefferson and Hamilton had different understandings of federal government. Banning (1983) in his analysis of the nationalists in the early 1780s highlights the fact that while Madison, first as representative of Virginia, tried to resist an extension of congressional authority, he came to a different understanding as financial pressure made it quite difficult for the confederation to keep an 'army in the field' during the War of Independence (1776–1783). Still, it was mainly Hamilton pressing fervently for national supremacy. In *The Federalist Papers*, a number of different reasons were enumerated in favor of a closer Union, ranging from dangers from foreign force and influence, to discord between the states that could lead to war, but also taking into consideration economic strength. To the federalists, the alternative to constitution was clear: political debility and social collapse (Banning 1974: 168). Few of the founding fathers were entirely happy with the Constitution and regularly major changes were demanded (Banning 1974: 178).

Charles Beard (1913) and other authors stress the economic interests underlying the creation of a stronger federal government. Following the insolvency of Congress during the War of Independence, it ceased to pay interest on public debt, and it was creditors who urged the establishment of a government 'capable of paying its debts'. The Congress had no power to tax as this was dependent on the states; the system of paper money was failing and fighting the war was expensive. Although Congress could contract loans, it could not guarantee repayment, as it was able to get money only from the requisition of states (Ferguson 1969: 243). For Hamilton and Morris, aiming at a stronger position of the Congress, threats like the Newsburgh Conspiracy (officers of the American Continental Army threatening no longer to protect Congress if they did not receive payment) were forceful arguments for demanding budgetary powers for Congress. Proposed as war measures, the Congress requested the states to grant a permanent duty on imports to be collected by the federation and the control of the federal debt became crucial not only in building a security for creditors, but also for building a basis for taxation and for ensuring loyalty to the union. Throughout the First Federal Congress (1789–1791), the logic of sovereignty was connected to taxation and to the service of revolutionary debt. As a consequence, the Bank of the United States became a national institution and bills of credit (money issued by states not backed by gold or silver) were prohibited by the Constitution[1] (Ferguson 1969: 256). But the union was expected to have effect also on the economy in general. In *The Federalist Papers* No 11, Hamilton highlights that:

> if we continue united, we may counteract a policy so unfriendly to our prosperity in a variety of ways. By prohibitory regulations, extending, at the same time, throughout the States, we may oblige foreign countries to bid against each other, for the privileges of our markets.

The Constitution delegated important powers to the federal level, like the coinage of money, and by prohibiting the collection of duties on exports or imports a single market was created, thus making the states more dependent on the Union. It was this economic program of Hamilton that evoked all kinds of conspiracy theories, fueling fears of 'government by money' and a subversion of popular will by 'paper creatures' (Banning 1974: 184). The creation of the financial system, according to the proposal of Alexander Hamilton, followed a period in time where the US was effectively bankrupt as a result of the debt accumulated during the War of Independence. In his *Report on Public Credit to Congress*, Hamilton demanded the establishment of the Bank of the United States, the mint, a securities market and the assumption of state debts by the federal government. The Coinage Act, passed by the Congress in 1792, established the United States Mint and regulated coinage by establishing the silver dollar as the unit of money in the US; but when the need for a medium of exchange exceeded the amounts available, banks and companies again started to print their own paper currency (1800–1865). Although, according to the Constitution, states were not allowed to issue their own currencies, banks issued notes as private entities.

The 'disordered' state of the nation's currency at the close of the war of 1812 was the main reason for chartering the Second Bank in 1812 (the charter of the First Bank, established in 1791, had expired in 1811 because of worries about its constitutionality) (Fraas 1974: 447; Rockoff 2000: 9), but the bank encountered numerous problems in returning to convertibility and in maintaining a national currency circulating everywhere with the same value. The reasons can be found in a balance of trade against the western and southern states and the inflation of 1817–1818, leading to a depreciation of notes issued by local banks and resulting in a flow of the notes of the Bank of the United States to the east. Throughout the nineteenth century, the US had encountered repeated economic crisis and bank failures, also a result of the lack of a common currency. It was especially the expansion to the west with the increasing demands for infrastructure that led to increased borrowing. The financial panic of 1837 and the recession between 1839 and 1843 made the incurred debt unserviceable, resulting also in state defaults.

Two facts are striking: on the one hand, it took more than a century to establish a single common currency within the monetary union, but on the other hand a common currency did not induce at the same time a Central Banking System. Monetary unification of the US was thus not completed until the twentieth century. Although America has had a monetary union since 1788 (with the exception of the Civil War), it was not until the 1930s with increasing federal fiscal transfers and bank deposit insurance that the system was able to adequately react to regional banking shocks.

A constitution and a common currency, these once were the stuff that European dreams were made off. Together with the completion of the single market, the creation of the common currency with the Maastricht Treaty was the paramount project of the European Union of the last two decades. Despite being conceived half-heartedly as it was, neither complemented by an economic, fiscal or social union, nor backed by a political union, it was envisaged as the major project of deepening. If the frequent currency crises that tormented single member states in the 1970s after the demise of Bretton Woods and in the 1980s had triggered the idea of a single currency, it is the fall of the iron curtain and the ensuing German reunification that opened the window of opportunity for the project's realization. In Europe, in the wake of the Fundamental Rights (1999–2000) and the Constitutional Conventions (2003–2004), a whiff of Philadelphia was sensed (Schmitter 2003: 73), but it was clearly dismissed after the negative referenda in France and the Netherlands on the Treaty establishing a Constitution for Europe in 2005. At best one could speak of a 'negative' constitutional moment. The famous speech of Winston Churchill in Zürich in 1946 on the need to create the United States of Europe had by then been forgotten, whereas integration was spurred by the pursuit of a customs union and the common market under the auspices of the regulatory policy of the Commission and the Council and, most importantly, of the judgments of the European Court of Justice. Not even the working group on economic governance in the frame of the constitutional convention, while suggesting better regulation of financial services in its final document, called for truly European economic governance. This has been a ubiquitous topic ever since the outbreak of the financial crisis.

It is doubtful whether such a constitutional moment could be created voluntarily by political elites. It seems rather to emerge from moments of threat, at critical junctures. While the US had this moment in the War of Independence and its socio-economic consequences, we may well ask whether the European Union is not living a similar moment now, the threat not being a military war but a battle unleashed by global financial markets that could ring the death knell for the supranational polity. When analyzing the introduction of a common currency in the United States, we may well ask if 20 years are not too short a time to really evaluate the success of the European currency and its contribution to European unity. Still, the example of the US makes us aware of two important issues: although diverging on the content of the constitution, federalists and anti-federalists had a common enemy, the British motherland. Today, the negative effects of the global financial system do not seem to unite the European states against this common threat, but as they are differently affected by the crisis, it becomes more of a disruptive force, probably better compared to the pre-Civil War era in the United States. We also learn that a common currency cannot work effectively as long as members have the possibility to defer from the rules, when it is in their economic interest.

The secession of 11 states in 1860–1861 was clearly a constitutional crisis in the United States. Whittington (2002: 2119) characterizes it as a time where the Constitution failed to order important political events, although the Constitution did not collapse but remained operative in the north. Preceding the secession was a time where an active Supreme Court interpreted the text of the Constitution and thereby delimited competences. On the bases of the 'necessary and proper' clause, the general welfare clause and the commerce clause, federal activities found a constitutional underpinning and the Supreme Court thus can be regarded as the motor of integration, although with some qualifications.

What can we learn from the American example? Although not confronted with the prospect of civil war, we nevertheless witness the disruptive effects of the economic crisis in European society. Although the Treaty of Lisbon repeatedly demands solidarity from the member states of the European Union, this solidarity is hardly visible in day-to-day politics. We are confronted with seemingly intractable problems of different economic systems. Both sides see the dangers of the other system for their respective economies: while the 'north' is afraid of the destabilizing economic and monetary effects of the unsustainable fiscal policy of the highly indebted countries for the whole Eurozone, also confronted with the high costs of rescue packages, the 'south' sees a dominating, austerity-imposing north, imposing ever stricter measures, unduly influencing national politics, without bringing the necessary growth. As the crisis lingers, the rupture deepens.

Defining the role of the nation (New Deal)

Ackerman in his analysis identifies a third constitutional moment for the US in the era of the New Deal under Franklin Delano Roosevelt. The 'New Dealers', as Sunstein calls them in his analysis, believed that institutional changes were necessary to allow for the federal government to deal with the multiple economic and social issues that arose during the Great Depression, holding the firm belief that the constitutional structure was closely associated with the protection of the distribution of wealth (Sunstein 1987: 423). The system of separated functions, enshrined in the system of checks and balances, led to an inactive government with only little flexibility to react and, therefore, little possibility to stabilize the economy and protect those at disadvantage in unmanaged markets. Roosevelt therefore demanded a 'second Bill of Rights', as new circumstances required the recognition of economic rights (Sunstein 1987: 438). The unprecedented rate of nullification of federal statutes were paralyzing government in the face of a harsh economic crisis and can thus can be qualified as a constitutional crisis (Whittington 2002: 2134).

The New Deal can be classified as changing traditional constitutional arrangements by introducing a different concept of the presidency and establishing a novel set of administrative actors (the so-called 'alphabet agencies', which allowed Roosevelt to allocate additional funding under the National Industry Recovery Act without the consent of Congress). The New Deal is important in two aspects: first, it led to a confrontation between the President and the Supreme Court, ending with success for the President after the Court-Packing Plan.[2] A shift in formal constitutional doctrines can be seen, as the Court reversed long-held positions on tax and commerce power (Scheiber 1977: 644) referring mainly to the Commerce clause, as it started interpreting federal powers rather broadly. All three branches of government then started working on the premise that the New Deal was legitimate (also by the will of the people, following the election result of 1936) and revolutionary reforms like the Wagner Act (National Labor Relations Act) and the Social Security Act were implemented (Kalman 1999: 2193). Whittington (2002: 2131) characterizes this phase of American history as a time when the Constitution, as it was understood by the Supreme Court, was besieged.

Another change emerging through the crisis was the new emphasis on redistribution. The first grant schemes emerged already during the 1880s, mainly alleviating the effects of the Civil War. With the New Deal, an emphasis was put on the social security system, putting in place a form of cooperative federalism, providing a mainly administrative role to the states (Scheiber 1977: 644). After 1945, grants were established, on the one hand, for the improvement of infrastructure (highways etc.) but also in the area of education and training. The Johnson administration set up 'block grants' (since 1966), like the 'Safe Streets' Crime Control Act providing large block grants for law enforcement and crime prevention (Scheiber 1977: 661). Increasingly these grants-in-aid incorporated explicit equalization formulas (Eichengreen et al. 1992: 139). They aim to approximate a 'uniform tax burden for the combined Federal, State and local taxes, which are necessary to support minimum levels of public service', taking into account the problems less affluent states might encounter in supporting a desired level of program service. Under the Reagan administration, the system of block grants finally replaced the revenues sharing program that had been in place since 1972. During the current crisis, the federal government had automatic stabilizers put in place to counter the pro-cyclical policy of the states and even provided for direct aid from the federal budget through the American Recovery and Reinvestment Act (ARRA)[3] (Trandafir and Ristea 2011: 403). The aim of the program was to create new jobs and spur economic activity by tax cuts, funding for entitlement programs (e.g., unemployment benefits) and funding for federal contracts and grants. The grants-in-aid amounted to $532 billion in 2010, $100 billion provided by ARRA. Through these grants, the federal government is able to provide significant stabilization during times of recession (Henning and Kessler 2012: 20).

In debates on the Eurocrisis, it has repeatedly been stressed that the US system of fiscal federalism does not provide for bailouts. The federal government has assumed the debt of states several times, especially during the early times of the federation until the 1830s. But during the crisis of the 1840s, renewed petitions were rejected. Without a large US banking portfolio, there was little risk of contagion and there were more financially sound states than indebted ones. This rejection established a 'no bailout' rule, albeit unwritten, leading to the inclusion of 'sound balance rules' in most of the state constitutions. With states like California tumbling into severe crisis after 2008, the question of bailout was again on the table, as no formal 'no-bailout' clause exists in American federal law. Still commentators hold the no-bailout rule credible even in the current crisis. As neither the Federal Reserve nor banks hold large amounts of state debt and depositors are covered through the Federal Deposit Insurance

Corporation (FDIC), defaults are unlikely to impose heavy duties on the federal budget, nor is a serious contagion likely. On the other hand, the US federal government grants and aid schemes like ARRA provide stimuli when states have to tighten their budgets (Henning 2012).

Unequal economic development, which may also in part be generated by the federation, destabilizes the system. At its core, the theory of fiscal federalism contends, therefore, that the central government has the basic responsibility for macroeconomic stabilization, as the instruments that lower levels of government have at hand are of limited effect, and the competition between state economies may even result in stronger market distortions (Oates 1999: 1121). Redistribution can thus have stabilizing effects within federations. Intergovernmental grants are a means to internalize spillover benefits across jurisdictions, and to create some kind of fiscal equalization that, according to Oates (1999: 1128), may also result in an avoidance of necessary regional adjustments. The grant policy of the United States aimed at redistribution and at equalizing fiscal capacities across states. Grants help to alleviate the disparities between resources and requirements among levels of governments. The goal was to facilitate the provision of public services like education (Musgrave 1997: 69).

When the crisis arrived in Europe one of the measures taken by the European Commission was to loosen the system of state aid prohibition, to allow for special measures in favor of banks. Because of the highly integrated financial markets in Europe, banks were especially vulnerable and remained so throughout the crisis. Meanwhile, a permanent Stability Mechanism has been installed and the Treaty has been changed to allow for this provision. The result of the European debt crisis is thus a turn to stricter rules for sound finances within the legal framework on the European and national level. Whether this is also a step towards an 'ever closer union' in the vein of fiscal federalism remains to be seen. In contrast to the New Deal, the new 'distribution' mechanisms to protect Eurozone Members from default are not backed by the 'public will', neither in the receiving nor in the donor countries.

Towards a genuine economic and political union – federation as the solution?

In his speech on the state of the Union 2012, Commission President Barroso envisaged a move of the European Union towards a federation of nation states. He does not call for an immediate treaty change, but changes will have to be made to the constitutional framework of the Union in the long run. Already Joschka Fischer (2000) in his Humboldt speech held that 'tension has emerged between the communitarization of economies and currencies, on the one hand, and the lack of political and democratic structures on the other' (Menéndez 2000: 127).

Menéndez stresses that the gradual integration without worrying about the picture of the polity that is being forged (the Monnet method) might be the root of present troubles. Since the beginning of the crisis, a number of urgent measures have been taken to provide the Union with possibilities to take action where the existing legal framework of the Treaty lacked a sufficient basis. With the introduction of the Monetary Union, a Stability and Growth Pact was installed demanding strict fiscal discipline from the members of the Eurozone concerning their national debts and deficits. Shortly after entering into the third stage of monetary union, France and Germany were unable to stay within the margins set by the stability criteria, and although this was a temporary problem the first arguments that emerged were concerned that the procedures envisaged by the Pact were insufficient to enforce discipline.

The problem returned with vehemence when at the beginning of 2010 it became obvious that the state debts of Greece were soaring and leading the country to the edge of default. A rescue package had to be set up, despite Article 125 TFEU, prohibiting bailout. It was based on Article 122 TFEU allowing for help financed from the EU budget in cases of 'natural disasters or exceptional occurrences beyond control'. This was highly controversial, but finally accepted on the basis that the potential collapse of the Euro was considered an emergency. Once it became evident that further members of the Eurozone were to follow the Greek path, the European Union established the European Financial Stability Facility with an accumulated volume of €740 billion Euro, including loans from the IMF (€250 billion). In contrast to the US, the member states of the Eurozone decided to bail out members in danger of default, as banks in all countries held a high amount of national debt and the effect of contagion was incalculable. This was clearly in breach of Article 125 TFEU. To establish the ESM, the treaty was changed by resorting to the simplified treaty revision procedure established by the Treaty of Lisbon.

Further changes in the legal framework will be necessary to push the European Union out of the crisis and allow for a return to 'normal' policy-making. In its 'Blueprint for a deep and genuine economic and monetary union' (COM(2012)777 final/2), the European Commission sets out a possible way forward. It identifies four major weaknesses of the initial EMU design: (a) the insufficient observance of regulation (like the SGP) by the member states; (b) the reliance on soft instruments (like peer pressure) for the coordination of national economic policies; (c) the strong yield convergence of national bonds despite differences in national budgetary performances; and (d) an inadequate coordination among the relevant authorities at all stages of the crisis in a nationally segmented financial stability architecture.

The measures taken so far combine better budgetary surveillance (the six pack and the proposed two pack), better economic policy surveillance (introducing a new Macroeconomic Imbalances Procedure and a new Excessive Imbalance Procedure in combination with the European Semester) and enhanced financial regulation and supervision (ESRB, EBA, EIOPA and ESMA, but also stronger prudential requirements for banks under the Capital Requirements Directive). In the long term, it is intended to establish an autonomous Euro area budget providing fiscal capacity for the EMU to support member states in the absorption of shocks. Commonly the theory of fiscal federalism provides a normative framework for the assignment of functions to different levels of government and the according appropriate fiscal instruments (Musgrave 1959; Oates 1972). Therefore, a federal system typically provides for redistribution from richer to poorer regions, stabilization and risk-sharing. Inman and Rubinfeld (1997: 44) highlight that federal systems encourage an efficient allocation of resources, foster political participation and a democratic community and protect basic liberties and freedoms. The issuance of Stability Bonds could create new means for governments to finance their debts. But most importantly a roadmap towards banking union was established, including a single rulebook, proposals for a single supervisory mechanism and a single resolution mechanism. But while measures like the ex-ante coordination of major economic policy reforms and a proposed Convergence and Competitiveness Instrument are possible without treaty reform, further obligations of the member states (like obligatory revision of national budgets, or a competence for the EU level to harmonize national budgetary laws with recourse to the ECJ in case of non-compliance), and especially the creation of a proper fiscal capacity and a redemption fund at the European level, are not possible without adapting the constitutional framework. These proposed changes are connected to institutional challenges: to create a strong fiscal capacity of the EU with a stabilization function, the Commission proposes to create a corresponding budget, new taxation power at the EU level and to provide for an EMU Treasury within the Commission.

To strengthen the accountability of the system is not possible without a deeper political Union with a stronger role for the European Parliament, with increased surveillance over the ECB insofar as it acts as a banking supervisor and co-legislation powers on taxation. These proposed measures move the Union further into a federal direction establishing the competence to 'tax and spend' (Börzel and Risse 2000: 53). Competences will be increasingly shared between the European Union and member states. Obviously, plans exist on how to overcome the operational crisis of the constitution by pushing the EU further in the federal direction, not merely as an 'emerging federation' (Börzel and Risse 2000: 53), but as a real 'federation of nation states' where only the power of last resort rests with the member states.[4] The model of European federalism thus increasingly seeks to embrace a new kind of cooperative federalism (Bellamy and Castiglione 1997b: 423). Although the changes may be profound, and when we return to normal policy after the crisis, a lot of issues will be handled very differently compared to before the crisis. It is still not clear whether this truly is a constitutional moment, as it is still far from evident that the 'crisis of constitutional fidelity' can be overcome at all.

A constitutional process, and if we characterize the transformation of the European Union towards a 'genuine economic and monetary Union' as such a transformative event, needs popular support (de Burca 2004: 563). The crisis brought new impetus to the discussion of various aspects of European democracy and legitimacy. The inception of the common currency has made every participating member's welfare more dependent on the actions of other members. This has manifested in growing opposition to the currency among many member populations and stressed the antagonism between economically dominant countries accused of imposing austerity on weaker eurozone countries, leading to the resurgence of national stereotypes (Theiler 2012). Nicolaïdis stresses that the crisis of the Union has magnified the pathologies of the national democracies, affecting each other in profound ways. 'The threats to democracy in the EU lie in the insularity of its Member States' governments and their refusal to face pervading democratic externalities' (Nicolaïdis 2013: 352). This links to different concepts of representative democracy and of political community and the need to develop a workable form of European 'Democracy' rather than a 'European democracy or a system of democratic states where some tend to dominate others' (Bellamy and Castiglione 2013).

David Cameron, the British Prime Minister, was right when stating in his speech on the European Union that the European Union is increasingly regarded as 'something that is done to people rather than acting on their behalf' (Cameron 2013). 'Secession' is nothing that is reserved to US history. In the EU, the financial crisis has triggered secessionist discourse in Britain, but also within member states by regions such as Catalunia, 'Padania' or Scotland. Last but not least, Euro-skeptic parties on the right and on the left enjoy, if to different degrees, electoral success in a number of member states. For instance, Austria's far right, despite creating several splinter groups in Parliament, is steadfast in its anti-Europeanism; in Greece, the austerity programs have fostered the rise of the far-right party, and in Italy the Lega Nord argued against the spending cuts of the Monti government as being imposed by Europe dominated by Germany. Trust in the European Union and solidarity amongst member states are probably the most regrettable losses suffered during the crises.

Conclusion

If anything is to be learned from American history, it is probably that (a) a constitution is only the beginning of a constitutional process and (b) a crisis in confidence is much more difficult to overcome and may have more severe disruptive effects than any operational crisis of constitution. As Castiglione (2004: 403) stresses, both the legitimacy and the democratic deficits need urgent attention in the European Union.

We may be living through a constitutional moment and the proposals for deepening the economic and political union point in this direction. At the same time, these proposals have to be implemented and accepted, which is only possible if the project is carried by popular support (as the political elites of the member states primarily have to respond to their national electorates). Giuliano Amato (2000), in commenting on the Humboldt speech of Joschka Fischer in 2000, stressed that the EU always had an engine, namely the Franco-German. But also Scharpf (1994: 35) mentions two points as critical for community building: the acceptance of a hegemon and the institutional separation of problem-solving and redistribution. Owing to its position as the largest member state and most successful economy, Germany could serve as a hegemon. However, acceptance of Germany's hegemony is far from clear. It is also questionable whether Germany would take on such a role single-handedly. But as Merkozy could not be translated into Merkollande, it may be intriguing to observe the German Chancellor's trips to Italy, Greece and Portugal officially to sustain the respective Prime Ministers in their austerity policy, whereas Rachman in the *Financial Times* notes a shift of the European capital from Brussels to Berlin (Rachman 2012). However that may be, even if Germany would accept such a role, popular support for the hegemon is beyond reach, as the many protest movements in Mediterranean member states demonstrate. What has become acceptable to or imposed on their leaders, though, is a commitment to sound fiscal policy.

This takes us to Scharpf's third point on the institutional separation of problem-solving and redistribution in EU politics. While such separation dominated the Union for many decades, problem-solving through regulatory politics being at the heart of supranational decision-making (Majone 1996) has become impossible in the crisis. The measures taken to bring the 'profligate sinners' back on the path of virtue implies strict conditionality in form of austerity policy. Such policy has deep re-distributional effects on member states, while the rescue of those plagued by sovereign debt requires credits or transfers from the haves to the have-nots. This reality dictates new approaches to decision-making that in the past were characterized by ad-hoc compensation through package deals. Quite obviously, it is impossible to compensate for a loss of sovereignty (Scharpf 1994: 38) emerging as a corollary of the conditionality inherent to the rescue packages.

Last but not least, in the current situation, while there may be clarity over costs, calculating future gains is a daunting task. Thus European crisis management would require a 'strategic' stepping back from its culture of compensation to overcome the joint decision trap and to gain a broader perspective (Scharpf 1994: 39). Such a perspective would have to focus on two main points: one regards the elaboration of creative long-term solutions, the fruits of which may take time to mature and be reaped; the other one is about generalized public support desperately needed for the implementation of the solutions envisaged. The key question is how to cross over from rational-egoistic bargaining to a spirit of solidarity or diffused reciprocity (Keohane 1985) or as a minimal requirement how to combine these two aspects. So the question, whether the European Union will rise from the crisis like a phoenix from the ashes, probably as a stronger federation, is still out there to be answered. At the moment, we witness it burning.

Notes

1 Paper money, not backed by reserves, was issued by the states and the Continental Congress to finance the War of Independence. This paper money was easily counterfeited and rapidly became devalued.
2 The plan of Roosevelt was to add one judge to the composition of the Supreme Court for every judge over the age of 70, thus breaking the conservative majority of the Court.

3 The ARRA also contained a 'Buy American Provision'. It provides that, unless one of three exceptions applies (non-availability, unreasonable cost and inconsistent with public interest), none of the funds appropriated by the Act may be used for a project for the construction, alteration, maintenance etc. of a public building or work, unless all iron, steel and manufactured goods used are produced in the United States.
4 Menéndez (2000: 136) points out that already now this cannot be ascribed only to either the state level or the European level, but is determined in a constant dialogue between these two levels.

Bibliography

Ackerman, B. (1991) *We the People! Transformation*, Cambridge: Harvard University Press.
Amar, A.R. (1998) 'The Constitutional Virtues and Vices of the New Deal', *Harvard Journal of Law & Public Policy*, vol. 22, no. 1, pp. 219–226.
Amato, G. (2000) 'A Strong Heart for Europe', in Joerges, Ch., Mény, Y., and Weiler, J.H.H. (eds.) *What Kind of Constitution for What Kind of Polity? Responses to Joschka Fischer*. EUI, pp. 119–124.
Banning, L. (1974) 'Republican Ideology and the Triumph of the Constitution, 1789 to 1793', *The William and Mary Quarterly*, vol. 31, no. 2, pp. 167–188.
Banning, L. (1983) 'James Madison and the Nationalists, 1780–1783', *The William and Mary Quarterly*, vol. 40, no. 2, pp. 227–255.
Barroso, José Manuel (2012a) Speech, State of the Union 2012 Address, Plenary Session of the European Parliament, September 12.
Barroso, José Manuel (2012b) 'European Federation is "Unavoidable"', CNN, October 1, Available: http://edition.cnn.com/2012/09/13/business/barroso-europe-federal-states.
Beard, Ch. (1913) *An Economic Interpretation of the Constitution of the United States*, New York: Macmillan.
Bellamy, R., and Castiglione, D. (1997a) 'Constitutionalism and Democracy – Political Theory and the American Constitution', *British Journal of Political Science*, vol. 27, no. 4, pp. 595–618.
Bellamy, R., and Castiglione, D. (1997b) 'Building the Union: The Nature of Sovereignty in the Political Architecture of Europe', *Law and Philosophy*, vol. 16, no. 4, pp. 421–445.
Bellamy R., and Castiglione D. (2013) 'Three Models of Democracy, Political Community and Representation in the EU', *Journal of European Public Policy*, vol. 20, no. 2, pp. 206–223.
Bellamy, R., and Schönlau, J. (2004) 'The Normality of Constitutional Politics: An Analysis of the Drafting of the EU Charter of Fundamental Rights', *Constellations*, vol. 11, no. 3, pp. 412–433.
Bestor, A. (1964) 'The American Civil War as a Constitutional Crisis', *The American Historical Review*, vol. 69, no. 2, pp. 327–352.
Börzel, T.A., and Risse, T. (2000) 'Who is Afraid of a European Federation? How to Constitutionalise a Multi-level Governance System', in Joerges, Ch., Mény, Y., and Weiler, J.H.H. (eds.) *What Kind of Constitution for What Kind of Polity? Responses to Joschka Fischer*. EUI, pp. 45–60.
Burca, G. De. (2004) 'The Drafting of a Constitution for the European Union: Europe's Madisonian Moment or a Moment of Madness?' *Washington and Lee Law Journal*, vol. 61, pp. 555–583.

Cameron, David (2013) Speech, January 23, Available: www.guardian.co.uk/politics/2013/jan/23/david-cameron-eu-speech-referendum.

Castiglione, D. (2004) 'Reflections on Europe's Constitutional Future', *Constellations*, vol. 11, no. 3, pp. 393–411.

Castiglione, Dario, and R. Bellamy (2004) 'Lacroix's European Constitutional Patriotism: A Response', *Political Studies*, vol. 52, no. 1, pp. 187–193.

Cohn-Bendit, Daniel, and Verhofstadt, G. (2012) *Für Europa! Ein Manifest*, München: Hanser Verlag.

The Economist (1997) 'Goodbye, Federal Europe?', November 13, Available: www.economist.com/node/352511.

Eichengreen, B., Obstfeld, M., and Spaventa, L. (1992) 'One Money for Europe? Lessons from the US Currency Union', *Economic Policy*, vol. 5, pp. 117–187.

Ferguson, J.E. (1969) 'The Nationalists of 1781–1783 and the Economic Interpretation of the Constitution', *The Journal of American History*, vol. 46, pp. 241–261.

Financial Times (2012) 'Germany and Europe: A Very Federal Formula', February 9, Available: www.ft.com/intl/cms/s/0/31519b4a-5307-11e1-950d-00144feabdc0.html#axzz2Ni3sjt1s.

Finkelman, P. (1996) 'The Dred Scott Case, Slavery, and the Politics of Law', *Nanzan Review of American Studies*, vol. 18, pp. 27–68.

Fischer, Joschka (2000) 'From Confederacy to Federation: Thoughts on the Finality of European Integration', Speech at the Humboldt University in Berlin, May 12, Available: http://goo.gl/wfTJd.

Fraas, A. (1974) 'The Second Bank of the United States. An Instrument for Interregional Monetary Union', *The Journal of Economic History*, vol. 34, pp. 447–467.

Gunderson, G. (1974) 'The Origin of the American Civil War', *The Journal of Economic History*, vol. 34, no. 4, pp. 915–950.

Henning C.R. (2012) 'California's Lesson for the Euro', *Prospect*, June 20.

Henning, C.R., and Kessler, M. (2012) *Fiscal Federalism: US History for Architects of Europe's Fiscal Union*, Working Paper Series, Peterson Institute for International Economics.

Inman, R.P., and Rubinfeld, D. (1992) 'Fiscal Federalism in Europe. Lessons from the United States Experience', *European Economic Review*, vol. 36, pp. 654–660.

Inman, R.P., and Rubinfeld, D. (1997) 'Rethinking Federalism', *Journal of Economic Perspectives*, vol. 11, no. 4, pp. 43–64.

Kaczorowski, R.J. (1987) 'To Begin the Nation Anew: and Civil Rights Congress, Citizenship, after the Civil War', *The American Historical Review*, vol. 92, no. 1, pp. 45–68.

Kalman, L. (1999) 'Law, Politics, and the New Deal(s)', *The Yale Law Journal*, vol. 108, no. 8, pp. 2165–2213.

Majone, G. (1996) *Regulating Europe*. London: Routledge.

Maltz, E.M. (1992) 'Slavery, Federalism, and the Structure of the Constitution', *The American Journal of Legal History*, vol. 36, no. 4, pp. 466–498.

Menéndez, A.J. (2000) 'Another View of the Democratic Deficit: Not Taxation without Representation', in Joerges, Ch., Mény, Y., and Weiler, J.H.H. (eds.) *What Kind of Constitution for What Kind of Polity? Responses to Joschka Fischer*. EUI, pp. 125–137.

Mundell, R.A. (1961) 'A Theory of Optimum Currency Areas', *The American Economic Review*, vol. 51, no. 4, pp. 657–665.

Musgrave, R.A. (1959) *Theory of Public Finance: A Study in Public Economy*. New York: McGraw-Hill.

Musgrave, R.A. (1997) 'Devolution, Grants, and Fiscal Competition', *The Journal of Economic Perspectives*, vol. 11, pp. 65–72.
Nicolaïdis, K. (2013) 'European Democracy and Its Crisis', *JCMS: Journal of Common Market Studies*, vol. 51, no. 2, pp. 351–369.
Oates. W.E. (1972) 'An Essay on Fiscal Federalism', *Journal of Economic Literature*, vol. 37, no. 3, pp. 1120–1149.
Oates, W.E. (1999) 'An Essay on Fiscal Federalism', *Journal of Economic Literature*, vol. XXXVII (September), pp. 1120–1149.
Paludan, P.S. (2013) 'The American Civil War Considered as a Crisis in Law and Order', *The American Historical Review*, vol. 77, no. 4, pp. 1013–1034.
Rachman, G. (2012) 'Welcome to Berlin: Europe's New Capital', *Financial Times*, October 22, Available: www.ft.com/intl/cms/s/0/01db45ba-1c32-11e2-a63b-00144feabdc0.html#axzz32q5fSTVO.
Rockoff, H. (2000) *How Long Did It Take the United States to Become an Optimal Currency Area*. Historical Paper 124, National Bureau of Economic Research.
Sala-i-Martin, X., and Sachs, J. (1991) 'Fiscal Federalism and Optimum Currency Areas: Evidence for Europe From the United States', *NBER Working Papers 3855*, National Bureau of Economic Research, Inc.
Scharpf, F.W. (1994) *Optionen des Föderalismus in Deutschland und Europa*. Frankfurt a. M.: Campus.
Scheiber, H.N. (1977) 'American Federalism and the Diffusion of Power: Historical and Contemporary Perspectives', *University of Toledo Law Review*, vol. 9, pp. 619–680.
Schmitter, P.C. (2003) 'Democracy in Europe and Europe's Democratization', *Journal of Democracy*, vol. 14, no. 4, pp. 71–85.
Sunstein, C.R. (1987) 'Constitutionalism after the New Deal', *Harvard Law Review*, vol. 101, no. 2, pp. 421–510.
Theiler, T. (2012) 'Does the European Union Need to Become a Community?', *JCMS: Journal of Common Market Studies*, vol. 50, no. 5, pp. 783–800.
Trandafir, A., and Ristea, L. (2011) *Fiscal Federalism: a Solution for the European Union during the Crisis?* The 6th edition of the International Conference European Integration Realities and Perspectives.
Walker, N. (2004) 'The Legacy of Europe's Constitutional Moment', *Constellations*, vol. 11, no. 3, pp. 368–392.
Weiler, J. (1982) 'Community, Member States and European Integration: Is the Law Relevant?', *JCMS: Journal of Common Market Studies*, vol. 21, no. 1, pp. 39–56.
Whittington, K.E. (2002) 'Yet Another Constitutional Crisis?', *William and Mary Law Review*, vol. 43, no. 5, pp. 2093–2149.
Die Zeit (2012). 'Eine verrückte Euro-Vision', October 4, Available: www.zeit.de/politik/ausland/2012-10/europa-manifest.

4 Disruption or consolidation?
Ideological orthodoxies and heresies

Jody Jensen

According to an article from the Khaleej Times on the World Economic Forum's summit in Dubai, terrorism is no longer the main concern of representatives of the international community. The predominant issue was, indeed, global financial instability, followed by issues of power shifts and China's rise, resource scarcity, inadequacy of global governance institutions, climate change, large-scale youth unemployment, cyber security and vulnerabilities created by new technologies (Lodhi 2012). These diverse issues were connected by the sense that the world is in a profound but uncertain transition, where the possibilities and challenges are manifold. Many participants agreed that the 'geopolitical risks were outpacing the international community's capacity to respond' and 'the weakness of global governance institutions emerged as a key concern at the summit' (Lodhi 2012).

What has not been working is the system of rules dealing with, among other things, financial issues and climate change. Pascal Lamy, head of the World Trade Organisation, claims that the political energy required to implement existing rules has been drained from governments in countries hit by the financial crisis and social stress. There is clearly a lack of leadership, as well.

The survey by the Global Confidence Index of 1000 experts from the private and public sectors reports that overall pessimism in the global economy remains (World Economic Forum 2013). Nearly 35 percent of the global experts polled said they lacked confidence in the global economy (Figure 4.1). This has actually increased from the previous year when the Eurocrisis was more prominent. Confidence in global governance is still low at only 21 percent. Most respondents pointed to the lack of trust in political leadership to deal with global risks to account for this pessimism.

The greatest disruptions that were predicted would be in the fields of geopolitics and economies, with societal disruption closely following (Figure 4.2). This does not reflect the geopolitical crisis that has arisen since March 2014 in Ukraine.

This survey reflects the views of 1500 executives who think the global economy got better from the end of 2013 until the first quarter of 2014. But this, again, does not take into account the rising crisis in Ukraine and the possible economic and security fallout.

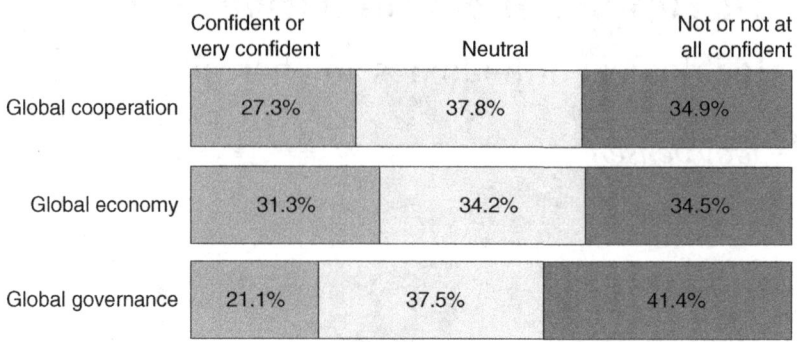

Figure 4.1 Confidence in the global economy, global cooperation and global governance. Taken from: www.weforum.org/content/pages/global-confidence-index.

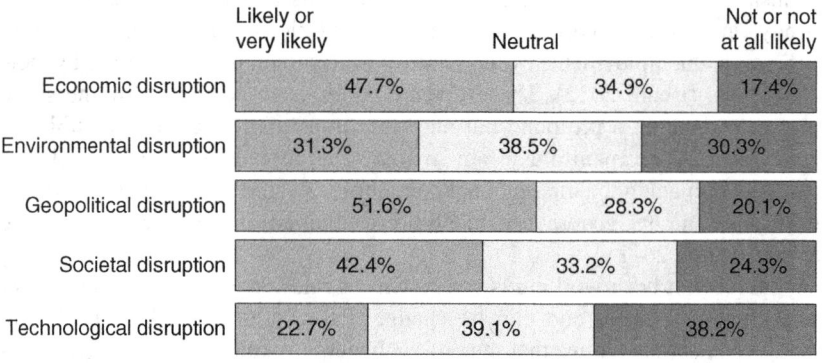

Figure 4.2 Predictions of greatest disruptions over the next 12 months. Taken from: www.weforum.org/content/pages/global-confidence-index.

Responses and failures

The concern lately of nation states, the EU and global multilateral organizations has been to minimize irrational panic in response to crises and I believe this *reveals a dysfunctional pattern of thinking*. The real challenge is not the particular crisis of the financial system, which everyone talks about, but it lies in the pattern of derivative thinking that has sustained the system and denied its problematic nature all along. Is the sovereign debt crisis in Europe, and its consequences for the financial system and societies, an indicator of a dysfunctional mode of thought in which we collectively participate today? Alternatively, can the crisis of confidence better be understood as a credibility crisis? A major danger is the current assumption that the only 'confidence' that needs to be (re)built is defined by market terminology and not by democratic terminology. Why are 'solutions' only being dreamt up after a crisis has struck? Does our way of thinking deny the existence of other systemic challenges and repress consideration of potential implications in other areas? Can a more vigilant analysis of the financial crisis as it evolves, and the language used in 'saving the system', help to *develop a framework to analyze emergent crises that have been subject to the same neglect through 'derivative' and not 'innovative' thinking.*

One of the key challenges is for new and innovative ways of thinking to resolve the threats to the sustainability of our social relations, environment and economies. New knowledge is required by the social sciences to meet the demands of technological innovation, management and public policy. New knowledge accumulation, or informational capital, would include the important contribution of civil societies.

According to the World Bank, financial crises have become more frequent over the past 30 years. Ninety-three countries experienced an astonishing 112 systemic banking crises between the late 1970s and the year 2000. Responsibility for the current financial crisis is avoided by two distinct processes, one in which individuals are blamed and the other in which the system as a whole is to blame. There is no question in the first case of blaming the system and none in the second of considering which individuals are to be held accountable for 'financial crimes against humanity'. Their behavior has been described at the least as financial extremism and at the worst as financial terrorism.

> The current crisis is perhaps more profound than previous episodes because it extends further to threaten the political and cultural legitimacy of global financial capitalism, and raises questions about the capacity of democratic institutions to respond effectively to the global reach of the crisis. It is not simply that bankers are vilified, but that cultures of finance in Wall Street and the City of London have been discredited.... Confidence in the capacities of financial and political institutions to find a way out of the crisis is currently lacking. The breadth and depth of crisis means that recourse to ideological preferences for 'free markets' or tougher public regulation no longer provide answers that are analytically satisfactory or sufficiently precise and fine-grained as guides to action. Similarly nation-based democratic structures appear slow, unwieldy and too self-interested to provide effective steering mechanisms to meet the challenges of financial reform. In meeting the analytical and practical challenges involved, it is necessary to re-think and reconnect understandings of politics and culture with the operation of markets.
>
> (Holton 2012)

There is more than one kind of foreign debt. Just as the markets and a few economists have shown us that we are living beyond our financial means and overdrawing our financial assets, scientists are warning us that we are living beyond our ecological means and overdrawing our natural assets and, as the environmentalists have pointed out: 'Mother Nature doesn't do bailouts.' The environmental business expert Paul Gilding named this moment, when both

Mother Nature and Father Greed have hit the wall at once, 'The Great Disruption' (Friedman 2009). Climate metaphors and terminology ('financial hurricane', 'financial maelstrom', 'financial cyclone', 'financial tsunami') are being used to frame the financial crisis and the response to it. This is an easy way of framing the crisis as beyond human control and responsibility.[1] Even in the context of systemic problems, it is interesting that the judgment-free term 'turbulence' in the market is used to describe the crisis. Such a metaphor frames the crisis as an act of nature or Act of God, clearly beyond human responsibility, whether individual or collective, which should instead be understood as a 50 or 100-year cycle problem, like flooding or hurricanes. So one view of the financial crisis, like the discredited view of global warming, is that it is not a consequence of human activity and, as with natural disasters, the concern is to minimize irrational panic in response (*Financial Times* 2008, *The Guardian* 2008b).

It is curious the way 'faith' is now vigorously encouraged by the most hard-headed economists and businessmen at the focus of the financial crisis. It is seen as central to a healthy recovery of the global economy. Economists, and those with governance responsibility, argue strongly that people should have faith, trust and confidence in the financial system which has abused that confidence. We now see that, all along, neoliberal capitalism was a form of mythology. That's why the triumphalism was necessary – you could not afford to have anyone challenge the system. Thomas Frank, in his book *One Market Under God* (2001), explains how neoliberalism entrenched its triumphalism into the political system of the US; how it marginalized and delegitimized all challenge and established hegemony in the so-called free world.

Another response to the crisis is connected to 'rapture' in the religious sense.[2] 'Rapture' is at least as important as creative response and human ingenuity. It is a response of faith-based governance, of the widespread belief in some form of divine 'bailout by God'. It is widely believed that the more fundamental or dramatic the complex of problems faced by humanity, the higher the probability of divine intervention. Therefore, it is extremely ironic that economists call for 'faith', 'belief' and 'trust' in an economic orthodoxy in a state of collapse today (Bunting 2008).

How can reliance on hope be distinguished from a false sense of what has happened and what needs to be done? One response can be described as the 'creative response of human ingenuity'. This is exhibited in many writers, like Homer-Dixon (2000), who subsequently recognized the inevitability of collapse of civilization as it is currently known (Homer-Dixon 2006), and Jared Diamond (2005) in his book *Collapse*. These authors, among others, believe the crisis is a reason to be optimistic.

It is strange, however, that such creative ingenuity has not been employed to anticipate the present or future crises, for example, by extending the global modeling work pioneered in 1972 for the Club of Rome. These efforts to analyze the evolution of the world problematique were undermined. The original study provoked many criticisms which falsely stated its conclusions in order to discredit it (Turner 2008). Despite the repeated substantiation of its conclusions, including warnings of overshoot and collapse, recommendations of fundamental changes of policy and behavior for sustainability were never taken up.

Economists have typically thought of markets as systems that are autonomous from politics, societies and cultures and function under the rationality of self-interest. Such confidence has been exhibited by traditional economic analysts in the market principle that many economists have been persuaded that even non-economic institutions, like the family or the state, could be analyzed as if they were markets. 'This way of thinking is problematic on many levels. The economics of markets does not explain whether institutions are seen as legitimate, or how far market participants trust each other' (Holton 2012). Nor does it grasp or address non-rational aspects of social and economic action – take greed, for example.

> Laissez-faire principles based on markets can not address the welfare needs of large sections of societies, and [in the past] the necessary reintegration took place through the growth of the welfare state which is now in contraction in Europe. Simultaneous with this contraction is the resurgence of financialization in the decades leading up to the present financial crisis and represent a renewed phase of laissez-faire, founded on financial deregulation.
>
> (Holton 2012)

In addition, the shift from face-to-face trading to electronic trading increasingly separates trading activities from a wider social context and orientation and magnifies the separation between finance and economics, and society. This results in highly destructive behavior on the parts of economic actors. This encourages malfeasance, destroys values, employment and trust. The major challenge, as a result, for regulatory agencies and governments, is how best to reintegrate markets with the values of social responsibility (Holton 2012).

Perhaps a more sociological approach, which sees markets as part of societies and linked with broader patterns of social change, needs to be taken. If we take an earlier example of just such political-ideological controversy, we need only look at the Polanyi–Hayek debate. Hayek became the founding father of a model of economic management which has brought us to the current crisis; Polanyi, with extraordinary prescience, warned that the crisis would come; he rejected the idea that the market is 'self-regulating' and can correct itself. There is no 'invisible hand' such as the neoliberals maintain, so there is nothing inevitable or 'natural' about the way markets work: *they are always shaped by political decisions.*

At the time Polanyi was writing, there were many who agreed with him that free-market capitalism was chronically and destructively unstable, with terrible political consequences; but in the 1970s and 1980s, Hayek's neoliberalism took hold in the US and Britain. The mantra was: Keep the state out and let the economy take care of itself. Alan Greenspan wrote enthusiastically in August 2008 that 'the past decade has seen mounting global forces (read: Adam Smith's 'invisible hand' globalized) quietly displacing government control of economic affairs'. He continued that the greatest danger facing the economy was that 'some governments, bedeviled by emerging inflationary forces, will endeavor to reassert their grip on economic affairs'.[3]

It is important here to identify the systemic role of actors (states), instruments (financial mechanisms and authorities), concepts and dynamics, as well as how long and short-term risk is managed in a context of both fear and a false notion of what has happened and why, engendered and exploited by fact and rumor. By employing the reasoning tools of finance, and its crisis, can we reframe our understanding of other imminent crises – for which there is a similar lack of preparedness and similar excuses for such lack?

There are critical views of the financial crisis that can help us to look at what is behind it. Larry Elliott argues that it is neither possible nor desirable to recreate the global financial system as it existed prior to the crisis (*The Guardian* 2008a). A Global Monetary Authority, equipped with the mindset that engendered the current financial malaise, would not have the observational skills or motivations to detect unfamiliar twitchings in the global system. In making a case for another Bretton Woods system of monetary management, Peter Mandelson recommended to inject confidence by regulating to control excessive risk-taking and heavy leveraging, and to improve the way ratings agencies work; and that certain financial products have become so complex that they are not understood by the very institutions that buy and trade them. This is a regulatory and professional failure of the first order (*The Guardian* 2008a).

The question is whether more vigilant analysis of the financial crisis as it evolves, and the language used in 'saving the system', can be used to develop a framework to analyze emergent crises that have been subject to the same neglect through 'derivative thinking' (*The Economist* 2008). This is key to a new approach to global modeling.

The great consolidation?

In a *New York Times* article, Ross Douthat (2010) looks beyond what he calls the 'anti-establishment theatrics' of populist protest to the deeper structures of political and economic power. He maintains that:

> From Washington to Athens, the economic crisis is producing consolidation rather than revolution, the entrenchment of authority rather than its diffusion, and the concentration of power in the hands of the same elite that presided over the disasters in the first place.

When considering the European situation, he writes that, for a week after the fiscal meltdown in Greece, all the talk was about the weakness of the European Union, the folly of its too-rapid expansion, and the failure of the continent's governing class to anticipate the crisis. After the Greek bailout of nearly a trillion dollars, and dictating economic terms to Athens that resemble 'the kind of thing a surrendering field marshal signs in a railway car in the forest at the end of a bloody war',[4] the EU's authority over its member states will be dramatically enhanced. The crisis that was created by rapid, perhaps incautious, elite-driven integration will have led, unrelentingly, to further integration and a more powerful elite. The public interest or public good has become too intertwined with private interests for the latter to be allowed to fail, and everything that has been done consequently to stop the panic in the Eurozone has only strengthened this symbiosis. Insiders have been further empowered at the expense of outsiders, and the interests of financial markets, bureaucrats and politicians are tied together as never before. It appears that the system only knows how to move in one direction towards further economic centralization. 'If consolidation creates a crisis, the answer is further consolidation. If economic centralization has unintended consequences, then you need political centralization to clean up the mess' (Douthat 2010). If a system of governance, like the EU, fails to prevent economic disintegration, then obviously it needs to be given more powers to prevent the next one, or the one after that. And once a system grows sufficiently complex, it doesn't matter how badly the 'best and brightest' (politicians, bureaucrats, economists) mess things up, every crisis increases their authority, because they seem to be the only ones who understand the system well enough to fix it. This is the perverse logic of meritocracy.

But theses 'quick fixes' tend to make the system even more complex and centralized, and more vulnerable to the next surprise, natural disaster or economic crisis. This is why, Douthat concludes, that despite all of the popular unrest and protest in Europe and abroad, 'this isn't the end of the "too big to fail" era. It's the beginning.'

Global financial crisis and democracy

> Many critics of economic globalization claim the processes of cross-border trade and investment together with cross-border capital markets operating within de-regulated markets undermine both national sovereignty and political democracy.
>
> (Holton 2012)

There has been too little analysis about the relationship between globalization and democracy. Without going into too much detail on definitions of globalization, suffice it to say that globalization is a multi-dimensional process which runs at different speeds in different contexts and in different spheres. Transnational, cross-border connections and interdependencies may advance globalization further in some aspects (economic and technological) while not as much in others (politics and regulation, governance in general, and societies). In the case of the EU, political integration does not match economic integration and for citizens at the national level there is no immediate political recourse for market and regulatory failures through a system of EU-level political institutions. The sovereign debt crisis stems from public bailouts of the banking system and leaves citizens at the mercy of powerful market players (global banks, multinational companies, bond markets) and political elites. Global business regulation remains organized within a complex, opaque confusion of national, regional and global regimes that elude or obstruct democratic accountability. Finance markets operate around the clock 24/7, facilitated by information technology; democracy, on the other hand, operates across days, months and years. This imbalance creates enormous tensions (Houlton 2012). Resolution of this cognitive disparity requires both greater transparency of global finance and its mechanisms and a greater commitment of financial actors like bankers to enter into dialogue with social forces and democratic institutions. Both markets and states have failed in this crisis and if the situation is not resolved it will continue to produce dysfunctional consequences. It cannot be resolved by returning to the same free markets and austerity measures. The social consequences and costs would be too great and there is no logic in trying to reform a system through the same structures and ways of thinking that created the crisis in the first place. One path or approach to better match financial globalization with effective political globalization might be to increase international political cooperation by listening to the concerns of citizens and not just elites.

The European crisis

The process of European economic integration reveals how the neoliberal economic model can undermine social solidarity, cohesion and democracy. Neoliberalism has not only eroded the power of nation states to plan and direct responses to fiscal and other challenges, but has silenced the voices of citizens as well at the national and European levels. This has led to what some analysts term the 'de-democratization' of 'a continent traditionally regarded as the cradle of social democracy' (Pianta 2013: 149).

> The institutional architecture of integration relied on a proliferation of technocracies – the European Central Bank, the increased power of the European Commission, more than 30 EU agencies, from the environment to judicial cooperation – which replaced national power structures embedded in established practices of democracy, such as parliaments, political parties, domestic public opinion, civil society, thus reducing the space for democratic control and contestation.
>
> (Pianta 2013: 151)

How decisions are made at the EU level has always been at the center of the discussions about the weakness of European democracy. Policy responses have generally led to a reduction of democracy as the expansion of the power of finance has been left unrestrained by European authorities. In addition, the European Commission, the IMF, ECB, ESFS and EMS do not have a built-in democratic framework for decision-making, transparency or accountability. The Fiscal Compact, the latest suggestion that would require a balanced budget in all member states' constitutions, could be the most dangerous threat to democracy at the national level yet, since it would take away an important leverage to support social cohesion while providing no room for a democratic debate on policy priorities at the European level (Pianat 2013: 156). Already, the governments of debt-ridden countries have been forced to implement harsh austerity measures against the interests and insistence of their citizens with dire consequences, as in Greece and Spain. This need not have been the case.

> In the past few years, a continental debate – uniting voices from a wide range of political organizations, trade unions, experts' groups and civil society forces – has pointed out [the alternatives]…: Protecting weaker European countries from the raids of speculation with extended responsibilities for the European Central Bank; cutting finance down to size with a return to strict regulation and the adoption of a financial transaction tax (first proposed by European civil society in the 1980s); a revision of the Growth and Stability Pact and of the Fiscal Compact, aimed at reversing austerity policies; Union-wide public expenditures, possibly funded by Eurobonds, targeted to converting European economies to sustainable production systems, given that other pressures (including climate change) call for a full scale reconversion of Europe's industrial setup; a large redistribution of income and wealth away from the 10% of richest Europeans, who in the last two decades have reaped huge benefits from the marketization of society.
>
> (Pianta 2013: 153)

Many, often contradictory, causes have been put forward for the recent events in Greece, Italy, Spain, Hungary, across Europe: economic (unemployment and neoliberal economic measures), political (institutionalized corruption and failure of education), cultural or ideological. The multitude and diversity of mobilizations in response to crisis seemed to agree that the fundamental causes of the crisis lie in the neoliberal policies and practices of the past decades that became increasingly virulent and destructive to large portions of societies. The most prominent reaction of commentators to street protests has been incomprehension (but also sometimes contempt and suspicion) because the framing of what needs to be done and how to do it appears to be fragmented along national, thematic and ideological lines.[5] This was and is a major criticism of the Occupy! movements. There is no one political center or organization directing the insurrections, no single ideology motivating them, no overwhelming demand put forward. The persistent question, 'What do they want?' often leads to the conclusion that the events are not political because they cannot be integrated into existing analytical frameworks. What seems to unite the protesters is simply refusal: 'No more, enough is enough.' A stubborn negativity characterized the insurrections. Is this a new type of politics after the decay of democracy? – insurrection and righteous 'indigNation'? When a biological system is jeopardized, the system begins to link more of itself to itself. Is this what we are seeing in emerging and expanding networks of protest, like Occupy! and other transnational, global protest movements?[6]

In addition to the insurrection that results from political invisibility and disempowerment, unregulated capitalism is charged by these movements with creating wealth but not effectively distributing it and that it takes no account of what it cannot commodify, neither the social relationships of family and community nor the environment, which are vital to human well-being and survival, and indeed to the functioning of the market itself. There has been a surprisingly sustained character to the European protests over time which could signal a new impetus for civil society input in the future of Europe debate.[7] Dissenting groups mobilize and form, submerge and re-emerge in new, diverse and innovative morphologies.

Crisis and democracy in Europe: new movements and democratic potential

> Shifting authority from states to markets, from national to global processes, has weakened the legitimacy and power of governments to control economic activities and social outcomes. The role of states in regulating production and distribution and in providing welfare services to society has been reduced; governments have become less and less able to implement decisions taken through the political process, weakening the mechanisms of democracy. The results have been worsening economic performance, social conditions, and political legitimacy in Western countries.
>
> (Pianta 2013: 148)

The protests we have seen across Europe and the world can be recognized as events of radical change only if the rules of politics change and this depends on who will uphold the possibility of changing the rules of what counts as political. There are certain moments in history when significant change is possible but not a certainty. It is very difficult for any single act or national response to actually set the 'momentum' for change in motion. But, as President Obama once claimed, when that historical wave arrives, it can be guided. We are in one of those moments now. This is the challenge that Greece, Spain, Portugal, Hungary, and now Ukraine, pose to the future of Europe debate as we witness the collapse of an economic orthodoxy that has dominated politics for nearly 30 years.

A recent study on the emergence of what is termed 'subterranean politics' conducted by the London School of Economics in four European countries (Germany, Hungary, Italy, Spain), and two trans-European studies (one focused on trans-European grassroots initiatives and one focused on trans-European initiatives and anti-austerity movements) tried to map what is not usually visible in mainstream political debates (Kaldor et al. 2012). They contend that 'This is one of those rare moments in history when subterranean politics "bubbles up" to the surface.' The demonstrations, protests, occupations and experiments with substantive and procedural democracy at the grassroots level were viewed as something new and different from what has occurred previously over the past decades. What is of special interest from 2011–2012 is the way the protests around

Disruption or consolidation? 63

Europe have 'struck a chord' and have had resonance in societies with diverse economic, political and social contexts. Subterranean political actors perceive the crisis as a political crisis rather than as a reaction to austerity. Subterranean politics, for example, was just as apparent in Germany, where no austerity policies were conducted, as in other countries where they were. The main findings from the report (Kaldor *et al.* 2012) are summarized here:

- *It is about politics, but not politics as usual.* What is shared across different types of protests, actions, campaigns and initiatives is extensive frustration with formal politics. Terms associated with subterranean political actions such as 'angry', 'indignant' or 'disappointed' are an expression of this frustration. Most of the protests were/are not about austerity, but rather about the failures of democracy as currently practiced. Subterranean political actors are concerned about democracy, but not as it is currently practiced. They experiment with new democratic practices, in the squares, on the Internet, and elsewhere.
- *It is about democracy, but not democracy as usual.* What was observed in the public displays of subterranean politics were collective projects of re-imagining democracy (its practices and its relation to everyday life). Participants stressed the subjective experience of participating in politics and pioneering new experiments of democracy to establish a direct relationship between them and the power structures they contest. This applies both to the assemblies and to new techniques of consensus building in public squares and campaigning for referendum (Italy), which was seen as an example of direct democracy.
- *The role of the Internet is seen as critical* at the level of mobilization, much of which was coordinated over social networks. The new political generation not only uses social networking to organize but the Internet has profoundly affected the culture of politics and political activism. Many activists are preoccupied with Internet freedom, particularly issues of anti-piracy. The term 'swarm intelligence', used to describe collective actions based on horizontality, replaceability and leaderlessness, is characteristic both of online activism and of the occupation of squares. Concern with process, accountability and transparency for many subterranean actors is more important than a program of specific demands.
- *Europe is invisible* and does not play a relevant role in the debates and protests studied. In the few instances in which it is 'visible', it tends to be regarded as part of the problem as much as part of the solution. Many regarded themselves as European in terms of life experience, and are concerned with and aware of global issues, but Europe as a political community or a public space only seems to exist for a small 'expert' minority.

One of the implications of these findings is that we must begin a European dialogue about the future, and (re-)problematizing the European construction needs to be a priority to redirect attention away from a focus on financial and debt crisis to the deeper crisis of European democracy. Another implication is the need to explain the gap between this activation at the grassroots level and the lack of political agency. One explanation, recognized by Habermas (2004) and others, is the lack of a recognizable and accessible European public sphere or space – a European Commons – that could provide a platform and an arena for common discussion and deliberation on shared problems. Because the EU is 'institutionally elusive', it makes it hard for social movements and concerned citizens to find an entry point to express opinions and demands to a defined center of power at the European level.

> With no common European 'demos' and no 'site' of European power, Europe-wide activism has been limited and has focused on rebuilding civil society connections, shared analyses, and proposals among experts' networks: A diagnostic perspective on the unacceptability of the liberal policies associated with the European crisis, rather than a prognostic agenda for change.
>
> (Pianta 2013: 155)

Is another Europe possible?

> Europe is in crisis because it has been hijacked by neoliberalism and finance. In the last twenty years – with a persistent democratic deficit – the meaning of the European Union has increasingly been reduced to a narrow view of the single market and the single currency, leading to liberalizations and speculative bubbles, loss of rights and the explosion of inequalities. This is not the Europe that was imagined decades ago as a space of economic and political integration free from war. This is not the Europe that was built through economic and social progress, the extension of democracy and welfare rights.
>
> (Another Road for Europe 2012)

Pianta (2013) believes that fragmentation has prevented the construction of a common frame of contention on Europe's crisis to emerge as a starting point for a new wave of activism. What is needed, he concludes, is 'a common discussion on how an alternative could be achieved through political processes – at the European and national levels' that has not yet begun. Perhaps 'government by discussion' – participatory public discussion – could help to identify appropriate reforms over reasonable timeframes, without threatening the foundations of Europe's system of social justice. The drastic measures that have been taken, with little or no public discussion and by and large rejected by Europeans, have played into the hands of extremists at both ends of the political spectrum (Sen 2012).

> Europe cannot revive itself without addressing two areas of political legitimacy. First, Europe cannot hand itself over to the unilateral views – or good

intentions – of experts without public reasoning and informed consent of its citizens. Given the transparent disdain for the public, it is no surprise that in election after election the public has shown its dissatisfaction by voting out incumbents.

(Sen 2012)

As long as a pro-active *demos* is missing from European governance, citizens will not be able to affect the top-down, technocratic, closed, unresponsive and opaque policies and policy-making structures that are today the EU (Jensen and Miszlivetz 2006; Miszlivetz 2012a, 2012b). There is a call for an institutional response to the protests and policies in Europe. Since its foundation as an elite project of politicians and experts, the EU's legitimacy has rested on output, not input, democracy (Scharpf 1999; Bellamy 2010); and wider publics have not been afforded the opportunity to act either in defense of or in opposition to specific EU policies.

This is because national political elites who have structured the debate in both national and European electoral arenas and who, in turn, were supposed to constitute the exclusive institutional channels for regular citizens' expression about such matters systematically kept EU policies outside electoral politics.

(Schmitter 2012: 22–23)

As the introduction to this chapter claims, we stand at a crossroads: this can be a good or a bad crisis for Europe. Are we to agree with the Austrian writer Robert Menasse (Boesler 2012), who concludes that democracy may no longer be the answer for Europe; that:

the present crisis and the way it is being addressed touches on the last taboo of democracies which believe themselves to be enlightened. This taboo is democracy itself ... Can it be that democracy as we have laboriously and inadequately learned it since 1945, and as we have become used to it, simply cannot function at the supranational level?

The outcome of conflict may force Europe and Europeans out of the comfort zone of the status quo, EU politics as usual. The crisis, in any case, has certainly moved large numbers of citizens out of their comfort zones and into the streets in attempts to rethink and redefine democracy, and to address in direct ways a new kind of Europe for the future.

Notes

1 Anthony Judge (2008) argues that: 'It is apparent that the earlier understanding of a "climate of change" is now itself being confused with "climate change".'
2 Bliss, beatitude; transport, exaltation; the experience, anticipated by some fundamentalist Christians of meeting Christ midway in the air upon his return to earth.

3 Greenspan later made a gigantic *volte-face* as he pleaded for the nationalization of banks.
4 The words of the *Washington Post* columnist Anne Applebaum.
5 European countries have suffered a highly uneven impact of the crisis and, while the pressure for social mobilization is modest in countries of Europe's centre, conflict is building up in the periphery. Moreover, different 'themes' of contention have driven recent activism.

(Pianta 2013: 155)

6 In addition to recent mobilizations, a dense network of organizations has long been working on European policy issues, including the question of democracy. These include the Seattle to Brussels network against trade liberalization, the Social Watch network on social issues, the Climate Action Network Europe on environmental challenges, European Alternatives on EU democracy, as well as lobbying groups such as Finance Watch and think tanks such as the Transnational Institute and the Corporate Europe Observatory (See, e.g., Pianta 2013: 154, and refer to Pianta and Marchetti 2007).
7 For example, Pianta (2013: 155) mentions the Blockupy Frankfurt (12 May 2011), Global Change (15 October 2011), the Florence 10+10Forum (8–10 November 2012), the European strike/day of action called by the European Trade Union Council (14 November 2012) and European mobilizations against the meeting of the European Council (end of March 2013).

Bibliography

Altman, D. (2007) *Globalization Story Still Has a Long Way to Go*, Available: www.opendemocracy.net/.

Another Road for Europe (2012) Available: http://gef.eu/future/another-road-for-europe/. Retrieved October 6, 2013.

Bellamy, Richard (2010) 'Democracy without democracy? Can the EU's democratic "outputs" be separated from the democratic "inputs" provided by competitive parties and majority rule?', *Journal of European Public Policy*, vol. 17, no. 1, pp. 2–19.

Bello, W. (2004) *Deglobalization. Ideas for a New World Economy*, Reading: Cox and Wyman.

Boesler, Matthew (2012) 'The REAL Eurozone crisis is about much more than debt', *Business Insider*, October 20, Available: www.businessinsider.com/europes-next-big-crisis-democracy-2012-10?op=1#ixzz2h8h51mHs.

Brundtland Report (1987) *Our Common Future*, Oxford: Oxford University Press.

Bunting, Madeleine (2008) 'Faith, belief, trust: this economic orthodoxy was built on superstition', *The Guardian*, October 6.

Cahn, Edgar (2013) 'Empathy, democracy and the economy', September 10, Available: www.opendemocracy.net/transformation/edgar-cahn/empathy-democracy-and-economy.

Cutler, A.C., Haufler, V., and Porter, T. (eds.) (1999) *Private Authority and International Affairs*, New York: State University of New York Press.

deAngelis, Tori (2004) 'Consumerism and its discontents', *Journal of Personality and Social Psychology*, vol. 35, no. 6, June, Available: www.apa.org/monitor/jun04/discontents.aspx. Retrieved October 6, 2013.

Diamond, Jared (2005) *Collapse: How Societies Choose to Fail or Succeed*, New York: Penguin.

Douthat, Ross (2010) 'The Great Consolidation', *New York Times*, May 16, Available: www.nytimes.com/2010/05/17/opinion/17douthat.html.

The Economist (2008) 'A Special Report', 11 October.
Elliott, Larry (2008) 'This primal scream of rage is a call for thorough overhaul', *The Guardian*, October 3, Available: www.theguardian.com/commentisfree/2008/oct/03/economics.banking.
Financial Times (2008) 'Need for action on the banking panic', September 25.
Frank, Thomas (2001) *One Market Under God*, New York: Anchor Books.
Friedman, Thomas L. (2009) 'The inflection is near?', *New York Times*, March 7.
Gilding, Paul (2011) *The Great Disruption*, New York: Bloomsbury Press.
Gill, S. (2000) 'Globalization, democratization, and the politics of indifference', in Mittleman, J.H. (ed.) *Globalization Critical Reflections*, Boulder: Lynne Rienner Press, pp. 205–229.
Graber, David (2009) 'Tactical briefing', *Adbusters*, February 10.
The Guardian (2008a) 'In defence of globalisation', October 3.
The Guardian (2008b) 'This panic is not irrational, it's quite rational', October 11.
Habermas, J. (2004) 'Why Europe needs a constitution', in Eriksen, E.O., Fossum, J.E., and Menendez, A.J. (eds.) *Developing a Constitution for Europe*, London: Routledge, pp. 17–33.
Handover, Paul (2011) 'The human side of enterprise. "The Great Disruption" by Paul Gilding', August 1, Available: http://learningfromdogs.com/tag/the-human-side-of-enterprise/.
Hayek, F.A. (1944) *The Road to Serfdom*, Chicago: University of Chicago Press.
Held, D., and McGrew, A. (eds.) (2002) *Governing Globalization: Power, Authority and Global Governane*, London: Polity.
Holland, S. (1994) *Towards a New Bretton Woods*, London: Russell Press Ltd.
Holton, Robert (2012) 'Culture, politics, and the global financial crisis', *The European Financial Review*, October 20, Available: www.europeanfinancialreview.com/?p=5628.
Homer-Dixon, Thomas (2000) *The Ingenuity Gap: How Can We Solve the Problems of the Future?* New York: First Vintage Books.
Homer-Dixon, Thomas (2006) *The Upside of Down: Catastrophe, Creativity, and the Renewal of Civilization*, Washington, DC: Island Press.
International Labour Organization (2011) *World of Work Report 2011*, Geneva: ILO.
Jensen, Jody (2010) *Globalizing Governance in a Multi-Stakeholder World*, Saarbrucken: Lambert Academic Publishing.
Jensen, Jody, and Miszlivetz, Ferenc (2006) 'The second renaissance of civil society in East Central Europe – and in the European Union', in Wagner, Peter (ed.) *The Languages of Civil Society*, New York, Oxford: Berghahn Book, pp. 131–158.
Jolly, R., Cornia, G.A., Elson, D., Fortin, C., Griffith-Jones, S., Helleiner, G., van der Hoeven, R., Kaplinsky, R., Morgan, R., Ortiz, I., Pearson, R., and Stewart, F. (2012) *Be Outraged: There Are Alternatives*, London: Oxfam.
Judge, Anthony (2008) 'Climate change as a metaphor of social change', December 5, Available: www.laetusinpraesens.org.
Kaldor, Mary, Held, David, and Quah, Danny (2010) 'The hydra-headed crisis', *Global Policy*, February.
Kaldor, Mary, Selchow, Sabine, Deel, Sean, and Murray-Leach, Tamsin (eds.) (2012) *The Bubbling-up of Subterranean Politics*, Available: http://eprints.lse.ac.uk/44873/1/The%20%E2%80%98bubbling%20up%E2%80%99%20of%20subterranean%20politics%20in%20Europe%28lsero%29.pdf.
Krugman, Paul (2009) 'The destructive center', *New York Times*, February 9, Available: www.nytimes.com/2009/02/09/opinion/09krugman.html.

László, Ervin (2006) *The Chaos Point: The World at the Crossroads*, Newburyport: Hampton Roads.
László, Ervin (2009) *WorldShift 2012: Making Green Business New Politics & Higher Consciousness Work Together*, Toronto: McArthur and Company.
Lefkofridi, Zoe, and Schmitter, Philippe C. (2013) *Transcending or Descending? European Integration in Times of Crisis*, unpublished manuscript.
Lodhi, Maleeha (2012) 'A world in transition', *Khaleej Times*, November 21, Available: www.khaleejtimes.com/kt-article-display-1.asp?xfile=data/opinion/2012/November/opinion_November52.xml&section=opinion.
Love, M.C. (2003) *Beyond Sovereignty. Issues for a Global Agenda*, Belmont: Thomson.
Lundberg, M., and Squire, L. (2003) 'The simultaneous evolution of growth and inequality', *Economic Journal*, vol. 113, no. 487, pp. 326–344.
Manifesto of Appalled Economists (2010) September 27, Available: www.paecon.net/PAEReview/issue54/Manifesto54.pdf.
Milanovic, B. (2005) *Worlds Apart: Measuring International and Global Inequality*, Princeton: Princeton University Press.
Miszlivetz, Ferenc (2012a) 'The multiple crises of Europe', in Bekemans, Léonce (ed.) *A Value-Driven Europe*, Brussels, New York, Oxford: Peter Lang, pp. 181–195.
Miszlivetz, Ferenc (2012b) 'Lost in transformation: the crisis of democracy and civil society', in *Global Civil Society 2012*, New York: Palgrave-Macmillan.
Monbiot, George (2008) 'This is what denial does', *The Guardian*, October 14, Available: www.monbiot.com/2008/10/14/this-is-what-denial-does/.
Pattberg, P. (2006) 'The transformation of global business regulation', *Global Governance Working Paper*, no. 18, Available: www.glogov.org/images/doc/WP18.pdf.
Pennings, Paul (2006) 'An empirical study of the Europeanization of National Party Manifestos, 1960–2003', *European Union Politics*, vol. 7, no. 2, pp. 257–270.
Pianta, Mario (2013) 'Democracy lost: the financial crisis in Europe and the role of civil society', *Journal of Civil Society*, vol. 9, no. 2, pp. 148–161.
Pianta, M., and Marchetti, R. (2007) 'Global Justice Movements. The Transnational Dimension', in della Porta, D. (ed.) *The Global Justice Movements. A Cross-National and Transnational Perspective*, Boulder: Paradigm, pp. 29–51.
Polányi, Karl (1944) *The Great Transformation*, Boston: Beacon Press.
Reidy, Chris (2012) 'The Great Disruption by Paul Gilding', January 30, Available: http://chrisriedy.me/2012/01/30/the-great-disruption-by-paul-gilding/.
Ruggie, J.G. (2001) 'Global-governance net: the global compact as learning network', *Global Governance*, vol. 7, no. 4, pp. 371–378.
Sakamoto, Y. (ed.) (1994) *Global Transformation: Challenges to the State System*, New York: United Nations University Press.
Saul, J.R. (2005) *The Collapse of Globalism*, London: Atlantic Books.
Scharpf, Fritz (1999) *Governing in Europe: Effective and Democratic?* Oxford: Oxford University Press.
Schmitter, Philippe C. (2012) 'European disintegration? A way forward', *Journal of Democracy*, vol. 23, no. 4, pp. 39–48.
Scholte, J.A. (2003) 'Governing global finance', in Held, D., and McGrew, A. (eds) *Governing Globalization*, Cambridge: Polity, pp. 189–208.
Sen, Amartya (2012) 'The crisis of European democracy', *New York Times*, May 22, Available: www.nytimes.com/2012/05/23/opinion/the-crisis-of-european-democracy.html.
Stiglitz, J. (2002) *Globalization and its Discontents*, New York, London: Penguin Books.

Stiglitz, J. (2010) *Freefall*, New York: W.W. Norton.

Turner, Graham (2008) *A Comparison of the Limits to Growth with Thirty Years of Reality*, Canberra: CSIRO, Available: http://meta-interlab.org/open-pdf/publications/Turner_Meadows_vs_historical_data.pdf.

Wallerstein, Immanuel (2000) 'Globalization or the age of transition? A long term view of the trajectory of the world system', *International Sociology*, vol. 15, no. 2, pp. 251–267.

Witte, J.M., Reinicke, W.H., and Benner, T. (2000) 'Beyond multilateralism: global public policy networks', *Internationale Politik und Gesellschaft*, no. 2, pp. 176–188.

World Economic Forum (2013) *Global Confidence Index*, Available: www.weforum.org/content/pages/global-confidence-index.

# Part II

Economic, financial and monetary aspects of the EU crisis

5 The cost of fiscal disunion in Europe and the new model of fiscal federalism

Guido Montani

Monetary union and fiscal disunion

The Maastricht Treaty was a slippery step forward. The proposal for a 'United Germany in a United Europe' produced an Economic and Monetary Union (EMU) without a fiscal union and without a federal government. The global financial crisis of 2007–2008 showed how fragile the European institutional architecture was. When at the end of 2009 the Greek budgetary fraud was discovered, a new stage of the financial crisis began: the crisis of sovereign debt. Now after a lot of shilly-shallying by national governments, the Monetary Union risks collapse and with the EMU so does the EU.

The crisis is made difficult by asymmetry in the EU: while Germany and some other countries, for the time being, have not been hit, other members of the Union are obliged to approve tough austerity policies. The European divide, between Northern and Southern Europe, is not new. It existed before the Maastricht Treaty, but today it is entangled with new problems, such as the challenge of global finance, the threat of climate change, the reform of the old welfare state and the development of a multipolar international system, with new big players like China, India and Brazil.

The first aim of the chapter is to show that the cost of fiscal disunion in Europe is the serious recession underway and, for some countries, a depression causing high levels of unemployment, social discontent and rising nationalism. But the economic and political cost of fiscal disunion will become immeasurable should the EMU break down. The second aim is to show that EU asymmetry can lead in two opposite directions: either the collapse of the European Union or a more perfect union, i.e. a Federal Union.

The difficulty of advancing towards the latter goal lies in ignorance of federalist principles. Frequently, a Federal Union is imagined as a super state, a centralized bureaucracy or a kind of European Leviathan. Sometimes federal institutions are identified with one of the existing federations, such as the USA, Switzerland, Canada, Germany, Australia and so on. But the variety of 'federalisms' in existence should suggest that federalism, as Wheare says, is founded on principles that can be applied to different historical contexts. The European Union is the first experiment in history of supranational integration. After the

Second World War, a group of nation states decided to abandon some of their sovereign powers in order to build a peaceful community. Today, if they want to advance towards a more perfect union, they must build a fiscal union and a federal government. The European fiscal union does not require a huge federal budget, as in the US; nevertheless, some new fiscal powers should be entrusted to the federal government. In short, we will try to show that a model of fiscal supranational federalism is possible and viable.

In order to explain the sovereign debt crisis in Europe, in section 2 we need to clarify the distinction between regional and international payments. In section 3, we show how it was possible to build a monetary union in the United States, drawing some lessons for Europe. In section 4, we analyse the main features of the euro crisis. In section 5, we discuss the kind of fiscal union the EU is setting up. Finally, in section 6, we see why the federal budget is crucial to avoid a centralized governance of the EU.

Interregional payments and international payments

Usually economists willing to discuss the costs and benefits of a monetary union take into consideration the theory of optimum currency area. The limit of this approach is that costs and benefits are considered only from an economic point of view. This is not the common sense notion of monetary union. Money also has a political aspect. In the last two centuries, ordinary people experienced that every nation state had its own money. A monetary union is similar to a national union. Within a national union, no balance of payments is necessary among different provinces and regions; the balance of payments is a notion concerning foreign trade and foreign payments. To work smoothly, a monetary union among different nation states should achieve the goal of removing the balance of payments constraints among the members of the union and establish a common balance of payments towards other countries. Therefore, we need to clarify the difference between interregional and international payments. In our opinion, the main difference concerns the kind of risk related to monetary and financial transactions: a regional payment runs only economic risks; an international payment runs economic risks and political risks.

In order to discuss the difference between economic and political risks we adopt the analytical framework proposed by Tibor Scitovsky (1969: ch. 8). Let us imagine a world economy, with one currency and one central bank. The political system is federal, with two regional governments and one central government. Moreover, let us imagine that our economy is in a state of simple reproduction, without growth. The national income is made up of the sum of both household and firm incomes; but the budget of each household and firm need not necessarily be in balance: somebody is indebted, because expenditures are greater than earnings; somebody else has credit, because the economic subject spends less than what it earns. Nevertheless, in the entire economy, the sum of credits and debts should be zero. Now, we will consider three kinds of financial assets: perfectly transferable, imperfectly transferable and foreign assets.

In our federal state, made up of two regions, C and D, we now imagine that all creditors live in C and all debtors live in D. Country C will have a surplus in its current account and D a deficit. Nevertheless, if financial assets – commercial papers, public bonds, company bonds, securities, mortgages – can circulate freely throughout the territory of the federation, the fact that C has a surplus and D a deficit in their current accounts does not create intractable problems in the financial and credit markets. The confidence of the creditors in the solvency of their assets does not depend on the region in which their debtors live. If the legal system of the federation guarantees that the creditor can collect its money in both regions and works efficiently, there is no reason to fear insolvency caused by the debtor's regional address. Within all countries, when business activities are taken into consideration, it may occur that a debtor is insolvent or a firm goes bankrupt. But nobody considers this event as the cause or consequence of a balance of payment deficit. If financial assets are perfectly negotiable in both regions (for instance, Federal Treasury Bonds), their value and their rate of return do not change according to the place in which they are held occasionally. In the long run, when creditors collect their money from debtors, the surplus in C and the deficit in D disappear. If financial assets are perfectly transferable in the entire economy, a balance of payments problem cannot arise.

Scitovsky considers this first case as 'the ideal situation'; the 'general case' is more realistic. Let us imagine that the ideal situation is upset by a slight economic crisis centred in region D: some firms are not able to sell their products and they dismiss some workers; it may even happen that a certain number of firms go bankrupt. In this new situation, the financial assets which come from D are considered insolvent or run the risk of insolvency. In C, creditors will accept financial assets from D only if debtors pay a higher interest rate (higher than the previous average interest rate) or the value of the assets is reduced. Therefore, the rates of interest become different in C and D where the debtors are obliged to pay a higher interest rate for the credit they require. This lack of confidence in region D's assets will have an impact on the real economy. A greater quantity of region D's income – where disposable income and employment decrease – should be paid to C citizens, where disposable income and employment increase. Region C's current account surplus will increase. The existence of imperfectly transferable assets emphasizes short-term imbalances. However, in the long term some re-equilibrating forces will appear. Consumers and firms in D are obliged, by the higher interest rates paid and by the lower disposable income, to reduce their expenses and consumption (of C products too; therefore C's surplus will be reduced). In C, the greater disposable income will allow more consumption (of D's products too; therefore D's deficit will be reduced). Moreover, some displaced workers from D may migrate to C, thus levelling the wage rate in the two regions. Some C capitalists may decide to invest in D, where the rate of interest is higher, hence reducing the gap between the two rates. At the end of the process, C is a little richer and D a little poorer. But these real effects do not represent an obstacle for C's debtors to pay their debts – capital and interest – to their C creditors, if the common legal system works effectively (if some firms fail, the loss hits their creditors, but private loss does not become a balance of payment problem). In the long run, the balance of payments will be in equilibrium again, even if a standing difference in per-capita income between the two regions survives. On the other hand, something similar – if panic is excluded – should happen in a nation state where debtors and creditors belong to a single administrative constituency and where, in the financial market, perfectly and imperfectly transferable assets are negotiated every day in the stock exchange and in other markets.

Now, let us consider the case in which C and D are not two regions of a federal state but two sovereign states, with a national currency and a national central bank. In this new political environment, financial assets of a foreign state can be traded in the other country only if they are evaluated in national currency. Unavoidably, the rate of exchange enters into the evaluation of the financial assets, which can no longer circulate freely between the two 'regions' (or 'states'). If two national currencies exist, the C businessman accepting an asset denominated in D's currency runs an extra risk: a change of the exchange rate. Indeed, at the expiration of the credit, it may occur that D's currency is devalued (i.e. with a unit of the C currency it is now possible to get more units of D's currency). This means that the C creditor, when changing his asset denominated in D currency into C currency, receives less local currency and buys fewer commodities. Therefore, a foreign asset involves a supplementary cost compared not only to perfectly transferable assets, but also to imperfectly transferable assets. The integration of the financial market of the two regions becomes very difficult because a decision by one 'sovereign' national government can change the value of the credit (or debt). In the last resort, when two countries have their own currency, the national governments can decide to make the national currency inconvertible or can declare default for its public debt, cutting the value of assets in the hands of foreign creditors to zero.

To sum up, a feature of interregional payments is economic risk for the creditor when the debtor has problems reimbursing the money received; international payments run a supplementary political risk caused by the sovereign power of a national government to change the value of the financial assets in the hands of the creditor. The aim of a monetary union among different states is to reduce to a minimum the economic risks among assets issued in different regions and countries and to completely remove the political risks.

The European crisis

The financial crisis broke out in the USA in 2007, and, in 2008, after the failure of Lehman Brothers, spread across Europe. The European Commission, between October 2008 and October 2011, approved €4.5 trillion – equivalent to 37 per cent of EU GDP – of state aid and measures for financial institutions (EC 2012b). The banks' private debts automatically became public debts, worsened public finance benchmarks and burdened European taxpayers. This was only the first act of the European drama. The second act started when it became clear to the international financial markets that the European Union did not have a European fiscal parachute or a European government. The eurozone had a better ratio of debt/GDP and deficit/GDP compared to the USA, but the 'US dollar zone' was better equipped to face the financial storm. In effect, off-the-cuff measures were taken by the Franco-German *directoire*, without a comprehensive policy goal. At a certain point, the very survival of the Economic and Monetary Union (EMU) was at stake. This second act of the crisis was typically European, though the IMF was involved in sharing the cost of European measures.

Here, our task is not to describe the several events and stages of the European crisis. Our aim is to show that: (a) from the beginning of the EMU, in 1999, to the eruption of the financial crisis, in 2008, financial integration and rates of interest convergence were in fact taking place; the euro crisis sharply stopped integration; (b) the sovereign debt and the banking system crisis are two interdependent phenomena; (c) there is an unavoidable link between monetary union and public finance, with the consequence that the political division of Europe causes its financial and banking division.

There is a lot of evidence of a process of financial integration in the eurozone. The ECB (2012) in its *Financial Integration in Europe* divides the member countries into 'surplus countries' (Belgium, Germany, Luxembourg, the Netherlands, Austria and Finland), with a current account surplus before the crisis, and 'deficit countries' (Ireland, Estonia, Greece, Spain, France, Italy, Cyprus, Malta, Portugal, Slovakia and Slovenia). The first evidence of financial integration is the trend of intra eurozone, cross-border financial transaction. The trend – including transactions with the rest of the world – of debt securities (from 200bn to about 1,300bn) and of other instruments (from 1,000bn to about 6,000bn) unambiguously increased from 1999 to 2008, the year of the Lehman Brothers' bankruptcy (ECB 2012: 105–106), but falls sharply after 2008. Moreover, also the relative share of cross-border transactions of deposits, loans and equity increased steadily. During the rising trend, one can conjecture that surplus countries purchased debt securities issued by deficit countries. The second piece of evidence is the location of savings and investments in the two groups of countries. In the years preceding the crisis, most of the saving was located in surplus countries while investments took place in deficit countries. Integrated financial systems 'allow funds to be channelled from those economic agents with a surplus of savings to those with a shortage and they allow risk to be traded, hedged, diversified and pooled' (ECB 2012: 39). In 1980, Feldstein and Horioka observed that international financial markets were not well integrated since savings and investments are highly correlated in the same country. On the contrary, in the EMU the evidence is that savings were mainly located in surplus countries and investments in deficit countries (ECB 2012: 104). The third evidence concerns the share of domestic banks and non-residents in total holdings of domestic sovereign debt. In nearly all countries of the eurozone the share of national governments' debt in domestic banks steadily decreased prior to the crisis – a process of portfolio diversification was taking place – but the trend was reversed after the crisis, with the exception of Germany. After the crisis, in deficit countries the share of non-residents in total holdings decreased while increasing in Germany, showing that Germany played the role of a financial safe-haven (Merler and Pisani-Ferry 2012b: 8). Finally, it is important to observe that a process of interest rate convergence had been taking place prior to the crisis, especially since 2000, when the international financial market was convinced that the EMU was an economically and politically viable project (ECB 2012: 20).

Now, let's consider the relationship between the sovereign debt crisis and the bank industry crisis. As we said before, the eurozone crisis was caused by the end of two groundless tenets: the first was that the EMU could work well on the basis of the fiscal rules of the Stability and Growth Pact (SGP); the second tenet was that the Lisbon Treaty was able to provide effective EU governance. It may be useful to remember that the Basel regulatory framework allowed for zero-risk weighting of sovereign bonds. Nevertheless, the international financial markets understood that the problem was not the macroeconomic health of the whole eurozone, but the specific national economic health of the member countries of the EMU, which were now unable to devalue their currency. In the USA, as we have seen, the integration of the national banking system – with the creation of perfectly and imperfectly transferable assets thanks to the existence of a federal political and legal system – occurred during the nineteenth century and was completed with the creation of the Federal Reserve System in 1913 so that, when the 1929 crisis erupted, the federal government was able, during the 1930s, to exploit monetary and fiscal policies to fight the Great Depression. On the contrary, in Europe the financial market perceived the frailness of the integration process and that the political risk had to be taken into account: a euro invested in Greece had a different risk compared to a euro invested in Germany, as was the case before the crisis. At that point the CDS on sovereign bonds, banks and some other industries increased (ECB 2012: 23), making refunding more expensive. Non-eurozone residents withdrew their deposits from the eurozone (ECB 2012: 52) and the rates of interest on new loans to households and to non-financial corporations sharply increased in deficit countries of the eurozone (ECB 2012: 46–47). The European banking industry was re-nationalized because 'the share of domestic sovereign debt held by domestic banks increased significantly between 2007 and 2011 in all countries' (Merler and Pisani-Ferry 2012a: 5). The vicious circle between sovereign debt and banks is very dangerous: at the beginning the national governments were obliged to rescue the ailing banks and to increase their public debt; the excessive public debt became risky, reducing the value of the assets held by banks; with reduced reserves, banks shrank credit to households and firms; the rate of growth of indebted countries slowed and the risk of default loomed dramatically above deficit countries in recession.

The debt–bank vicious cycle is only the technical aspect of a more general European crisis. The real origin of the European crisis was political. The Lisbon Treaty instituted ineffective and undemocratic governance. The main powers were located mainly in the European Council, led by the Franco-German *directoire*. In 2009, the disclosure of the adulteration of Greece's public finance accounting opened the eurozone sovereign debt crisis. In effect, it was very soon clear that the Commission did not have the power – political and financial – to solve the Greek crisis and that the other governments were not disposed to pay for Greek debt. In January 2010, Prime Minister George Papandreou asked the EU for €10bn in aid, but the German government refused this request. At last, after dithering and disputes, and the involvement of the IMF, aid of €110bn was granted but with drastic conditionality clauses, which plunged the Greek economy into deep depression. The history of the Greek crisis is a good example of how the intergovernmental system of governance is structurally asymmetric and inefficient. There were two reforms, already underway or under discussion, which could have stopped the infection of other banks in the EU and removed the risk of national defaults. The first reform was the creation of a banking resolution authority, complementing in this way the reform of the financial supervision framework decided in 2010, on the basis of the European Commission's proposal (the European Systemic Risk Board, the European Banking Authority [EBA] and other supervisory authorities). This first set of supervisory authorities did not have the power to seize the ailing bank when it was still functioning, to remove its management and eventually to wind it down, liquidate or merge it. National governments did not agree to surrender this power to EU institutions, because the decision of the European resolution authority could have had an impact on national budgets. The second reform under discussion was the creation of Eurobonds. This proposal was already included in the Monti Report on the completion of the single market. The Report observed that 'the government bond market is still fragmented, as debt issuance remains at national levels' and no European national bond could compete on the global financial market. 'The recent fall of the euro during the Greek crisis reflects capital outflows from Europe towards US-Treasuries, which even the quality of the Bund was not able to contain. Europe clearly loses from its lack of a global asset.' The proposal of the Report was that:

> borrowing at large scale through a European body, and then lending to member states, may represent a balanced solution. Lending to member states should not exceed a given level of a country's GDP (the same for all member states) so that, for financing needs not covered through this mechanism, governments would continue to issue their own, national debt for which they would remain individually responsible.
>
> (Monti 2010: 63)

The European Council did not accept these reforms, because the German government refused any proposal leading to a 'transfer union': the German government accepted only to pool a limited quantity of money in the EU purse, but the deficit countries had to accept severe fiscal austerity conditions. And, since the money at the disposal of the EU to save the weak member states was granted slowly and parsimoniously, the crisis spread from Greece to Ireland, Portugal,

Spain and Italy. An economist, who detected the frailty of the European banking system in advance, writes:

> Even though it is impossible to know counterfactuals, had the western European banking sector been less fragile at that time, it is very possible that a different course would have been taken involving Greek debt restructuring as early as 2010, and everything afterwards would have developed very differently. Put bluntly, the moral hazard created by the Greek package is largely a consequence of the failure or unwillingness of European policymakers to resolve the European banking crisis in 2009.
>
> (Véron 2011: 5)

Was a 'different course' possible? Only future historians will answer this difficult question. Here we can only propose a conjecture. Since 1950, with the ECSC, the initiative for more European integration was always taken by France and Germany, but France, as a winner of WWII and member of the UN Security council, led. In effect, de Gaulle could theorize 'l'Europe des patries' led by France. During the present financial crisis, it became clear that the economic power of reunified Germany was crucial. So France had to accept willy-nilly the German austerity policy. At a certain point, a 'gaullism allemand' seemed to inspire the German government for a new 'Europe des patries', since a project for a Federal Union was not on the table. Jürgen Habermas says that the traditional European vocation of Germany was replaced by 'an undisguised leadership claim of a "European Germany in a German Europe"' (Habermas 2012: 133). The German government, however, by pushing the austerity policies too far, caused a further division between virtuous and profligate countries and put at risk the very survival of the EMU. The reversal of this strategy came about only when the German government realized that Germany itself could become the victim of the European catastrophe.

Whatever the political explanation of the crisis is, it is necessary to find a way out. And since the main hurdle seems to be unfamiliarity with the principles of federalism, in the following sections we try to show that a European fiscal union is possible and viable.

The European fiscal union and Hamilton's problem

Fiscal federalism is the field of public finance that studies the appropriate allotment of fiscal revenues and expenditures among different levels of government. Nevertheless, the bulk of the literature on fiscal federalism assumes, implicitly or explicitly, US institutions as the model. We need to overcome this. At present, the USA is a centralized federation, with roughly two thirds of tax revenues collected by the federal government. This degree of centralization can be explained by the fact that US citizens accept to share with other citizens some 'national' duties (for instance, military service and income tax) and some 'national' services (for instance, Medicare and Medicaid). In short, the USA is a nation in which the federal institutions are considered a means for a decentralized form of government.

The EU is not a nation, but a supranational union of national peoples. Therefore, we should look for a supranational model of fiscal federalism in which, presumably, the degree of solidarity among citizens of different nations is lower than the degree of solidarity among citizens of the same nation state. Since implementation of the crucial principles of federalism can produce different effects in different societies, we need to draft a new model that fits Europe's needs. Alexander Hamilton, the Secretary of the Treasury, was the first to understand and theorize the problem of a fiscal system subdivided among different governments. Therefore, we try to redefine what is known as Hamilton's paradox (Rodden 2006), or Hamilton's problem (Fiorentini and Montani 2012: ch. 6), to stress that a solution is possible. In order to have a well-run monetary union, the main principles for a European model of fiscal federalism are: (a) the relative autonomy of monetary policy from fiscal policy; (b) hard budget constraints for every level of government; (c) a limited transfer union; (d) an autonomous federal budget (this fourth principle will be discussed in the last section).

Autonomy of monetary policy from fiscal policy

The no-bailout clause for the ECB is clearly stated in the Maastricht Treaty; the Lisbon Treaty inherited it. The ECB, according to this clause, cannot purchase directly member states' debt. This clause is necessary in order to make the ECB independent from the will of national governments: its statutory goal is price stability. Notwithstanding, during the crisis many economists (for instance, De Grauwe 2011a, 2011b; Bradford DeLong 2011) strongly supported the view that the ECB should intervene in the market buying national bonds under attack, fully playing its role as lender of last resort to save not only the banking industry but also the European system of public finance. The German government and the Bundesbank always refused this proposal. Let's consider their point of view.

In a nation state, if the Central Bank issues an excessive quantity of paper money that causes inflation, a vertical distribution of income among different groups of citizens is the result, because there will be some groups able to defend their purchasing power and other weaker groups whose real income will be eroded by price increases. In a monetary union, an inflationary process can provoke not only a vertical redistribution of income but also a horizontal transfer of income among countries. A hidden horizontal transfer of income in the long run can destroy a monetary union. In a nation state, this problem is seldom detected. In the USA during the 1970s and 1980s, the inflation rate sometimes reached two digits, but none of the 50 states protested.

In the EMU, the degree of tolerance to inflation changes drastically from country to country. The same problem can arise even without inflation. When a crisis bites and the EMU risks collapse, the ECB should play the role of lender of last resort, because a liquidity crisis can easily become a solvency crisis, both for the banking industry and for some governments. Only the ECB can provide an unlimited amount of cash. The significance of this can be tested by the present condition of the US and UK economy, which have a higher debt/GDP and deficit/GDP than the eurozone but are not besieged by international finance. The objection is this: if the ECB buys an unlimited amount of some national debt, this opens the doors for a new debt issuance. De Grauwe correctly observes that one should distinguish the role of the institution providing liquidity from the institution charged with the regulation and supervision of bond issue.

> The ECB assumes the responsibility of lender of last resort in the sovereign bond markets. A different and independent authority takes over the responsibility of regulating and supervising the creation of debt by national governments. To use a metaphor: when a house is burning the fire department is responsible for extinguishing the fire. Another department (police or justice) is responsible for investigating wrongdoing and applying punishment if necessary. Both functions should be kept separate.
>
> (De Grauwe 2011a: 9)

This can be accepted, with two qualifications. The first is that the principle that the ECB cannot bail out national governments is to be maintained, but it should be admitted that when the integrity of the eurozone is threatened the ECB can act as lender of last resort. If the EMU crumbles, the ECB crumbles. At present, Europe is in a dangerous situation because the EMU was set up without a fiscal union or a federal government. Monetary policy can only be really autonomous if public finance is independent from private finance. If the house burns, the ECB must play the role of the 'fire brigade' supplying the liquidity necessary to stop the fire; but the 'police department' has the duty to prevent a pyromaniac from setting the house on fire.

The second qualification concerns the ECB, which must not only guarantee price stability to the eurozone, but also financial stability. In fact, the request of a 'banking union' is an attempt to fill the present gap. In short, the ECB should become responsible for a European resolution authority and a guarantee scheme for EMU bank customer deposits, as proposed in 'Towards a Genuine Economic and Monetary Union' by the President of the European Council (Van Rompuy 2012). The European Commission has already proposed a provisional scheme for a banking union (EC 2012a).

Hard budget constraints

In a competitive market, a company fails when it is not able to meet its debts. This company has hard budget constraints. If this company has a reasonable expectation that somebody – for instance, a benevolent government – will bail it out, it has a soft budget constraint. If we transpose this concept into a political system, we have hard (or soft) budget constraints that can be taken as a measure of the degree of centralization or decentralization. If the central government is financially strong, in the sense that the bulk of financial resources are centralized, usually local governments have soft budget constraints, because they can rely on the bailout of the central government in the case of an unsustainable deficit. On the other hand, in an anarchical international order, a sovereign state burdened with unsustainable debt has no alternative to default. In a federal state, which is a system of independent and coordinate governments, the principle of hard budget constraints should be applied to every level of government, from the local to the central government. Autonomy involves responsibility. This is theory; in practice it is very difficult to find a federation in which this principle is fully applied (for a survey, see Rodden *et al.* 2003).

After the Maastricht Treaty, the European governments considered the SGP as a guarantee for the fiscal probity of the member states of the EMU. When the crisis came, the Greek case was considered more of a scandal than a political problem for the eurozone. Only after many haphazard measures and mistakes did it become clear that the existence of the EMU was at stake and that a comprehensive reform – a fiscal union – was necessary. The principle of hard budget constraints is never mentioned in the official documents, but the declared goal is to achieve the full fiscal responsibility of national governments. The Treaty on Stability, Coordination and Governance, approved by the Council on 31 January 2012, the so-called Fiscal Compact, is in effect a reinforced SGP: it includes the main decisions taken during the crisis, with some important new innovations.

In 2010, the Commission proposed the European semester in order to involve the national governments, the national parliaments and the European Parliament in a process aimed at strengthening the coordination of macroeconomic policies and the formation of national budgets. During the first semester of every year, the EU member states debate and coordinate *ex-ante* their fiscal policies, growth policies and structural reforms, fixing medium-term objectives. The intrusive power of the Commission in national economic policy is strongly increased. The aim is to steer the economies of the member states towards a level of debt and deficit below the default risk and to avoid pro-cyclical economic policies. The Fiscal Compact establishes a legal framework and allows more power to the Commission to implement medium-term objectives:[1] The member states of the EMU have to put in their constitution or in their national legal system the balanced budget rule, which is incorporated into the jurisdiction of the Court of Justice. If the Commission observes that a member state has failed to comply with the agreed medium-term objectives, the matter will be brought to the Court of Justice by one or more governments and the judgement of the Court is binding.[2] The recommendation of the Commission on the corrective measures can be opposed only by a reversed qualified majority of the Council.

The European Parliament approved a resolution, called 'two pack' (13 June 2012), which increases the control power of the European Commission over the eurozone countries' fiscal policy, but these powers will be subject to more democratic control – by means of delegate acts – and the budget cuts suggested by the Commission should not be made at the expense of killing off investments with growth potential, not least those in education and healthcare. Moreover, the Parliament proposes an institutionalized mechanism to allow for a national default, in order to provide legal protection for any member state that is at risk of default. The member state is required to submit a debt settlement plan for approval by the Commission in which all creditors have to make themselves known to the Commission.

In sum, the supranational powers of the Commission (the police department) are greatly increased, allowing both an *ex-ante* power to implement national plans for growth and yearly budgets and an *ex-post* power, thanks to the new powers of European jurisdiction, to punish the countries of the EMU in breach of the agreed medium-term objectives. Moreover, and this regulation is crucial to set in motion the hard budget constraints, an institutional mechanism for a national orderly default system is established. With these measures, the political risk of a sovereign debt default is turned into an economic risk (similar to the risk a creditor must bear for a private company default). Finally, the default of one member state should not be confused with its expulsion from the EMU. The expulsion of a member state is nothing but the admission of the failure of the EU which, according to Art. 3 of the Lisbon Treaty, 'shall promote economic, social and territorial cohesion, and solidarity among Member States'. The leaders of the EU should explain to their voters that European citizens not only have rights, but also duties.

A limited transfer union

During the New Deal, the US government created some crucial welfare state institutions at the federal level. In Europe, welfare state institutions have firm national roots. Citizens in member states feel a higher degree of solidarity towards their fellow citizens than towards other European citizens. In the 1990s, the German federal government bailed out Saarland and the City of Bremen; the German reunification was a kind of bailout of the Eastern Länder, but in 2010 the German government refused to bail out Greece. The German government does not accept hidden or unverifiable transfers of revenue from country to country, as in the cases of an ECB or national debt bailout. Of course similar behaviour can be seen in other EMU countries. This does not mean that the degree of solidarity among European peoples is zero. Some new institutions were set up to come to the rescue of distressed states, but not without intergovernmental control and conditions.

In 2010, the European Commission created the European Financial Stability Mechanism (EFSM), an instrument that allows the European Commission to borrow money on the capital market, thanks to the guarantee of the EU budget, in order to aid distressed countries. The EFSM has a borrowing capacity of €60m. In the same year, the national governments created the European Financial Stability Facility (EFSF) as a temporary intergovernmental instrument to borrow money on the capital market. It has a lending capacity of €440bn. It was utilized to provide financial assistance to Greece, Ireland, Portugal and Spain. Since 2012, the permanent intergovernmental instrument of solidarity is the European Stability Mechanism (ESM). It can borrow money on the basis of its own capital: €80bn granted by the EU member states and a callable capital of €620bn. It will have effective lending capacity of €500bn.

The institutional structure and the goals of the ESM are similar to the IMF. The fund of €80bn is the founding capital of EU member states and will have an impact on their gross sovereign debt level but not on their budget deficit. Since it can issue its own bonds, its debt will not be consolidated with that of member states. The callable capital will not have an impact on the sovereign debt of member states as long as there are no losses to record (caused by some EMU member state's default). The goal of the ESM is to lend money to distressed countries, at a rate of interest lower than the usually unsustainable rate the financial market asks for a failing country, but a little higher than the normal market rate and not without conditions. The ESM can recapitalize banks directly and reduce the spread in interest rates on bond issuances among eurozone countries. It is interesting to see what happened with Greece.

> The three-year bilateral loans granted [by the EFSF] to Greece in May 2010 have indeed increased the sovereign debt of each EMU member state. In fact, each country has been forced to issue new bonds in order to be able to grant Greece a loan. Yet, given that Greece pays them interest at a rate higher than that at which they themselves are borrowing on the money markets, these new issuances of debt have not increased their public deficit because the costs of issuing have been balanced out by the interests paid by Greece.
> (Fernandes and Rubio 2012: 4)

Therefore, the impact of the ESM on the national budgets of the EMU member states, if we exclude a dramatic default, will be limited to the cost of the founding capital. Since the ESM is able to guarantee that each member state under stress can raise money at a given (though at a penalty cost) rate of interest, its function will be similar to that of a Eurobond. The real difference with a traditional loan is that the ESM will impose restructuring financial plans, similar to those imposed by the IMF, as happened for Greece, Ireland and Portugal.

The ESM as an instrument is not considered powerful enough to face all the European problems. In effect, some reasonable doubt exists on its capability to face the default of some big countries, such as Spain or Italy. Moreover, many debtor countries think that it is unfair that in a monetary union some countries can raise money at very low interest rates (like Germany) and others are obliged to face unsustainable rates. In the US, the 50 states can find specific difficulties in borrowing on the market, but the spread in interest rates is not so high as in the EMU, because the federal government greatly reduces their financial needs thanks to federal grants. In the EU, the 'federal' budget is too small to provide significant aid to member states.

One way to solve the problem of a 'common and fair rate of interest' for every country is the creation of Eurobonds. There are two interesting proposals. The first, originally drawn up by Delpa and von Weizsäcker (2010) and adopted by the European Commission (EC 2011), is that the EU countries pool up to 60 per cent of GDP of their national debt assuming a joint liability for the common European debt. The national debts beyond the Blue bond allocation are considered Red bonds, for which the issuing national government is fully liable. Of course, the Red bonds will pay a higher interest rate, thus pushing the issuing government to converge to the 60 per cent level. The advantages of the Blue bonds proposal are several:

> The euro area Blue bond market could amount to 60% of euro area GDP (about €5,600bn), which is about five times the current market for the German Bund and almost as large as the US Treasury debt market (about $8,300bn). All things being equal, greater liquidity in bonds reduces the borrowing costs.
>
> (Delpa and von Weizsäcker 2010: 4)

Notre Europe (2012: 38–41) proposes a similar, but more gradual scheme. A European Debt Agency would issue 10 per cent of GDP eurozone of member states' debts. A discount window would allow euro area states to borrow up to 20 per cent of GDP relatively easily, but for tranches above 20 per cent the interest rate will be raised and the distressed country must agree to an adjustment programme.

The second alternative is a redemption fund, based on the proposal made by the German Council of Economic Experts (2011). The EMU member states should pool their debts exceeding 60 per cent of GDP into a European fund. EMU members are jointly liable for redeeming their part of the debt in 20–25 years, but have the advantage of paying a low interest rate since the European Redemption Fund (ERF) can issue its own bonds. The condition for EMU members to take part in the ERF is that they should devote part of their tax revenue to pay their yearly lump amount to the ERF and deposit collaterals. The German government prefers this second alternative – and also the European Parliament supports it – but it has the drawback of leaving the EMU at the end of the transitory period of 20–25 years without European bonds. In fact, for a smooth functioning of the European financial and banking system a 'perfectly transferable' asset – similar to the US Treasury Bonds – is necessary.

Federalism is neither centralization nor decentralization

The abovementioned three principles of the European model of fiscal federalism show that the EU is embarking on a different path from the one chosen by the US. In Europe, the bulk of public revenues are allocated at national level and the EU budget is only about 2 per cent of total EU revenues. In fact, the small EU budget is basically ignored in the debate over the fiscal union. The proof is that the next Multiannual Financial Framework 2014–2020, at present under discussion, does not forecast any significant change from that amount (about 1 per cent of EU GDP). This is a grave error both of the national governments and of the European Parliament: if a fiscal union is to be set up in the next few years – and this step is necessary to save the EMU – it will not work properly and frequent reparations will be required in order to avoid a new dramatic crisis.

Here attention will be drawn to the relationships between the three features listed previously and the EU budget. A fiscal union is a set of constitutional rules regarding the apportionment of fiscal resources among independent and coordinated governments. But, as Wheare (1967) says, if federalism is to operate not merely as a matter of strict law but also in practice, the European level of government should have autonomous financial resources. The solution to this problem is the creation of a federal budget, which entails a federal government (a reformed Commission, with a Ministry of Finance) responsible before a bicameral parliament – a chamber of representatives and a chamber of national governments. Let's consider again the three features already discussed under this new perspective.

Autonomy of monetary policy from fiscal policy

As we have already seen, the autonomy of monetary policy from fiscal policy involves the full responsibility of the ECB for the functioning of the European banking industry. A banking union must be set up, with a resolution authority and a euro area deposit guarantee fund. At present, the supervision system is rooted at the national level. The EBA needs information from national supervisors to intervene. 'The limited supervisory role of the EBA is, of course, related to the absence of financial means at EU level to support banks in difficulty. Taxpayers' resources remain firmly in the hands of national governments and parliaments' (Marzinotto *et al.* 2011: 4).

The same observation should be made for the deposit guarantee fund because the bank industry should contribute to the fund with an insurance premium, in order to avoid public finance authorities being obliged again to rescue the banking industry should a new crisis arise.

> A euro area deposit insurance scheme would go a long way to breaking the existing link between banks and their national sovereigns which tends to become a vicious circle in times of crisis. The [fund] would ultimately have to be backed by euro area fiscal capacity.
>
> (Marzinotto *et al.* 2011: 6)

Unfortunately, the proposal under discussion in the EU (Van Rompuy 2012) is that 'the ESM could act as the fiscal backstop to the resolution and deposit guarantee authority'. If the financial stability of the eurozone is considered a European public good – as it is – the fiscal backstop should be the EU budget and not the ESM, which is a life belt for distressed countries. To these observations one must add that the intergovernmental decision-making system is too slow in the case of crises. The ECB must make very quick decisions consulting the European Finance Ministry, which is of course politically responsible before the European Parliament for the utilization of the taxpayer's money.

Hard budget constraints

The set of financial and accountability constraints included in the Fiscal Compact are a necessary guideline for a sound fiscal policy in EMU member states. But these rules will be applied and work smoothly only if each government has enough fiscal resources, given the expectations and needs of their citizens.

Unfortunately, in the EU member states, a dysfunctional equilibrium exists between national political commitments and national fiscal resources. After WWII, during the first decades of European integration and the NATO military protectorate, European governments were able to build a satisfactory welfare system, granting high levels of employment and good public services. Today, European governments must face new challenges, such as new military commitments for peace keeping and peace enforcing, in the framework of the UN, and the ecological reconversion of their old system of production. Moreover, globalization is relentlessly eroding the financial basis of the European fiscal system. The liberalization of capital movements allows financial capitals to fly where profit perspectives are higher and risks lower. International direct investments go where tax rates are lower. Global competition among national fiscal systems increases the fiscal burden on the working and middle classes, as the increasing rates of indirect taxation (like VAT) compared with the decreasing rate of corporate taxation show. Income inequalities are increasing everywhere (see Fiorentini and Montani 2012: chapters 3 and 6). Therefore, national governments can recover their power to tax only at the supranational level, in the EU with a federal government and, when it becomes possible, at a global level.

National governments strongly resist devolving more fiscal powers to the EU, but are unable to supply the public goods citizens need. The national waste of European resources causes less growth, more unemployment and more poverty in the EU. This waste is clearly substantiated in a report by three members of the European Parliament (Haug *et al.* 2011) who show how miserable and antidemocratic the management of the EU budget is. For instance, the EU decided to create an External Action Service in order to set up a European foreign policy. But, at present, the EU member states employ 94,000 staff members while the US has only 22,000. The European system of central banks employs 44,000 people while the US Federal reserve banks employ 18,000. In the defence sector, split into several national systems, the European system employs 2 million people, but the potential effectiveness on the battlefield is lower than that of the US, as the Afghan and Libyan deployments have exemplified.

The EU budget is not a piece of the transfer union, because its main function is to provide European public goods, which benefit all the Union's citizens. But the EU national governments do not accept the obvious fact that a federal budget is the most effective way to collect European taxes, to reduce the risks of economic cycles and to exploit economies of scale for the provision of European public goods. The size of the federal budget is considered a taboo. The first and last study on this problem was the McDougall Report drawn up for the European Commission in 1977. According to this report, the EU budget should reach 5–7 per cent of GDP, but it took the US as a model. Today, a suitable size for a European federal budget could probably be more modest. Here, it is necessary only to recall that the EU budget must be financed with 100 per cent of its own resources: with an ensemble of a financial transaction tax, a VAT, a carbon tax, a corporate tax and an income tax. Moreover, the growth plan 'Europe 2020', proposed by the European Commission, must be financed as soon as possible if the EU wishes to save the EMU and to avoid further years of distress for European citizens. The decision, taken by the European Council on 27–28 June 2012, to launch a 'European Growth Pact' of 1 per cent of EU GDP is only a timid step forward: €55bn are reallocated structural funds, already in the EU budget; only the increased lending capacity of €60bn of the EIB is a really new measure, together with the first issue of project bonds (€5bn), already approved by the European Parliament. All in all, the effectiveness of the EU budget for the growth and stability of the European economy is greatly underrated. Thanks to the principle of co-financing, European expenses stimulate national investments too and, in fact, the EU budget coordinates all EU investments in a more effective way than administrative rules.

A limited transfer union

The debate on the transfer union disregards the fact that the size of the EU budget is part of the problem. The EU budget finances the provision of European public goods, such as Galileo, a number of industrial and scientific research projects and, hopefully, the growth plan 'Europe 2020'. These expenses, together with other policies, such as the structural funds, favour convergence among rich and poor regions and increase the welfare of European citizens. If the size of the EU budget is not enough to create an effective convergence, the hard budget constraints for national governments become a straitjacket: austerity policies provoke recession and fiscal unsustainability. When the EU budget fails to guarantee a convergence process, distressed countries seek the help of the ESM and, if the financial strength of the ESM is not enough, the integrity of the eurozone is threatened. Hard budget constraints are not the only criteria for assessing the efficiency of a fiscal union: an efficient fiscal union should also guarantee the real convergence of diverse and dissimilar national economies (as Art. 3 of the Lisbon Treaty states).

Moreover, instead of the ESM, which is an intergovernmental instrument, the same function can be carried out better by the EFSM, which is financed by the EU budget and is under the control of the European Commission. The problem with the EFSM is that its financial capacity is small because the EU budget is small. But from a European point of view, the best place to put the European taxpayers' money is the EFSM not the ESM.

Finally, let's consider the question of Eurobonds. Apropos, we should distinguish between the problem of national debt management and the structural needs of a 'perfectly transferable financial European asset'. For national debt management, the proposal of the creation of the ERF is likely the most appropriate.

But the EMU needs a permanent transferable financial asset for two reasons: (a) to avoid a new double crisis, of the national debts and the banking industry; (b) to attract capital from outside Europe and make the eurozone a competitive global financial market. From this second point of view, the best solution is for the European Commission, if the EU budget is financed by its own fiscal resources, to issue its own bonds, pure Eurobonds, not only project bonds. The rules of the Fiscal Compact should be applied at the European level too. The budget of the EU must become flexible, with some slow deficits and surpluses according to the phase of the economic cycle, like the national budgets. The European citizens and financial investors should (and probably will) buy pure Eurobonds as alternatives to national bonds.

A fiscal union without a federal budget is like a sailing ship without the mainmast. The omission of the size of the EU budget in the plans for the European fiscal union reveals that the compliance of hard budget constraints at national levels will rely more on administrative rules than on effective and agreed upon processes of economic convergence among the national economies. This approach may cause political and social protests against Brussels' bureaucracy and the national governments which support these policies. To avoid this danger, the creation of a federal budget and a democratic European government are necessary. The citizens will accept to give more fiscal powers to the EU if they trust the new federal government, and the political parties which support it, in the European Parliament. This will require time to be fulfilled and real political leadership, but it is possible because a proper federal budget can decrease the fiscal burden of European citizens.

At present, the national political leaders, with their disagreements, wavering and errors, have brought the EMU to the verge of collapse. Their duty is to get out from this quagmire as soon as possible by setting up the necessary institutional reforms to save the EMU; this urgent decision must be coherent with the creation of a federal government, fixing the stages and the date for its establishment. Human institutions were never born perfect. The US states, in spite of their federal constitution, caused a civil war before finding the way for a more perfect union. In Europe, we have already had two bloody civil wars; now we must work incessantly to save the European construction and render it more perfect.

Notes

1 The budget of the member states must be in balance or in surplus; only a structural deficit of 0.5 per cent of the GDP is tolerated; if the debt exceeds 60 per cent of GDP, it should be reduced at an average rate of one twentieth per year as a benchmark.
2 The Court may impose a lump sum or a penalty payment that shall not exceed 0.1 per cent of the GDP of the non-compliant state.

Bibliography

Bodenhorn, H. (1992) 'Capital Mobility and Financial Integration in Antebellum America', *The Journal of Economic History*, vol. 52, no. 3, pp. 585–610.

Bradford DeLong, J. (2011) 'The ECB's Battle against Central Banking', *Social Europe Journal*, 1 November.

Cebula, R.J., and Zaharoff, M. (1974) 'Interregional Capital Transfers and Interest Rate Differentials: An Empirical Note', *The Annals of Regional Science*, vol. 8, pp. 87–94.

De Grauwe, P. (2011a) *The European Central Bank: Lender of Last Resort in the Government Bond Markets?* CESifo Working Paper No. 3569, September.

De Grauwe, P. (2011b) 'Europe Needs the ECB to Step up to the Plate', *Financial Times*, 19 October.

Delpa, J., and von Weizsäcker, J. (2010) *The Blue Bond Proposal*, Bruegel Policy Brief, no. 3.

EC (2011) *Green Paper on the Feasibility of Introducing Stability Bonds*, Brussels, 11 November.

EC (2012a) *Proposal for a Directive of the European Parliament and the Council Establishing a Framework for the Recovery and Resolution of Credit Institutions and Investment Firms*, Brussels.

EC (2012b) *New Crisis Management Measures to Avoid Future Bank Bail-outs*, Press Release, Brussels, 6 June.

ECB (2012) *Financial Integration in Europe*, Frankfurt am Main.

Feldstein, M., and Horioka, C. (1980) 'Domestic Saving and International Capital Flows', *The Economic Journal*, vol. 90 (June), pp. 314–329.

Fernandes, S., and Rubio, E. (2012) *The Budgetary Cost of Solidarity in the Eurozone: Getting Things Clear and into Perspective*, Notre Europe Policy Brief, no. 35.

Fiorentini, R., and Montani, G. (2012) *The New Global Political Economy. From Crisis to Supranational Integration*, Cheltenham: Edward Elgar.

German Council of Economic Experts (2011) *Assume Responsibility for Europe*, Annual Report 2011–2012, Berlin.

Habermas, J. (2012) *The Crisis of the European Union. A Response*, Cambridge: Polity Press.

Haug, J., Lamassoure, A., and Verhofstadt, G. (2011) *Europe for Growth. For a Radical Change in Financing the EU*, Brussels and Paris: CEPS and Notre Europe.

Ingram, J.C. (1959) 'State and Regional Payments Mechanism', *The Quarterly Journal of Economics*, vol. 73, no. 4, pp. 919–932.

James, J.A., and Weiman, D.F. (2010) 'From Drafts to Checks: The Evolution of Correspondent Banking Networks and the Formation of the Modern US Payments System, 1850–1914', *Journal of Money, Credit and Banking*, vol. 42, no. 2–3, pp. 217–265.

Marzinotto, B., Sapir A., and Wolff, G.B. (2011) *What Kind of Fiscal Union?* Bruegel Policy Brief, no. 6, Brussels.

Merler, S., and Pisani-Ferry, J. (2012a). *Who's Afraid of Sovereign Bonds?* Brueghel Policy Contribution, no. 2, Brussels.

Merler, S., and Pisani-Ferry, J. (2012b) 'Hazardous Tango: Sovereign-Bank Interdependence and Financial Stability in the Euro Area', *Banque de France – Financial Stability Review*, no. 16.

Monti, M. (2010) *A New Strategy for the Single Market. At the Service of European Economy and Society. Report to the President of the European Commission Josè Manuel Barroso*, Brussels.

Notre Europe (2012) *Completing the Euro. A Road Map towards Fiscal Union in Europe. Report of the Tommaso Padoa-Schioppa Group*, Paris.

Pfister, R.L. (1960) 'State and Regional Payments Mechanism: Comment', *Quarterly Journal of Economics*, vol. 74, no. 4, pp. 641–648.

Robertson, R.M. (1964) *History of the American Economy*, New York: Harcourt Brace.

Rockoff, H. (2003) 'How Long Did It Take the United States to Become an Optimal Currency Area?', in Capie, F.H., and Wood, G.E. (eds.) *Monetary Unions: Theory, History, Public Choice*, London: Routledge, pp. 70–103.

Rodden, J.A. (2006) *Hamilton's Paradox. The Promise and Peril of Fiscal Federalism*, Cambridge: Cambridge University Press.

Rodden, J.A., Eskeland, G.S., and Litvack, J. (eds.) (2003) *Fiscal Decentralization and the Challenge of Hard Budget Constraints*, Cambridge Mass. and London: The MIT Press.

Scitovsky, T. (1969) *Money and the Balance of Payments*, London: Unwin University Books.

Van Rompuy, H. (2012) *Towards a Genuine Economic and Monetary Union. Report by the President of the European Council Herman Van Rompuy*, Brussels, 26 June.

Véron, N. (2011) *Testimony on the European Debt and Financial Crisis*, Bruegel Policy Contribution, Brussels.

Wheare, K.C. (1967) *Federal Government*, Oxford: Oxford University Press.

6 From democratic dissatisfaction to financial crisis

Dóra Győrffy

Following the financial crisis, the ideal of democracy seems to be losing attractiveness. In several countries, the populist measures, which eventually led to the crisis, were the outcome of democratic politics as electoral considerations dominated policy-making at the detriment of long-term sustainability. Excluding vote-maximizing considerations from economic decision-making thus seems to be the order of the day in Europe as the reform of economic governance increases the power of European institutions over almost every aspect of economic policy.

The public does not remain unaware of decreasing national discretion. In the creditor countries, there is considerable outrage over the large-scale financial help to the periphery. It appears that democratic control over taxpayers' money is greatly reduced. In the periphery countries, the strict conditionality, which comes from the bailout packages, strongly constrains the discretion of democratically elected leaders over economic decisions.

Based on the above, it is unsurprising that trust in the EU and national governments is in steady decline. Figure 6.1 shows the changes in the satisfaction with democracy and the level of trust towards the European Union and national governments.

The growing skepticism towards democracy by both elites and regular citizens raises disturbing questions about human freedom and autonomy. However, its relationship to the financial crisis is almost never mentioned. In the following, I will attempt to uncover the links between democratic dissatisfaction and financial imbalances. The main argument of the chapter is that by reflecting decreasing trust in the political system, democratic dissatisfaction leads to a shortening of time-horizon in society, which in turn increases the attractiveness of short-term, populist measures. Accumulating public and private indebtedness is a manifestation of this problem.

The chapter will discuss the background of indicators such as trust and satisfaction with democracy in order to understand their meaning. Then it will provide a theoretical framework showing the relationship between lack of trust and short-term thinking. The theory will be illustrated by data on indebtedness in the original euro-zone countries and new EU member states (EU-12 and CEE-10). Finally, the case of Hungary will be used to illustrate how such results come

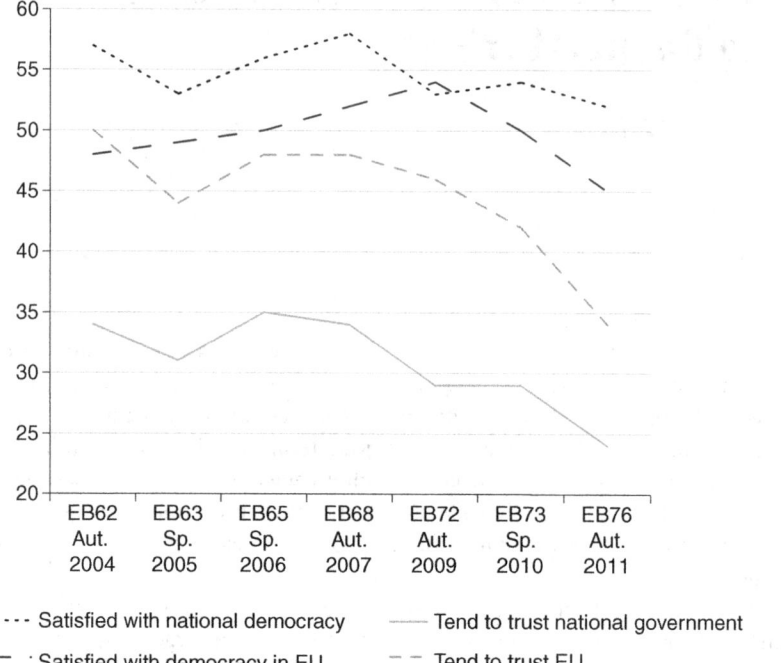

Figure 6.1 Trust and satisfaction in the EU, 2004–2011 (percent of respondents) (data: Eurobarometer 65, 76, 77).

about from the policy process. The conclusion will discuss the main implications of these trends.

The debate over measuring political support

Before proceeding to discuss the consequences of declining trust in democracy, first it is important to discuss what the indicators such as trust in government and satisfaction with democracy actually mean. In the following, I will provide a brief overview of the debate over these measures focusing on the meaning of satisfaction with democracy.

The focus on political support can be traced back to the work of David Easton, who argues that the level of trust in government is a key factor in the functioning of the political system (Easton 1965). In assessing support, he differentiates between specific support, which relates to short-term outputs, and diffuse support, which means 'a reservoir of favorable attitudes or good will that helps members to accept or tolerate outputs to which they are opposed or the effect of which they see as damaging to their wants' (Easton 1965: 273). These ideas strongly resonate with the ideas of Gamson (1968: 45–46), who claims that:

when the supply in the reservoir is high, authorities are able to make new commitments on the basis of it and, if successful increase such support even more. When it is low and declining, authorities may find it difficult to meet existing commitments and to govern effectively.

Indicators such as 'Trust in government' or 'Satisfaction with democracy' aim to measure this kind of support.

Critics of the indicator, however, have noted that when an individual answers the question whether they trust the government or are satisfied with democracy, it is not at all clear what they mean. The most thorough critique of the indicator is given by Canache et al. (2001), who claim that in the literature the satisfaction with democracy measure is used in a variety of ways. Some authors consider it as an indicator of specific support, while others as an indicator of diffuse support – these two interpretations are clearly contradictory. There is a pragmatic third way of interpreting the indicator (Clarke et al. 1993) through looking at it as a summary measure of support for political community, regime, incumbent authorities – satisfaction with the existing political system. Canache et al. (2001: 508) note that empirical evidence favors this interpretation. However, this also means that the measure is so ambiguous that inferences from its use become meaningless.

In response to the above criticism, Anderson (2005) claims that, although it is indeed impossible to separate specific and diffuse support, it does not mean that the indicator is meaningless. He takes the pragmatic position that 'in the absence of a better item [which the authors, incidentally, do not supply], the satisfaction with democracy measure is a reasonable (albeit imperfect) indicator that we can use to test our theories' (Anderson 2005: 10). He also suggests that triangulation of evidence and different methodologies are most appropriate to assess the theories.

The most recent empirical examination of the problem is a longitudinal study done by Wagner et al. (2009) on the determinants of the satisfaction with democracy. They find that controlling for various variables, a better rule of law, lower corruption, a smaller shadow economy, better checks and balances, and a better institutional quality generally all lead to a higher satisfaction with democracy score (Wagner et al. 2009: 37).

Based on the above, in the following I will interpret the satisfaction with democracy indicator as a summary measure of institutional performance and show how it lies at the root of financial imbalances. However, knowing its limitations, I will also use a case study in order to uncover processes through which this variable contributes to outcomes.

The relationship between public trust and the time horizon of decision-making

When uncovering the consequences of democratic dissatisfaction and distrust in the system, first it is important to look at what trust means. In an attempt to provide a cross-disciplinary understanding of trust, Rousseau et al. (1998: 395) define trust as 'a psychological state comprising the intention to accept vulnerability based upon positive expectations of the intentions or behavior of another'. This implies that when acting upon trust we cannot be certain that the other party will not abuse this trust.

Lack of certainty does not mean that trust implies blind faith. When accepting vulnerability, the actor uses the information available on the other party. In this sense, there are rational elements of trust such as experiences from past interactions or the understanding of the motives of the other party. However, it is also important that the picture is necessarily subjective, since no one can be certain that she knows all the relevant facts about the other party's past or motives. This makes belief an essential ingredient of trust, which facilitates action on the basis of incomplete information (Möllering 2001).

Social science literature distinguishes between particular and general trust (Uslaner 1999: 126–127). Particular trust means that people trust only those who are part of the same community – such as family members or those with the same religious faith. This kind of trust is based on personal knowledge, the necessity of repeated cooperation and shared identity, which reduce the danger of an abuse of trust. In contrast, generalized trust means that most people, including those outside one's social group, can be trusted. As society became larger and more complex, this kind of trust gained increased significance since this makes cooperation among strangers possible. From the perspective of aggregate economic outcomes, it is generalized trust which matters, since this form of trust makes anonymous exchange possible.

The written and unwritten rules of society contribute to generalized trust and increase the predictability of interactions among members. According to Offe (1999: 73–75), institutions can generate trust through enforcing the values of truth-telling, promise-keeping, fairness and solidarity, which contribute to trust. Such an outcome is not the result of a single institution but rather the joint effect of a set of institutions. Truth-telling and the provision of information are ensured, for example, by the freedom of the press, public court proceedings and accounting standards. Promises are enforced by contracts and independent courts. Equality before the law and equal political rights foster a sense of fairness. Finally, state redistribution towards the less fortunate generates the feeling of solidarity. The success of institutions in these endeavors can give rise to 'moralistic trust', which claims in a normative sense that most people should be trusted. This is a variety of the Golden Rule, which requires 'you do unto others as you would have them do unto you' (Uslaner 2008: 103). Not attributing the intention of exploiting trust to the other party follows from this rule. According to Uslaner (2008: 117), moralistic trust is the real foundation for generalized trust.

The importance of institutions generating trust underlines the fact that everyday life governance, which is the output side of the political system, is at least as important as the input side, elections. In the absence of good governance,[1] generalized trust cannot emerge and the institutions cannot fulfill their role in coordinating the interactions of citizens. If the state is widely seen as corrupt, there is no equality before the law and public services increase rather than decrease life opportunities, the non-privileged groups are unlikely to have strong motives to respect the rules.[2]

The above consideration is particularly important once we recognize that, in the emergence of rule-following behavior, the legitimacy of norm or its creator is particularly important. In his overview about rule compliance, Hurd (1999) differentiates three different motives for following the law: coercion, self-interest and the legitimacy of the rule. He claims that the most efficient is the third, when internal convictions rather than external pressure create obedience. Physical coercion is not only expensive but also leads to resentment and resistance to the law and authorities (384–385). Self-interest is somewhat better in motivating voluntary compliance, but in the long-term it is likely to fail since it encourages continuous cost–benefit analysis about following the rule – once it appears too costly, there seems to be no reason to obey.[3] In contrast, rule compliance based on legitimacy does not calculate and obedience becomes habitual – in this case breaking the rule has psychological costs and thus requires special consideration (388). If this is missing, and following the rules is not in someone's interest, rule-avoidance becomes the norm since it is clear that the state cannot have a policeman for every citizen.

Based on the above, it is clear that institutional trust has a particularly important function in creating generalized trust. Without institutional trust, the risks of cooperating with strangers increase greatly. If business partners cannot be certain that contracts are enforced, they will require much more guarantee for signing a contract than in an environment where respecting the rules is the norm. This not only increases transaction costs, but it also results in an uncertain, unpredictable environment, where long-term plans are unrealistic. It is very risky to invest in a place where contracts are not enforced by independent courts and respect for private property rights cannot be taken for granted. In such an environment, short-term survival becomes the major objective for those who cannot leave, and rule-breaking and corruption become the widely accepted means towards this objective.

In a low-trust environment, the evasion of rules is generally fostered by perceptions about success. This has been analyzed empirically by Csepeli *et al.* (2004: 222), who found that in contrast to Western Europe, in Eastern Europe perceptions of success are much less associated with talent and hard work than with dishonesty. If success is associated with rule-breaking, and weak institutions are seen as unlikely to punish trespassers, people will have much less internal resistance to do the same, and a vicious cycle emerges among low trust, wide-spread rule-evasion, radical uncertainty and short-term thinking.

Politicians, who expect to gain votes during elections, cannot remain impervious to the prevalence of the above cycles. Since long-term promises are not credible, in the absence of strong external pressure, they answer to the short-term objectives of citizens by short-term solutions in order to gain votes. These, however, rarely intersect with the requirements of sustainable development.

The possibilities for short-term solutions are almost endless. In the socialist system, the state generally looked the other way rather than punished trespassers. The leaders of the system attempted to reduce the social stress due to shortages and the resulting low level of consumption through allowing private deals, very often involving the use of state resources. State authorities were willing to overlook these dealings and show leniency, although this was unpredictable and they could change their mind and apply the law in its full rigor at any time (Kornai 1992: 451–452). While the second economy indeed improved the standard of living, it also implied a lasting heritage about the disregard for rules shared by both citizens and authorities.

Improved living standards can also be achieved by increasing public or private debt. In order to improve their popularity, democratic governments can increase spending or cut taxes – both leading to budgetary imbalances; but while the first option generally benefits the poor, the second option benefits the taxpayers. If the rise in deficits is not feasible for some reason, loose financial regulation makes it possible to increase present consumption at the cost of the future without directly influencing state finances.

The likely failure of the above strategies already at the medium term further increases the distrust towards the institutions and strengthens the short-term orientation in society. If external pressure forces policy-makers to consolidate finances, the short-term sacrifices further increase dissatisfaction. There is thus no easy way out of the vicious cycle regardless of whether a responsible or irresponsible path is taken.

Institutional trust and indebtedness in the European Union

On the basis of theoretical considerations, we can hypothesize that lack of trust towards the government or the political system will manifest itself in increased debt levels, which reflects a strong preference for the present over the future.[4] In the following, I will illustrate this hypothesis in the old and new member states of the European Union. Institutional trust in the analysis is measured by the satisfaction of democracy indicator. While this is not a perfect measure, as discussed above, I view it in a pragmatic sense as an approximate measure of the level of satisfaction with the political system. Although it is clearly sensitive to daily politics and scandals, looking at longer periods can smooth out these factors.

Figure 6.2 shows the relationship between satisfaction with democracy and fiscal balance during the period 1998–2007. Both measures signal averages during the ten years. This period is particularly good for examining the hypothesis of this chapter because in order to qualify for the euro deficit was below 3 percent by 1998 in every country.[5] Following the introduction of the euro, there was no external force to discipline these countries – risk premiums converged to Germany.[6] At the same time, the Stability and Growth Pact also failed to discipline euro-zone members following the no-vote in the ECOFIN to the fining of Germany and France in 2003. This means that neither market nor bureaucratic

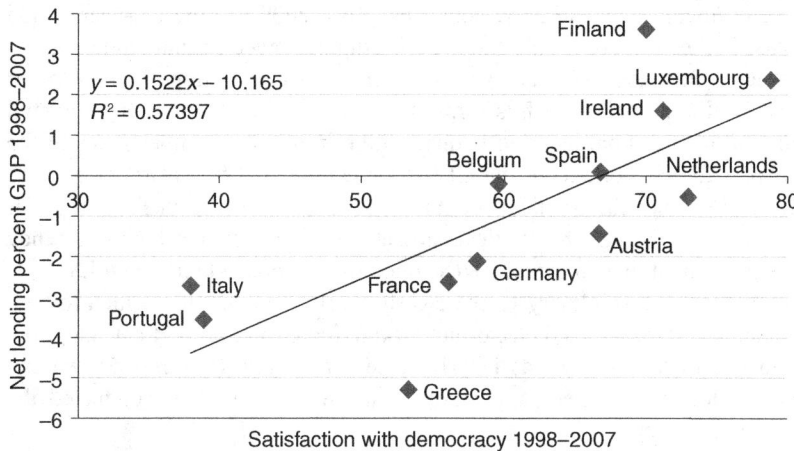

Figure 6.2 Satisfaction with democracy and fiscal balance in the EU-12, 1998–2007 (data: Eurobarometer No. 49, 51, 53, 56, 58, 59, 61, 63, 65, 68, European Commission 2012: 180).

discipline worked in this period, which means that internal factors were decisive in the trends in fiscal balance. Figure 6.3 supports this hypothesis and shows a strong relationship between satisfaction with democracy and fiscal position.

The relationship between institutional trust and indebtedness is much less evident in Eastern and Central Europe (EU-10). Given the inheritance from the Communist period, trust is notoriously low in these countries – as shown by Figure 6.3, satisfaction with democracy rarely reached 50 percent even in those countries which have the highest level of satisfaction, such as Slovenia or the

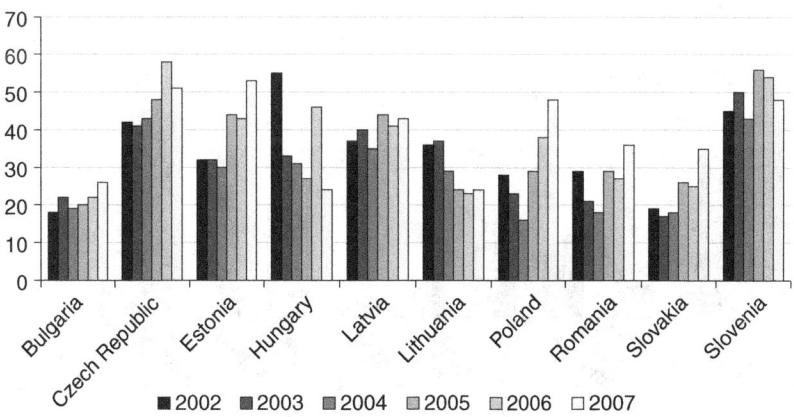

Figure 6.3 Satisfaction with democracy in the CEE-10, 2002–2007 (data: Candidate Countries Eurobarometer 2002.2, 2003.4, 2004.1, as well as Eurobarometer 63, 65, 68).

Czech Republic. This implies that the majority of the population in not satisfied with the political system in these countries (Rose 2009). In the ten-year period examined in the euro-zone, only Italy and Portugal showed similar tendencies.

In spite of low levels of trust, we can observe a declining trend in the level of public debt (Figure 6.4), which is surprising in light of the theory. One potential explanation for this contradiction is that, unlike in the old member states of the EU, market forces worked for the CEE-10 countries and fiscal processes were influenced by other factors than internal pressures. This is especially true for those countries, such as the Baltic States and Bulgaria, which had a currency board arrangement, which can be undermined by irresponsible fiscal policy.

While external disciplinary forces clearly worked, there still seemed to be a way to appease a dissatisfied electorate through increasing present consumption. If we take a look at the trends in private sector lending (Figure 6.5), we can observe a clear rise in debt, especially in those countries that conducted the strictest fiscal policy.

A simple correlation between public debt and private debt in Figure 6.6 provides some evidence for the presence of a substitution effect. However, the relationship is rather weak given two outliers: Romania and Hungary. Credit growth in Romania was much smaller than could have been expected based on its low public debt, while in Hungary both public and private debt soared during the period under examination. In the case of Romania, weak institutions and lack of a currency board providing credibility constrained access to the international financial markets and thus placed limits on becoming indebted. Still, in anticipation of its EU accession, there was a lending boom, but given the very low base and a later start, the expansion could not reach the proportions it did in other countries of the region (Hudecz 2012). The Hungarian case is the reverse – as a former leader of the transition, the country had access to international financial markets, and both the public and the private sector made use of this opportunity. As will

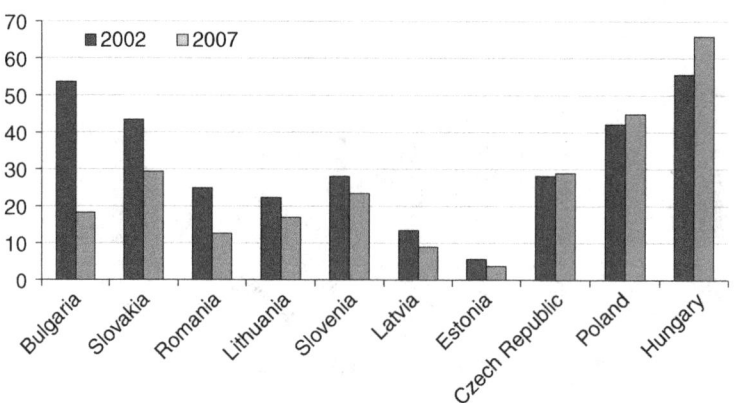

Figure 6.4 Public debt in the CEE-10, 2002–2007 (% of GDP) (data: European Commission 2012: 184–185).

Democratic dissatisfaction to financial crisis 101

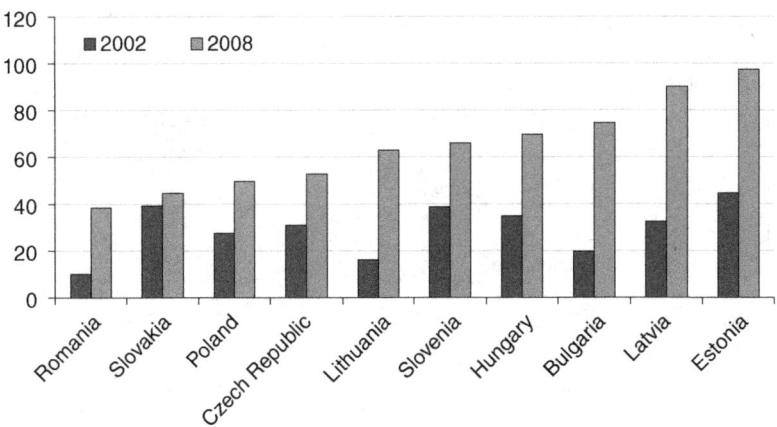

Figure 6.5 Credit to private sector in the CEE-10, 2002–2008 (% of GDP) (data: World Bank Data Catalog, available: http://data.worldbank.org/indicator/FS.AST.PRVT.GD.ZS).

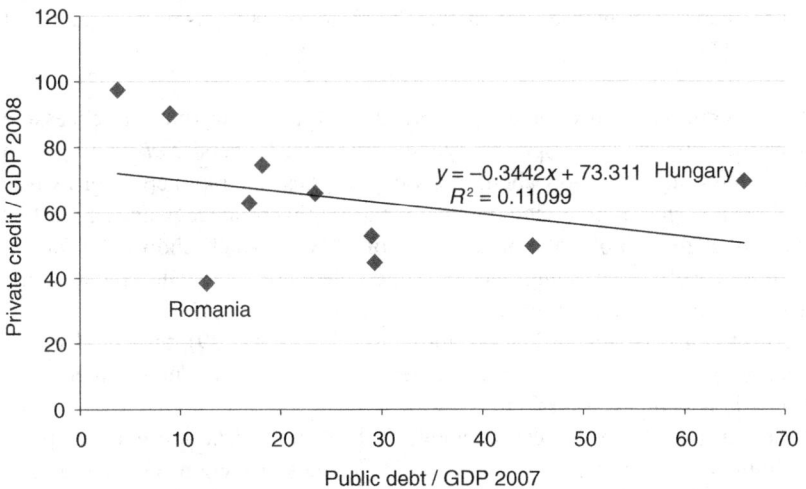

Figure 6.6 Public and private debt in the CEE-10, 2007/2008 (data: see Figures 6.4 and 6.5).

be shown in the next section, the case is an extreme illustration of the theory of trust and economic policy. In the regional context, however, the total lack of restraint makes it an outlier.

Removing the two outliers from the sample yields a very strong correlation between public and private debt, as shown by Figure 6.7. This provides some evidence for the hypothesis about the substitutability of welfare spending and credit.

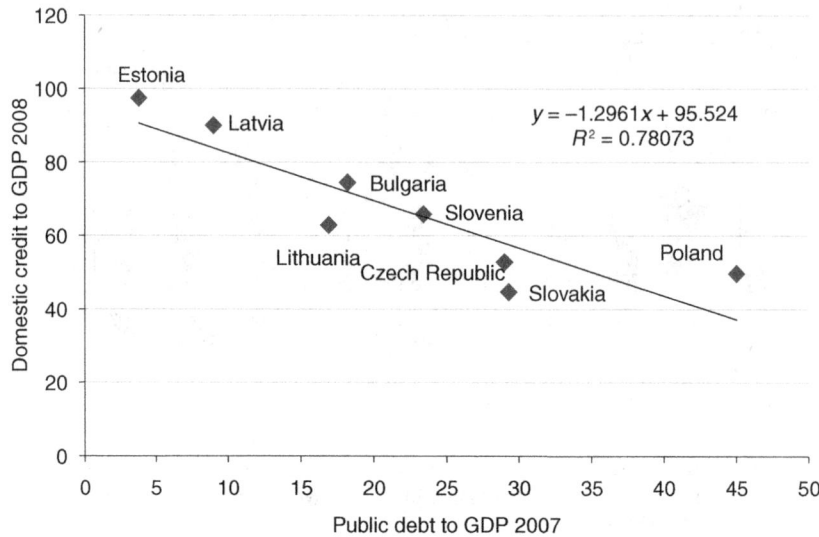

Figure 6.7 Public and private debt in the CEE-8, 2007/2008 (data: see Figures 6.4 and 6.5).

The hypothesis that access to cheap private credit can substitute for excessive welfare spending is also supported by the findings of Hilbers *et al.* (2007), who provide a thorough overview about the policy responses to rapid credit growth in the post-communist region, and conclude that they were inadequate, with a few exceptions such as Poland. For the case of Latvia, which shows the largest reduction in welfare spending and the largest increase in private credit, Bohle (2010: 8–9) suggests clear political motives in encouraging private indebtedness. Based on the assessment of Darvas and Kostyleva (2011: 29), the country also had the weakest financial regulation framework in the region, and between 2003 and 2007 it became even weaker.

Based on the above, we can conclude that, in the absence of external pressures in the euro-zone between 1998 and 2007, the satisfaction with democracy shows a strong correlation to fiscal performance that provides illustration to the theoretical considerations. In the CEE-10 countries, this relationship is much less evident partly because of the much stronger market discipline in these countries. However, a possible reason for the parallel rise in private sector credit is the popularity considerations of governments. Csaba (2009) calls these trends the new macroeconomic populism.

While the above correlations illustrate the predictions of the theory, they say nothing about the causal mechanisms. For this purpose, case studies are particularly valuable. In the next section, I will examine the case of Hungary, which can be considered as an extreme illustration of the theory given the parallel rise in public and private indebtedness.

Distrust and the dominance of short-term policies in Hungary

Distrust has been prevalent in Hungary for many decades. Under communism, both interpersonal and institutional trust were eroded. Given the all-pervasive nature of bureaucratic coordination, the system was essentially built on distrust: neither fellow citizens (who might be agents of the regime), nor the state (operating without checks and balances) could be trusted (Kornai 1992). Following the collapse of communism, transition resulted in new grievances that perpetuated distrust. While a thorough overview would require a separate analysis, four major reasons can be mentioned for this outcome.

The first important factor relates to the 'material losses' due to the transformational recession. The loss of output between 1989 and 1993 amounted to 18 percent (UN ECE 2003: 112), leading to decreasing consumption and rising unemployment. Real total consumption expenditure reached its pre-transition levels only in 2000 (UN ECE 2003: 113). By 1996, employment decreased to 69.8 percent of the 1989 level, although the unemployment rate fluctuated around 10 percent (UN ECE 2003: 115, 117). Rising inequality accompanied these processes: over the transition, the Gini-index rose by 19 percent (Kornai 2006: 229).

'Subjective feelings of injustice' aggravated the objective losses. The old elite were generally perceived to have fared much better during the transition than the population as a whole. While the dominance of incumbents in the privatization process is only partially true, it remains a widespread perception (Laki and Szalai 2006).

'Unrealistic expectations' of the new system can similarly contribute to the general disillusionment. Transformation was originally perceived as a way to close the gap in living standards with the advanced West. As this did not materialize, disappointment was coded into the system. In spite of the considerable increase in living standards, as measured by the availability of various consumer goods (EBRD 2007: 6), nostalgia for the previous regime has remained widespread – even in 2004, 60 percent of Hungarians thought that the old regime was better (Rose 2006: 39)

'Failures of the new system' are also a source of justified disillusionment. Endemic corruption, policy and institutional failures contribute to a sense of skepticism regarding the new system. Over 70 percent in Hungary believe that there is more corruption in the new system than in the old regime (EBRD 2007: 51). The strong general distrust towards the new regime and especially towards the representative institutions such as the parliament and the political parties is shown by Figure 6.8.

Overall, given the above factors, the distrust that characterized the old socialist regime did not disappear with transition. In the following, I will show how such dissatisfaction showed up in Hungarian policy-making, especially following accession to the EU.

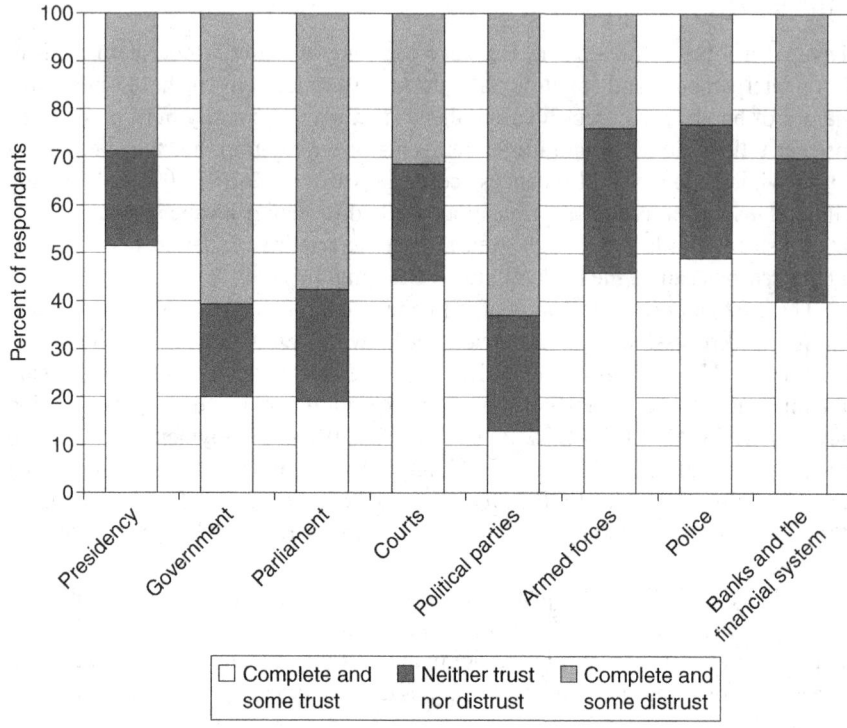

Figure 6.8 Trust in public institutions in Hungary, 2006 (source: EBRD 2007: 51)

The early phase of Hungarian transition

During the early phase of transition, lack of trust did not seem to influence policy. In the 1990s, Hungary was among the leaders of post-communist transition – it had signed an association agreement with the EU already in 1991 and was the first country to submit its membership application in 1994. This early period was characterized by a widespread consensus among the major political actors over the main tasks of transformation – the establishment of democracy and market economy that would eventually lead the country into the European Union. Furthermore, the idea that, for a small, open economy, export-led growth is the way to sustainable development was also widely shared. This consensus was also supported by the public – while in 1991 only 23 percent of the population expressed satisfaction with the economic situation, 72 percent was positively hopeful for the future (Rose 2005: 31–33).

These factors proved to be very important in the transformation of the economy, especially in the decisions over privatization and the hardening of the budget constraints for companies. Given the high level of inherited debt, which was 73 percent of the GDP in 1989, the major objective of privatization was to generate revenue for the state and additional capital for enterprises. This practically meant the sale of enterprises to foreign investors and thus helped the country to step on the path of export-led growth (Mihályi 2001). Hungary's experience stands in sharp contrast with the experiences of most other transition countries where various public distribution schemes were tried before selling to foreigners. Besides the creation of real owners, the hardening of budget constraints was also seen as essential for the functioning of a market economy. The measures to reach this objective amounted to a microeconomic shock therapy for the economy (Csaba 1998: 1382). In January 1992, four major laws were introduced which aimed at hardening the budget constraints for all actors in the economy and ending the situation of circular indebtedness in the economy.[7]

Foreign-dominated privatization and the hardening of budget constraints in the economy were very successful in bringing about the fast adjustment of domestic production. Hungary was the major beneficiary from foreign direct investment among the transition countries until 1995 (UN ECE 2003: 127). At the same time, the radical measures also had costs. During the early 1990s, over 30,000 companies went through some form of bankruptcy procedures (Ábel and Szakadát 1997: 640), which had far-reaching consequences. As discussed in the previous section, during this period employment dropped by 30 percent, unemployment rose to over 12 percent and the loss in GDP was close to 20 percent. The wave of bankruptcies affected the banking sector as well, and the share of non-performing loans reached 32 percent of total company loans by 1993 (Ábel and Szakadát 1997: 643).

The transformational recession resulted in fast disillusionment from the transition and soon led to the collapse of the elite consensus. The loss of employment opportunities and rising popular dissatisfaction placed increasing demands on the welfare system of the country. In response to these pressures, the government considerably eased regulations regarding disability pensions, early retirement and maternity benefits, thus sowing the seeds for future problems in the economy. The pressure to consolidate the banking system further contributed to the erosion of the earlier commitment for lowering state redistribution. By 1994, consolidated expenditures reached 60.8 percent of the GDP up from 55.8 percent in 1991 (László 2001: 846). The upcoming elections were not favorable for fiscal restraint either and gave a further reason for the government to postpone fiscal consolidation. Massive overspending, however, did not save the government: the Hungarian Democratic Forum still suffered a devastating defeat at the elections, which were won by the Hungarian Socialist Party.

While a large fiscal deficit and the accompanying current account deficit due to foreign financing required immediate action, the government postponed harsh measures in order to prepare for the municipal elections that were held in October that year. The problems were addressed only in March 1995 after financial crisis hit Mexico, and it was feared that Hungary would be the next to fall. The surprise package implemented by the new minister of finance, Lajos Bokros, relied on monetary, fiscal and income policy to stabilize the economy (Kornai 1996). The main elements were a one-off devaluation, the introduction of a crawling peg exchange rate, the levying of an 8 percent import surcharge and nominal wage freeze in the public sector. Structural reforms played only a marginal role and instead there was an across-the-board type cut, reducing primary expenditures from 51.9 to 41.6 percent of GDP. After the package, the process of privatization, which was stopped before the elections, was resumed in order to generate revenue to cover the debt burden. Similarly to the earlier years, the privileging of foreign strategic investors for the buying of banks and other large enterprises was an explicit governmental policy.

The package achieved its main objective and Hungary avoided a financial crisis without entering into a recession or suffering further employment losses. The devaluation of the exchange rate and the nominal wage freeze greatly improved the competitiveness of the economy and kept the country on an export-led growth-path – the value of merchandise exports doubled between 1995 and 1999 (UN ECE 2003: 121). As a result, by 1997 growth resumed and Hungary was second only to Poland in recovering its industrial output to reach its pre-transition level by 1998 (UN ECE 2003: 114). No other transition country achieved this before 2000. The country also maintained its reputation as one of the leaders of the transition, signaled by the highly positive evaluations from international institutions from the EBRD to the European Commission.

These results, however, came at a serious social and political cost. Inflation jumped to 28 percent, eroding real wages, which fell by a total of 18 percent in 1995 and 1996. The reduction of entitlements, such as introducing needs-based family allowances or tuition fees in higher education, aimed to signal the importance of individual responsibility in the new regime but their main result was the triggering of a serious resistance to the package. The opposition denied that such harsh measures were necessary, and Bokros soon became the least popular figure in the country. After the crisis was over, he was forced to resign from his post in 1996. While a three-pillar pension system was introduced by his successor in 1997, no further major reforms took place for a decade.

The shock administered by the Bokros package had long-lasting influence on Hungarian economic policy-making and strongly contributed to the dominance of short-term decision-making during the next decade. First, the country avoided a financial crisis and thus Hungarian policy-makers never learnt the dangers of irresponsibility in the age of capital mobility. Instead, the unpopularity of the package and the loss of the following elections in 1998 made them extremely reluctant to introduce fiscal restrictions. Promising material benefits to buy support became the norm for all parties before the subsequent elections. Second, as the opposition took advantage of the difficult situation of the government and exploited the resistance to the measures, the consensual policy-making characterizing the early phase of transition turned into open hostility among the major forces. These developments eventually eroded the results of the package.

Governance without trust

Following the turn of the millennium, the consequences of low trust became manifest in Hungarian policy-making. While the early consensus regarding economic transformation had already broken down in the 1990s, the closure of EU accession negotiations in 2002 meant that an important external anchor also disappeared. The period after 2000 can be characterized by the permanent election campaign and the lack of any major reform. The dominance of political factors in budgetary decision-making is well documented by Ohnsorge-Szabó and Romhányi (2007: 265). They calculated that, in the absence of politically motivated spending since 2000,[8] public debt would have been 36.9 percent of the GDP in 2006 instead of 66 percent. During this period, the fiscal deficit fluctuated between 6.5 and 9.4 percent (European Commission 2012: 181).

On the surface, the persistence of electoral considerations after 2000 is due to two factors: the large number of elections and referenda in this period and the intensifying antagonism between the major political parties after the closing outcome of the 2002 elections that brought the Hungarian Socialist Party back to power.[9] However, if we look deeper, three factors can be identified that contributed to the dominance of election cycles in economic policy-making. First, in line with the theoretical considerations, in a low-trust environment, support can be bought only through short-term material benefits and, therefore, regardless of the ideological leaning of the parties, overspending was the norm rather than the exception. This phenomenon also implies that the public remained unaware of the consequences of irresponsible fiscal policy, and fiscal illusion was rampant.[10] Second, the institutional structure provided ample opportunity for the political class to manipulate the budget according to electoral considerations[11] as well as contributed to the fiscal illusions of the electorate.[12] Policy-makers had no incentive to strengthen these institutions as that would only make vote-buying more difficult for them. Finally, during this period there were no external factors to enforce discipline and the international financial markets provided ample financing to cover imbalances.

The period between 2000 and 2008 in Hungary demonstrates the difficulties of long-term oriented economic policy in a low-trust environment. The imbalances, which were due to populist electoral politics, were temporarily reduced in the mid-term through sub-optimal revenue-increasing measures that led to a worsening business environment. The increase in taxes and the administrative measures to fight the informal economy substantially increased administrative costs and created an unfavorable environment for investment. Small and medium-sized enterprises were particularly hard hit since they did not have the means to lobby individual exemptions from taxes or regulations (OECD 2008: 147). As this sector employs 69 percent of the labor force in Hungary, it is unsurprising that, after Malta and Poland, Hungary had the third lowest employment rate in the European Union at 57.3 percent in 2007. Low employment in turn affects both growth and the fiscal balance. As labor is underutilized, growth prospects of the country decline. Low legal employment also means low contribution to the budget, while at the same time entrenches demand for high welfare provisions. These provisions then have to be financed by high taxes on those who work, which provides considerable incentives for tax evasion and little incentive to work legally. These developments undermined public trust in the state even further and thus created a vicious cycle between lack of trust and low growth.

The situation was further worsened by rapid credit growth, which took place mostly in foreign currency.[13] The major reason for foreign indebtedness was the large interest rate differential between loans in domestic currency and in euro. Given the weak credibility of Hungarian economic policy due to the above reasons, domestic interest rates remained steadily high – as a result, between 2004 and 2007, euro loans were cheaper by 6.5 percent for housing and 15.5 percent for consumption goods (Darvas and Szapáry 2008: 40). The high interest rate influenced foreign currency lending through the exchange rate channel as well – the forint remained strong and stable in relation to the euro, which contributed to the underestimation of exchange rate risk by borrowers. As the credit boom created the illusion of prosperity, it is unsurprising that the sharp increase in foreign currency borrowing was not countered by effective policy measures.[14] The growing indebtedness in foreign currency made the country extremely vulnerable to any change in market sentiment and the volatility of the currency.

Overall the unhindered manifestation of short-term policy-making as a consequence of low levels of trust led to the emergence of large fiscal imbalances, high public and private debt as well as a high share of foreign currency loans. Under these conditions, it is unsurprising that, following the collapse of Lehman Brothers in September 2008, the subsequent freeze of the global financial markets and the sharp devaluation of its currency, Hungary was the first EU country that had to turn to the IMF for help. As a consequence, the country had to implement significant fiscal cuts in the midst of the subprime crisis,[15] deepening the collapse of output, which reached –6.3 percent in 2009. Following a decade of resistance by the political elite, in the context of the bailout package, the parliament adopted strict fiscal rules constraining the growth of debt and established a fiscal council to provide independent assessment of budgetary policy and evaluate legislative proposals based on their budgetary impact.

The political consequence of distrust: the majoritarian turn under Viktor Orbán

The mismanagement of the economy and the subsequent pain of adjustment during the financial crisis swept away the Socialist government in the 2010 elections. The center-right Fidesz in coalition with the Christian Democrats received a two-third majority in the Parliament on the basis of promises of an alternative economic policy, which involves no further restrictive measures but promotes growth instead. While they promised a radical turnaround, the short-termism of the earlier period only intensified as checks and balances in the institutional framework were removed.

The program of the new government relied on a mix of conservative and nationalistic elements. During its first year in office, it introduced the flat tax, substantially increased benefits to families with children, as well as loosened labor market regulations and welfare benefits in order to encourage employment. While these measures copied the earlier Slovak reform program (Győrffy 2009), they did not produce the same results given the parallel measures, which aimed to compensate for the loss of state revenues. Unlike in Slovakia, the reduction of taxes on labor was not matched by similar cuts in state expenditure. Instead the government de facto nationalized the second pillar of the pension system and special taxes were introduced for banks and multinational companies. The problem of foreign currency indebtedness was addressed through a long moratorium on evictions as well as the possibility of repaying the foreign currency loans at an exchange rate well below the market rate (Hudecz 2012: 400–407). The method of implementation aggravated the negative impact of these steps as they were mostly introduced in an ad hoc manner without consultations or impact studies.

Many of the measures were deemed unconstitutional and thus the government also took step to eliminate institutional checks and balances and thus increase its discretion over policy-making. Steps towards this objective included the nomination of party members to the posts of President and the head of the State Audit Office, as well as the elimination of the newly established Fiscal Council. The power of the Constitutional Court was also curbed following its resistance to retroactively endorse laws. While the inclusion of a 50 percent debt rule in the new Constitution could seem like a step towards rules-based fiscal policy, in reality the government made sure that the rule applies only to future governments.[16]

The impromptu decision-making and the weakening of institutional checks and balances greatly increased uncertainty for all actors and undermined confidence in the rule of law. So although the government was able to reduce debt from 81.4 (2010) to 78.5 percent (2011) and maintain a deficit below 3 percent (European Commission 2012: 49, 210), growth remains way below the regional peers, below 1 percent in 2012 and 2013. An important reason for this is the lack of confidence from global and domestic investors, which is manifested in the country's downgrade into speculative category, a weakening exchange rate, outflow of foreign capital, increasing risk premium and growing difficulties in obtaining credit for both companies and households.[17]

Overall, Hungary can be considered a primary example of how lack of institutional trust makes short-turn decision-making a constant feature regardless of who is in power. While lack of trust could be compensated by elite consensus and an external anchor during the early years of transition, following the disappearance of these factors distrust manifested itself in growing financial imbalances. As the global financial crisis made the continuation of such policies impossible, short-termism assumed a new form and manifested itself in attacks against multinational companies and banks. The sad consequence is the continuation of a vicious cycle between distrust and economic performance.

Conclusions

This chapter attempted to show how dissatisfaction with democracy lies at the root of the present crisis. The relationship to fiscal performance was most evident in the original member states in the euro-zone, where lack of external discipline implied that internal factors were dominant in determining outcomes. Although this was not the case in the new member states of the EU, there is some indication that, in countries which faced strong external pressure to conduct responsible fiscal policy, private lending played a substitute role to public lending. By examining more closely the case of Hungary, I attempted to show how these outcomes emerge from the policy process. The case is particularly illuminating given the variety of short-term measures to appease the electorate − reckless spending, loose financial regulations, tax cuts and finally attacks on banks and multinationals were all popular and all extremely harmful to the long-term prospects of the country.

The major implication of this study is that democratic dissatisfaction is an important root of the crisis. This means that in managing the crisis and building more resilient economies this factor cannot be neglected. While stronger external discipline takes a central role in managing the crisis especially in the EU, this is unlikely to be sufficient to bring about discipline given the wide variety of shapes short-term populist measures can take. As we could see in the case of Hungary, rule of law and considerations of procedures are very easily dismissed in the name of urgent crisis management. Such measures however can easily become counterproductive as they further undermine confidence and thus make recovery slower.

As the world struggles to resolve the financial crisis, governance reforms should be on the forefront of the agenda. Only a high-quality government can tackle the financial crisis effectively and contribute to lengthening the time horizon of thinking in society, thus precluding the need to gain votes through destructive, short-term measures.

Notes

1 The concept of good governance became widespread following the failure of the neo-liberal agenda about minimizing the role of the state. It is generally defined in terms of respect for democracy, human rights, rule of law as well as transparent and efficient state administration. For a more thorough overview about the concept, see Weiss (2000) and Rothstein and Teorell (2008).
2 A good example for this idea is the research by Hellman and Kaufmann (2004). Based on data from 6500 companies in 26 transition countries, they find that those firms which feel that they have disproportionately small influence on regulations directly affecting them have a negative view about public institutions, are less likely to pay taxes and are more likely to engage in corrupt practices. Paying taxes or paying bribes appear to be substitutes.
3 It is important to note that Hurd (1999: 386) does not accept references to enlightened self-interest, since if everything can be considered self-interest, then the concept becomes empty. In his definition of self-interest, the individual does not accept moral responsibility for others, which means that her relations are purely instrumental. This

does not exclude cooperation, but it does imply that the relationship in itself is not valued, only the benefits it yields.
4 Naturally I do not mean to imply that other factors, most importantly investment, do not drive tendencies of indebtedness. The hypothesis is that other things (such as investment needs) being equal, countries with low level of trust will be more likely to accumulate debt than high-trust countries.
5 With the exception of Greece, which introduced the euro in 2001.
6 Between 2002 and 2007 there was less than 1 percentage point difference in long-term interest rates within the euro-zone (European Commission 2012: 126).
7 The law on the central bank prohibited the monetary financing of the budget deficit. The law on financial institutions introduced the prudential, safety, transparency and disclosure requirements of the Basle Convention. The law on accounting required companies to comply with international accounting standards. Finally, the bankruptcy law introduced an automatic trigger, which obliged debtors under criminal law to initiate bankruptcy procedures if they were in default for more than 90 days.
8 Among others these include subsidized credit for housing, increase in the public sector wage bill, increase in pensions and other social security benefits.
9 These included municipal elections in the autumn of 2002, referendum on accession to the European Union in May 2003, European parliamentary elections in May 2004, referendum on dual citizenship and hospital privatization in December 2004 followed by the parliamentary elections in 2006.
10 This was manifested in a Gallup survey between the two rounds of parliamentary elections in 2006, which showed that only 18 percent of the voters of the winning party considered the high fiscal deficit (close to 10 percent that year) a serious economic problem.
11 The major problems of the institutional framework concern the overly optimistic planning of the budget, the lack of restrictions during the adoption phase to increase spending, the discretion of the government to change the budget during the execution phase as well as the lack of transparency. The extreme weakness of the Hungarian institutional framework for budgeting even in a Central European comparison has been noted by a number of observers. See Gleich (2003) or Kraan et al. (2007).
12 The attempts in 2004 and 2005 to hide the budget deficit through creative accounting are examples of this relation. For these measures see Kraan et al. (2007: 12).
13 By 2008, the share of foreign currency lending approached 70 percent of total household loans. For a detailed overview about the buildup of these loans see Hudecz (2012: 381–386). I rely primarily on his assessment in the following discussion of the main causes of foreign currency lending in Hungary.
14 The complete lack of response to the growth of foreign currency lending is unique in the CEE region, as shown by Bethlendi (2011:211). Based on interviews with the participants, the reluctance of the government to constrain the credit boom is documented by Szentkirályi (2011). This was especially important, since financial supervision in Hungary is separate from the independent central bank, and the supervisory body (PSZAF) is under the authority of the Ministry of Finance.
15 The measures included:

> (i) a nominal wage freeze and the elimination of the 13th monthly salary for all public sector employees; (ii) the elimination of the 13th monthly pension for all early retirees and a cap of the 13th monthly pension to HUF 80,000 for other pensioners; (iii) postponement or elimination of indexation of selected social benefits; and (iv) across-the-board cuts in other spending allocations to ministries (0.5 percent of GDP). Within the capital expenditure envelope, priority will be given to investment projects co-financed by EU structural funds. On the revenue side, the authorities have already announced that tax cuts previously envisaged for 2009

will be postponed until sufficient fiscal space has been created through expenditure restraint. Under the program, the authorities will also not make any changes in the tax code that could lead to a net revenue loss.

(IMF 2008: 10)

16 The Law on Financial Stability postponed the obligations under the debt rule to 2016.
17 Gross fixed capital formation has been declining since 2009 and is expected to decline even in 2013, when it is forecasted to recover in all the other countries in the region (European Commission 2012: 69).

Bibliography

Ábel, Isván, and Szakadát, László (1997) 'A bankrendszer átalakulása Magyarországon 1987–1996 között' [The Transformation of the Banking System in Hungary Between 1987 and 1996], *Közgazdasági Szemle*, vol. 44, no. 7–8, pp. 635–652.
Anderson, Christopher J. (2005) 'Good Questions, Dubious Inferences, and Bad Solutions: Some Further Thoughts on Satisfaction with Democracy', Working Paper No. 116, Center on Democratic Performance, Binghamton: Binghamton University.
Bethlendi, András (2011) 'Policy Measures and Failures on Foreign Currency Household Lending in Central and Eastern Europe', *Acta Oeconomica*, vol. 61, no. 2, pp. 193–223.
Bohle, Dorothee (2010) 'East European Transformations and the Paradoxes of Transnationalization', *EUI Working Paper* SPS 2010/01, Badia Fiasolana: European University Institute.
Canache, Damarys, Mondak, Jeffery J., and Seligson, Mitchell, A. (2001) 'Meaning and Measurement in Cross-National Research on Satisfaction with Democracy', *Public Opinion Quarterly*, vol. 65. no. 4, pp. 506–528.
Clarke, Harold, Dutt, Nitish, and Kornberg, Allan (1993) 'The Political Economy of Attitudes toward Polity and Society in Western European Democracies', *Journal of Politics*, vol. 55, no. 4, pp. 998–1021.
Csaba, László (1998) 'A Decade of Transformation in Hungarian Economic Policy: Dynamics, Constraints and Prospects', *Europe-Asia Studies*, vol. 50, no. 8, pp. 1381–1391.
Csaba, László (2009) *Crisis in Economics?* Budapest: Akadémiai Kiadó.
Csepeli, György, Örkény, Antal, Székelyi, Mária, and Barna, Ildikó (2004) 'Blindness to Success: Social Psychological Objectives Along the Way to a Market Economy in Eastern Europe', in Kornai, János, Rothstein, Bo, and Rose-Ackerman, Susan (eds.) *Creating Social Trust in Post-Socialist Transition*, New York: Palgrave Macmillan, pp. 213–240.
Darvas, Zsolt, and Kostyleva, Valentina (2011) 'The Fiscal and Monetary Institutions of CESEE Countries', Bruegel Working Paper, no. 2.
Darvas, Zsolt, and Szapáry, György (2008) 'Euro Area Enlargement and Euro Adoption Strategies', *Economic Papers*, no. 304, Brussels: Directorate General for Economic and Financial Affairs.
Easton, David (1965) *A Systems Analysis of Political Life*, New York: John Wiley and Sons.
EBRD (2007) *Life in Transition: A Survey of People's Experiences and Attitudes*, London: EBRD.
European Commission (2012) *Statistical Annex of European Economy, Spring*, Brussels: Commission of the European Communities Directorate General for Economic and Financial Affairs.

Gamson, William A. (1968) *Power and Discontent*, Homewood, Il: The Dorsey Press.
Gleich, Holger (2003) 'Budget Institutions and Fiscal Performance in Central and Eastern European Countries', *Working Paper*, no. 215, Frankfurt: European Central Bank.
Győrffy, Dóra (2009) 'Structural Change without Trust. Reform Cycles in Hungary and Slovakia', *Acta Oeconomica*, vol. 59, no. 2, pp. 147–177.
Hellman, Joel, and Kaufmann, Daniel (2004) 'The Inequality of Influence', in Kornai, János, and Rose-Ackerman, Susan (eds.) *Building a Trustworthy State in Post-Socialist Transition*, New York: Palgrave Macmillan, pp. 100–132.
Hilbers, Paul, Ötker-Robe, Inci, and Pazabasioglu, Ceyla (2007) 'Analysis of and Policy Responses to Rapid Credit Growth', in Enoch, Charles, and Ötker-Robe, Inci (eds.) *Rapid Credit Growth in Central and Eastern Europe: Endless Boom or Early Warning?* Houndmills and New York: Palgrave Macmillan, pp. 84–136.
Hudecz, András (2012) 'Párhuzamos történetek. A lakossági devizahitelezés kialakulása és kezelése Lengyelországban, Romániában és Magyarországon' [Parallel Stories. The Development and Management of Foreign Currency Household Lending in Poland, Romania and Hungary], *Közgazdasági Szemle*, vol. 59, no. 4, pp. 349–411.
Hurd, Ian (1999) 'Legitimacy and Authority in International Politics', *International Organization*, vol. 53, no. 2, pp. 379–408.
IMF (2008) 'Hungary: Request for Stand-By Arrangement – Staff Report', *IMF Country Report*, no. 361.
Kornai, János (1992) *The Socialist System: The Political Economy of Communism*, Oxford: Clarendon Press.
Kornai, János (1996) 'Kiigazítás recesszió nélkül' [Stabilization Without Recession], *Közgazdasági Szemle*, vol. 43, nos. 7–8, pp. 585–613.
Kornai, János (2006) 'The Great Transformation of Central Eastern Europe: Success and Disappointment', *Economics of Transition*, vol. 14, no. 2, pp. 207–244.
Kraan, Dirk-Jan, Bergvall, Daniel, Hawkesworth, Ian, and Krause, Philipp (2007) 'Budgeting in Hungary', *OECD Journal on Budgeting*, vol. 6, no. 3, pp. 1–61.
Laki, Mihály, and Szalai, Júlia (2006) 'The Puzzle of Success: Hungarian Entrepreneurs at the Turn of the Millennium', *Europe-Asia Studies*, vol. 58, no. 3, pp. 317–345.
László, Csaba (2001) 'Vargabetűk az államháztartási reform tízéves történetében (1988–1997)' [Twists and Turns in the Ten-year History of Hungarian Public Finance Reforms (1988–1997)], *Közgazdasági Szemle*, vol. 48, no. 10, pp. 844–864.
Mihályi, Péter (2001) 'The Evolution of Hungary's Approach to FDI in Post-Communist Privatization', *Transnational Corporations*, vol. 10, no. 3, pp. 61–74.
Möllering, Guido (2001) 'The Nature of Trust: From Georg Simmel to a Theory of Expectation, Interpretation and Suspension', *Sociology*, vol. 35, no. 2, pp. 403–420.
OECD (2008) *Reforms for Sustainable Growth: An OECD Perspective on Hungary*, Paris: OECD.
Offe, Claus (1999) 'How Can We Trust our Fellow Citizens?', in Warren, Mark E. (ed.) *Democracy and Trust*, Cambridge: Cambridge University Press, pp. 42–87.
Ohnsorge-Szabó, László, and Romhányi, Balázs (2007) 'Hogy jutottunk ide: magyar költségvetés, 2000–2006' [How We Got Here: Hungarian Fiscal Policy 2000–2006], *Pénzügyi Szemle*, vol. 52, no. 2, pp. 239–285.
Rose, Richard (2005) 'Are Bulgaria and Romania up to EU standards? A New Europe Barometer Evaluation', *Studies in Public Policy*, no. 418, Glasgow: Centre for the Study of Public Policy.
Rose, Richard (2006) 'Diverging Paths of Post-communist Countries: New Europe

Barometer Trends since 1991', *Studies in Public Policy*, no. 418, Glasgow: Centre for the Study of Public Policy.

Rose, Richard (2009) *Understanding Post-communist Transformation: A Bottom Up Approach*, London: Routledge.

Rothstein, Bo, and Teorell, Jan (2008) 'What is the Quality of Government? A Theory of Impartial Government Institutions', *Governance: An International Journal of Policy, Administration and Institutions*, vol. 21, no. 2, pp. 165–190.

Rousseau, Denise M., Sitkin, Sim B., Burt, Ronald S., and Camere, Colin (1998) 'Not So Different After All: A Cross-discipline View of Trust', *Academy of Management Review*, vol. 25, no. 3, pp. 393–404.

Szentkirályi, Balázs (2011) 'Ki a felelős a devizahitelezésért?' [Who is Responsible for Foreign Currency Lending?], 18 October, Available: http://index.hu/gazdasag/magyar/2011/10/18/ki_a_felelos_a_devizahitelezesert/.

UN ECE (2003) *Economic Survey of Europe 2003*, no. 2, Geneva, Switzerland: United Nations Economic Commission for Europe.

Uslaner, Eric M. (1999) 'Democracy and Social Capital', in Warren, Mark E. (ed.) *Democracy and Trust*, Cambridge: Cambridge University Press, pp. 121–150.

Uslaner, Eric (2008) 'Trust as a Moral Value', in Castiglione, Dario, van Deth, Jan W., and Wolleb, Guglielmo (eds.) *The Handbook of Social Capital*, Oxford: Oxford University Press, pp. 101–121.

Wagner, Alexander F., Schneider, Friedrich, and Halla, Martin (2009) 'The Quality of Institutions and Satisfaction with Democracy in Western Europe – A Panel Analysis', *European Journal of Political Economy*, vol. 25. no. 1, pp. 30–41.

Weiss, Thomas (2000) 'Governance, Good Governance and Global Governance: Conceptual and Actual Challenges', *Third World Quarterly*, vol. 21, no. 5, pp. 795–814.

7 The origin and characteristics of the Euro crisis and solutions

Tibor Palánkai

General background

The Euro crisis has broad, global connections and roots, particularly as far as its origin and generating causes are concerned. The crisis began as a global financial crisis and at the beginning many believed that Europe could avoid it more or less unscathed. The opposite happened, and the structural deficiencies of the Eurozone played an important role.

One of the main developments of the last 40–50 years was the emergence of global integration that was based primarily on market integration, liberalisation and deregulation ('negative integration'). This was particularly spectacular in terms of the integration of financial markets. The creation of parallel regulatory structures ('positive integration') was largely missed, which is the basis of the general regulatory crisis of global capitalism.

In general terms, global integration calls for multi-level governance (global, regional, national, local), which in the context of increasing interdependence means the emergence of a new structure where the constitutional foundations of sovereignty remain largely unchanged, but at the same time, it challenges the functional or operational autonomy of states by sharing decisions, and pursuing certain policies in a shared way. This is an interrelated and overlapping multi-player system, which tries to give answers to the complex processes of integrating economies through regulation, direction and surveying of it in different fields and levels.

Serious deficits appear at all levels of governance, both in terms of institutional structures and competences, and the efficiency and coherence of regulation. It is clear that the main deficiencies lay in weaknesses at the global level. The restructuring and reform of global institutions is slow and contradictory, and that particularly applies to international monetary institutions (IMF, World Bank). Institutions and mechanisms to regulate global financial markets are particularly lacking. The coherence and coordination between the global and lower levels is weak, but the national or local regulatory deficits are equally responsible for the crisis.

The EU, with relatively developed regional integration, is not an exception – in spite of its institutions, policies and competences, it was not able to avert the crisis; on the contrary, deficiencies were to a large extent responsible for extending and deepening the crisis and clearly applies to the present Euro crisis.

When we analyse the present crisis, one cannot forget about the fundamental changes in the international monetary system, starting from the 1970s, often identified as the collapse of the 'Bretton Woods system'. What is more important, however, is the elimination of the stabilising mechanisms of the gold standard. From the 1970s, gold was definitely and irrevocably de-monetised; and instead the use of credit monies became prevalent. The traditional gold mechanism was replaced by strict monetary policies that were generally called *monetarism*. Paradoxically, by the time global integration emerged, gold was replaced by national credit. Clearly, gold was global in character, but was unable to fill the requirements of the present global economy.

Monetarism means control over the money supply, with an independent central bank, and intervention into the monetary and financial markets. It is a principle and a practice that is an organic part of the modern market economy. It is an extension and sophistication of regulated markets that is often falsely identified with market fundamentalism.

The normal operation of the economy assumes two basic monetary conditions: liquidity and stability. By credit monies, price stability gains special importance, and becomes the basic priority of economic policy. Liquidity should be secured so as not to negatively affect stability and can only be achieved by the strict control of the money supply. An excessive supply of money may lead to inflation, while the drive for stability is paid by deflation and recession.

Inflation is an abnormal state of the economy. It is destructive for both consumers and producers. It is bad for growth, for savings, investments, profit and welfare. It destabilises equilibrium, undermines competitiveness and should be avoided. Controlling inflation and stability is of primary concern for everyone. After the collapse of the gold standard, the gold price mechanism should have been substituted by monetarism, i.e. strict anti-inflationary monetary policy.

Economic stability, however, should not come at the expense of economic growth or economic dynamism. Economic growth assumes flexible pricing and prices serve an important dynamising function and price stability should be defined in this context. 'Desirable inflation' reflects that objective, which according to the IMF and other international monetary institutions, can be fixed around 2–3 per cent of annual price increases (some allow up to 3.5 per cent because even at this rate it will not produce detriments to inflation. These numbers appear in the inflation targeting policies of national banks all over the world.

The ECB follows the same pattern. The main task of the ECB is to safeguard 'the maintenance of price stability', which the Bank defined as 'keeping inflation between 0 and 2%', and monetary policies must be subordinated to this. This target is in harmony with the broad economic policy guidelines of the Council (Issing *et al.* 2001).

In plans for the Euro, monetarist considerations were very clearly formulated. The single currency, for Germany in particular, was acceptable only if it was not more inflationary than the German national currency had recently been. This in general coincided with the interests of all the other member countries.

It should be noted that setting desirable inflation rates is nominally limited by price increases. More important is so-called optimal or equilibrium inflation, which is the basic determinant of welfare and competitiveness. It is possible that in one country inflation is 'only' 2 per cent, but if productivity stagnates this could lead to the erosion of real incomes and competitiveness. At the same time, prices may increase by 5 per cent, but with 7 per cent growth of productivity, both welfare and competitiveness may improve. Under these circumstances, excessive efforts to curb inflation may lead to a slowdown in the economy. The Maastricht criteria neglect these connections and they are particularly negative from the point of view of catching-up in the emerging economies of new members. Many argue that monetary policy restrictions are as binding as the gold standard. It is true that in order to escape from the crisis, monetary restriction is insufficient. As the present Euro crisis demonstrates, dynamising the economy is of utmost importance.

Besides liquidity and stability, economic growth, extended to *sustainable growth based on competitiveness*, is the basic demand for any economic policy. This requires a *complex and comprehensive definition of sustainability*, including both monetary and fiscal stability that assumes the sustainability of economic growth. Sustainable growth implies monetary stability, both in terms of inflation, and budget and balance of payments equilibrium. Monetary stability cannot be achieved without sustainable growth. This can be extended to social and environmental sustainability as well. We all know that economic growth within the present energy framework is environmentally unsustainable (that is the notion of sustainable development as distinguished from sustainable growth); and as the examples of Greece and Spain demonstrate, present stabilisation programmes are socially unsustainable. We can also bring into the picture the sustainability of democratic political structures as well. The notion of a *European model of democratic eco-social market economy* is a nice objective, but we are still far from its realisation, not to speak of its sustainability.

In order to stabilise and curb inflation, monetary policy from the beginning was connected to the requirement of a balanced budget. Monetary stability, therefore, was closely connected to fiscal stability. This implied a revision of Keynesism, which by the strict control of expenditures raised a serious dilemma for the welfare state. Consequently, strict monetary control could be connected to deregulation and liberalisation. It is not by chance that 'monetarism' became a term of abuse (a false narrative about the conflict between state intervention and market freedom) even among experts.

In the initial arsenal of monetary policy, the control of the money supply is a primary objective. It became quickly evident, however, that this was not enough. The quantitative control of national currencies applied during the 1970s, but by the 1980s had lost relevance. This was particularly due to the rapid global integration of financial markets and was gradually replaced by inflation targeting, which from the 1990s was accepted by a growing number of central banks.

Inflation targeting concentrates directly on price stability, even if there is a divided opinion over its efficiency. After the revival of monetarism in the 1960s and 1970s, inflation targeting became the mainstay of the European Central Bank.

The monetary framework of integration

In connection to both global and regional integration, three main monetary conditions should be met: (1) convertibility of currencies; (2) monetary stability: stability of prices, exchange rate stability; (3) liquidity (availability of money). These conditions are considered as extensions of the integration requirements of stability and liquidity.

The convertibility of national currencies is one of the basic conditions of trade integration (no free trade without free exchange of currencies). After WWII, in global terms, this is what the IMF and GATT aimed for, and several supporting measures were applied to promote steps towards both trade and monetary liberalisation. From the point of view regional integration, different levels of convertibility were assumed: free trade area or customs union – current account convertibility (trade and income transfers); common market – capital account convertibility (direct investments), but short-term, speculative transfers remained restricted; single market – full convertibility (characteristic only among the EU countries, due to the goals of the four freedoms).

In Europe in the 1950s and 1960s, when the two free-trade-based integration organisations (EEC and EFTA) were created, the monetary framework was provided by the 1958 convertibility (on current account) of the major European currencies. It was not by chance that by 1968, when the common market was implemented, the requirements of capital account convertibility were fulfilled. EFTA did not aim at a common market, at least in terms of freedom of movement of labour (achieved among the Scandinavian countries), while the free movement of capital was secured among these countries due to the extended OECD frameworks.

Originally, a customs union was associated with fixed rates. Later, it was replaced by the notion of 'stable exchange rates' that already assumed a kind of monetary policy coordination or intervention primarily to defend exchange rates. By the end of the 1960s, the requirements for exchange rate stability were more or less secured by the IMF.

With the emerging crisis of the international monetary system, new solutions should be sought. In the EC, by implementation of the common market, the necessity of closer monetary cooperation arose. At end of the 1960s, several plans were worked out on economic and monetary union among the EC member countries. The first attempt, based on the Werner Plan, was launched on 1 January 1971 with a deadline for implementation by 1980 (with the creation of a common currency). The project collapsed after a few months due to the monetary crisis of 1971 and the outbreak of the oil crisis took it decisively off the agenda.

Exchange rate stabilisation, however, remained more certain. The main forms of stability and flexibility set bands for the fluctuation of rates, and were connected with certain types of central bank interventions. Differences were basically in the width of bands and intensity and scope of intervention. In the EC, in the framework of the European Monetary System, the Exchange Rate Mechanism was such a stabilisation scheme. Over time, the ERM changed, but the full participation of all members has never been achieved. Recently, the ERM2 has applied to some non-Euro members.

The other very close form of monetary stabilisation is the currency board.

> In its strictest definition, a currency board is an arrangement in which one country pegs to another currency at a fixed level and the issue of domestic currency is fully backed by the foreign currency. One could even say that a currency board is a form of unilateral and reversible monetary union. In a currency board regime, a country gives up sovereignty in monetary matters.
> (Giordano and Persaud 1998: 154)

In addition, the currency board is seen as an institution that 'would be purely passive, with no monetary policy role of its own, nor any commitment to, or clear definition of, the monetary or institutional development' (Padoa-Schioppa 1994: 157). Such currency boards have been created in Estonia, Bosnia and Bulgaria, pegged to the German mark, and in Hong Kong and Argentina, pegged to the dollar.

Exchange rate stabilisation was broadly used also as a tool for anti-inflationary policies. By the 1980s, many came to believe that economic policies could implement monetarist principles more decisively and effectively through exchange-rate stabilisation than through the regulation of the internal money supply. Monetary discipline linked to external (stable) exchange rates is called 'external monetarism'. It was generally believed that in the framework of monetary integration, particularly in countries where inflation is rising rapidly, the fixing of exchange rates can be a tougher and more efficient tool than national currency targets.

All in all, the experiences of the 1980s undoubtedly showed that it was no longer possible to achieve better economic performance with more flexible exchange rates. Inflationary effects were not accompanied by higher growth or improved performance in terms of employment.

> There is more than circumstantial evidence to indicate that participation in the exchange rate mechanism served, at least for a large part of the period under consideration, as an important additional instrument in the fight against inflation; and this seems to be particularly true of France, Italy and Ireland. Participation in the ERM acted as an external constraint on domestic monetary policies, while the exchange rate has also been used, as an instrument of disinflation.
> (Tsoukalis 1993: 195)

In spite of stabilisation measures, under the circumstances of global integration and the growing freedom of movement of capital, the control of monetary processes remained highly inefficient. The global movements and transactions make any national monetary control extremely difficult.

> With the development of global currencies, credit cards and the like, even the most powerful state has lost unqualified authority over money supplies and exchange rates. Nor can a state successfully assert supreme and exclusive rule over the global financial flows that pass through its jurisdiction (or do they?). Electronic commerce, intra-firm trade, offshore financial centres, derivatives and hedge funds have all substantially compromised state abilities to raise tax revenues.
>
> (Scholte 2005: 189)

Laszlo Csaba (2010: 226) calls attention to the role of private actors in money creation and argues the impossibility of control of the money supply by state authorities.

> The new operational order of money markets, since the emergence of eurocurrency markets in the 1970s and the general extension of electronic markets, has gotten out of the control of governments ... the practice of using 'immaterial' currencies and doing extra-territorial business have become general. There is no tool or procedure by which one or another government could eliminate competition between business locations, and – using the terminology from old textbooks – could harmonise between the 'real needs of the markets' and the actual money supply. For a long time, the latter has not been created or controlled by the central banks but by private actors. The national economy as a closed unit exists only in descriptions in introductory textbooks.

In this context, private actors (primarily commercial banks and the TNCs) play a decisive role in money creation and business practice. In fact, the failure of central monetary authorities was dramatically demonstrated by the present financial crisis.

In summary, the major deficiency of the present monetary and financial system is that the harmonisation between liquidity and stability has spectacularly failed, and the same applies to the requirements for growth. None of these factors proved sustainable, and there was a clear lack of necessary institutions and policies. The measures taken to combat the crisis were generally badly timed and often not only failed to cure the maladies, but rather aggravated them.

The Euro crisis

The Euro rests on the strong foundations of a real economy. The EU members are characterised by a high intensity of relations, and strong interdependence of

The origin of the Euro crisis and solutions 121

their economies in all fields (production or finance). Between 1960 and 2007, the share of foreign trade in the GDP of member countries increased from 20 per cent to more than 40 per cent, and the share of internal trade in their GDP reached 25 per cent (it was 7–8 per cent in 1960). These proportions are about 80 per cent in the case of Hungary, and the same applies to other Central European countries, and also Belgium and the Netherlands. The proportion is evidently lower in the case of larger countries, but the high intensity and interdependence apply to them as well.

Since the 1970s, we have experienced a strong and rapid transnationalisation of the European business sector, and TNCs are the main actors of the integration processes. Europe is part of the developed world with a high level of competitiveness, even if in relative terms and in certain fields it needs to cope with serious weaknesses.

By the 1990s, the Single Market was largely implemented and the Single Currency logically followed from its measures and structures. According to Padoa-Schioppa (1989), the single market undertakes an impossible task, that of reconciling the four priorities of economic policy, namely free trade, completely free movement of capital, fixed exchange rates and 'national autonomy in following monetary policy'. 'These four elements form what I call an "inconsistent quartet": economic theory and historical experience have repeatedly shown that these four elements cannot coexist, and that at least one has to give way' (Padoa-Schioppa 1989: 373). Thus, in the interests of the normal functioning of the single market, monetary integration, or EU-level centralisation of monetary policy, is required. This is achieved with the EMU. The introduction of the Euro resulted in substantial savings in transaction costs and stability. In any speculation about the future of the Euro, these implications should not be forgotten.

Monetary stability and the international position and roles of a currency are always closely related to the state of the real economy. After WWII, the dollar standard operated smoothly and the stability of the American economy was preserved (rapid productivity increase), the control of inflation was secured, and the dollar fulfilled the role of an anchor currency. The connection with gold was of course important, but in itself was enough only when the economies were competitive. The competitiveness of the EU is far from satisfactory, and expectations of the Lisbon Treaty to become the most competitive global economy were not fulfilled.

In order to analyse the real character of the Euro crisis, we need to clarify its nature and basic characteristics. Normally, classical financial crises are usually based on the devaluation of the currency, both in internal (inflation) and in external (exchange rate) terms, in the loss of confidence and the restriction of liquidity. This is only partly the case with the Euro. In fact, developments of the last decade have proved that the Euro was one of the strongest and most stable currencies, and that has not changed dramatically, even during the recent crisis.

It is true that in the last ten years, the Euro in terms of inflation failed to keep the 2 per cent ceiling, but the 2.2 per cent average inflation performance between 1999 and 2010 proves that price stability was maintained. In 2011, inflation in the Eurozone climbed to 3 per cent, but still managed to remain within the parameters of a 'desirable inflation rate'. In spite of the crisis, there is no soaring inflation. In 2011, in the leading countries of the Eurozone (Germany, France, Italy, the Netherlands), inflation was between 2.2 and 2.6 per cent, and even the high inflation countries (Belgium, Portugal, Slovakia, Finland) remained at 3.4–3.6 per cent.

Although in the first year of its existence, the Euro started with substantial devaluation, exchange rates were later stabilised and, in historical perspective compared with 'strong' currencies, the exchange rate fluctuation was fairly moderate. If we take the estimated purchasing power parity (ppp) of 1:1.25 to the dollar, even in these years, the over-valuation of the Euro remained unchanged (in the second half of 2011, the Euro rate to the dollar was around 1.35–1.40), and did not change dramatically during 2012 either. Of course, the weakness of the dollar should be taken into account, and the devaluation to some other currencies (Swiss franc) was more marked, but there was no dramatic loss of value or collapse of the currency, even if trust remains shaken. The external trade and payments of the Union are more or less balanced; the trade balance of the Union fluctuated around roughly +/−1 per cent of GDP in recent years, and in 2012 was in surplus. This definitely does not indicate crisis.

The present Euro crisis is practically nothing more than a budgetary or debt crisis or, put another way, it is a sovereign debt crisis. And it should be added that it affects only some of the southern countries (Greece, Italy, Spain and Portugal) and Ireland, even if it threatens the stability of the whole Eurozone. Historically, the budgetary balance of the Union member countries reflected their general economic performance. In the 15 years before 1973, the average 0.5 per cent budget deficit of the Community countries was considered a balanced budget. The 1973 crisis had dramatic impacts on the budgets, and in the following ten years, the deficit was above 6 per cent of GDP. Keynesian economic policies were abandoned, and most of the countries turned to more strict budgetary policies (often called monetarism or Thatcherism).

In addition to curbing inflation, the budget was balanced by the 1990s, which is another success story of the integration. (This was not the case for promoting economic growth and employment.) By 2000, nine countries of the Eurozone produced budget surpluses, which meant 0.1 per cent surplus for the Eurozone and 0.8 per cent for the whole EU. Strict budgetary policies played an important role, but the drop of oil prices contributed to the process. In some countries, the substantial privatisation revenues also helped.

In the ten years following the introduction of the Euro, with some fluctuation and divergences, budgets remained stable. Between 2001 and 2005, in the Eurozone and in the whole EU as a whole, budget deficits were around 2.4–3.1 per cent, and fell back to 1.7 per cent in 2006 and to 0.9 per cent in 2007. In 2007, from the EU25, eight countries (Denmark, Sweden, Finland, Spain, the Netherlands and Luxemburg, and two new members, Estonia and Cyprus) were in surplus. Ireland and Slovenia had balanced budgets. That promising trend, however, proved to be short.

The 2008 global financial crisis brought dramatic changes in EU member states' budgets. By 2009, the EU27 budget deficits tripled compared to previous years, and reached 6.8 per cent (6.3 per cent for the Eurozone). Surpluses disappeared in all countries, and only Germany, Denmark, Sweden, Finland, Germany and Estonia remained below the 3 per cent threshold. The deficit was around the average in France, Italy, Netherlands, Slovenia, Slovakia, Poland and Hungary (4.4 per cent), but the country produced a record 9.2 per cent deficit already in 2006. By 2009, several countries reached or even surpassed the 10 per cent deficit level in their GDP, which can rightly be termed a 'crisis'. From the Eurozone countries, this applied to Greece (15.4 per cent deficit), Ireland (14.4 per cent), Spain (11.1 per cent) and Portugal (9.2 per cent). Similarly high deficits were produced by the UK (11.4 per cent), Lithuania (10.2 per cent), Latvia (9.2 per cent) and Romania (8.6 per cent). In 2010–2011, the budgetary crisis continued. The American budget deficit, which was below 3 per cent before 2007, by 2008 jumped to 6 per cent and by 2010 reached 12–14 per cent. In 2011, only Sweden produced a surplus (0.9 per cent), but the average of the EU27 increased further to 7.3 per cent. The high deficit countries failed to improve their performance and some countries' positions further deteriorated.

The budgetary crisis dramatically contributed to the increase of indebtedness, particularly in some countries. The debt level of the EU27 from 2001 increased from 60 per cent to 80 per cent by 2010. In 2011, besides the new members, only Denmark, Sweden, Finland and Luxemburg produced a debt below 60 per cent. Ten years ago, the deficit level of the new members was below 50 per cent, and Hungary also managed to keep below the 60 per cent ceiling. In 2011, for different reasons, the Hungarian deficit reached a crisis level of 80 per cent (in fact already by 2009), although it remained far below the level of some highly indebted countries (Greece – 165 per cent; Italy – 120 per cent; Ireland and Portugal – 108 per cent).

The sovereign debt crisis of the EU partly reflects the consequences of the 2008 global financial crisis, but in several countries irresponsible government and bank policies also played an important role. In most of the countries, the bank rescue actions were financed by state budgets and that applied also to the consumer demand inducing measures against the recession. Under these circumstances, the increase of deficits and the public debt was unavoidable, and this is clearly demonstrated by the tripling of EU deficits after 2009. In several countries, the situation was aggravated by irresponsible governmental policies (Greece – acceleration of state expenditures), or banks by producing housing bubbles (Spain and Ireland). It should be stressed, however, that the performance of northern members, in many respects, is excellent, and the problems of competitiveness and structural weaknesses are characteristic mostly of the southern members. But as the four southern countries' (Greece, Italy, Spain and Portugal) share is 24 per cent in the total GDP of the Union, it is large enough to shake the whole Eurozone.

The EU economy entered a dangerous downward spiral. The majority of commercial banks were saved, but the brunt of the sovereign debt crisis fell back onto their shoulders, particularly for those banks who owned the state debt and the treasury bonds of the highly troubled countries. This undermines trust in the whole banking system and dangerously limits financing capacities and willingness. Without investment, there is no chance for growth or recovery and in the end little chance of overcoming the crisis.

Causes and diagnoses

The causes of the Eurozone crisis are complex and manifold. Beyond the general global components, there are others with 'European' origins that follow from the decisions and policies of the EU and national governments. They are based on: shortcomings in the construction of the EMU institutions and policy coordination; missing institutions and facilities in dealing with crisis; lack of necessary foresight, concepts and strategies; mistaken conceptual assumptions, particularly about the role of market mechanisms and national policy; setting criteria that do not fit the situation; deficits in regulation at both the EU and national levels; lack of proper recognition and management of the discrepancies between common monetary and national fiscal policies; growing diversities in terms of levels of development and structures (increasing gap in competitiveness), or of traditions and values; slow and late decisions and reactions to challenges. Half solutions or fire extinguishing, which rather deepened than solved the crisis. Necessary steps subordinated to election considerations. Damaging political compromises.

According to many, the roots of the crisis lay in the original wrongly built architecture of the EMU, particularly its failure to face crisis situations. The Maastricht criteria (and the SGP) give absolute priority to price stability supported by fiscal stability requirements. These expressed the firm intention of the decision-makers to implement the EMU and especially the single currency with a low and controllable level of inflation. In fact, among macro-performance factors, only inflation was singled out, while others (e.g. budget deficit, indebtedness) were only apparently target criteria. The monetary conditions were thereby comprehensively tightened, thus severely restricting the traditional field of play of economic policy. With interest rate convergence, the range of instruments available for exchange-rate stabilisation was reduced, and it was not possible simply to replace monetary policy with budgetary instruments either. Since devaluation was automatically ruled out, the traditional means for improving the balance of trade and payments were lacking. Moreover, it was not possible to operate by restricting or increasing the national debt.

The strict prescription of the monetary criteria was an attempt to reduce member countries' room for manoeuvre in economic policy in order, theoretically, to improve performance in the sphere of the real economy. It was assumed that approximation in the performance of the different countries would enforce greater discipline in economic policy.

There are discussions about the relevance of set targets in Maastricht. Different modelling attempts indicate that the objective of around 2 per cent direct inflation can be maintained by the fiscal targets of 3 per cent budget deficit and

60 per cent debt in GDP. One of the shortcomings of the Maastricht criteria is, however, that it lacks growth targets. It may be understandable politically, but not in economic terms. If we accept that an average growth rate of about 2.5–3 per cent was silently assumed, then serious doubt arises about its relevance. In the last more than one decade, the average growth rate of the core countries was rather around 1–1.5 per cent, while the new members produced about 4–5 per cent growth. These substantially differ from the basic assumptions and mean that the targets fit neither to the old nor to the new members. It became clear that, with largely diverging growth performance of the countries, the uniform monetary and fiscal targets ('one size fits all') raise serious problems of consistency.

One of the main mistakes was related to false expectations about the disciplining role of the markets. Among the initial assumptions, there was an overwhelming belief in the disciplinary power of the markets. Accordingly, since devaluation is not possible, money markets can be expected to exercise even stricter selectivity with regard to national governments and restrain them from irrational behaviour. Financial markets are perfectly capable of discriminating among governments, as among private borrowers, on the basis of creditworthiness. In Europe, EMU will sharpen this credit-risk discrimination by shifting the markets' attention from inflation, current-account imbalances and other warnings of currency changes to the narrower question of budget deficits and the accumulation of public-sector debt. As a result, the arithmetic of public finance will come into much clearer focus. So according to these expectations with the integration of money markets, market evaluation of national budgetary policies becomes more refined. There may be stronger political pressure for more effective budgetary policy, which could contribute to the improvement of the efficiency of public services or stricter enforcement of fiscal discipline. In reality, market mechanisms failed to prevent the crisis. They are not able to discipline in advance, but they rather punish afterwards. When the assumed 'disciplining' mechanisms entered into force, it was too late, and they rather pushed countries into a downward spiral.

In fact, markets with low or negative real interest rates gave the wrong signals, and encouraged rather than prevented the accumulation of debt. For 7 of the 13 years of the Euro's existence, the base rate was lower than general inflation. This means negative real interest rates, and they were quite substantial in southern members and Ireland for many years. The basic rate was above 4 per cent for only a few years when one could speak about measurable real rates. While in Southern Europe and in Ireland inflation was mostly above 3 per cent, which meant they 'enjoyed' continuously high negative rates. At the same time, as the danger of devaluation ceased, risk premiums dropped and all the Eurozone members received favourable credit ratings (the problematic countries were upgraded). In reality, instead of 'disciplining', governments could increase their debt with diminished risks.

Added to this is the irresponsible and undisciplined behaviour of national governments. The rules were neglected and broken not only in the present crisis countries, but also in the core countries as well. Strict credit limits were not taken seriously. Germany itself was one of the first to breach the stability pact's ceiling in 2002–2003. For every irresponsible borrower, there is a reckless lender (often German bank). Excessive deficits for some imply excessive surpluses in others. The Euro's design was flawed without fiscal integration or a central bank to act as a lender of last resort. If so, what is needed is greater mutual support: joint Eurobonds to mutualise at least some of the debt, as suggested by the European Commission, and perhaps a change in the statute of the European Central Bank.

From the beginning there was agreement that for monetary integration an independent central bank was needed that had the necessary jurisdiction. Independence means that the bank could not be instructed by national governments or EU institutions. National monetary policy, in fact, is often subordinated to short-term government and electoral interests, and governments have bought votes with policies that, in the longer term, have had inflationary effects. 'It is difficult to avoid the conclusion that there is a strong link between central bank independence and price stability. Germany and Switzerland have the two most independent central banks, and enjoy the lowest inflation rates' (Emerson and Huhne 1991: 68).

The recommendations expressed the conviction of experts and decision-makers that there really is a close connection between the central bank's independence and low inflation, although there was some disagreement on this point. The bank has to possess all the attributes of national central banks in order to fulfil its function. The single currency must be a guaranteed legal tender. In the financing of national debt and deficits, three important golden rules must be followed: (1) no possibility of financing deficits by printing money, (2) no possibility of financing deficits from privileged sources, only from the money markets, (3) no possibility of rescue action (bailouts) to help governments in trouble.

It was assumed that if governments could not count on a community safety belt ('no-bailout rule'), combined with a strict community competition policy, that irresponsible behaviour would be prevented. But just as market discipline proved false, the same applied to government policies. So when the crisis broke out, the situation was aggravated. National banks lost the possibility to rescue and pump money into the economy, but no possibility was created to do that at the ECB level either. The no-bailout rule was relevant in terms of avoiding inflation, even if such rules do not curb the policies neither of the FED nor of the Japanese central bank. The recent crisis made clear that this rule should be used with care and in a flexible way. The insistence on strict application of no bailout limits the restoration of necessary liquidity, which hinders the re-start of economic growth and creates serious deflationary impact.

Besides the creation of liquidity by national central banks, the other main failure of national policies was the elimination of the possibility for exchange-rate intervention. The exchange rate is a special type of price mechanism that serves to bring the different national economies into equilibrium, equalising price levels. This may operate automatically, but in recent decades it has been actively used by governments since it was assumed that devaluation compensates for the decline in competitiveness. It was hoped that exchange-rate corrections could counterbalance the comparative cost disadvantages. Profitability immediately improved with devaluation, and producers were able to remain in the market. Obviously, if exchange rates are 'irreversibly' fixed, and exchange rate mechanisms disappear, then equilibrium can be restored in different ways, and managing them requires new forms and methods.

With the elimination of the possibility of exchange rate corrections, the maintenance of competitiveness finally becomes directly dependent on the flexibility of prices and wages. This leads to fundamental changes in the operating mechanisms of the macro-economy, and macro-level economic policies are confronted with new requirements. Many argue, however, that if a country devalues:

> it not only makes its exports cheaper, but it makes its imports more expensive. Its costs rise. If wage bargainers react by pushing up pay settlements, it may not be long before the rise in the level of domestic costs and prices has eroded the initial gain from the devaluation. Devaluation makes a country cheaper for a time, but it also pushes up inflation. It is thus more like postponing an adjustment than actually making it.
>
> (Emerson and Huhne 1991: 13)

Devaluation has short-term and transitory impacts and can genuinely improve competitiveness only if the increase in real wages is less than the increase in producer prices and productivity.

> In open economies, the competitiveness gain acquired by devaluation is likely to be small since imported inputs and final goods will rise in price immediately. If, in addition, real wages are sinking downwards, discrete realignments would destabilise the price level even more.
>
> (Pelkmans 1997: 290)

Thus, the EMU's exchange-rate mechanism does not represent an irreparable loss. The only advantage of devaluation is that it smoothly transfers welfare losses to society (the reduction of real incomes by devaluation and inflation). With devaluation, real incomes ultimately decrease, though gradually and less painfully. As experience shows, it is socially more acceptable than direct cuts in incomes. A 1 per cent cut in income could set a city on fire, while even a 5 per cent real income loss due to inflation could be silently accepted. Devaluation only treats symptoms, and does not cure the disease.

Many believe that the main problem was rather the failure to find the new national 'policy mixes' which conform to monetary integration. With the raising of monetary policy to the EU level, the role of other economic policy spheres gains in importance for individual countries. Besides the control of national fiscal policies, there are other areas, such as income policy or structural policies, which could and should be given more prominent roles. For the time being this does not seem to be happening, at least not to the extent that it did formerly in Germany, where the Bundesbank could count on the well-established cooperation between the trade unions and business organisations.

Most governments neglected the importance of responsible income policy by breaking the link between incomes and productivity. This lead to catastrophic consequences from the point of view of competitiveness and contributed to budgetary problems (Balassa-Samuelson effect). Theories of the optimal currency area assume that exchange-rate correction mechanisms are replaced by flexible income factors, including wages and interest rates. The social and political aspects of the problem, however, were neglected. No one recognised the importance of income policies neither at the national or at the EU level.

The role and importance of development and structural policies (increasing competitiveness) was also underestimated. It became clear that neither strict monetary policies nor market mechanisms could automatically increase competitiveness. On the contrary, they could worsen competitiveness. Economic development always depends on the interests and behaviours of the main actors, from entrepreneurs to governments. Cheap money can be spent on innovation, development or re-structuring of the economy. But it could also be used for increasing incomes, for buying votes or investing in real estate speculation. We have examples for very different types of approaches among the member states.

Of course, investors usually follow short-term profit interests, and the same short-term thinking could be followed by politicians. This could easily overwrite the long-term interests of companies and countries. The dilemma could be solved by well-considered and coherent development and structural policies. The new situation, in fact, should have re-valued national and EU policies. Europe 2020 is good in terms of outlining certain strategic principles and directions, but only makes recommendations. The political will, competencies and financial resources to support them are, however, missing and have far-reaching consequences.

The EU is characterised by increasing diversity as a result of southern and eastern enlargements. The differences appear in the size of the countries, levels of development and economic structures, economic performance and state of stability, level of global (and EU) integration, social and political structures and situations, state of internal ethnic and minority problems, pattern and consequences of historical development, and cultural, moral or religious traditions.

Many argue that one of the main problems of the Eurozone is that it brings together countries with very different levels of development and socio-economic structures. Indeed, these differences raise several problems. But at the same time, similarly large differences exist in most classical federations and they manage fairly well with a single currency. The assumption is, however, that there are proper federal policies coherent with the local ones, and substantial social and regional transfers (cohesion), as well as broad policy coordination. This is mostly missing in the Eurozone, and it is too simple to answer with the slogan for 'more Europe'. Instead, real federal solutions would be needed. In reality, there is a long way to go and intermediary solutions are needed. Multi-track Europe is a reality, but it is not a relevant and desirable solution.

It is also clear that it is not simply a question of good common policies and policy coordination. The social, political and legal elements are equally important, and the state of democracy, the credibility of the country and its government, the reliability of policies and legal systems, the general political and investment atmosphere are all factors that need to be taken into account.

We can say that the EU is committed to a model of democratic, eco-social market economy, which under the circumstances of stiff global competition tries to balance political, social and environmental considerations. At the same time, Europe is structured by several types of models, like the Anglo-Saxon, Scandinavian or Mediterranean, and even the new members can be distinguished by Baltic, Central European or Balkan models of development. Historical and religious traditions and moral values are equally important.

The normal functioning of the market assumes 'good' ethical behaviour. It is enough to mention some basic differences in business moral and taxation attitudes in different regions and cultures. Some keep to the rule that 'my word is my contract', while others do not and this occurs independent from different 'cultural' backgrounds. No one likes to pay taxes, but some feel that tax evasion is something wrong, 'free riding' at the expense of others for access to vital public services. At the same time, for others it is a kind of national 'sport', and there is no guilt attached to it. These aspects must be included in analysis of the causes of the crisis.

The role of speculation should not be forgotten. Some tend to blame the whole crisis and its consequences on speculators who are not just guilty but criminally responsible. Others claim that speculation is part of normal market operations and companies and governments are responsible. These views emphasise the 'cleansing' role of speculation, and speculators are clearly more efficient than sending in marines in corrupt political regimes (Indonesia or Argentina). Most agree, however, that some legal regulation is needed to avoid the worst consequences.

The experience so far draws attention to the dangers of a 'one-size-fits-all' monetary policy. This arises especially in connection with the policy of uniform interest rates in relation to differing growth and inflation rates. But the question of speculation as a corrective mechanism could be approached in broader terms, and conclusions should have been drawn for both EU and national policies.

Solutions and perspectives

In light of the crisis, it became clear that fundamental changes and reforms are needed both in terms of institutions and policies and also in attitudes and practices. The main lines of reform can be:

- more efficient control of national budgets, and better coordination of policies;
- new institutions and funds, particularly dealing with emergency situations;

- changes in status and competences of the European Central Bank;
- refining of principles and concepts related to the operation of EMU;
- efforts to reconcile stability with social aspects, improving democracy both at national and at EU levels;
- steps taken towards political union, towards federal structures ('more Europe').

EMU raised monetary policy to the EU level, while budgetary policies, apart from the conditions defined in the Stability and Growth Pact, basically remained within the competence of national governments. 'The EMU block will be almost unique among the world's currency unions in having no central fiscal authority with a substantial role in taxing and spending' (Crawford 1996: 299).

In order to secure sustainable monetary stability, balancing national budgets has primary importance. That was the main aim of the *Stability and Growth Pact* (SGP), which was approved in the framework of the Amsterdam Treaty, according to which member states committed themselves to a stability programme planned to last for several years. The member states must continue to prevent deficits in excess of 3 per cent of GDP, but in the medium term they aim to achieve 'balanced budgets'. If a given country does not fulfil the budgetary indices, it receives a warning from the Council. In the event of non-fulfilment, at the end of a special procedure, the member state can be required to make a deposit of 0.2 per cent of its GDP in a non-interest-bearing Community account. If the member state is unable to put its budget in order within two years, this deposit is converted into a non-returnable fine. The penalty is not automatic, but can be imposed with the approval of a majority of the Eurozone members. If the country is hit by a recession, it can be exempted from 'punishment'.

There were efforts and steps to refine the SGP and make it more flexible, but its main deficiency was that it largely remained a guideline or expectation, and no efficient or determined efforts were made to enforce it. This particularly applied to large countries (Germany and France), and their breaking of the rules had no negative consequences. Resulting from the crisis, several decisions were taken to improve the control of national budgets. The first step was made in September 2010 in the framework of a 'new architecture of economic governance' and the 'European Semesters' were launched. Accordingly, economic and budgetary policies should be coordinated bi-annually with the Commission, and should harmonise with both the SGP and with Europe 2020. Coordination provides important information and guidance to national governments and parliaments with application to enforcement mechanisms. Financial sanctions may be applied through suspension of transfers from structural funds.

The European Semester was further strengthened by the March 2011 Council decision in the framework of the *Euro Plus Pact* where measures were taken to improve European governance and policy coordination. Hungary and three other members (UK, Sweden and Czech Republic) abstained from the Pact. Hungary objected to the plans for company tax harmonisation, as not relevant since it is a national competency. The subscribers committed themselves to work out measures to improve competitiveness.

Real progress was achieved in budgetary control at the December 2011 Council meeting. Decisions about a 'Fiscal Union' strengthened monitoring procedures, and gave the Commission the possibility to veto the budgets of member states. Targets are more decisive and precise, according to which structural deficits should not surpass 0.5 per cent of GDP, and national governments should decide how to prohibit increases in public debt. The efficiency of these legislations is controlled by the European Court. It is important that sanctions become automatic and can be suspended only by majority decisions. The related changes in the EU treaties were vetoed by the UK, but ways to avert and solve crises were opened where non-Eurozone countries could also join. Of course, all of this depends on implementation.

Gradually, 'life boats' have been built. In May 2010, *the European Financial Stability Facility* (EFSF) was created by the 16 Eurozone members and with a centre in Luxemburg. The main aim is to secure monetary stability through temporary financial help to the troubled Eurozone members. Credit capacities were set at €440bn, and there is a €780bn guarantee from member countries behind it. The EFSF was replaced by the *European Stability Mechanism* from 2012, which is a permanent rescue fund for financially troubled countries. Its credit capacities are increased to €500bn, and non-Eurozone members can also join. The ESM provides mid-term financial support with strict conditions. It is not a bank, and it lacks even the autonomy of a monetary fund. Decisions are made with a 'supermajority' (85 per cent), which excludes the veto of some small countries. It is similar to the IMF TARP rescue programme.

In the first years of crisis, the European Central Bank contributed about €600bn to rescue commercial banks. Its role, however, was limited. It could buy government bonds only on secondary markets through commercial banks, and the amount was limited to €20bn per week. These activities from 2012 were gradually extended, and the possibility of 'unlimited' intervention was welcomed by the financial markets. The treaties still do not allow direct interventions; these still should be made indirectly through commercial banks. This means increased liquidity connected with ESF facilities. The 'no bailout' rule still limits the classical central bank functions of ECB as unlimited lender of last resort. This would require changes to basic treaties and the status and authorisation of the ECB. It would be difficult to gain support from all members for this. The issuing of Eurobonds is still rejected by Germany based on excessive fears about the impact on inflation.

All agree that the final solution to the crisis is possible only through economic growth and that long-term and sustainable growth is needed. So far the financial conditions required for this are missing, and the same applies to clarification of the role of the private sector and state intervention.

Policies so far have failed to address basic contradictions. It is clear that the short-term stabilisation measures (restrictions) do not stimulate economic growth, and many countries experienced a downward spiral with no hope of improvement. Stabilisation policies have so far concentrated on rescuing the banking sector, or some of the highly indebted governments, but everybody agrees that the real spheres of industry and trade are also in trouble. We face a recession, and in spite of some upturns, we are not out of the woods yet. There were some demand-stimulating measures, but they have proved unsatisfactory.

There is broad agreement that stimulation of the economy should be connected to structural modernisation. The European Parliament, already in 2009 under the Headlines of 'New Agreement for Promotion of European Recovery', called attention to the opportunity that the crisis should be used for supporting structural change, and the development of knowledge-based and environmentally conscious economies.

Stabilisation so far has been characterised rather by short-term demand-stimulating measures (Keynesism) than on long-term innovation and structural modernisation (Schumpeterism). There were certain efforts taken in the latter direction, but so far they have failed, partly because of resistance from the business sector (automobile industry), partly because governments were hesitant about the Schumpeterian dilemma of 'constructive destruction', which may imply increasing unemployment, even if it probably would have been a transitory price to pay.

Both the strategies and financial resources are lacking, and that applies to both the EU and national levels. The EU decision for €120bn may help (recapitalisation EIB by €10bn, which creates €60bn new investment capacities + structural funds), but all depends on investments of the private sector. It is clear that a favourable investment atmosphere is needed, and even a low base rate (0.75 per cent) and the 'unlimited' credit offered by the ECB to the commercial banks is not enough.

Many feel and propose that there are huge opportunities for greening of economies, and in changing energy structures. As Peter Felcsúti, the former general director of Raiffeisen Bank Hungary stated:

> This uncertain state lasts till the appearance of such a technological-technical innovation, which could be the driving force of the processes. This can appear in the form of green technology, namely environment friendly, or just as energy innovation. Formerly, such forces were, for example, the railways, electrification, or explosive spread of IT technologies.
>
> (Kocsi 2011: 20)

All agree that the present growth path based on hydro-carbons is unsustainable in the long run and may increase the risk of environmental catastrophes, influencing mankind's future existence. The search for new, renewable energies, however, is too slow, and the determination for change is lacking both on the side of the main energy companies (too many investments are frozen in the present structures) and on the side of government, for whom the present energy mix is one of the main sources of tax revenue. New resources would need investment. Europe, with its growing dependence on hydro-carbon supplies, potentially could be a winner, and it has all the scientific and technical capacities for such a change. Strategies and determination are the first steps, but it should be done sooner rather than later.

Finally, structural reforms cannot be avoided. The positions of member states are different; some have progressed, others lag behind. The present social, health, pension and educational systems are unsustainable in most of the countries. Normally, reforms should have been implemented under favourable economic conditions, but most governments did not feel the urgency to do so. Crisis can enforce radical solutions, but could easily become socially unsustainable and the best possible solutions could be missed again.

One should stress that the Euro is not a magic bullet, neither a blessing nor a curse. Greece and Ireland experienced crisis not because they are members of the Eurozone, but because of their faulty and irresponsible economic policies. One has to pay for bad economic policies in or out of the Eurozone. It is another question about keeping to the disciplinary rules that provide a better chance for avoiding mistakes. In Hungary, 100,000 people could have been saved from the Swiss franc exchange rate loss if the country had joined the Eurozone in 2008, as was realistically assumed. Hungary was not in a worse situation compared to Slovakia or Slovenia, but the political will and the corresponding policies were not in place.

There are question marks about the future of the Euro and in fact about the whole EU venture. The real economic foundations are unchanged, and there are substantial economic, social and political interests in maintaining it. Collapse would mean unforeseeable consequences and astronomical and intolerable losses. According to the UCB Bank calculations, in the first year the collapse of the Euro in the peripheral countries would cost about 40–50 per cent of GDP, while this loss in the core countries could reach 20–25 per cent. This would mean trillions of Euro (*The Economist* 2011). In these circumstances, the whole European project might collapse. Survival is not only a European issue. There are strong global interests at stake as well. The collapse of the Eurozone cannot be excluded, but there is only a slight chance of this occurring.

The measures for a 'Fiscal Union' and recently concerning the 'Bank Union' assume some radical changes that may imply a move towards federal structures. There is no doubt that a sufficiently operating economic and monetary union needs political integration. The possibility of the Commission vetoing national budgets and imposing automatic sanctions could limit national fiscal autonomy and would require changes in the basic treaties that may raise national objections. The same applies to the Bank Union, which extends rescue facilities to commercial banks. The Bank Union would guarantee the bank deposits of citizens, but assume strict union oversight and control that could hurt strong national and local interests. Countries can bargain for 'sovereignty or solidarity', but the necessary public support remains uncertain.

No doubt, in the future, the integration of budgetary policy is unavoidable in order to deal with asymmetric shocks and promote stabilisation. So-called fiscal federalism will be inevitable. One important characteristic of fiscal federalism is that cohesion transfers are largely automatically carried out by the budgets of the various federal states by means of progressive income tax and social benefits. Income is redistributed from richer regions and social strata to poorer ones. From the fiscal point of view, it is a weakness of the EMU that the EU budget does not contain these automatic mechanisms. On the other hand, community transfers from the various 'cohesion and structural funds' do not come close to the amount that is likely to be needed and is typical in federal states. In contrast to the structural funds' 0.46 per cent share of GDP, such 'cohesion transfers' in other federations amount to 3–4 per cent of GDP.

In spite of proposals for a common Eurozone budget, the extension of the EU budget towards a real federal budget, which would assume a substantial increase in size, both in terms of financing (own resources – EU taxation) and in expenditures with satisfactory cohesion transfers, and balancing and corrective mechanisms (automatic stabilisers), has little chance in the foreseeable future. The EU is in a multi-track integration, and that would hardly change even in the middle-term perspective. A multi-speed Europe could be acceptable, particularly if there are strong enough locomotives towards a future federation.

A 'federalist future' is not only desirable, but it is necessary as well. As the fate of constitutional treaty confirmed, it cannot be an elite venture. It needs broad agreement and support from civil society and citizens. 'Europe's future depends not just on governments putting forward the right policies, but on the capacity of democracies to bring about peaceful change. If the burden gets too heavy, the political system collapses' (*The Economist* 2011: 6). Sustainable growth is needed for sustainable financial stability, but this assumes sustainable social and political stability as well. This is an urgent task if we want a strong and prosperous Europe. In the twentieth century, we have already experienced the derailment of history (Nazism and Bolshevism). This should not happen again.

Bibliography

Crawford, M. (1996) *One Money for Europe? The Economics and Politics of EMU*, London: Macmillan Press Ltd.

Csaba, L. (2010) 'Paradigmaváltás az európai gazdaságpolitikában?', Available: www.csabal.com/downloads/paradigmavaltas_az_europai_gazdasagpolitikaban.pdf.

The Economist (2011) 'Staring into the Abyss, Special Report on Europe and its Currency', 12 November.

Emerson, M., and Huhne, C. (1991) *The ECU Report*, London: Pan Books.

Giordano, F., and Persaud, S. (1998) *The Political Economy of Monetary Union. Towards the Euro*, London: Routledge.

Issing, O., Gaspar, V., Angeloni, I., and Tristani, O. (2001) *Monetary Policy in the Euro Area: Strategy and Decision-Making at the European Central Bank*, Cambridge: Cambridge University Press.

Kocsi, Ilona (2011) *Rém? Álom? Kapitalizmus? [Nightmare? Dream? Capitalism?]*, Budapest: Alinea Kiadó.

Padoa-Schioppa, T. (1989) 'The European Monetary System: A Long-Term View', in Giavazzi, F., Micossi, S., and Miller, M. (eds.) *The European Monetary System*, Cambridge: Cambridge University Press.

Padoa-Schioppa, T. (1994) *The Road to Monetary Union in Europe*, Oxford: Clarendon Press.
Pelkmans, J. (1997) *European Integration (Methods and Economic Analysis)*, Heerlen, Open University of the Netherlands: Longman.
Scholte, J.A. (2005) *Globalization: Critical Introduction*, Basingstoke: Palgrave Macmillan.
Tsoukalis, L. (1993) *The New European Economy*, Oxford: Oxford University Press.

Part III
Landscape in the 'peripheries'
Inside and outside the EU

8 Anatomy of the Euro-crisis

Annamaria Artner

The Eurozone crisis is seen mostly as the crisis of the less developed, peripheral countries of the zone, namely Portugal, Ireland, Italy, Greece and Spain (PIIGS). This chapter would like to prove that this is false. The crisis originates from the heart of the capitalist production, i.e. from the developed or 'core' countries, but the globalization of the market mechanisms makes it possible to shift the crisis from core countries to the periphery. The analysis begins here with a theoretical approach to the crisis.

The crisis, that is to say the manifestation of the inevitably cyclical depreciation of capital, is strongly connected to the distribution of the value added between profits and wages. Every production cycle, be it short ('business') or long ('Kondratiev'), is divided into extensive and intensive periods of growth. During short cycles, production grows on the basis of a given set of technology or 'technological paradigm'. In this extensive period, the demand for labour grows, hence wages grow as well, and an inflationary pressure is born. Wage increases lift the wage rate (or unit labour cost), reduce the rate of profit and diminish competitiveness. The decrease of the profit rate can be counterbalanced, at least for a while, by increasing the amount of profit through multiplying investments at the same level of technology. The decrease of the rate of profit, however, stimulates inventions, technological upgrading that pays with a higher rate of profit or 'extra profit' for those entrepreneurs that apply the new, productivity-enhancing technologies first. This process depreciates the capital of other companies that still apply the older technologies and compels them also to upgrade their technologies. Thus, intensification becomes general. More and more companies replace their technology with newer, more developed forms and the cycle enters the second phase, i.e. the intensive period. However, as productivity grows, there is more and more tangible technology (fixed assets) and less labour, and increased productivity spreads to more and more participants, the competition becomes more fierce, prices decrease and the extra profits of the first inventors gradually disappear. The consequence is that the added value relative to the invested capital decreases. The rate of profit relative to the invested capital decreases too in general and on average. The shrinking of the rate of profit can be, at least partly, counterbalanced by keeping wages down. This pushdown on wages is possible because, thanks to the more productive technology, the demand for labour decreases and unemployment goes up and inflationary pressure is low in the intensive period.

The end result of the cycle is that the rate of profit relative to invested capital and the share of wages relative to the value added decreases. The reduction in the rate of wages, however, evaporates the effective demand of the population relative to output. Markets reach their saturation point, overproduction appears and crisis breaks out. This breaking out of the crisis, however, is usually postponed by a 'pseudo demand' boom. It happens as spontaneously as the above-described cycle. As in the intensive phase, more and more capital becomes outdated (uncompetitive) and demand decreases because of growing unemployment as a consequence of the productivity-enhancing innovations, and more and more 'idle' capital lies in the banks in the form of money waiting for better possibilities for profit making in the real economy. This 'idle' capital represents 'dead' capital, loss and crisis.

The money then lent out by banks, thereby increasing demand, increases the debt of wage earners. The problem of the insufficient demand caused by low wages is hidden by the artificially increased ('pseudo') demand, and outdated technologies can survive for a while. The crisis accumulates while the GDP grows, hiding the growing crisis under apparent growth. The debts, however, will never be repaid as markets become saturated and growth is exhausted. At this point, the crisis breaks out in the form of credit crisis and 'toxic assets' of the financial institutions.

In the era of global capitalism, investment allocation policies of transnational corporations rule the global economy. The obsolete or second and third line technologies are transferred to the low-wage peripheral economies in the form of foreign direct investments because, with the lower wages in the periphery, outdated technologies can be made profitable. The two periods of the production cycle divide in space but unite in time (Rozsnyai 2002). The extensive period shortens or even disappears in the core countries and the intensive period becomes almost continuous there. The extensive period occurs mainly in peripheral countries, and continues for a longer period of time. Hence, the technological lag, lower productivity and competitiveness, the steady inclination to inflation and indebtedness are preserved or even exacerbated in the periphery and crisis inevitably reappears from time to time. In the Eurozone, this shift of the crisis to the periphery happened in this way, aided by the common currency.

Theory and reality

According to the theory of Optimum Currency Area (OCA) that was developed in the early 1960s, the primary condition of an OCA is the close-to-equal ability of members to successfully react to external shocks. This requirement presupposes that the members of the currency union are similar in structural factors, like competitiveness and productivity, and inclination to inflation; also the rate of change of these structural features are the same or at least very similar. The European policy, however, which was driven by the interests of transnational capita, quickly put aside the original considerations. As elaborated earlier (Artner and Róna 2012), first the 'interim solution' to the management of the problem of the sequencing was allowed, the problem of abandonment of the sovereign monetary policy was eliminated and so on.

It cannot simply be said that the Eurozone was a creation purely of political will, a mistake or an unreasoned step in the development of European integration. Every political step is fed by certain interests. The creation of a common currency was in the very interest of the largest trading and financial actors who were interested in profiting from global markets.

The common currency general has a long history. It was one of the indispensable conditions of the emergence of national markets. Reliable money has always been the core requirement for international commodity trade and the flow of capital. National markets and states emerged and were fed by international trade: the capitalist system of production historically came into existence as an international system.

The need for a stable international monetary order has produced solutions since the silver and gold standard, through to the Bretton Woods system or the creation of pseudo-currencies like SDR. In general, and as history teaches, the international monetary system that rests on a common currency is advantageous for the more competitive and disadvantageous for the less competitive (nations, regions). This is because the latter cannot increase their competitiveness in line with the former, and hence are forced to internal devaluation if they want to survive in the common currency system. Towards this goal, a decrease of wages and prices is required, i.e. internal devaluation. This internal devaluation is harmful to both social peace and national capital. This is why neither the gold standard nor the Bretton Woods system were long-lived. Even the US did not undertake the sacrifice of internal devaluation to a sufficient extent for the sake of a stable international monetary system, and suspended the convertibility of the dollar into gold, thereby breaking Bretton Woods in 1971.

On the other hand, a stable international currency is very advantageous for those that are able to act on the international market and to gain profit from it, e.g. transnational companies. In spite of the fact that transnational corporations are frequently also multinational, they are still connected to national states. Certain states have more ties with, or stake in, transnational corporations; others have only a few or none. In this way, the hierarchy and competition within the capital itself appears as the hierarchy and competition of nations that can lead even to conflict or war between nations. The nation state cannot be eliminated by market forces since it was formed by market forces. On the basis of the market economy (i.e. a profit-making system of production), the nation state can be eliminated only by war, as history proves. But even this type of elimination in capitalism cannot be maintained in the long run.

The common currency of the United States, the country which was the source of the idea of the 'United States of Europe', was borne with and by the independent Union in 1783, and was defended by a civil war. The European states, however, were already well-founded historical nations when the need of global capital required their unification. This is a project that is not feasible in the given socio-economic frames. This contradictory situation bears the gloomy possibility of war since global capital has governed itself into a historical crisis again. War is a possibility because the crisis is a crisis of the global capital that demands profound changes in the world that have hardly been possible before without the possibility of some kind of war.

At the beginning of the present crisis, the partial and apologetic explanations of the crisis and the problems of the Eurozone ruled the scientific field. The political will, the skill or even ethical behaviour of government leaders, companies and consumers was criticized. Even now, after more than four years of the crisis, the debate is about 'suitable' economic policy. The neo-Keynesian solution is gathering ground, demanding more state intervention, protection of the poor and/or debt abolition, at least partially. These changes may remedy the problem to a certain extent, but they are unable to solve the problem of capital accumulation, which is the essence of economic activity and at the same time is the cause of all crises. The processes that have evolved in the Eurozone tell the story and prove that the original OCA theory and history are correct about the monetary integration of differently developed nations.

Inflation

Contrary to expectations, the harmonization of inflation did not occur after the introduction of the Euro. The peripheral countries of the Eurozone (like Portugal, Ireland, Italy, Greece, Spain – the PIIGS) became more expensive, as the Balassa-Samuelson effect says, especially compared to strong economies like Austria, the Netherlands, France and first of all Germany. From Figure 8.1, one can see that the divergence of inflation rates has accelerated since the creation of the Eurozone. What is more, the divergence has continued after the crisis in spite of austerity policies. Only Ireland was able to decrease its inflation rate relative to Germany, and even this position has weakened since the middle of 2010.[1]

This phenomenon was not independent from the free movement of capital. Capital could easily flow from the stronger economies to the peripheral countries and be invested with more profit than in the country of origin. This had further consequences that deteriorated the situation of peripheral countries.

External balance

In general, the competitiveness of peripheral countries suffered a decline that resulted in a declining external balance (trade, income and payment), increasing indebtedness of consumers, companies and states. All of this hampered innovation that was already insufficient even before these effects were felt.

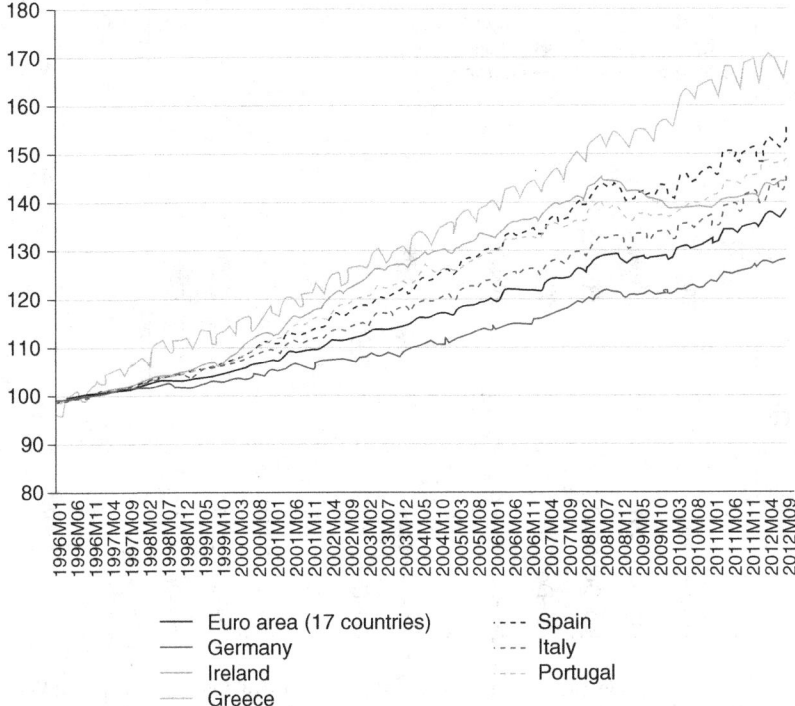

Figure 8.1 Harmonized index of consumer prices, January 1996–September 2012 (1996 = 100) (Eurostat Online Database).

Balance of trade

As Figures 8.2 and 8.3 show, between 1999 and 2007 the deficit in extra-EU trade (i.e. trade with the non-EU countries) increased significantly in the case of Spain and Greece; it stagnated in Portugal; the growth of Ireland's trade surplus came to a halt; and in Italy the surplus turned into a deficit. As for the intra-EU trade, the loss is more marked, since the balance deteriorated in all five countries. Only Italy somewhat improved the balance and achieved a modest surplus in 2007–2008, but this quickly faded. Until the outbreak of the crisis, the export surplus of Germany showed a dynamic, and constantly increasing trend in the intra- and, albeit at a slower rate, extra-EU trade as well. The crisis mitigated the problem mainly through the decrease of the imports of the PIIGS.

Between 2000 and 2007, Germany's total exports in goods (intra- and extra-EU) tripled, while the most successful exporter of the PIIGS, namely Ireland, increased its surplus by less than 20 per cent only. The PIIGS's balance of trade with Germany is even more informative. It was more or less in equilibrium; small import or export surpluses were achieved by the five countries before

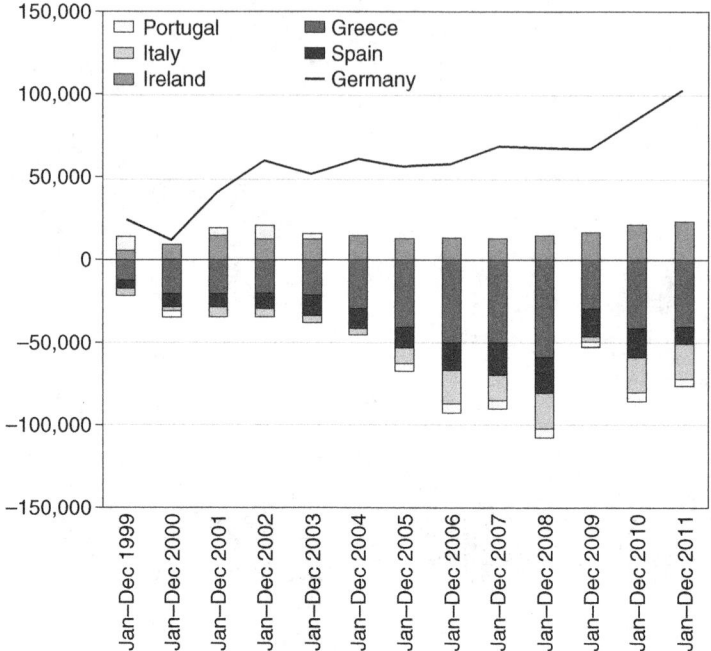

Figure 8.2 Balance of non-EU27 trade, 1999–2011 (millions of Euro) (Eurostat Online Database).

1999. As so much else, this situation has also changed after the creation of the Euro. Trade surpluses disappeared and deficits have substantially grown. In most of the period between 1999 and 2011, the deficit of the PIIGS combined in relation to Germany was much higher than the deficit of the whole Eurozone (Austria, Belgium, Finland, France, Germany, Greece, Ireland, Italy, Luxemburg, Portugal, Spain and the Netherlands) with Germany (Figure 8.4).

In 1999, 14.8 per cent of total German trade surplus derived from the five peripheral countries and this proportion has doubled in half a decade to reach 28 to 29 per cent in 2005–2007. Since the first year of the crisis, this share has decreased, but it was still higher (18.4 per cent) in 2011 than in 1999.

Income balance

Figure 8.5 clearly shows how the income balance of the PIIGS deteriorated (further) as well after entry to the Eurozone, while the balance of Germany rose steeply upward since 2002.

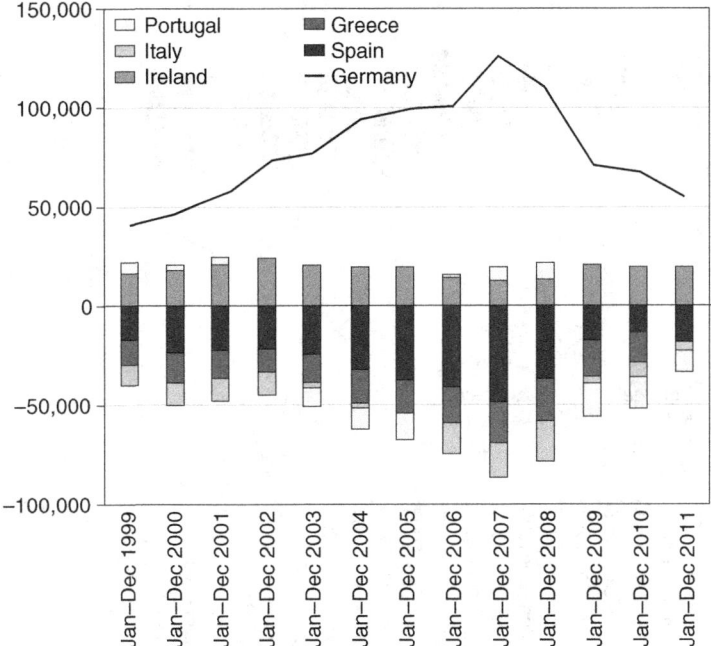

Figure 8.3 Balance of trade with EU27, 1999–2011 (millions of Euro) (Eurostat Online Database).

Balance of payments

After the accession to the Eurozone, all five countries' balance of payments (balance of goods, services, incomes, current transfers and capital) declined compared to Germany, whose balance changed from a deficit into a briskly rising surplus (Figure 8.6).

Indebtedness

The low interest rate of the Euro, together with the higher inflation rate in the peripheral countries, resulted necessarily in booms in real estate and consumer goods because negative real interest rates were very advantageous for profit making. The boom of the 1990s led by the information technologies had already wound down and large amounts of capital lay idle in the financial sphere. This surplus capital found its way into production through the banks and other financial institutions in the form of credit. Without this U-turn, the global crisis would have appeared earlier. With this credit boom that increased consumption, the obsolete production structure could be maintained. All the countries involved in the transatlantic economy were participants in the processes that led to the crisis in 2008, though not with the same consequences due to their differing national

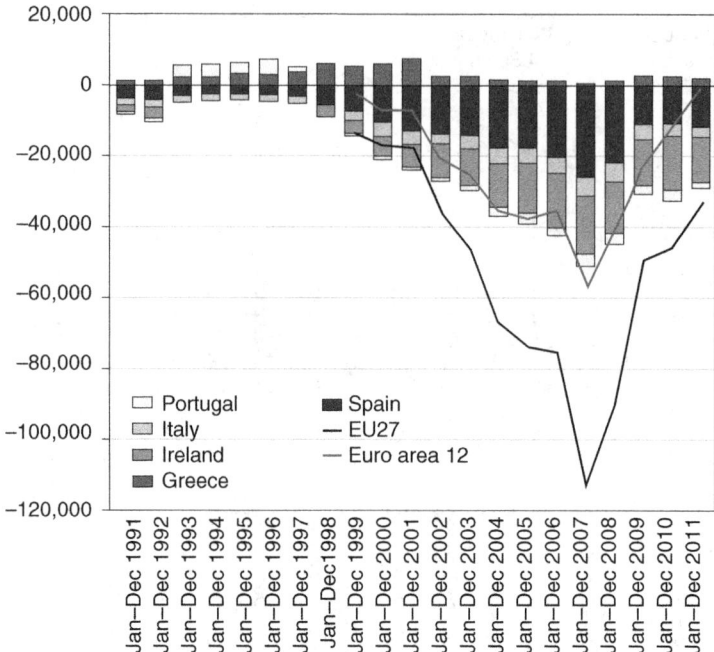

Figure 8.4 Trade balance with Germany, 1999–2011 (millions of Euro) (Eurostat Online Database).

economic, political and historical features and, most importantly, their different levels of participation in the hierarchical division of labour in the global economy.

As pointed out earlier (Artner and Róna 2012), debt was incurred, above all, by the population, rather than the public sector. The rise in public debt is largely due to the bailout of the banks. This is illustrated also by the Cyprian example where the close-to-bankruptcy situation was elaborated mainly by the inevitable recapitalization of Cypriot banking institutions that had lost a lot after the 50 per cent 'haircut' on Greek debt in 2012.

The indebtedness of the population relative to GDP in the PIIGS had increased already before the creation of the Eurozone, but a similar trend can be seen in Germany as well. After 1999, however, the situation changed: while the indebtedness of the population of the PIIGS relative to GDP continued to grow at an accelerating pace (with the exception of Portugal having already a high level of debt), the German population's financial obligations began to fall, and this trend persisted until the crisis.

There is no over-indebtedness without over-lending. The low interest rates of the Euro, on the one hand, and the high profits realized in investment bubbles in the PIIGS, on the other, tempted banks in the Euro member states to pour money into the financial sphere of the PIIGS. As Figure 8.7 shows, between 2004 and

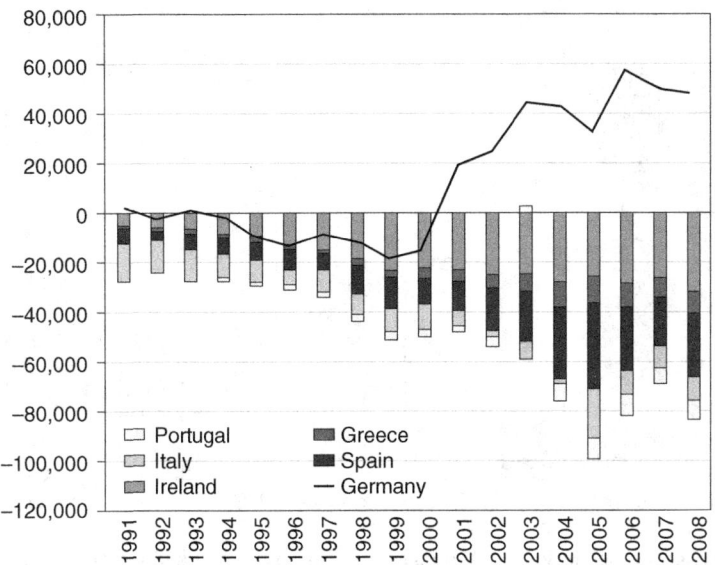

Figure 8.5 Current account, balance of income, 1991–2011 (millions of Euro) (Eurostat Online Database).

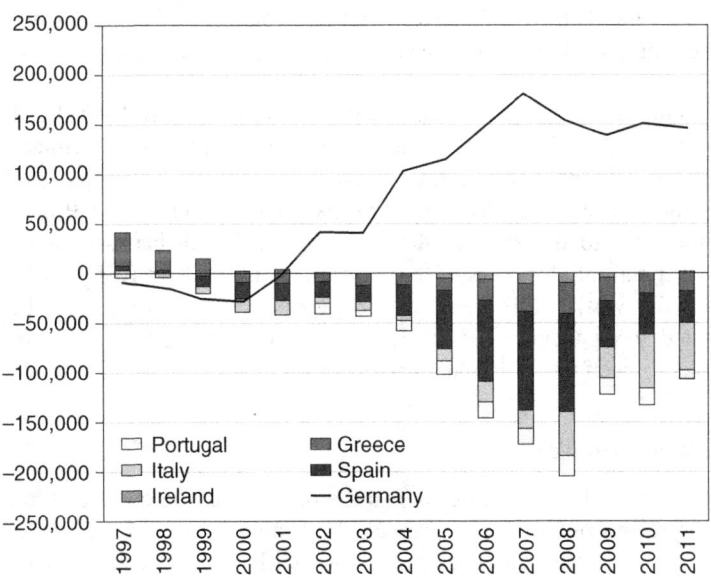

Figure 8.6 Balance of payments: current and capital account, 1991–2011 (millions of Euro) (Eurostat Online Database).

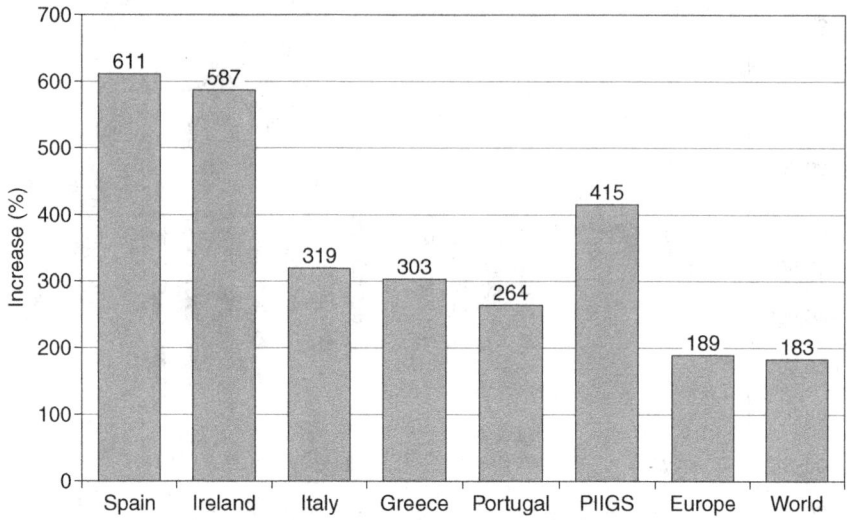

Figure 8.7 Increase of the consolidated foreign claims of the French and German banks together in the PIIGS between June 2004 and March 2008 (percent).

2008, when the bulk of the credit boom occurred, the consolidated foreign claims of French and German banks in the five peripheral countries of the Eurozone increased more than five times larger than their total claims in the world or in Europe.

According to the Bank of International Settlements in December 2010, 1,571 billion Euros, or nearly half of the consolidated foreign claims of the European banks, were claims on debtors within the Eurozone, and more than a quarter of these (or 12.1 per cent of all claims of the European banks) were in the PIIGS. At the same time, the total claims of the German and French banks together represented 53 per cent of all claims of the European banks in the PIIGS. At the end of 2010, the five weak Eurozone economies represented 17.8 per cent of the total consolidated foreign claims of the German banks, and 20.6 per cent of the French banks respectively (BIS Quarterly Reviews).

Deterioration in competitiveness

As a result of the credit boom that postponed the outbreak of the crisis and hid the need for the reconstruction of the capital, the competiveness of the PIIGS deteriorated in the 2000s. As less developed economies have a tendency towards higher inflation, the Euro inevitably appreciated in the PIIGS; while the low Euro interest rates induced a boom in demand. The boom in the economy pushed up wages (Balassa-Samuelson effect) and – as a result – the public welfare expenditures as well. The increase of productivity has not, however, kept pace with this because of the extensive growth in production on the basis of given technologies that provided sufficient profit for producers. This resulted in an increase in unit labour costs relative to the Eurozone and outside it as well. For these reasons, the Euro helped these processes to a great extent. We can say that the Euro has been the catalyst and the amplifier of the deteriorating competitiveness of the PIIGS.

Increasing development gap

A very important critique of the Eurozone is that the convergence of developmental levels came to a standstill exactly when the countries in question became members of the Eurozone. Previously, Ireland rapidly had approached the average of the 12 members of the Eurozone (Euro12), but the rate of convergence slowed after 1999. The catching up of Greece was particularly strong up to 2003 (the GDP grew by 5.9 per cent in that year), most probably under the influence of the early years of the Euro and the impact of Olympic preparations, but after that period the trend breaks. Similarly, the catching up of Spain also lost momentum. In Portugal, the former trend of catching up reversed, while the lagging behind of Italy has accelerated. As a mirror image, Germany's position shows an improving trend throughout the period (Figure 8.8).

The divergence of the developmental levels is summarized in the standard deviation of the GDP/capita of the Euro12 (Figure 8.9). Between 1999 and 2007, the standard deviation of the nominal GDP/capita grew by 78 per cent, real value by 36 per cent and the purchasing power standard (PPS) value by 75 per cent. Only the crisis has brought a temporary change in this trend, but it proved to be short-lived, especially in the case of the nominal and PPS values.

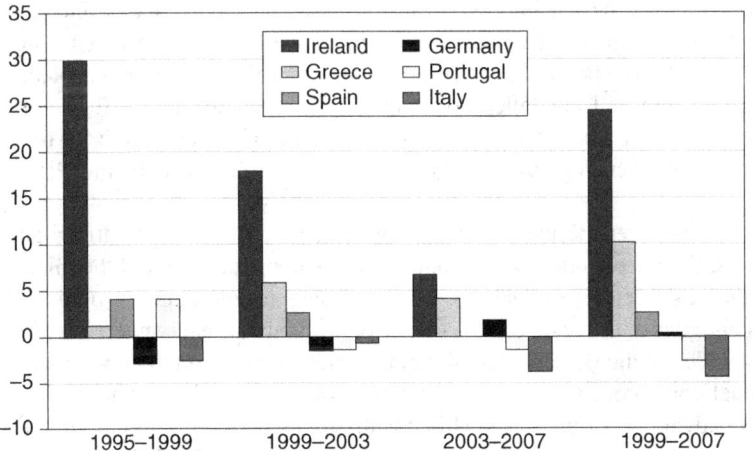

Figure 8.8 Change in share of national GDP/cap to Euro12 average, 1995–2007 (percentage point) (Eurostat Online Database).

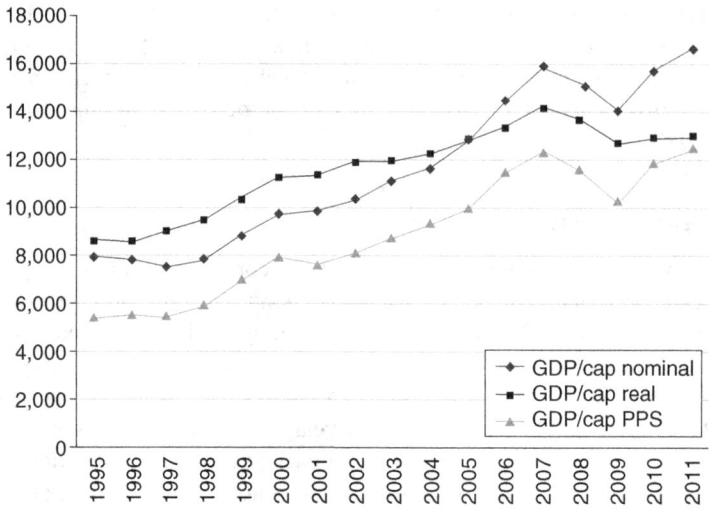

Figure 8.9 Standard deviation of GDP/cap in the Eurozone 12, 1995–2011 (Euro per inhabitant) (Eurostat Online Database).

Conclusion

As the above data reveal, the Eurozone has been harmful for the less developed members while it has helped the stronger ones become even stronger: inflation rates diverged, the real effective exchange rate of the inherently less developed countries became 'overvalued', their population became heavily indebted, their external balance deteriorated and their catching up stopped. They have suffered a drop in competitiveness primarily because of this and the associated increase in the wage/GDP ratio (unit labour costs), but it would not have taken place (or not to this extent), and not have caused problems similar to present problems, if their equilibrium had not fallen apart due to their position in the Eurozone. At the same time, the strongest nations, Germany first of all, profited a lot from the situation, experiencing just the opposite results from those in the PIIGS countries.

Developments over the past decade show that, in contrast to intentions and expectations, the introduction of the common currency neither served the micro-level of the real sector (production), nor promoted technological progress in weaker economies and, thus, not only did it not bring about real convergence but it actually widened the developmental gap further. Only the countries with large transnational companies and a very strong position in the global economy were able to take advantage of the Euro, while the disadvantages in the form of deterioration in competitiveness were left to the weaker countries. This led to the crisis in the form of imbalances and indebtedness of the PIIGS. This also implies that neither the hierarchy of competitiveness within the Eurozone nor the possibility of future crises can be eliminated by any kind of stronger budgetary discipline or better regulation of finances.

Note

1 According to the Balassa-Samuelson effect, the increase of productivity and wages are higher in the tradable goods sector than in the non-tradable goods sector, but as labour is mobile this rise in wages pushes up wages in the non-tradable sector as well. This leads to a rise in inflation. As the productivity of the non-tradable sector of the less developed economies is less than that of the more developed economies, this means that the former tend to have higher inflation.

Bibliography

Artner, Annamária, and Róna, Péter (2012) 'Euros(c)eptic: The Theory of the Optimum Currency Area and the Practice of the Euro', *Romanian Journal of European Affairs*, vol. 12, no. 2, June, pp. 80–98.

Rozsnyai, Ervin (2002) *Az Imperializmus Korszakváltásai* [*Epoch Changes of Imperialism*], Budapest: Rozsnyai Ervin.

9 Does austerity prevail over democracy?

Two bad models: Italy and Greece

Federico Rampini

Europe fell back into recession in 2012/2013, as a consequence of the 'shock-therapy' it inflicted upon itself. Whereas the first recession of 2008/2009 was 'made in the USA', the second and most recent one is entirely manufactured in Europe. It is the result of wrongly conceived austerity policies. It should not be depicted as a 'crisis of the euro', first because the United Kingdom (not a Eurozone member) is under the same strain due to the tight fiscal policies of the Cameron cabinet, second and foremost because the collapse of the monetary union is unlikely, after a decisive showdown by the European Central Bank (ECB) in the summer of 2012. But this is not the point. The impact of the European crisis has been especially hard on workers and the middle class, with unemployment rates at historically high levels since the 1980s in most countries – albeit with notable exceptions like Germany, Austria, Holland and the Scandinavian countries – and a decline in the purchasing power of wages and pensions. Has the European Left anything to say about this? Not much, until the autumn of 2013, despite the fact that France, the second largest member of the European Union, has had a Socialist president since May 2012. A slight change in the mix of economic policies occurred in Germany with the formation of a *Grosse Koalition* [large coalition] after the elections of September 2013. With the Social-Democratic Party (SPD) joining the Christian Democratic Party of Angela Merkel, the political agenda has indeed shifted to the left, as we shall see, but only insofar as these changes are reserved to Germany itself, not its weaker partners in the Eurozone.

The crisis of the single currency that dominated the agenda until the summer of 2012, and the need to avoid its collapse as well as the default of some member countries, reinforced German hegemony. The German chancellor, Angela Merkel, accepted, although reluctantly, to play a dominant role in the bailout of Greece and in other indirect forms of support to the weaker members of the monetary union: the so-called PIIGS (together with Greece these include Portugal, Ireland, Italy and Spain). In exchange, Ms Merkel imposed on the whole Eurozone a tight austerity. This austerity is not 'neutral' in its impact on the distribution of wealth and income. It is somehow ironic that a country like Germany, which we identify with the European 'social model' at its best, is forcing its neighbors to dismantle parts of their welfare state. (This term has usually a wider meaning in Europe than in the US and includes not only subsidies to the unemployed or aid to the poor but also entitlement expenditures for pensions and healthcare.) Government spending has been cut and taxes have been raised on workers and the middle class everywhere from Paris to Rome, from Madrid to Athens. If the example of Greece is of any help, being the first country that has been forced into a massive austerity program, it is not encouraging: this ferociously tightening policy is a recipe for disaster. Pro-cyclical spending cuts accelerate the downward spiral into recession. When the GDP decreases, tax revenues fall, deficits rise, exacerbating the crisis of confidence instead of healing it. It's 1937 all over again: the year when in the US Franklin Delano Roosevelt put a stop to the New Deal policies and decided to tackle the federal deficit instead, with the result that the US economy plunged back into recession.

As if the human costs of European austerity were not enough, another price has been paid in terms of democracy. Greece was the first country to experience this crisis with the severe limitation of its sovereignty. When the former prime minister George Papandreou wanted to submit the austerity plan imposed by the EU to a national referendum, the two main 'shareholders' of the EU decision-making process, Angela Merkel and then French president Nicolas Sarkozy, were outraged. When the G20 summit opened in Cannes (France) on November 4, 2011, the euro was under attack. Investors in the global financial markets were alarmed by the prospect of a prolonged political debate among the Greeks. Merkel and Sarkozy – or 'Merkozy' as the center-right duo were called in Europe – pressured Papandreou to cancel the referendum which he had already announced to his fellow citizens. Soon afterwards, the Greek prime minister resigned. His successor, Lucas Papademos, was an unelected technocrat: a former banker at the European Central Bank (ECB) in Frankfurt, Germany. The Greek democracy was therefore 'suspended' by Merkozy and the financial markets. Papademos held office from November 2011 till May 2012. Following the May 2012 elections and the victory of the conservative party New Democracy, he was replaced by the Harvard-educated economist Antonis Samaras.

Something similar happened in Italy, with consequences that proved even more dramatic. The third largest economy in the Eurozone and one of the founding members of the EU back in 1957, Italy got rid of Prime Minister Silvio Berlusconi in November 2011 not because the progressive opposition won the elections – there weren't any – but because the extravagant and dangerous tycoon-turned-politician was ousted by Merkozy, the ECB and the financial markets. Berlusconi was the victim of his incompetence: having governed Italy for almost nine years in the last decade, he was absorbed by his huge conflicts of interests, his judicial problems, his decadent personal life, and paid no attention to the constant weakening of the Italian economy's competitiveness. As a result, in the summer and fall of 2011 investors became very nervous about the Italian public debt, at 120 percent of the country's GDP. Berlusconi's European partners were unwilling to tolerate his antics anymore. No matter how beneficial the outcome may have seemed at that time, Berlusconi, too, was ousted by a supra-national and un-democratic diktat. This has had consequences, as we saw with the February 2013 elections. Because the Italian Left played only a marginal role in his resignation, Berlusconi was replaced by a government of technocrats that seemed at times to be more accountable to Germany, the European Commission and the ECB than to Italian citizens. Prime Minister Mario Monti, in charge from November 2011 till April 2013, is a very decent man, a well-respected economist and a former European commissioner in charge of antitrust policies. But Monti had to govern with the parliamentary support of both the right-of-center parties (mostly the Partito delle Libertà, led by Berlusconi) and the Democratic Party on the left. Mr Monti's policies were disappointing, for anyone hoping to see a real change after Berlusconi. His 'austerity package' was the usual mix of tax hikes which burdened even more the middle class, and spending cuts that strained the welfare state, education, healthcare, scientific research. In the Italian austerity policies, there has been no meaningful rebalancing of social injustice. Little has been done to tackle rampant tax fraud, which in Italy is mostly concentrated in wealthy groups and privileged élites (small businesses and many liberal professions like doctors and lawyers). Italy, after Greece, was under a similar 'suspension' of its democracy, with the only beneficial result avoidance of utter financial disaster: a sovereign bankruptcy.

It is surprising to see how little 'European' the policies implemented in the EU are to tackle the so-called debt crisis (the mere definition of the current recession as a 'debt crisis' is obviously misleading, as if unemployment and impoverishment were sideshows to more important fiscal and financial issues). In the US, public discourse, especially among Republicans during the 2012 presidential campaign, 'European' became a synonym for 'socialist'. Mitt Romney repeatedly accused President Obama of trying to 'turn the US into another European Welfare State', where the government is supposed to take care of its citizens 'from cradle to grave'. These accusations resonate powerfully in these times, when the American conservatives can argue that 'European socialism' is going bankrupt. The 'entitlement society' is depicted in the US as utterly devoid of energy, dynamism or the ability to innovate. Sadly, many Europeans share this pessimistic view of their 'model'. Even if there is little sympathy or attraction (even among European moderates and conservatives) towards a US-style free market, with an extreme flexibility that translates into insecurity, many Europeans feel that their own social compact and their tradition of Keynesian deficit spending are doomed. What will happen if the European governments end up believing what the American Right says about them? And how is it possible that one of the best regulated, 'cradle-to-grave Welfare' countries, i.e. Germany, wants its European partners to be less and less like itself? This is, at the end of the road, the outcome of the structural reforms that Ms Merkel has extracted from Italy, Spain, Greece: more US-style flexibility and insecurity, less spending for education, research, healthcare, pensions, public services.

To understand this impasse, one has to look at the contradictions of the European Left. Europe has a few success stories to exhibit in today's global economy, and they bear the marks of progressive policies. First and foremost, there is

Germany: a country whose population is less than one third compared to the US and only one fifteenth of the Chinese population, and yet has managed to be either the first or the second largest exporter in the world, almost on a par with China and often outranking the US, over the last decade. Germany has been able to run a trade surplus with China whereas the US has a massive trade deficit. The German economy remains remarkably competitive even as it has preserved its high salaries, very powerful labor unions, a generous welfare state, and with some of the toughest environmental regulations in the world. It is, in many respects, the perfect antithesis to all the dogmas of the Republicans and free-market conservatives all over the world. Germany is not a lonely and exceptional case. Austria, Holland and Switzerland (albeit not a EU member) are similar in their social compact and economic performance. Scandinavian countries, some of which have higher per capita income than the US, are among the most egalitarian societies in the world. The fact that the gap between their wealthiest and their poorest citizens is much narrower than it is in the US, or in China, has not prevented Scandinavian economies from thriving. Thanks to their investment in education – their high-school students are among the best performing in the world, on a par with South Koreans, as measured by the OECD-PISA rankings – Scandinavians consistently rate among the 'most satisfied' people, when interviewed in international surveys about their own results in the global economic competition. Also, German and Scandinavian economies have proved that you can thrive in the global economy without having to pay outrageously high wages and superbonuses to your chief executives. Sweden is the utmost proof that social justice is not at odds with competitiveness: this country ranked fourth in the world in The Economist's Democracy Index (2010) even as it ranked second in the global competitiveness index measured by the World Economic Forum. In fact, Germans and Scandinavians vindicate the concepts exposed by Wilkinson and Pickett (2009). Egalitarian societies have more 'social capital', i.e. reciprocal confidence among citizens and faith in government, which makes them safer, happier, less crime-ridden and exceptionally competitive.

And yet, Europe does not seem to want to profit from these lessons of its own best champions. Specifically, the European Left has not been strengthened by the Great Contraction of 2008–2013 (Rogoff and Reinhart 2009). Why? One reason is linked to what happened when the German Left was in power. Gerhard Schroeder, the last social-democrat who was chancellor, reformed the welfare state in order to make it leaner and more efficient, by reducing waste, trimming benefits and subsidies for the long-term unemployed. He was a latecomer to the Third Way of Bill Clinton and Tony Blair. His moderate left-of-center policies opened a rift inside his own party, and some of the most progressive social-democrats followed Oskar Lafontaine in a new leftist party. The memory of that internal infighting and of the schism has stained Schroeder's reputation. Even more so, his personal ethics have proved controversial: when he retired from office, he promptly accepted the nomination by his friend Vladimir Putin to the board of a large Russian energy company. That lucrative position seemed an outrageous payout and a flagrant conflict of interest: when he was still in power,

Chancellor Schroeder had been very active in promoting business links between Germany and Russian energy corporations.

Socialist parties in Sweden and Denmark have their own problems. Both countries steered to the right, although the policies implemented by conservative governments do not differ much from the socialist tradition. One explanation is that you can have only so much egalitarianism, welfare state and government spending. Tax rates in Northern Europe are among the highest in the world. The US seems an exotic tax haven, when you compare the highest marginal tax rates that are paid by most German or Scandinavian citizens, not only the wealthiest ones. French President Hollande captured headlines in the world media when he raised the top marginal tax rate on income to 75 percent, and movie actor Gerard Depardieu applied for Russian citizenship in order to escape taxation in his country. Moreover, the 'German model' has proved less successful when mimicked in Southern Europe. Italy has grown a vast and inefficient bureaucracy, often despised as a 'parasitic' and 'privileged class' even by the voters of the left. Tax fraud is rampant in Southern Europe, enshrined in a culture of mistrust towards the government. One of the reasons why Ms Merkel has been so tough in dealing with the looming sovereign default of Greece is the perception of many Germans, including blue-collar union members, that they would have to sacrifice their hard-earned savings in order to bail out wealthy Greek citizens who evade taxes, investing their capital in offshore shelters, or Greek civil servants who can apply for early retirement when they are 55, and enjoy other perks funded by the EU. Alas, this is not really a caricature. When the social-democrat Schroeder was chancellor, his government worked hand-in-hand with the labor unions to build the foundation of today's strong and competitive German economy, by trimming down some of the most expensive welfare programs. Denmark has been celebrated all over the world for its 'flexi-security' system, which draws from the same philosophy that inspired Bill Clinton's 'welfare-to-work'.

In France, Italy, Spain, Greece, the parties of the left share the same problem: advocating a reduction in economic inequalities is necessary but it is not enough. For sure, progressive taxation and other redistributive policies are necessary ingredients to inject purchasing power into the working poor and the middle class. The engine of growth will not restart without a strong Keynesian policy. But this cannot be achieved just by creating new public deficits, especially if any 'stimulus package' goes into feeding the same old bureaucratic dinosaurs. This is a major cultural problem for the left, especially in Mediterranean countries: we have inherited from the last decades a very low 'social capital'. Trust in public institutions, civil servants and the government runs at its lowest point ever. High-profile corruption cases have instilled the suspicion that any new public spending will be an opportunity for further waste or fraud by the political elite.

Therefore, a new strategy for growth must not only take a distinct egalitarian approach, it should also explore non-traditional, non-governmental tools. Ideas like Benefit Corporations, social entrepreneurship, could find a fertile ground in Europe. These economic and social innovations might be able to reignite the passion that the European Left invested a century ago in creating the cooperative movement, a 'third economy' that wanted to emerge as an alternative to Big Business on the one side, and government-owned corporations on the other side.

Today the impetus towards new forms of economic organization is supported by a growing environmental awareness: a vast majority of Europeans understand that they have to explore a sustainable path to growth, that growth cannot restart just by turning back the clock and reviving old patterns of wasteful overconsumption. The left still has a 'cultural competitive advantage', in its tradition of shared universal values, global solidarity, and an international approach to common economic challenges. At the very beginning of the era of globalization '2.0', i.e. when Western countries were negotiating with China for its membership in the World Trade Organization, the French Socialist Jacques Delors (who was president of the European Commission) advocated a new 'social contract' as the indispensable framework for trade agreements. Delors had a clear view at the beginning of the 1990s. He understood that developed Western countries could use their leverage to accelerate a positive evolution in emerging countries towards human rights, labor rights, environmental protection. As the recent wave of social unrest in China proves, this is still a very hot issue, and one that the European Left must rediscover from its own legacy.

The 2013 elections in Italy have shown that the left pays a very high price if it chooses the easy path of 'politics as usual'. The general elections held on February 24 and 25, 2013, were a disaster for the Democratic Party and its allies of the radical left (Sinistra Ecologia Libertà). The Democratic leader, Pierluigi Bersani, was considered until late 2012 as a super-favorite and should have won an easy victory. Instead, he won with the slightest of margins, and only thanks to a controversial 'majority premium' enshrined in the electoral rules. He was able to master a clear majority only in the House, not in the Senate. The real winner was the Movimento 5 Stelle (M5S) led by former comedian Beppe Grillo, who did not even exist a few years ago and came out as the single largest political party in 2013 with 25 percent of the popular vote. Berlusconi had a strong showing too, coming in a close second to Bersani in terms of elected representatives.

The 2013 campaign was brutal to the left. The Democrats and their allies campaigned mainly on labor and economic issues, advocating progressive taxation and an 'equality agenda'. But the message of M5S proved much more effective, denouncing political corruption and government waste. Grillo attracted disappointed voters both from the left, the center and the right of the political spectrum, especially among the young. His rhetoric is populist and anti-European. He wants to hold a referendum to exit the euro. He opposes immigration, thereby capturing the xenophobic vote that previously went to the Northern League. His denunciation of austerity policies as both destructive and imposed by Angela Merkel resonate among many Italians. Some of his proposals – a 20-hour work week, a guaranteed salary paid by the government to all Italian citizens – sound unrealistic, irresponsible or pure demagoguery. And yet he triggered a wave of enthusiasm, participation, new-style political commitment, by a bold use of the Internet. He proved that he could overcome Berlusconi without ever appearing on a TV talk show.

Grillo brought into the Italian Parliament a new generation of very young representatives, many of them women. His message has been perceived as 'revolutionary' because he wants to get rid of a whole 'nomenklatura': the professional politicians who are despised as parasites. The left bears a terrible responsibility for the success of populism. Just a few months before the general elections, a scandal hit the most ancient bank in Italy (and in the world), the Monte dei Paschi di Siena. Corruption, fraud, all the usual ingredients were there. And in this case the left was the culprit. The city of Siena has always been governed by progressive politicians, formerly the Communists, then the Democrats. The local bank was deeply involved in politics and controlled by the 'red nomenklatura'. This scandal, not the first one to hit the Democrats, seemed to confirm Grillo's message: that there is not a great difference between Berlusconi and his traditional adversaries, all of them being included in the 'rotten politics as usual'. This is populism at its best, but Grillo has a point. His victory is another setback for the whole European Left.

Meanwhile, the so-called 'euro crisis' had already been stopped by another Italian, the president of the ECB, Mario Draghi. In July 2012, in a conference in London, he declared that the Central Bank would do 'whatever it takes to save the euro'. That message was clear enough. It meant that the ECB would resort to its own brand of 'quantitative easing', by purchasing Spanish or Italian bond, if this became necessary to stem a confidence crisis. That statement proved effective. But supporting the euro and avoiding an implosion of the monetary union does not address the fundamental issues of growth, job creation, education, inequalities. Socialist France is itself under serious economic stress and unable even to reach the deficit reduction target that is requested by the EU 'fiscal compact'. President Hollande desperately needed to find an ally in a leftist government in Italy, in order to counterbalance Ms Merkel's hegemony. The result of the Italian election was a disappointment in that respect, too. The new prime minister, Enrico Letta of the Democratic Party, has been supported by the left, the center and the right. The only large party that chose to oppose Letta's government was the M5S, at least until November 2013 when Berlusconi was ousted from the Senate after being sentenced for tax fraud. In November, the conservative Partito della Liberta split, with a small fraction of moderates still supporting Letta's government and the others following Berlusconi in the opposition ranks. For the vast majority of Italians, what matters is that under Prime Minister Letta nothing changed: Italy maintained the same austerity policies, the recession continued, unemployment (especially among the youth) escalated to new historically high levels. In his first year of his tenure, Letta has been unable to establish himself as an alternative voice in Europe advocating for a change in economic policies. France, Italy, Spain have not been able to unite their efforts and to counter-balance the influence of Germany.

The only positive change happened recently in Berlin, after the elections. In the negotiations that led to the new coalition, the SPD was able to put a minimum wage of 8.50 euros, higher pension entitlements and further investment in childcare for small children on the government's agenda. Angela Merkel, inaugurating her third mandate as chancellor, seemed almost eager to accept the requests of her junior partner. The outcome is almost paradoxical: whereas Germany continues to preach austerity abroad, its own policy mix reverted to the 'European social model' at its best. But this contradiction further strains the relations between different countries inside the Eurozone. The weaker economies are becoming even less competitive due to the advantage Germany has from lower funding costs (bank interest rates are higher in the periphery of the Eurozone). The exchange rate of the euro, which has been very strong compared to the US dollar (usually above 1.30 during 2013) does not hamper German exports, but it is unsustainable for small businesses in France, Italy and Spain. In the spring of 2014, a new European Parliament will be elected, with stronger constitutional powers than the previous ones. This might be an important opportunity to have a 'continent-wide conversation' about the consequences of austerity, and the social compact. Several polls indicate that public opinions in major countries (France, Italy, Holland) are shifting in favor of anti-European parties. After having inflicted damage upon democracy on a national level, austerity might have the same effect on pan-European democracy.

Bibliography

Rogoff, Kenneth, and Reinhart, Carmen (2009) *This Time Is Different: Eight Centuries of Financial Folly*, Princeton: Princeton University Press.

Wilkinson, Richard, and Pickett, Kate (2009) *The Spirit Level: Why Greater Equality Makes Society Stronger*, New York: Bloomsbury Press.

10 Yugoslav and EU decline

The dynamics of dissolution and sovereignty reframed

Stefano Bianchini

In times of crisis, nationalism emerges as a strong cohesive factor of social groups. This trend has been experimented with in Europe repeatedly during the twentieth century and, once again, in the new millennium since 2008, as a new financial and economic crisis has deeply affected the world.

The mechanism is very simple and to a large extent unsophisticated. Basically, the homogeneity of a social/cultural group (in modern times the 'nation', whatever this word may mean), together with a territorial sovereignty rigorously asserted, is claimed as a pivotal factor able to guarantee the best conditions for resisting the adversities and uncertainties of the changes imposed by the crisis, and for re-establishing the pre-existing social stability and wealth.

Actually, this process is based on a great political (and cultural) illusion, since there are no old answers to new problems and no possible return to the pre-crisis social stability/wealth; neither is there unconditional sovereignty in the context of globalization. The illusion, however, does work. It speaks to emotions, and policy makers basically refer to it in order to preserve power, mobilize consensus and the support of people, who are emotionally inclined to positively react to such suggestions.

In other words, nationalism seems to provide a powerful shield for groups, since it is perceived as an effective tool able to guarantee the collective sense of belonging, when identities are challenged by the changing times. The implementation of this process is primarily pursued through the imposition of hierarchical (patriarchal) homogeneity within a group with a harsh corresponding definition of the boundaries of inclusivity. Nationalism, then, becomes a vehicle of exclusivity, where male dominance, racism, and xenophobia are nurtured. It, therefore, reinforces the identification of 'otherness' as a social factor of group threat by establishing the basis for confrontations, conflicts, and wars. This identification is particularly promoted by policy makers lacking a vision of the future, having no courage to pursue radical reforms, and/or believing they will be able to attract an easy consensus, while simultaneously confident that they will maintain control over the events. The Yugoslav experience in the twentieth century is, in this sense, indicative in many respects.

The Yugoslav crisis, 1980–1987

When a deep economic crisis erupted in the Yugoslav federation in early 1980, the political institutions of the country were put immediately under stress since the powerful personality of Tito was disappearing (as a consequence of his sickness) and the Soviet invasion of Afghanistan was, once again, perceived in Belgrade as a warning against its independent policies. The new rotation presidency began to work under these conditions in May 1980, when Tito died. Therefore, the Yugoslav federation experimented with something that was institutionally unknown in the communist praxis so far: namely, a collective negotiation of interests in a time of crisis, without a recognized leader able to embody the unity of the country and impose, if necessary even with violence, its own strategy and vision.

The eight members of the collective presidency represented de facto the interests of the six republics and the two autonomous regions, although they were intended to mirror the general Yugoslav interest. The setting up of the government and the conduct of its activities were regulated by a balanced ethnic ratio, visible in the distribution of the ministries. As a result, the relations within the institutions rapidly made clear that a 'Yugoslav synthesis' would be produced by the ability to negotiate and mediate the different interests expressed by its territorial administrations: in short, Yugoslavia de facto adopted an 'intergovernmental method' of governance.

Meanwhile, the economic crisis that affected the country was characterized by high (for the time) international debt (worsened by the rapidly increasing rate of the US dollar), high expenses in unproductive investments, a huge bureaucratic mechanism that oppressed the free development of cooperation among the self-managed enterprises, the social services, and the local communities.

We do not need to enter here into the causes of the crisis, as they have been widely discussed and analyzed in Yugoslav and international literature in the last decades (Horvat 1985, Korošić 1989a, 1989b, Goati 1989, Bianchini 1984, 1989, Cohen 1995, Woodward 1995, Lampe 1996, Allcock 2000). For the purposes of this article, rather, we will draw the attention of the reader to the *political* reactions to the crisis.

Under the pressure of international financial organizations, the government led by Milka Planinc since 1982 adopted a set of restrictive measures (*Asahi Shimbun* 1982, Bartlett 1987). Some of them immediately impacted the standard of living of the population (e.g., the reduction of electricity); others had far-reaching consequences since the decline of imports denied Yugoslavia, among others, the access to innovations in communication technologies. The growing isolation of the country, in stark contrast to the openness of the previous decades, did not facilitate the internal negotiation of interests. On the contrary, discrepancies increased and different visions began to clash (Brera 1985).

In a brief sketch of the debate, there were two main constraints: the first was ideological, the second was territorial. The ideological constraint refers to the 'social contract' that the political power had established with the population:

a set of social services and guarantees were offered in terms of social welfare, with a limited participative mechanism through self-management, in exchange for a soft, but undeniable party dictatorship. The crisis made clear that this system had become too costly. The reform of the welfare system, with the inevitable financial cuts, would exacerbate social tensions and imply further radical political reforms to make the changes acceptable to the people. This perspective appeared to many party leaders to be in conflict with the socialist ideology, either because social guarantees were part of its strategy, or because the introduction of a multiparty democracy would lead to a radical rejection of the legacy of the October revolution. The reading of the official documents produced in 1982–1985 by the two commissions that were established with the aim of exploring the conditions under which an economic (the so-called Sergej Kraigher Commission) and a political reform (the so-called Josip Vrhovec Commission) would have been possible clearly emphasized this deadlock and finally made evident the general impasse of Yugoslav politics.

The territorial constraint was, to a large extent, a consequence of the previous one. With the deepening of economic difficulties (inflation, decline in the standard of living, of the quality of production, of export and imports) and the persistent uncertainties in defining a shared way out of the crisis, the economic protectionism of the republics and regions began to grow, affecting the unity of the Yugoslav market. A conference promoted in Maribor already in January 1982 by the Center Kardelj was the first public expression of a concern that was emerging within the party. The conference adopted a convoluted terminology by referring to the 'social and economic aspects of the "intra-national" relations' (where the term 'intra-national' was about the republics and regions of Yugoslavia). Nonetheless, the meaning of the debate was clear: the decision of the government to classify the international debt by republics, making public only the total amount of the Yugoslav debt while economic relations were gradually confined within the territorial units of the country, making it certain that the economic crisis could trigger a chain reaction from protectionism to nationalism (Jugoslovenski Centar za teoriju i praksu samoupravljanja 1982). In other words, the potential spreading of the belief that the best way to face the crisis was to defend local production in order to avoid the impact of the consequences stemming from the unbalanced development of the republics and regions appeared to have a highly detrimental effect on the future of the country already at the beginning of the 1980s.

Actually, the administrative units of Yugoslavia reacted by reproducing, to a lesser degree, the attitude adopted by the Yugoslav government. The latter, with its restrictive measures, unintentionally encouraged the republics to adopt similar behaviors: as Yugoslavia was becoming more isolated from the international economic world (after two decades of openness), the republics did the same within Yugoslavia. This double protectionism was detrimental to the country as a whole, since the crisis occurred in times when interdependency increasingly characterized global economic relations. Yugoslavia, with its non-aligned policy, was already permeated by this interdependency, which was the first step towards globalization. As a result, Yugoslavia 'suspended' its ties with the world when interdependency was becoming a pivotal factor of development. Meanwhile, its administrative units (namely republics and regions) increasingly began to refer to the Yugoslav institutional system as merely a broader arena for negotiating national interests, without necessarily achieving a shared synthesis. In sum, without democratic reforms and a legally accepted democratic dialectic, which was considered ideologically incompatible, the political leaders operated under the belief that the only authorized dialectic was that of the territorial interests of republics and regions, which were also understood as a crucial factor for the legitimization of power. The consistent implementation of this rationale paved the way for the transformation of protectionism into nationalism.

Republics and regions began to distance themselves: some of them looked for opportunities outside Yugoslavia, others were determined to preserve the *status quo* in terms of employment, production, services, even if they were increasingly costly, ineffective and inadequate (or detrimental) to the general economic needs of the country. The sense of solidarity within the federation deteriorated with the diminishing availability of financial resources. The mechanism for redistribution in support of less developed republics and regions was increasingly affected by both declining funds and growing demands from the economically disadvantaged areas of the country (Šetinc 1990, Dizdarević 2009).

Self-management suffered as well from the gradual disarticulation of social, economic, and political relations within Yugoslavia. Forced to cope with elephantine bureaucratic procedures, enterprises had additionally to deal with the terrible slow pace of the public administration (municipalities/regions/republics) any time they wanted or needed to develop their market interests in other territories of the federation. Actually, ideological reasons suggested submitting the contractual relations of enterprises, operating in different administrative units, to the negotiation between public powers. The aim was to avoid the establishment of 'domestic colonial relations' of dependencies. The outcome was a continuous delay in the decision-making process, which affected the economic productivity and the functioning of the market by encouraging enterprises to give priority to local investments. Furthermore, when relations among republics worsened, this trend became even more visible as it contributed significantly to the reduction of the domestic market, affecting the distribution of goods, increasing social inequalities and the existing gap between developed and undeveloped areas, social polarization and discontent (Djeković 2010, Perović 1988, *Samoupravno sporazumevanje u udruženom radu* 1981, Bianchini 2003: 44–56).

The particular combination of institutional ineffectiveness and economic crisis contributed to the belief that the responsibility for the declining standard of living was identified both in other republics and in the lack of transparency and democratic standards. For example, the Slovenian elite increasingly blamed the re-distribution of resources (jointly decided in Belgrade) for the underdeveloped regions/republics, by ambiguously identifying the Serbian and the federal government. Intellectuals of the Serbian Academy vehemently criticized a supposed economic and cultural discrimination against the Serbs outside of Serbia, while

Milošević began to mobilize the Serbs against the leadership in Vojvodina, Kosovo and, then, Slovenia through mass demonstrations (the so-called '*događanje naroda*' or people's events). Quickly, the social and economic crisis became a forceful incubator of self-victimization and nationalist resentment against the 'others'.

This briefly sketches the historical phase that characterized Yugoslav developments from Tito's death to early 1987. The economic crisis deepened social differences within the federation and multiplied the contrasts among territorial, cultural, political interests, affecting governance as a whole. Since the decision-making system was based on a de facto unanimity of votes among the representatives of republics and regions, agreement was increasingly difficult to achieve, while the worsening of the economic situation required quick decisions. The sense of powerlessness became progressively rooted in the population and merged with general dissatisfaction. It was the most undeveloped area of Yugoslavia, namely Kosovo, which first expressed a social and rapidly nationalist discontent, already in 1981. Under these conditions, the expectations for radical change intensified, although the sense of this 'radicalism' differed greatly within the party and the country. This background paved the way for a new phenomenon in communist leadership that materialized in April 1987 when Milošević decided to play the nationalist card against Kosovar Albanians and to extend it against his party adversaries, no matter what institutional consequences might occur.

The long-lasting perception of a deadlock decision-making system generated, mainly in the Serbian elite, the idea that the constitutional system had to be changed, even by force. As a result, polarization in the whole of Yugoslavia strengthened and the room for mediating opposing interests quickly vanished: nationalism became the ideological mainstream most able to coagulate the active support of groups, and Milošević became the most powerful leader ready to advocate and force a change in the rules. An atmosphere of mistrust and threat poisoned the relations among republics and regions, and other leaders were led to, or attracted by, the will to preserve their power by protecting/expanding the prerogatives of their territorial autonomy. Inevitably, the dismemberment of the country began to occur.

Finally, the acceleration of national tensions and the need to offer politically convincing answers to social and economic imbalances roughly led (between January and March 1991) to a consensual decision by the leaders of Serbia, Croatia, and Slovenia to go their own way and dissolve the federation. Nonetheless, they proved unable to agree on how to split the country, making the war inevitable.

The European crisis since 2007

Approximately twenty years later, a new financial and economic crisis, which started in the United States, rapidly crossed the oceans and affected the whole world. On the European continent, the effects of the crisis interacted with, among other things, a broad political uncertainty determined, on the one hand, by the aspirations for greater integration in the light of EU enlargements and, on the other, by the reluctance of EU member states to agree about the content and prospects of such integration. From this perspective, a key question is whether and to what extent the mechanisms that deepened the Yugoslav crisis in the first half of the 1980s may offer some lessons when looking at the behavior of European policy makers as the 2008 global economic crisis began to affect Europe. Although the two contexts are very different in nature and content – Yugoslavia as a socialist federation with the dictatorship of the proletariat and a very atypical economic system, and the EU an atypical framework of convergence of democratic and market economy countries – there are still similarities that require consideration.

The economic crisis clearly revealed the limits of Yugoslavia's communist ideology that restricted the room for effective action to be taken to redress the situation. Nonetheless, it is also true that the 2007 global economic crisis marked the failure of the neoliberal economic theory and practice advocated by the Chicago school, substantially implemented through *Reaganomics* and *Thatcherism*, and which dominated the capitalist world since the 1980s, but particularly after the fall of the Berlin wall. This ideology, which suggested shock therapy to post-socialist transition countries, and encouraged easy access to credit and bank investments in an uncontrolled system of funds in stock markets that inspired a rigid implementation of the *Washington consensus*, proved to be the main cause of bank insolvency, collapse in construction sectors, family bankruptcy, and turmoil in the currency market. This fueled an unexpected public bailout in the economic and financial spheres (Duménil and Lévy 2009, 2010, Harvey 2009). As a reaction, a sort of 'new Keynesism' has been evoked by the spreading awareness that some rules should be imposed on markets, especially on the new *virtual* markets. Furthermore, governments have started to consider new forms of control and taxation, in order to restrict the banks' preferences of investment in exceptionally volatile funds, instead of sustaining production. In addition, the decline of available resources, climate change, and the increasing need for energy have strongly contributed to the spread of the belief that the nineteenth century idea of unlimited development was impossible. Sustainability, the search for renewable sources of energy, state policies for saving banks from bankruptcy after 2008 (including nationalization), increasing state intervention in the economy, and the demand for new forms of regulation of the market economy have all characterized the end of the neoliberal ideology that has predominated the world since the 1980s.

The end of an ideology, however, does not necessarily mean that a convincing alternative will emerge, offering successful answers to pressing questions. In the Yugoslav socialist experience, the crisis of self-management placed local policy makers in a sort of deadlock as they were ideologically unprepared to abandon self-management and accept either the patterns of the Soviet command economy or the Western capitalist market. Similarly, thirty years later, the crisis of neoliberal ideology has taken place in a political environment unprepared to react with the support of a convincing alternative vision which requires to go far beyond the nation state, since the impact of globalization and interdependency, the public interference in economy, and the reconsideration of the notion of development still evoke conflict in terms of theories, suggestions, and pressures from powerful lobbies.

Actually, as the crisis presented a global dimension, the leaders of the world's economic powers have intensified their contacts in different forms, either bilaterally or multilaterally (G8, G20, etc.), in order to explore the possibility of a political convergence. Meanwhile, however, most Western leaders were likely to adopt urgent protectionist measures, the implementation of which stood in contrast to existing global competition. In the specific case of the EU, the attempts of (and the claims for) protecting existing national economies, when a process of gradual integration was still under way, endangered the prospects for the single market (Crumley 2009, Münchau 2009, Amato and Bonino 2009: 1, 10, *International Herald Tribune* 2009: 6).

In sum, despite the differences between Yugoslavia and the EU, in both cases an ideological crisis has occurred in parallel with both protectionist tendencies and institutionally inadequate frameworks. In fact, when the global crisis erupted in 2008, the EU (after the inclusion, with some restrictions and reluctance of Romania and Bulgaria) was still looking for an institutional alternative after the failure of the referenda in France and the Netherlands of the Constitutional Treaty. Even the new – but less ambitious – Lisbon Treaty soon came under criticism, being initially rejected in a referendum by Ireland, then contested by the presidents of Poland and the Czech Republic, while also the Constitutional Court of Germany was invited to express its opinion. In all these cases, the re-nationalization of policies was their common (and predominant) feature. In other words, the global crisis caught the EU in a moment when its institutional adjustment was marked by uncertainty and the content of its deepening put under question. At the beginning of the 1980s, Socialist Yugoslavia found itself in a similar situation as the economic crisis made evident that an institutional adjustment was needed, even if the existing balance of powers among republics and regions would have been affected.

Thirty years later, after a phase of enthusiasm for the integration process that characterized the beginning of the millennium, EU member state leaders asserted a limited 'absorption capacity' of the EU, a sort of fatigue from enlargements that required the deferring of further steps in integration. In early 2006 the Bavarian Prime Minister Stoiber claimed that the absorption capacity of the EU should be the 'decisive criterion' for EU further enlargements and the European Parliament on 17 March 2006 called the Commission to submit a report by the end of the year in order to define the notion of 'absorption capacity'. As a reaction, the Commissioner for Enlargement, Olli Rehn, and the High Representative for Common and Security Policy, Xavier Solana, had to reiterate publicly the EU commitment towards the inclusion of the 'Western Balkans' as the notion created concerns in South Eastern Europe. In October 2006, the Center for European Policies Studies issued a paper that strongly criticized the notion, which however monopolized the political narratives in the years to come (Emerson *et al.* 2006). Actually, these statements revealed that the dichotomy between integration and nation state sovereignty was remerging in popularity, taking advantage of the contentious trajectory experimented in the institutional readjustment of the Union after 2005.

Announced in France during the electoral campaign for the referendum on the Constitutional Treaty, when the criticism against the 'Polish plumber' dramatically contributed to the final results, the nationalist concerns against the freedom of movement of the EU citizens within the common European space rapidly escalated. The press noticed a return to nation state supremacy even earlier. The *International Herald Tribune*, in March 2006, connected the failure of the EU referenda with divisions emerging in EU member states before the second Iraqi war, coming to the conclusion that the EU was unable (once again) to 'speak with one voice in foreign affairs' (Bennhold and Bowley 2006, Matlack 2006).

Furthermore, the authors of the comment, Katrin Bennhold and Graham Bowley, recorded several events that revealed the resurgence of new protectionisms within the EU, with a negative impact on its 'four freedoms' (capitals, goods, services, and people). By referring to the governments of France and Spain, which opposed the transnational merger of water and power companies (Gaz de France/Eni or E.ON and Endesa), Bennhold and Bowley reported that globalization – with the great new economic competitors like China, India, and Russia – raised new challenges, suggesting that the EU join forces instead of weakening itself by accepting slower integration and applying forms of economic nationalism. By contrast, a few years later, two parallel phenomena began to operate simultaneously within the EU.

On the one hand, in order to preserve their consensus or, at least, to limit their fall in popularity, policy makers tended to react to the global crisis by concentrating on domestic economic problems, 'playing to their voters' concerns, rather than trying to defuse them, often attacking the European Commission in Brussels for policies aimed at opening and integrating markets further' (Bennhold and Bowley 2006). On the other hand, the growing sense of social and political uncertainty – aggravated by threats of terrorist acts promoted by al-Qaida and its affiliated Islamic extremist groups – paved the way to an increasingly uncontrolled rejection of 'otherness', extra-communitarian migrants or even EU co-citizens, by endangering specifically one of the EU 'four freedoms' (namely, the free movement of people), while racism and xenophobia began to be nurtured by populist and rightist parties (Michalski 2006, Menon and Wright 2001, Balibar 2001, Noiriel 2001).

Gradually, a highly disruptive social and economic mixture has surfaced, affecting particularly (though not exclusively) the older EU member states. Reading newspapers from the years 2008–2011 is, in this respect, extremely enlightening. Actually, a sequence of two phases of economic nationalism took place, the first lasting up to the end of 2009 and the second beginning in 2010 with the Greek crisis.

In 2009, the main tendency was characterized by governmental invitations to people to consume national products, as well as by the adoption of a set of protectionist measures in industry and banking. The Centre for Economic Policy Research of the Bocconi University in Italy drew attention to state financial supports granted to industries only under the condition of preserving local jobs, while the nationalization of banks was followed by decreasing credits for transnational operations. Similar events occurred in France, Great Britain, Germany, and Italy, and the international press regularly reported on that (*La Repubblica* 2009: 22). It is, however, true that, despite the alarm, this tendency was at least formally rejected in the declaration against protectionism signed in April 2009 at the London G20 summit, and partially contained by international interests and commitments of big transnational corporations (Leaders' Statement 2009). Nonetheless, the implementation of protectionist economic policies remained an issue in 2009.

In 2010, the emphasis increasingly fell on the advocacy of national interests, particularly within the EU, when the crisis affected first Greece and later Ireland, threatening the stability of the Euro. In particular, the risk of state insolvency (that might involve, after Greece and Ireland, Portugal, Spain, and even Italy) posed a crucial question, namely to what extent the management of the common currency and solidarity within the Euro-club could be maintained (Beck 2009, Münchau 2010: 9). The protracted reluctance of Germany to define a European strategy for supporting the new government in Athens offered a tangible expression of a new economic nationalism. At the beginning, this reluctance was due to Ms Merkel's primary concern for the local elections in North-Rhine Westphalia in early 2010. But later, even when she accepted to create a EU-IMF joint financial aid package, the conditionality imposed for accessing it led to the general impression that she was pursuing an austerity, which mirrored the German vision of monetary policy. Particularly, this austerity plan was aimed to achieve, in a few years, a sharp restructuring of governmental budget deficits through restrictive measures, including cuts in public expenditures and salaries, together with tax increases.

This strategy has been criticized in many respects. In some cases, its social implications could have devastating effects on the government stability of member states compelled to apply the new program. The US Administration feared negative repercussions on consumers and restrictions in the domestic markets, jeopardizing the fragile economic recovery at the global level. Moreover, the package of aid – though quite relevant – would have been sufficient to help small countries (like Greece, Ireland, and Portugal), but not large economies such as Spain and Italy. Finally, the whole strategy did not provide a redesign for European financial, fiscal, and economic policy that would strengthen the Euro; rather, an expanding German economic policy in the eurozone, a sort of 'German Europe', was increasingly recognized (Beck 2010, Vinocur 2010: 2).

In fact, a new 'German question' started to emerge for several reasons: the more restrictive measures imposed by Berlin and – more or less reluctantly – applied in countries risking insolvency, the more the Euro was identified with

German policy by the financial speculation, which underestimated the complexity of negotiation and harmonization required by the eurozone decision-making process. As a result, the slow pace of the EU reaction in achieving consensus among member states did not comply with the rapid pace of the speculation. Meanwhile, the currency rate weakened or stabilized according to how public statements of German leaders were welcomed by the markets. In this context, German entrepreneurs began to consider whether it would be preferable for them to split the Euro into a hard and soft currency, the first identified with Germany and Northern Europe, and the second with France and the Mediterranean. Moreover, German taxpayers became increasingly reluctant to loan money to countries threatened with insolvency, although German banks were particularly exposed in Ireland and Spain so that the bankruptcy in those countries would have had a dramatic impact on them (Fischer 2010, Spiegel 2010: 1, Chapffin and Peel 2010: 3).

This contradictory atmosphere and the tensions triggered by concerns over potential domino effects in European financial performances affected the sense of EU solidarity and contributed to undermining the process of integration, whose institutional framework was still under construction. The Euro crisis has been, therefore, perceived by many economists and policy makers, such as Giuliano Amato, Jean-Paul Fitoussi, Jacques Attali, Giorgio Napolitano, and Jože Mencinger, as a lever able to pave the way to EU dismemberment.

In this regard, Ulrick Beck has repeatedly warned against economic nationalism; according to him, the German unwillingness to concede credits to their neighbors in difficulties mirrors the vision where each state manages alone its financial problems in such a way that the economic and financial sovereignty of each member state should not affect others. Therefore, he said, 'mutual nationalisms' were emerging that reject giving more competencies to the EU in economic, fiscal, and financial matters to the detriment of common currency solidity. Beck (2008) warned already in 2008 about the negative impact of nationalism in the era of globalization and he has returned to these issues (Beck 2010: 1, 27). From this perspective, although scenarios with a Euro at risk or even collapse remain unpredictable, the European sense of belonging and the whole integration process arrived at a crucial crossroads where future prospects were seriously put in question.

Matching the EU crisis with post-Yugoslav instability: the challenges to governance in times of uncertainty

From this angle, the consequences generated by the European financial crisis do not appear so different from some of those which troubled Yugoslavia in the early 1980s. In fact, mechanisms of dissolution are in action, although it remains to be seen how powerful they will be in the EU context. The length of the crisis will definitely play a crucial role in the evolution of the events. The more the crisis is prolonged without a clear political perspective, the more the risk of dissolution will become tangible, as member states might be attracted by the hope/illusion/calculation that it is more convenient and effective to face the challenges of the crisis without the conditionality of neighbors and 'unfinished' supranational institutions. This belief would be reinforced by both an overestimation of state capacities to face global economic challenges and the confidence of preserving the people's consensus in a ballot. Indications in this respect are already visible.

In this context (worsening economic performance not only in Greece – whose prospect for recovery appears negligible – but also in Portugal, Ireland, and Spain), while EU members states are unable to agree on a shared strategy for growth, a sense of powerless that generates insecurity and social tensions is spreading and multiplied by demographic changes and the mobility of people on the continent. All together these factors are producing new waves of nationalism and xenophobia.

After centuries of strict state borders, the Schengen treaty, the common currency, and EU enlargement have radically transformed the cultural and political configuration of Europe in less than a decade, while an increasing flow of migrants from outside the EU has taken place. Schengen actually represented a revolution for European citizens in cultural terms. In Bauman's words, Schengen is the revenge of nomadism against the solidification of the nation state based on 'soil' and 'blood' (Bauman 2000: xx). The freedom of mobility for EU citizens, their possibility to study, work, and vote for local administrations in any of the member states has challenged the post-Westphalian state control over citizens. The porosity of borders, together with a shared common currency and the EU expansion eastwards, have therefore provoked a tremendous shock in societies nurtured for more than two centuries by nationalism, confrontation with neighbors, and territorial pretentions. Culturally, part of the population did not have, and does not have, effective tools for interacting with these changes, stemming from mobility, integration, and globalization. Therefore, they simply reject them, as a threat to their 'stability' and 'identity', even if they were/are illusory. They become prey to emotional feelings that look at the 'otherness' as a menace. These feelings can take different political expressions. On the one hand, they endorse a parochial self-exclusiveness in terms of culture and territory; on the other, they promote an aggressive polarization between 'us' and 'them'. (Ethno-)Nationalism, racism, and xenophobia are the most relevant expressions of these feelings and they emerge either separately or in a peculiar combination.

As said, EU member states (and particularly the old member states, but not necessarily only them) are experiencing a growing wave of these feelings. The campaigns against migrants, the 'Polish plumber', Muslims, the Roma, as well as outbursts of anti-Semitism (that can be easily identified in the behavior of some policy makers or political parties in the Netherlands, France, Italy, Denmark, Austria, Sweden, Hungary...) are all expressions of both a fear of 'otherness' and a lack of political imagination on how inclusiveness should be carried out in a framework of European integration. Merkel's public declaration, in October 2010, that multiculturalism has miserably failed in Germany has fueled new arguments in those who oppose the reality, namely, the fact that societies develop and transform themselves (Friedman 2010, Kanli 2010, Heathcote 2010: 7).

The electoral campaign of President Sarkozy against Schengen may have a dramatic impact on the European project. This campaign actually comes after a tense confrontation between Italy and France that has been provoked by the waves of migrants who reached the Italian coasts from Tunis and Libya (where the social and political life was exacerbated by the uncertainties of the Arab revolutions) and rapidly moved to France. The Schengen suspension imposed by Paris was immediately followed by the rightist government of Denmark, who established similar measures on the borders with Germany. Despite the fact that these events were later minimized, the decision of Sarkozy against the visa-free Schengen zone, with the hope of attracting rightist votes in his confrontation with Hollande, is a serious confirmation of the inability of present European leadership to cope culturally with reality. Looking back to the past, they contribute to merging illusions on territorial sovereignty with a lack of vision for economic recovery. The deep social dissatisfaction with the ineffectiveness of state and EU institutions (the latter being paralyzed by the long-term negotiations among member states, but criticized by them as the 'Brussels bureaucracy') could ignite a new powder-keg. As a result, in such a disputed social and cultural context, the EU values of tolerance, respect of human rights, and empathy are increasingly challenged. Moreover, EU domestic tensions generate an external perception of inconsistency, weakening not only the inner process of integration, but also the confidence towards successful EU accession in candidate or potential candidate countries.

This is a new phenomenon, since the period between 1993 and 2005 has been characterized by an opposite trend: the perspective of enlargement was carried out together with the deepening of the integration process. After 2005, however, the integration processes have stagnated and may be at risk of rolling back, while the enlargement is increasingly under criticism with the absorption capacity aiming to suggest cautious approaches and postponements for the future.

Despite this resistance, Croatia joined the EU in 2013 and the status of candidate countries has been given to Serbia and Montenegro. Apparently, the aforementioned negative trend is invalidated at least where enlargement is concerned. Actually, the situation in the Western Balkans remains uncertain because it is affected by the contradictory contents of the peace treaties. Imposed by the US and the EU between 1995 and 2001, they mediated between opposing national interests of warlord parties, without unambiguously rejecting the rationale of the wars. In other words, the dichotomy of disintegration and integration remained an open issue in the post-war relations between entities, territories, and administrative competencies, by affecting governance as a whole. So, the accords have been mainly perceived on the ground as temporary solutions, a necessary way for stopping violence while postponing the settlement of accounts to an undefined future (Bianchini *et al.* 2007).

At the same time, awareness that a risky ambiguity characterized the peace treaties as well as concern that this situation would reproduce persistent instability in SEE have suggested to the European Commission and the European Council that they encourage the EU accession of the Western Balkans since the Thessaloniki summit in 2003. Ideally, in fact, the inclusion within a broader project of European integration represented an alternative to the nationalist rationale of the war, and an effective strategy for regional stabilization, consistent with the origins of the European integration process since the European Coal and Steal Community was established.

Truly, since 2001, the behavior of the political elites in the post-Yugoslav space was mainly oriented to supporting the prospect of EU accession. Even more recently, the campaign of the Croatian government against corruption, the dialogue between Serbia and Croatia symbolically confirmed by the meeting of the two presidents in Vukovar, the prospect of a Serbian–Kosovar dialogue, the joint Serbian–EU resolution at the UN on Kosovo, the first Bajram celebration in Banja Luka as well as the 'Yugoslav' cooperation in the railway system, in justice and home affairs through judges and mutual police assistance, all confirm that a process of dialogue, softening tensions, and gradual rapprochement was under way during 2010.

Despite the ideological criticism that arose in Croatia, the notion of 'Yugosphere' – which was used by Tim Judah in *The Economist* in 2009 – is going to mirror a trend that has been reinforced by improving economic and trade cooperation at the regional level. As paradoxical as it may sound (but similar to what happened after 1929 and before Hitler's economic expansion in the middle of the 1930s), the global economic crisis has contributed to strengthening economic relations and market exchanges in the post-Yugoslav space, as a defensive factor (Judah 2009, 2010: 22–25). As a result, the Western Balkans may be considered an area that – after a long period of suffering in the twentieth and twenty-first centuries – will recover.

However, the whole region is still caught in the trap of persistent nationalism that is able to undermine the efforts made so far. Needless to say, Kosovo–Serbia relations remain uncertain and affect the multilateral cooperation activities promoted by regional organizations (like RCC, CEI, AII, etc.); Macedonian–Greek relations still seem far from a shared solution, which can trigger negative effects for domestic Macedonian–Albanian cohabitation, which was threatened by a wave of violent events. Alternative visions of the future for the Bosnian–Herzegovinian state still persist in the two entities, reproducing an institutional ineffectiveness with very high administrative costs that put prospectively under question the existence of the state.

Interestingly enough, the appeal to nationalist arguments has gradually, but constantly, declined in the public speeches of policy makers in the Western Balkans during the first decade of the twenty-first century. The main reason for this turn should be identified not only in the political changes that occurred after the death of Tuđman, the defeat and arrest of Milošević, and the retirement of Izetbegović, but also – if not mainly – because of the intensification of relations with the EU, thanks to the signing of the Stabilization and Association Agreements, the general interest in submitting applications for accession, the

EU–Croatian negotiation for enlargement, and the gradual visa liberalization between the EU and Western Balkan countries. In other words, the strengthening of EU–Balkan relations had an effect on the public statements of the local political elite.

By contrast, during the same period, the appeal to nationalist arguments has increased within the clergy of different religious beliefs. Religions, particularly the Croatian Catholic Church, the Serbian Orthodox Church, and the Islamic Community of Bosnia-Herzegovina, have intensively exploited religious and civil ceremonies (often ambiguously confused to such an extent that civilian holidays are celebrated in temples with the attendance of public servants and policy makers) in order to raise the voice of clergy in support of both a patriotism ethno-nationally depicted and a national identity religiously defined. Particularly, clergy like to emphasize in their sermons that the nation is under threat, by recurring to self-pitying tones mixed with warnings against abortions, decreasing birthrates, heterosexual family decline, secularization, and relativism. Sometimes, the morality of the society is put in question by evoking the legacy of communism in order to explain most recent phenomena, as corruption or criminality. In the end, the religious clergies are increasingly trying to identify themselves with nationalist narratives, by keeping 'fear' of the 'other' alive that hinders forgiveness, empathy with the suffering of the 'others', and the development of tolerance. In doing so, their discourse impacts on the still fragile and emotionally reactive imagination of populations that perpetuates the legacy of war, victimization, and the sense of collective wounds, despite the passing of time and the integrative conditionality generated by the binding negotiations with the EU (Stabilization and Association Agreements, the opening of chapters for accessing countries, etc.).

As a result, the overall situation remains vulnerable: on the one hand, the polarization between the rational values of integration and the emotional attractiveness of nationalist isolation is exacerbated in terms of political cultures far beyond the political agendas; on the other, the global economic crisis is increasingly affecting the sense of solidarity within the EU, as well as deepening the social inequalities both in the EU and in the Balkans (Bianchini 2010). The risk is that the efforts made in stabilizing the Balkans can be jeopardized, while the European integration processes are put in question by the inability of member states to identify proper fiscal and financial measures consistent with the transnational function of the common currency. Matching the European crisis with Balkan instability can trigger far-reaching consequences, as the experience of Socialist Yugoslavia has shown (Lévy 2010, Fischer 2003).

Yugoslav society was actually deeply intercultural. Interculturality is deeply encoded in the European societies as well, and it is bound to increase, since complexity and interdependence are the main characteristics of post-modern societies. At the same time, in both the Yugoslav and the EU case, the main obstacle in designing reforms able to guarantee effective institutions (when the crisis concerns ethno-cultural diverse groups of people) stems to a large extent from the predominant mindset of the nation state and national sovereignty, regardless of the ethnic or civic interpretation of the nation. This predominance is understandable, since it has forged the last two centuries of European history and thought; it has promoted cultural and religious homogeneity, standardized languages, a sense of belonging within rigorously defined borders that have generated a sense of security and inclusiveness for those who were considered part of the nation. This process, however, has been deeply contradictory: challenging the divine right paved the way to the development of democracy; yet by stressing the supremacy of the 'nation' it has generated racism, xenophobia, and totalitarianism.

This complex but well-rooted background contributes to making clear why the nation state is still so reluctant to step down from the role it has historically played so far. Meanwhile, however, the world has dramatically changed. A deep social diversification, globalization, and interdependence provide new frontiers in terms of social aggregations at the supranational level and economic competition at the world level. Within this framework, the European Lilliput-nations face a crucial dilemma for their future: closing themselves locally, or accepting integration and mobility. According to Bauman, this is the time when the construction of knowledge of the self, based on homogenous identities, is going to liquefy, making possible a process of fusion of the nation state.

Homogeneity (of language, culture, religious, sexual orientation, economic interests…) has been presented by media and policy makers, in the textbooks and by a number of intellectuals, as the cornerstone of stability and the prospective development of the nation. The legacy of patriarchy and its social hierarchical relations has been reinforced and re-legitimized under the new conditions of modernity. In doing so, people have been encouraged to think that the national collective identity is fixed and its perpetuation is a lever of collective security. When policy makers feel themselves in trouble, they regularly resort to national identity and sovereignty. In this perspective, the rigidity of borders becomes a powerful tool for reinforcing such perceptions of the group and the state.

By contrast, identities are always under transformation. They produce unexpected métissages, hybridizations, nomadisms, which multiply the complexity of a society, establish new networks of relations, interact with diasporas, produce a diversification of life styles; even the forms of families proliferate either because of sexual orientations or because of different social needs, or simply thanks to the improvement of medicine and science. The rhythm of changes of these phenomena has intensified dramatically after the fall of communism, the growing world's interdependence and globalization. Both the introduction of the Euro and the Schengen treaty are to be considered under these lenses. Both revolutionary in content, the Euro challenges the economic, fiscal, and financial powers of the member states; Schengen questions the social perception of homogeneity nurtured for centuries by the nation states. As seen, the reaction of EU political leaders, when forced to face the global economic crisis and the wave of migrations, tends to suggest measures which are more reminiscent of protectionism (culturally and economically), rather than aimed to develop transnational solidarity. This behavior encourages the rooting of neonationalism (Gingrich and Bank 2006). At the moment, the phenomenon is particularly evident in the old

EU member states: Finland, Sweden, the Netherlands, Denmark, France, Italy, Austria, the United Kingdom, but – among the new ones – Hungary is also a clear example.

Neonationalism has a double face, because it promotes both an anti-EU feeling on behalf of the restoration of sovereignty in existing nation states, and a separatist perspective within the existing nation states (as, for instance, in Belgium, Italy, Spain, and the United Kingdom). Moreover, neonationalism is permeated by racist and xenophobic ideas to such an extent that a successful Finnish party has decided to be called the 'True Finns Party'. The reference to 'true' reveals the presumption that 'true' and 'false' Finnish citizens exist; then, it suggests that only the party in power can assign the quality trademark of 'true' to the others, and finally it claims a fixed Finnish identity – based on criteria established by the party – which represents a rigid construction of the Finnishness, defined ex-post. Frankly speaking, I cannot see any cultural difference between these ideas and those promoted by Radovan Karadzic and Slobodan Milošević in support of Serbianness, of Janez Jansa on Slovenianness, of Tudjman and Susak on Croatianness, among others. Even in the Yugoslav case, before and during the war, there were parties that claimed both to represent the 'true' values of the nation and to have the monopoly of their definition. Their aggressive vision of their own self was initially directed to intimidate intellectuals and ordinary people, supposedly belonging to their nation, who did not recognize themselves in that vision. As soon as homogeneity was re-established within the group, the military confrontation with the 'other' set the agenda.

In this sense, and similarly to Yugoslavia at the beginning of the 1980s, the EU after 2005 is facing a new/old phenomenon that is resurfacing. I am referring here to the competing dynamics of neonationalism and integration, with a double impact on the transnational/European level and the national/intercultural level, since multiple cultures are increasingly a peculiarity of both local and continental societies. As a result, the polarization, which may escalate to conflict, concerns alternative visions of the state, as the neonationalists' main features are isolation, exclusivity, parochialism, racism/xenophobia, anti-Europeanism, fixed borders, and sedentary people, while the integrative perspective is based on inclusivity, openness, nomadism, networking, porous borders, and a 'Europeanness' derived from the further accomplishment of euro-effectiveness, communitarian governance (rather than intergovernmental), Schengen mobility, networking, consistent implementation of the four freedoms, etc.

In conclusion, radical changes (in economic, social, cultural, religious, linguistic terms) are pushing in a direction that restricts the room for nation state homogeneity, while restructuring societies with pluralities. Nonetheless, resistance to this trend is powerful and confirms that nationalism, as political culture, is not just a matter which concerns primarily, if not exclusively, Eastern Europe. The communist collapse, the European enlargement, and globalization have made evident how this issue goes beyond the violence that provoked the Yugoslav dissolution, or the ideology of various political parties in the post-communist societies: rather, it affects the governance of Europe as a whole, particularly in times of deep economic and social crisis. As seen, the Yugoslav experience shows that an intergovernmental mechanism of governance is ineffective when a federation faces deep economic and financial crisis. Nonetheless, the EU member states are still negotiating their strategy of economic recovery and euro-protection following a similar intergovernmental path. But the world is rapidly and radically changing: the transformations under way require strong efforts in search of unexplored solutions, great intellectual courage, and political vision. Regretfully, they all appear to be lacking in contemporary European leadership.

Bibliography

Allcock, John B. (2000) *Explaining Yugoslavia*, New York: Columbia University Press.
Amato, Giuliano, and Bonino, Emma (2009) 'La minaccia protezionista', *La Repubblica*, February 23.
Attali, Jacques (2010) *La Repubblica*, April 28, p. 7.
Asahi Shimbun (November 8, 1982).
Balibar, Étienne (2001) *Nous, citoyens d'Europe?, Les frontières, l'État, le peuple*, Paris: La Découverte.
Bartlett, Will (1987) 'The problem of indebtedness in Yugoslavia: causes and consequences', *Rivista Internazionale di Scienze Economiche e Commerciali*, vol. XXXIV, nos. 11–12, November–December, pp. 1179–1195.
Bauman, Zygmunt (2000) *Modernità liquida*, Laterza: Bari.
Beck, Ulrich (2008) 'Nation-state politics can only fail the problems of the modern world', *The Guardian*, January 15.
Beck, Ulrich (2009) 'This economic crisis cries out to be transformed into the founding of a new Europe', *The Guardian*, April 13.
Beck, Ulrich (2010) 'El e-nacionalismo alemán', *El País*, April 9, Available: www.elpais.com/articulo/opinion/e-nacionalismo/aleman/elpepiopi/20100409elpepiopi_13/Tes.
Bennhold, Katrin, and Bowley, Graham (2006) 'News analysis: in EU, nation states appears to be back', *International Herald Tribune*, March 2.
Bianchini, Stefano (1984) *La diversità socialista in Jugoslavia. Modernizzazione, autogestione e sviluppo democratico dal 1965 ad oggi*, Triesta: Editoriale Stampa.
Bianchini, Stefano (ed.) (1989) *L'enigma jugoslavo. Le ragioni della crisi*, Milano: Angeli.
Bianchini, Stefano (2003) *Sarajevo, le radici dell'odio*, Roma: Edizioni Associate, 3rd extended edition.
Bianchini, Stefano (2010) 'Crisi economica globale e stabilità balcanica. Economia, politica e riforme: quale impatto sulla sicurezza regionale?', *PECOB's Papers Series*, no. 3, September.
Bianchini, Stefano, Marko, Joseph, Nation, Craig, and Uvalić, Milica (eds.) (2007). *Regional Cooperation, Peace Enforcement and the Role of the Treaties in the Balkans*, Ravenna: Longo.
Brera, Paolo A. (1985) 'L'économie yougoslave face au programme de stabilisation', *Revue d'études comparatives est-ouest*, vol. XVI, no. 1, pp. 121–152.
Chapffin, Joshua, and Peel, Quentin (2010) 'Merkel's sacrifices secure fragile triumph', *Financial Times*, October 31, p. 3.
Cohen, Lenard J. (1995) *Broken Bonds. Yugoslavia's Disintegration and Balkan Politics in Transition*, Boulder: Westview Press.

Coimbra Group (2001) *Migration, Minorities, Compensation. Issues of Cultural Identities in Europe*, Brussels.
Crumley, Bruce (2009) 'Protectionism on the rise in Europe?', *Time*, February 4, Available: www.time.com/time/world/article/0,8599,1876944,00.html.
Dizdarević, Raif (2009) *From the Death of Tito to the Death of Yugoslavia*, Sarajevo: Sahinpašić.
Djeković, Liliana (2010) 'Privredna kriza i privredna reforma u Jugoslaviji', in Korošić, Marijan, (ed.) *Quo vadis Jugoslavijo?* Zagreb: Naprijed.
Duménil, Gérard, and Lévy, Dominique (2009) 'The crisis of neoliberalism and the US hegemony', *Kurswechsel*, no. 2.
Duménil, Gérard, and Lévy, Dominique (2010) *The Crisis of Neoliberalism. From Subprime Crash to the Great Contraction*, Harvard: Harvard University Press.
Emerson, Michael, Aydin, Senem, De Clerck-Sachsse, Julia, and Noutcheva, Gergana (2006) 'Just what is this "absorption capacity" of the European Union?', *CEPS Policy Brief*, September.
Fischer, Joschka (2003) 'From confederacy to federation: thoughts on the finality of European integration', in Poole, Peter A. (ed.) *The EU's Eastern Enlargement*, Westport: Praeger.
Fischer, Joschka (2010) 'Euro crisis has left Angela Merkel with much to fear', *The Guardian*, November 4, Available: www.guardian.co.uk/commentisfree/2010/nov/04/euro-crisis-angela-merkel.
Friedman, George (2010) 'Germany and the failure of multiculturalism', *Stratford Global Intelligence*, October 19, Available: www.stratfor.com/weekly/20101018_germany_and_failure_multiculturalism.
Gingrich, Andre, and Bank, Marcus (eds.) (2006) *Neo-nationalism in Europe and Beyond*, New York: Berghan Books.
Goati, Vladimir (1989) *Politička anatomija jugoslovenskog društva*, Zagreb: Naprijed.
Harvey, David (2009) 'Is this *really* the end of neoliberalism?', *Counterpunch*, March 13, Available: www.counterpunch.org/harvey03132009.html.
Heathcote, Edwin (2010) 'Down, socially cleansed and out in Paris and London', *Financial Times*, October 30, p. 7.
Horvat, Branko (1985) *Jugoslavensko društvo u krizi*. Zagreb: Globus.
International Herald Tribune (2009) 'The peril of "Buy American"', June 4, p. 6.
Judah, Tim (2009) 'Yugoslavia is dead, long live the Yugosphere', *LSEE Papers on South East Europe*, November.
Judah, Tim (2010) 'Ja sam otac Jugosfere', *Globus*, no. 1027, August 13, pp. 22–25.
Jugoslovenski Centar za teoriju i praksu samoupravljanja (1982). 'E. Kardelj', *Drustveno-ekonomski aspekti medjunacionalnih odnosa u Jugoslaviji*, Ljubljana: Delavska Enotnost.
Kanli, Yusuf (2010) 'Multiculturalism', *Hürriyet Daily New*, October 25, Available: www.hurriyetdailynews.com/n.php?n=multiculturalism-2010-10-25.
Komisija za probleme ekonomske stabilizacije (1982) *Polazne osnove dugoročnog programa ekonomske stabilizacije*, Beograd: Dokumenti Borba, April.
Komisija za probleme ekonomske stabilizacije (1983) 'Zaključni deo dugoročnog programa ekonomske stabilizacije', *Savremena Praksa*, prilog br. 966, Beograd, July 14.
Korošić, Marijan (1989a) *Jugoslavenska Kriza*, Zagreb: Naprijed.
Korošić, Marijan (ed.) (1989b) *Quo vadis Jugoslavijo?* Zagreb: Naprijed.
Lampe, John R. (1996) *Yugoslavia as History. Twice There Was a Country*, Cambridge: Cambridge University Press.

La Repubblica (2009) 'La crisi frena le riforme e aumenta i nazionalismi', March 13, p. 22.

Leaders' Statement (2009) *The Global Plan for Recovery and Reform*, G20 Communiqué, London, April 2.

Lévy, Bernard-Henry (2010) 'Kriza tek dolazi'a s njom i moguci raspad Evrope', *Globus*, December 21.

Matlack, Carl (2006) 'Europe's utilities stay close to home', *Bloomberg Businessweek*, February 27.

Mencinger, Jože (2009) *The Global Financial Crisis and the European Union*, paper presented at the international conference 'The EU, Russia and the Global Crisis', Forlì, April 17–18.

Menon, Anand, and Wright, Vincent (2001) *From the Nation State to Europe?* Oxford: Oxford University Press.

Michalski, Krzysztof (ed.) (2006) *What Holds Europe Together?* Budapest: CEU Press.

Münchau, Wolfgang (2009) 'Europe and the protectionist trap', *Der Spiegel*, February 13, Available: www.spiegel.de/international/europe/0,1518,druck-607457,00.html.

Münchau, Wolfgang (2010) 'Europe's choice is to integrate or disintegrate', *Financial Times*, May 3, p. 9.

Noiriel, Gérard (2001) *État, nation et immigration. Vers une histoire du pouvoir*, Paris: Belin.

Perović, Blažo (1988) *Jugoslovenstvo i nacional-feudalizam*, Beograd: Gardoš.

Poole, Peter A. (2003) *The EU's Eastern Enlargement*, Westport: Praeger.

Reichenberg, Neil E. (2001) *Best Practices in Diversity Management*, UN Export Group Meeting on Managing Diversities in the Civil Service, New York, May 3–4.

Samoupravno sporazumevanje u udruženom radu (1981) Beograd: Marksistički Centar.

Savezni društveni savet za pitanja društvenog uređenja (1985) *Kritička analiza funkcionisanja političkog sistema socijalističkog samoupravljanja*, Beograd.

Šetinc, France (1990) *Uspon i silazak*, Zagreb: Globus.

Spiegel, Peter (2010) 'Trichet warns on EU treaty deal', *Financial Times*, October 31, p. 1.

Vinocur, John (2010) 'Pondering the German question', *International Herald Tribune*, May 4, p. 2.

Woodward, Susan (1995) *The Balkan Tragedy*, Washington, DC: The Brookings Institution.

Žagar, Mitja (2006/2007) 'Diversity management and integration: from ideas to concepts', *European Yearbook of Minority Issues*, vol. VI, pp. 307–327.

Part IV
Citizenship and democracy in Europe

11 The crisis of the Euro, the crisis of the European Union and the crisis of democracy in Europe

Philippe C. Schmitter

There is nothing new about crises in the process of European integration. One could even say that they have been an integral part of it and, moreover, they have had a positive effect. The usual reaction by member governments has been to increase the authority and expand the tasks of the institutions of the European Union (EU) and its predecessors (EEC/EC) in order to resolve (or at least to respond to) the crisis.

The underlying reason for this is obvious. It begins with the unprecedented nature of the process of integrating sovereign national states peacefully into a regional organization. The actors involved have an intrinsic difficulty in acting rationally because it is so difficult to assess the costs and benefits of possible courses of action: first, because the range of alternatives (especially given the presumption of peaceful negotiation among relative equals rather than violent imposition by the strongest) is so different from analogous choices made during their respective processes of national integration; second, because, however well considered their policies and well-intentioned their implementation, they are bound to generate unexpected and, often, undesired consequences; and third, if these were not enough, the EEC/EC/EU has repeatedly changed its overriding goal from providing regional security, to promoting trade in industrial goods, to subsidizing agriculture to encouraging cross-national investment, to liberalizing financial flows to coping with the competitive pressures of globalization – not to mention the more recent ones of coordinating police cooperation, control of borders, visa and asylum requirements, energy networks, transport systems and foreign and security policy. Each time the EU has expanded its *compétences*, the stakes in the game have involved ever more complex packages of policies whose interactive effects and emergent properties have proven more difficult to predict. And, if all this were not enough, one of the greatest successes of European integration has been the incorporation of new member states – 22 in addition to the original 6. Each time this has occurred, the effects on existing policy commitments and the likelihood of agreeing upon new ones has become less predictable.

The present crisis of the Euro and the 'sovereign debt' of several of its member states is a near perfect example of how causal complexity, unanticipated consequences and decisional uncertainty can have a significant and cumulative impact on regional integration. Some 41 years ago, in an article revising the neo-functionalist approach, I imagined four successive 'good' crises that the EU might face in the future and that might drive the process further (Schmitter 1970). What each was supposed to do was to build upon frustrated or disappointed member expectations in the pursuit of some common objective. This would compel actors to redefine either the tasks or the level of authority (or both) of regional organizations by reaching a collective agreement that would 'spill over' into previously unsatisfactory or ignored policy areas. What has (heretofore) made the EU unique is precisely this capacity to exploit successive crises positively by repeatedly breaking out of its momentary zone of organizational indifference. At least until now, no other regional organization has acquired this dynamic characteristic.

My fourth 'transcending' crisis was virtually identical to what is presently occurring with regard to the Euro. *In theory*, I argued it should compel actors in member states: (1) to engage in more comprehensive policy coordination across sectors and policy arenas, thereby, institutionalizing at the supra-national level the mechanisms of policy harmonization, budgeting and taxation characteristic of a federal government; and (2) to break out of predominantly national political alliances and form more salient supra-national ones, thereby, laying the foundation for the establishment of the most important missing element in the Euro-polity, namely, a distinctively European party system. *In short, this was supposed to be the crisis that would drive the EU from economic to political integration.*

Unfortunately, *in practice*, the outcome – at least, so far – has been just the opposite. Member governments seem to be retreating to more restrictive and nationalistic calculations of interest. Led by overt German recalcitrance (but supported quietly by other 'Northern' states), there has been little sign of the sort of cross-national partisan solidarity or the need for comprehensive policy coordination that I had anticipated. Some members have even experienced the revival of extreme right-wing nationalist parties and movements that are overtly contrary to any further 'spill-overs'. A few of them even advocate outright withdrawal, not just from the Euro, but from the EU as such. The emerging Euro-polity seems further than ever from acquiring its distinctive party system. Moreover, mass publics – rather than favouring more integration in gratitude for the benefits it has given them – have by-and-large expressed hostility to the prospect.

Could it just be that the 'good' crisis that I imagined 40 some years ago has turned out to be a very 'bad' one? For not only is the crisis of greater magnitude at the supra-national level than expected, but it also seems to have penetrated more deeply and negatively into national political institutions and public opinion. *It is even plausible to imagine a vicious triangle emerging: first, the collapse of the Euro; then, the collapse of the European Union and, finally, the collapse of democracy in its member states.*

Let us look at these three crises to assess how serious their implications are and how closely they may be related to each other.

The Euro-crisis

If it were just a matter of sustaining the existence and value of the Euro as the common currency of 17 EU member states, the solution seems to be falling (slowly and painfully) into place. Europeans have discovered that they may not yet have a common identity, but they do already share a common fate – and the Euro binds them to it. The cost of unravelling these ties is simply too uncertain and threatening. If this implies accepting a range of previously unthinkable policies – from issuing Eurobonds, to creating a Europe-wide system of deposit insurance and banking supervision, to allowing unlimited purchases of sovereign debt by the European Central Bank, to empowering the Commission to monitor and supervise national budgetary and fiscal policies, to granting to the European Court of Justice extensive powers to review compliance and punish infractions by member states, even to mutualizing a fixed proportion of the debts of member countries – the Euro-zone members will probably agree to pool the risk in order to reduce the spread in interest rates among them and to protect the value of the Euro vis-à-vis other currencies. To make these commitments credible, they will have to have a firm legal foundation and probably some source of EU 'own' resources – perhaps in the form of an earmarked tax on financial transactions. This may sound like an enormous transfer of national sovereignty to a remote and complex set of supra-national institutions. And it is.

What just might tip the balance is if one EU member (probably Greece, but possibly Cyprus as well) were to defect or be expelled from the club. The ensuing economic catastrophe could serve to convince even the most reluctant of its other members to accept the mega-package deal outlined above. One hopes that this will not happen, but accepting 'the Mother of All Spill-Overs' just may take such a shock.

But what if the real problem were not the Euro? What if the crisis runs deeper and long precedes the decision to establish a common currency? Economic growth and real wages in Europe began to decline already in the 1980s. The accelerated expansion of both public and private credit also pre-dates the introduction of the Euro. Something fundamental seems to have changed in the nature of capitalism during the last quarter of the twentieth century – at the end of the so-called '*Trente Glorieuses*' years of uninterrupted economic growth, greater income equality and enhanced social protection. How much the integration of Europe contributed to this unprecedented prosperity is debatable, but one cannot question the fact that the EEC/EC/EU was credited not only with maintaining a security community among the states of the region, but also with creating a climate for superior economic performance and social justice.

For the last 20–30 years, the EU has become associated with gradually declining to negative outcomes. Ever since the Single European Act in 1986 and the Maastricht Treaty in 1992, its policies have conformed closer and closer to neo-liberal doctrinal principles of financial liberalization and market deregulation. And in the last two to three years, the Euro and the policies of the ECB have been specifically (and accurately) perceived as mechanisms for enforcing austerity and accused of fostering not just lower growth and greater inequality, but also decline in real incomes, as well as massive increases in unemployment. If this were not enough, international capital markets discovered that the government bonds rapidly accumulated by those member states that could no longer devalue their currencies to enhance competitiveness had reached such a magnitude that they might not be repaid – and these speculators started treating them as equivalent to private or corporate debt by demanding a premium for the greater risk involved. Much of this might have occurred without the common currency, but it has been blamed for it.

If this scenario is correct, it suggests a fundamental and irreversible rupture of the social contract – whether the explicit result of corporatist concertation or the implicit outcome of pluralist pressures – that has characterized the European political economy in the post-war period. Globalized finance capitalism has made it impossible for states to raise sufficient revenues to cover the expenses of such a contract – so they have to borrow and borrow more to meet the expectations of their citizens. The level of taxation on middle and lower classes has reached saturation point and it has become impossible to tax the rich since they have so many means of hiding income or shifting it to foreign sites. If that were not enough, the implacable demography of an aging population is raising the costs of retirement and health policies – and these older people continue to vote at a time when younger ones are abstaining more and more. In other words, saving the Euro might be futile if this deeper contradiction is not addressed.

In principle, the European Union could survive without a common currency. It did so rather well for four decades. Admittedly, the failure of monetary integration would probably signal an end to aspirations for eventual political integration – but this would not be regretted by many of its citizens (especially those living in Great Britain and Denmark).

Obviously, a great deal would depend on how the Euro went under. A gradual negotiated retreat or one that left it the common currency of some sub-set of member states would be more tolerable. However, this seems highly unlikely and a chaotic *sauve-qui-peut* would trigger enduring political and legal recriminations that would make policy-making in other areas virtually impossible. If nothing else, the Euro-crisis has exposed a highly salient and deep cleavage between Northern creditor and Southern debtor countries that will be hard to overcome – especially since it has been accompanied by a revival of stereotypes about national character and historical resentments about German domination. Prior to this, the underlying cleavage structure was basically pluralist with different sets of winners and losers across changing policy arenas – held together by the Franco-German duopoly, with the former providing the ideas and the latter the money. This time there is a clear and cumulative pattern of conflict, and France and Germany are not in sufficient agreement to overcome the gap.

But the most serious threat to the EU may emerge precisely because its members are successful in saving the Euro. The only way of accomplishing this seems to be *via* the devolution of extraordinary *compétences* upon its institutions, especially the Commission and the ECB. Not only would they have to substantially increase the number of their functionaries and experts but, in order to be credible, these additional commitments would also have to be funded through 'own resources' that would not depend on periodic member approval – something that has heretofore been denied on such a scale. Whether through a fee on financial transactions, an increment to the VAT tax or a flat Euro-levy, it would definitely raise the sensitive issue of the EU's democracy deficit. Up to now, this issue has been finessed on the grounds that the EU was either just another inter-governmental organization or a supra-national regulatory agency. But such a massive transfer of sovereign authority and financial resources would definitely raise the eternal issue of 'No Taxation without Representation' and require the introduction of new mechanisms of democratic participation and accountability, or the legitimacy of the whole operation would be constantly challenged. The classic formula of increasing the powers of the European Parliament has failed in the past and would be even more insufficient under such circumstances. So far, the various packages of proposed fiscal, budgetary and regulatory measures to save the Euro have completely ignored the imperative of political legitimation. Presumably, the dominant approach rests on the assumption by technocrats that the rescue of the Euro will be 'self-legitimating'. Europeans will be so grateful for what has *not* happened to them that they will not ask how it was done and what its cost was.

The crisis of European democracy

Democracy in Europe has long been a national or sub-national product and, therefore, the collapse of the EU would not seem to threaten its viability. Elsewhere, I have even argued that its multi-layered and poly-centric system of 'supra-national governance' has had some negative effects on the practice of domestic democracy. *Ergo*, getting rid of it might even help to improve the quality of democracy at the national and sub-national levels.

The EU has long had an ambiguous relation to democracy. It requires something like a liberal, representative, constitutional version of it (along with respect for human rights, rule of law and capacity for administering EU directives and regulations) as a condition for membership, but it does not itself practice this type of democracy. As some wag once put it, 'if the EU were to apply to join itself, it would be rejected'. By applying strict conditionality to the post-Communist Central and Eastern European candidates, it undoubtedly contributed to the relatively rapid and successful consolidation of democracy there, and its subsequent role with regard to pending candidates from South Eastern Europe seems also to have been positive. But its feeble efforts to democratize itself, mainly by directly electing European deputies and increasing their parliamentary powers, have been insufficient to overcome the basic impediment that its government, the Commission, does not reflect the partisan preferences expressed by European voters and its Commissioners are chosen by opaque negotiations among member governments.

With or without the EU, however, European national democracies have been in trouble for several decades. The paradox of these times is that, precisely when so many aspiring *neo*-democracies emerged to the East, the *archeo*-democracies of the West were entering into crisis. Their citizens started questioning the very same 'normal' institutions and practices that new democratizers were trying so hard to imitate. And they tended to find them deficient, to say, outright defective. The list of morbidity symptoms is well-known (if not well-understood): citizens have become more likely to abstain from voting, less likely to join or even identify with political parties, trade unions or professional associations, more likely not to trust their elected officials or politicians in general and much less likely to be satisfied with the way in which they are being governed and the benefits they receive from public agencies (Schmitter and Trechsel 2004).

None of these symptoms can be attributed directly to the EU, but that does not mean that they could not get worse in its absence. Again, a great deal depends on how the EU goes into demise and what consequences this triggers. A 'soft landing' that leaves intact many of its treaty-based obligations does not threaten the established security community and protects much of the basic structure of regional trade, and investment might have little impact. Again, this seems unlikely. A 'hard' landing will involve many unfulfilled contracts, multiple law suits, considerable disruption in trade and capital flows and, of course, lots of resentment – not just between individuals and firms but between national states. And these are very likely to be polarized along geographic, cultural and political lines – with the Northern 'hard-working and abstemious' creditors pitted against the Southern 'lazy and spendthrift' debtors.

One clear signal has already emerged. Voters in national elections during the past three years have demonstrated an unprecedented propensity for throwing incumbents out of office. Historically, European democracies were built upon hegemonic parties that ruled for long and consistent periods of time. Now, there are no more ruling parties, only governing ones. Whether of the centre-right (e.g. France, Italy, the Netherlands, Denmark, the Czech Republic, Hungary) or of the centre-left (e.g. Portugal, Spain, Ireland, Slovenia, the United Kingdom, Finland), the tenure of virtually all European governments has become precarious. Moreover, citizens have shifted an increasing proportion of their votes to fringe populist parties of either the right or left. Such populisms are an intrinsic, if periodic, temptation in all democracies. They are the side product of systems of sclerotic and oligarchic political parties that have become incapable of representing existing citizen preferences or articulating credible future projects for the polity as a whole. They are not so much anti-democratic, as they are less politically liberal, sometimes 'supra'-constitutional and often economically imprudent. Even when they do not succeed in occupying governing positions, they can push more established, centrist parties into adopting items from their platforms, thereby making it increasingly difficult for them to form coalition governments.

Democracy in Europe was already changing before the Euro-crisis and the EU-crisis emerged. It will survive both of them, but in so doing it will have to become even more different from the one that Social Democrats and Christian

Democrats built after World War II. It will have to find (and institutionalize) a new social contract and a more regulated political economy – not to mention novel channels of democratic participation and mechanisms for accountability to citizens.

Conclusion

The crisis is not over and its consequences will be felt for some time to come. Which means that there is an opportunity to turn an apparently bad crisis into a good one. Moreover, the instrument for doing so already exists in the form of that unprecedented (but still not accomplished) delegation of *compétences* to the Commission, the European Central Bank and the European Court of Justice. What will make the difference will be the purpose for which these supra-national institutions will exercise those powers.

What if the EU, instead of promoting orthodox neo-liberal policies of fiscal balance, budgetary austerity, lower welfare provisions and greater labour market flexibility at the national level, switched direction and became an aggressive supra-national agent of growth and job creation via the issuing of Eurobonds guaranteed by all member states and the launching of a programme of European scale public works in energy and transport – even in research and development – financed by the European Investment Bank? There does seem to be a critical mass of dissident economists (and plenty of social scientists) in favour of this, as well as an emerging coalition of national governments (of the right in Spain and Portugal, of the left in France and of Technocrats in Greece and Italy). Even the centrist Dutch government recently made similar noises by questioning the sacrosanct status of the 3 per cent barrier on budget deficits. Whether this proves sufficient to nudge the German government and with it the Board of the ECB and, eventually, the European Council in such a new direction remains to be seen. But if it is sufficient and (even more problematic) if it is successful, then the EU would re-acquire and greatly strengthen its association with economic prosperity and social justice – that famous European Model of Society that Jacques Delors was so fond of invoking. Seen from this (admitted improbable) perspective, the current Euro-crisis could just be the detonator of that 'Transcending Cycle' that I imagined 40 years ago.

Bibliography

Schmitter, Philippe C. (1970) 'A Revised Theory of Regional Integration', *International Organization*, vol. 24, no 4, pp. 836–868; also published in Lindberg, L., and Scheingold, S. (eds.) *Regional Integration: Theory and Research*, Cambridge, Mass.: Harvard University Press, 1971, pp. 232–265.

Schmitter, Philippe C. (2007) 'The Vices and Virtues of Populism', *Aspenia*, vol. 12, no. 35–36, pp. 42–48; also published as 'I populismi: vizi e virtù', *Aspenia*, vol. 12, no. 36, 2007, pp. 71–78; also published as 'Los vicios y virtudes de los "populismos": un balance general', *El Debate Político. Revista Iberoamericana de Análisis Político*, Año 3, No. 4/5, November 2006, pp. 208–214.

Schmitter, Philippe C. (2004) 'Will EMU Make It Easier or More Difficult to Democratize the EU', in Torres, F., Verdun, A., Zilioli, C., and Zimmermann, H. (eds.) *Governing the EMU*, Florence: EUI, pp. 99–110; also published in Torres, F., Verdun, A., Zilioli, C., and Zimmermann, H. (eds.) *EMU Rules: The Political and Economic Consequences of European Monetary Integration*, Baden Baden: Nomos, 2006, pp. 101–110.

Schmitter, Philippe C., and Trechsel, Alexandre (eds.) (2004) *The Future of Democracy in Europe Trends, Analyses and Reforms*, Strasbourg: Council of Europe Publishing.

12 The life and death of democracies

Stuart Holland

Default on a dream

In 2004 the American political scientist Jeremy Rifkin published a book called *The European Dream*, where he wrote that, unlike the United States, the European Union appeared to be a model of an emerging 'soft power' in a hard world. Already an economic giant, with a single currency stronger than the dollar, it lacked the arrogance in world affairs of the US. It had emerged from the ashes of WWII with a project for peaceful unification of hitherto warring states. All its members were democracies. With the end of the Cold War, most former satellite states of the defunct Soviet Union already had joined it. It had drawn up a Charter of Fundamental Rights, which was to be part of a new Constitution for Europe. It seemed a model for what might in due course be a new global order (Rifkin 2004).

Yet, within months of Rifkin's claims, something went wrong. The Constitution for Europe was serially rejected by those electorates given the chance to vote on it. Since 2009 Europe has less than fulfilled Rifkin's dream. Rating agencies which had ranked toxic debt as safe as government bonds until the subprime crisis threatened banks and hedge funds with collapse turned their sights on European governments whose debt, in key cases, had soared to salvage them. Threats to the single currency, which Helmut Kohl had presumed would lock Germany into a democratic Europe, instead proved to be the template for resurgence of German hegemony, with debt-distressed member states succumbing to the claims of Angela Merkel that there was no alternative to saving them other than an austerity which denied the very principles of achieving rising standards on which the Rome Treaty, founding a European Community, had been based.

The outcome, by 2012, was a Stability Treaty agreed by 25 of the then 27 EU member states that national governments should submit their budgets to European technocrats before these were submitted to their parliaments and that they should commit themselves to 'budget balance' as a principle, despite this being as progressive a response to crisis as a return to the gold standard. This was matched by another principle that would have satisfied Milton Friedman, that European governments should govern only by market criteria, rather than those for social welfare, which was a denial not only of Keynesian reasoning but also of the principles of Marshall Aid from which Germany herself had been a key beneficiary, and of the European Social Model to which nation states emerging either from dictatorship in southern Europe, or in the former Soviet Union, had assumed that the then European Community and later European Union was committed.

The path towards this had been laid by the earlier failed attempt to impose a European Constitution, which was rejected by the electorates of every member state to which it was put for ratification, yet then recycled as a Lisbon Treaty, and later endorsed by the Irish electorate only on the basis of an offer they could not afford to refuse. For an austerity pact, of itself, will not placate financial markets, which, by 2012, became increasingly aware that, without growth, the European economy could not reduce its debt and deficits. For example, when Standard & Poors downgraded nine Eurozone member states in January 2012, they stressed that the three key reasons were: (1) simultaneous debt and spending reduction by governments and households, (2) thereby weakening economic growth, and (3) prolonged dispute among European policymakers on what to do about it (*The Telegraph* 2012).

What went wrong?

Some economists had warned that a monetary union without significant fiscal transfers could risk disintegration. Yet this ran against the determination of British governments, since Clement Attlee, not to cede sovereignty on fiscal and monetary policy to Europe. This coincided, during the Eurozone crisis, with the determination of Germany under Angela Merkel not to agree to a 'transfer Union' by which German taxpayers would subsidise the rest of Europe.

Some authors drew on the case that had been argued in the blueprint for a European Community, the Spaak Report, that integrating economies with unequal efficiencies would aggravate structural, social and regional inequalities and need active offsetting policies to counter this (Spaak 1956, Holland 1980). Meanwhile historians, political scientists and other commentators have asked why the Keynesian full employment commitment which was consensual when the European Community was founded, and which survived for nearly two decades, was displaced by monetarism as a dominant institutional ideology within the EU. This occurred despite the fact that a founding aim of the Rome Treaty was rising standards of living, and that the first revision of the Rome Treaty in the Single European Act of 1986 committed it to social cohesion, with the internal market, as the 'twin pillars' of the Community.

Borrowing as credit and debt as guilt

Gestalt psychology has stressed that there are not 'facts of the world', rather what is perceived depends on the perceiver (Jastrow 1899). Such perception reflects the values, dispositions and beliefs that one has consciously or less than consciously acquired since early childhood (Bourdieu 1977, 1984, 1990, Oliveira and Holland 2012). This also is relevant to perceptions of borrowing and credit which may be less than consciously trapped by language (Wittgenstein 1953), as with the German and Dutch word for debt – *Schuld* – being the same as for guilt, whereas the inverse perception of borrowing as credit has resonance in Latin in the *Credo* of the Creed and in belief. Such a dual meaning of *Schuld* was stressed by Nietzsche in his *Genealogy of Morals* (Nietzsche 1887) in which he also observed that there was a tendency in Germany among strong creditors not only to want repayment from weak debtors, but also to demand penitence for their guilt and to punish them if they did not seek redemption.

Some of this was echoed in the language used in reaction to the Eurozone crisis, as in the title of a proposal from the German Federal Council of Economic Advisers in 2011 of 'Redemption Bonds' by which EU member states would redeem all national debt over and above the 60 per cent of GDP nominally allowed by the EU's Stability and Growth Pact within 25 years (GCEE 2011). The proposal was less severe than the measures being demanded short-term by the German government. It also had the merit that it could 'at a stroke' resolve the Greek debt crisis by reducing its national debt by two thirds. This included the inference that bond holders do not necessarily 'want their money back', even after 25 years, since holding onto bonds guarantees return on their investments. This is the case with the British Treasury, which is still rolling over bonds which had been issued to finance the Napoleonic Wars.

From the onset of the Eurozone crisis, Angela Merkel sought to 'ban' discussion of bonds to mutualise debt at lower interest rates than governments needed to redeem their national bonds. Her opposition to this was rational in the sense that she and most German public opinion were opposed to fiscal transfers to other member states, less rational in that German banks were highly exposed to peripheral country debt and less rational again in that exit of weaker economies from the Eurozone would mean an appreciation of the euro for the stronger economies still in it and less competitiveness for their exports (ETUC 2011, Münchau 2010, Varoufakis and Holland 2010).

Consistent with different *Gestalt* perceptions of the same phenomenon and Wittgenstein's case that the meaning of words depends on their use, there are multiple meanings of the word 'bond', ranging from negative implications, as in bondage, through to 'my word is my bond', implying trust, or as a bond implying a reciprocal obligation on lenders and borrowers rather than simply debt dependence, such as the French for a bond being *obligation*. Positive meanings rather than presuming that investment in them is equivalent to guilt can be observed in bonds being known as *buoni* in Italian, or *boni* in Spanish. In the British case, bonds are known as *gilts* and therefore presumed to be 'as good as gold', both before and after Britain was on the gold standard, even if the original meaning was derived from the paper on which they were issued being gilt edged rather than consciously dropping the 'u' from guilt.

A bond can mean bonding together, as in *Bund* in German, and achieve a positive connotation in political terms. Such as postwar Germany becoming a *Bundesrepublik* rather than a *Reich*, and redesignating its institutions accordingly, such as a *Bundesbank* rather than *Reichsbank*, and a *Bundesverfassungsgericht* for its constitutional court. While postwar Germany was committed to 'bonding' with other nations in the construction of a European Union in which, in the words of then French foreign minister Robert Schumann, another war between Germany and France not only would be 'morally unthinkable' but also materially impossible, contemporary Germans now view their single currency in terms of a 'bondage' (Guérot 2012).

Splitting, denial and projective identification

There is a parallel with what Melanie Klein (1952) conceptualised as the related concepts of 'splitting', 'denial' and 'projective identification'. For Klein (1932, 1952), the notion 'splitting' of what was good from what was bad was then projected onto either someone or something else. She developed this from her studies in child psychology. This conceptual framework was seen by many psychologists and psychoanalysts to be relevant to not only child psychology but also to other forms of behaviour (e.g. Rosenfeld 1950, Segal 1950, Bion 1963). Schneider (1975) and Richards (1989) have related splitting and projective identification to market behaviour where rating agencies 'split' from recognising that subprime and other financial derivatives could be toxic and 'projected' them as safe as government bonds. Dinnerstein (1978) extended 'splitting' in terms of 'splits between heart and head, feeling and reason, private and public' (Dinnerstein 1978: 130) where private is deemed good and public bad.

Splitting and displacement have been endemic to the Eurozone crisis, for this was not caused by high debt levels as such, but by the speculation of banks and hedge funds in subprime and other financial derivatives which led to their threatened collapse and to European governments salvaging them. Two of the countries hit hardest by the crisis, Spain and Ireland, had much lower levels of debt before the financial crisis than Germany. Splitting and displacement were also relevant to the presumption in Germany during the Brüning government (in the early 1930s that led to support for the Nazi party) that austerity was needed to avoid the hyper-inflation that followed WWI. Yet little has been learned from this during the austerity policies demanded by the German, Austrian, Dutch and Finnish governments in response to the Eurozone crisis. The Stability Treaty introduced on their initiative in March 2012, and agreed by 25 of the EU's 27 member states, claimed the need to 'encourage and, if necessary, compel' a member state to reduce a deficit' (EU 2012). The governor of the European Central Bank proposed that governments that did not meet austerity debt and deficit levels should have their voting rights in European councils suspended.

Policies imposed since the onset of the Eurozone crisis by the Troikas of the IMF, European Central Bank and European Commission replicated those of the Brüning austerity measures by insisting on repayment of debt, credit restrictions and, even more severely than the Brüning measures, public sector investment, wage and salary cuts. This has been accompanied also by a rise of the extreme right in several countries, including not only some of those recently emerging from communism, but also in the Netherlands and Greece.

Delving deeper

While this chapter is highly critical of the response to the Eurozone crisis by the Merkel government, key figures in German politics also have been so. The former foreign minister, Joschka Fischer, claimed that since Germany twice destroyed Europe in the twentieth century, it would be a tragedy if it were to do so again by failing to ensure the success of a European union that had been designed precisely to avoid a repeat of this (Fischer 2012). In September 2011, Sigmar Gabriel, national chairman of the German Social Democratic Party, criticised the 'failed Eurozone crisis management' of the Merkel government for assuming that the problems have basically been caused by a lack of fiscal discipline at the national level, and that the solution is primarily to be sought by spending cuts, arguing that only common liability by governments for Eurozone debt could eliminate instability in financial markets (Spiegel 2011). This called for courage granted that German public opinion was overwhelmingly opposed to a 'transfer union' by which Germany would assist other member states in difficulty (Guérot 2012).

This merits delving deeper into what progressive Germans confront. For postwar Germany there was 'good' in splitting from the 'bad' of a Nazi Reich, but this has been difficult. Successive German chancellors – other than Adenauer and Willy Brandt – declared that it was time for Germany to 'throw off' guilt for its Nazi past and to be recognised as a fully-fledged western democracy. The Eurozone crisis has offered the first occasion since WWII for German public opinion to displace guilt for Hitler causing WWII and for the Holocaust. Germany is projected as 'good' because it is in surplus and this implies (with unconscious echoes of Nietzsche) that the rest of Europe is 'bad' because of debt and should redeem itself through austerity, even if this incurs pain by doing so.

Weber's misguided legacy: the Protestant Ethic

The dual meaning in German – and Dutch – of *Schuld* as both debt and guilt relates also to Weber's (1905) concept of the Protestant Ethic and widespread misperception that it was this that gave rise to capitalism. Few enough German, Austrian or Dutch people may have read Weber, yet many are aware of the association of the two words Protestant Ethic that also has relevance now to the question of debt and deficits in the Eurozone. The common *Gestalt* perception is that hard-working and high-saving capitalism was the outcome of such an ethic and in contrast to Catholic self-indulgence and profligacy, which is 'wrong'.

For Weber, the *Geist* or spirit of capitalism was the triumph of rationality over tradition and he associated this with Protestant countries such as England, Germany and Holland, yet this 'displaced' the fact that modern banking did not originate in these countries, but in Catholic Italy. One of the main challengers to Weber was Richard Tawney, who was also a critic of the values of 'the acquisitive society' which had stemmed from possessive individualism with the rise of capitalism (Tawney 1920). In his 1926 *Religion and the Rise of Capitalism*,

Tawney argued that Protestantism adopted the risk-taking, profit-making ethic of capitalism, rather than that capitalism was due to it. He also, with justification, claimed that there was plenty of capitalist spirit in fifteenth-century Italy, or in Catholic South Germany and among Catholics as well as Protestants in Flanders.

Tawney's case was that the development of capitalism was due less to Protestantism than to the trading successes of Venice in the Mediterranean and Near East and the discovery by the Medici that they could lend deposits made to them by successful Tuscan merchants. Religion either was coincidental or, in the case of Medici popes, compliant in displacing the earlier Catholic denunciation of usury.

Robertson (1933) also criticised Weber for presuming that the values of the Protestant Ethic in terms of diligence and good works were opposed to those of Catholicism. He recognised that the Jansenists prescribed to their flocks that the Christian life was one of toil and not pleasure. The Jesuits stressed a similar work ethic, as well as what more recent management theory has deemed 'reflective practice' on effective performance (Argyris and Schön 1996, Lowney, 2003).

Amintore Fanfani (2009) parallels Robertson's criticism of Weber but from a different perspective in evidencing that key early Protestant leaders, including both Luther and Calvin, actually opposed capitalism. Calvin condemned as unlawful any gain obtained at a neighbour's expense, such as from interest on lending. Through the sixteenth and seventeenth centuries, continual prohibitions of usury were issued by the synods of the Huguenots and by those of the Dutch Reformers, whose ethical code also condemned excessive labour as diverting time and energy from the service of God.

Jacob Viner, one of the most eminent twentieth-century economists, also used Scotland as a case study to demonstrate that, where Calvinism was a state religion, it tended to abet rather than aid the rise of capitalism (Viner 1978). He pointed out that, until well into the eighteenth century, and only after economic union with England, Scotland was a desperately poor country and contemporary commentators often remarked on the lack of economic initiative and ambition in the population and on a general lack of entrepreneurship.

Crowell (2006) also has posed one of the main criticisms of Weber in terms that are consistent with the later Wittgenstein's claims that the meaning of words lies not 'in themselves' but in their context and their use, illustrating that how Weber's use of the term 'spirit of capitalism' was so arbitrary as to expose him to challenge by a range of critics. As he puts it: 'After all, how is one to define spirit? It is a bit like asking someone to define the word blue. It is up to interpretation, based on context, tone and timing of the use of the word' (Crowell 2006: 8).

Where there is relevance now from Weber's analysis of the Protestant Ethic is that both Luther and Calvin claimed that the relationship between man and God was direct and that there was a need to redeem original sin by good works in one's lifetime. In this sense, Protestantism was dyadic, whereas Catholicism was triadic. Catholicism allows for intermediation and remission of guilt by a priest, and remission of guilt can avoid repression and denial. This is what has been lacking in Europe since the onset of the Eurozone crisis: there has been little effective triangulation between an increasingly powerful Germany and other member states on alternatives to austerity.

Soft and hard power

In his *Between Two Ages: America's Role in the Technetronic Era*, Zbigniew Brzezinski (1970) argued that: 'The nation-state as a fundamental unit of man's organized life has ceased to be the principal creative force. International banks and multinational corporations are acting and planning in terms that are far in advance of [such] political concepts' (Brzezinski 1970: 246). The 1975 report to the Trilateral Commission on 'The Crisis of Democracy' observed that US 'hard power', post Vietnam, would confront limits and proposed that there was a need to 'reconstitute democracy' and to 'carry through a basic mutation in [the] model of social control [to] experiment with more flexible models that could produce more social control with less coercive pressure' (Crozier *et al.* 1975). The soft power thesis was taken up by Rifkin. But the reality of 'more flexible models' when these involve the 'labour market flexibility' of the 'structural reforms' which became part of the *pensée unique* of European institutions, even before the adoption of a single currency, is that this is hard power undermining the pluralism on which effective democracy depends.

For example, the insider–outsider case for labour market flexibility as advocated by the influential Nobel economic committee member Assar Lindbeck and the British economist Denis Snower challenged the social partnership model of *Mitbestimmung* and the *Sozialmarktwirshaft* that Christian Democrats in postwar Germany, such as Ludwig Ehrhart, had seen as vital to preventing the undermining of trades union rights that had followed the National Socialist seizure of power (Ambrosius 1977, Becker 1980, Lindbeck and Snower, 1988). Lindbeck and Snower's thesis was that protective employment legislation means that trade unions can defend high wages and benefits against outsiders who would be prepared to work for less, and that such insider privilege undermines competitiveness, but there was no evidence for such a claim (Esping-Andersen and Regini 2000, Kelly 2005, Howell *et al.* 2007). Lindbeck and Snower offered none at all, rather than algebra based on undemonstrated premises. This was then falsified when Hans-Werner Sinn (2003) of the influential Münich Ifo Institute declared Germany to be 'the sick man of Europe' because it defended insider privileges just when Germany was about to overtake America as the world's largest exporter.

This unfounded thesis influenced the case that Germans needed to work harder and German companies needed to restrain wages, as in the peremptory demand in 2004 of leading employers (Siemens, DaimlerChrysler, Volkswagen and Bosch) that employees should work from four to five more hours per week with no increase in pay, while since the later 1990s there has been near to no increase in real wages in Germany (Münchau and Atkins 2004). This then hit other European economies since it reduced German demand for imports and thus other countries' exports. While the adoption of a single currency meant that the only way in which its periphery then could adjust its trade was by deflation and unemployment rather than devaluation.

The Constitution for Europe

The central principle of democracy is choosing between alternatives and safeguarding the right both to assent and to dissent. An increasingly hegemonic Germany, insisting on a Stability Treaty that could compel governments to submit to its criteria, can be challenged on this. The path taken, however, was already prepared by the former president of France, Valéry Giscard d'Estaing, in not only accepting an invitation to prepare a report on what could be the premises for a Constitution for Europe, but by then demanding one.

This involved an extension of the principle of qualified majority voting in the supranational logic of Jean Monnet, which Attlee had rejected in favour of international cooperation. Agreed upon by national parliaments, it would bind governments in a minority on such a qualified majority vote, with higher weighting for larger member states, to accept policies to which their national parliaments had not agreed rather than enable diversity with a confederal framework in which they could choose not to adopt policies which did not suit them or to which they were opposed in principle.

Rather than a statement of principles which could guide a European Court of Justice, brief enough for anyone to read and understand, such as the Constitution of the United States, the Giscard proposal of a Constitution for Europe had the clarity and charisma of an out-of-order telephone directory. It summarised decisions already made by successive European Councils at vast length but many of its cross references to these led nowhere since they had not even been properly edited. Delivering copies to every household in France reinforced public opinion in its rejection since it summarised what governments had done rather than what people wanted. What people wanted, as evidenced by a Gallup poll after its rejection, was not less Europe but commitment to a Social Europe and that governments should act to achieve this (Manchin 2005).

When it appeared clear that the twin referenda in France and the Netherlands might reject such a proposed Constitution for Europe, on the basis that they wanted more proactive policies for such a Social Europe, Michel Barnier, then French foreign minister, reported that there was no alternative 'Plan B' in the event that it failed. Some heads of government realised what was happening, and called for a new constitution which could more centrally reconcile the need for effective decision-making at a European level with safeguards for national democracy.

The initiative on this was taken by Romano Prodi, who, like Giuliano Amato, was persuaded of the case for inverting qualified majority decision-making, which would bind governments in a minority, in favour of an enabling voting procedure which could take majority decisions but not impose them on governments either dissenting from them or not yet ready to adopt them (Holland 2003). This did not occur. In all key respects, the so-called Lisbon Reform Treaty, agreed by heads of states and governments in December 2007, was a recycling of the Constitution which the French, Dutch and Irish electors had rejected. What transpired was not dissimilar from the somnabulance that Keynes (1919) observed in the negotiation of the Treaty of Versailles which:

> had this air of extraordinary importance and unimportance at the same time. The decisions seemed charged with consequences for the future of humanity; yet the air whispered that the word was not flesh, that it was insignificant, of no effect, dissociated from events.
>
> (Keynes 1936: 4)

What Keynes described was Kleinian displacement and denial, less in the manner of Freud's (1900, 1912, 1915) claim that the conscious represses unconscious sexual desire than in Schopenhauer's (1818) recognition, anticipating later Kleinian analysis, that it can repress any unwelcome thought or feeling. As if a nightmare, the Constitution for Europe was rejected in the three referendums, while less than veiled threats were offered to Ireland for its second round that, if it rejected it, it could be expelled from the Union itself. This was displacement in the sense that, if those prepared to ignore the outcomes of the referenda were asked whether they were democrats, they would strenuously affirm that they were despite the evidence. In Kleinian terms, they had 'comprehensively disconnected' democratic choice from those of a majority of the French, Dutch and Irish electorates, while these were the only electorates in the EU at the time given a choice on whether or not to accept the Constitution.

Europe therefore should be careful to avoid double standards in the manner in which it claims that others should adopt its democratic values, as in Silvio Berlusconi's claiming that Islam is backward because it never had a Renaissance without knowing that it did, or that the beginnings of the Renaissance in Italy were in the multi-cultural environment of the twelfth-century Norman Kingdom of Sicily where both Arabs and Jews were not only tolerated but their intellectual influence welcomed and fully integrated into the legal system as magistrates and as influential advisers at court (e.g. Abulafia 1977). This is also evident in Berlusconi's contradiction of the principle that democracy implies an independent media and judiciary by combining the press and television that he owns with indirectly controlling the rest as head of government, and denouncing Italian judges for seeking to bring cases against him for corruption.

Rousseau, Mill and democracy

Rousseau and John Stuart Mill inveighed against democracies that were limited to minority elites, such as in eighteenth century and early nineteenth century England, but both Rousseau (1762) and Mill (1861) realised that a majority could permanently exclude the rights of a minority. The most striking example for France, in

Rousseau's time, was the Huguenots. In England, both in the eighteenth and nineteenth centuries, the inverse lack of rights was for Catholics. This only now is being addressed in the twenty-first century in the UK in the proposal that a Catholic or someone of any religious denomination might be its head of state.

Mill's economic and political liberalism is not in question, yet he protested in his *On Representative Government* against what could be no less than a 'tyranny of democracy' on two key grounds (Mill 1861). The first was that, if voting were only on a simple majority basis, this could deny a minority the outcome that they wanted. Mill's second reason concerned the electoral process. In his time, as now, the British voting system was on the basis of 'first past the post'. This allows for 'winner takes all' in the sense that the candidate gaining most votes for himself or herself wins outright, even if such a vote is a minority of those cast and the total votes for other candidates vastly exceed it.

This is replicated by governments which may take office with the support of only a minority of the electorate. At the apogee of their parliamentary power, Margaret Thatcher and Tony Blair won parliamentary elections with less than half and later nearer a third of those entitled to vote, with a high level of abstentions on the grounds that no party likely to win represented what those who abstained wanted from governments. As Robin Cook, a former Leader of the House of Commons, warned, this can disenfranchise a majority of the population from the political process (Cook 2003).

Mill responded to this with the case for proportional representation. As a member of parliament for some time, before exiling himself to France, he knew that proportional representation had near to no chance of being agreed by the political elite of mid-nineteenth century Britain. He therefore recommended that both it and 'first past the post' should be adopted, as well as that certain individuals should be elected on what would amount to a 'merit' list in terms of intellect and integrity. In the alleged 'Mother of Parliaments' in Britain, however, it is not electors who determine who should be selected on such alleged merit to its second chamber in the House of Lords, but through appointment on recommendation to the head of state by the head of government. There is also the 'whipping' system by which governing parties in the UK can sanction their members of parliament by 'withdrawing the whip' from them and not supporting them in a further general election, which usually has fatal consequences for independent candidates who wish to contest the status quo.

Against this, governments clearly need coherence. But if this demands support without differentiation of degrees of consent and dissent, this also becomes what one of the most conservative of all twentieth-century politicians, Lord Hailsham, protesting against the democratic mandate for the postwar Labour government, called an 'elected dictatorship'. Margaret Thatcher, priding herself on her democratic values, imposed this not only in central government but also by suspending the autonomy of local governments; the same relates to her claim that there is no such thing as society, rather people and their families, and a more plural governance framework enabling effective choice by both political and civil society was denied.

Formal and effective democracy

India is the world's largest democracy, and rightly proud of it. But the elite of Britain, for centuries, not only presumed to rule India without its consent, but for just as long presumed that it could not learn democratic values. There were questions as to whether such an élite really wanted its former colony to survive its transition to democracy, or fail. While Clement Attlee, as Labour prime minister, was seriously concerned to assure that it should succeed, he did so against the determined opposition of Churchill, whose defence of democracy against Hitler excluded it to Eastern Europe at Yalta, and to British colonies (Harris 1982).

Will Hutton (2002) has pronounced that China needs to learn from Western Enlightenment values and adopt plural institutions separating a legislature, executive and judiciary. But if China were to announce tomorrow that it had adopted a bicameral parliamentary system in which all members of its second chamber would be appointed by its head of state on recommendation by its head of government, as is the case now in the UK with the House of Lords, it would be denounced as a travesty of democracy.

Most proportional representation in continental Europe works on the principle of a 'transferable vote' in successive electoral rounds until one candidate gains an absolute majority of the votes cast, whether in an election to a national parliament or assembly, or for the president of a republic. This has more merit in terms of claiming to be representative than the British principle of 'first past the post', yet means that electors may be voting for a candidate whom they do not want. This was clear in the French presidential election where Le Pen eliminated Lionel Jospin in the first round. This meant that many electors in the second round were voting for their second worst choice for president in Jacques Chirac. This may result in Rousseau's claim that electors may vote for the better of two bad alternatives yet in between elections remain as unfree as before (Rousseau 1762).

In terms of a distinction between formal and effective democracy, there is also the issue of whether proportional representation achieves its aim if electoral constituencies are unequal in terms of the number of those entitled to vote. If they are, this would mean that their boundaries would have to be changed for every election. This condition for formal democracy may have negative implications, however, for effective democracy. If a constituency does not have a boundary coinciding with that of a local or regional government, it becomes an abstraction, meaningful only at the time of an election, and not between them.

For such reasons, in the UK, the boundaries of parliamentary constituencies are regularly changed by a Boundary Commission, which nonetheless retains them within the boundaries of local governments. Many of their decisions are arbitrary, unchallengeable in practice, and do not seek to gain a strict equality in the voting population. It was due to such boundary changes that the Labour Party in 1951 first saw its majority reduced to four, and then lost a second election despite the fact that its overall vote had risen and it was the largest party in the country (Harris 1982). The decisions of the unelected Boundary Commission had denied electors the outcome for which they voted. Effective democracy also depends on how large constituencies are. For example, in European elections they are very large, including entire regions of countries, but those formally representing such regions are not as effectively accessible as a member of a parliament elected by a local constituency.

What is vital is that governments should be able to reinforce rather than reduce democracy in those countries which pioneered it. Especially now, Europe needs to overcome both displacement and denial and learn from cases like the US in the Depression that recovered with Roosevelt's New Deal.

Learning from the New Deal

One of the striking failures of European governments has been the inability to learn from the New Deal, not least since: (1) its success inspired the postwar Marshall Aid programme from which Germany herself was a key beneficiary; (2) it both recovered faith in democracy and reinforced it at key levels within society; (3) that its best known programme, through the Tennessee Valley Authority, both created jobs in and enhanced the environment for its least developed and least competitive member states; (4) it was not financed by the Keynesian deficit spending to which key European governments are so strenuously opposed, but by bonds shifting under-utilised savings into social and environmental investments.

Contrasts between the New Deal and the European responses to the 2008–2009 financial crisis, and then the Eurozone crisis, are marked (Selznick 1949). Rather than only salvaging banks and shareholders, the US Emergency Banking Act of 1933 insured people's deposits in banks. This helped restore the public's confidence in the nation's banking system. Rather than only proposing a Banking Union which might or might not gain greater regulation of banks, and reduce speculation with depositors' funds, the Glass-Steagall Act of 1936 demanded a separation of commercial banking from speculative investment banking. Rather than waiting for a recovery of private sector investment, which had been as low as only $2 billion in 1933, the National Industrial Recovery Act of 1933 enabled the US to directly undertake public investment projects. Although challenged by the US Supreme Court, as were several measures of the first 'hundred days' of the New Deal, the Works Progress Administration of 1935 invested and spent over $10.5 billion and employed 8.5 million workers from 1935 to 1941. It built 77,000 bridges, 664,000 miles of road, 285 airports, 122,000 public buildings including hospitals and 11,000 schools as well as dams, reservoirs, water control and irrigation systems, parks and playgrounds.

Rather than allowing youth unemployment to rise over to 50 per cent, as in Spain and Greece during the Eurozone crisis, Roosevelt introduced the Civilian Conservation Corps of 1933 to create jobs in environmental protection and renewal for single men between the ages of 18 and 25. It took only 37 days from his inauguration on 4 March 1933 to start the programme which employed some three million men for six months, sometimes renewable, from 1933 to 1941 and, from May 1933, former veterans. It improved millions of acres of federal and state lands, as well as parks. New roads were built, telephone lines strung, and some three billion trees planted, which was crucial in countering the earlier Dust Bowls by retaining water and holding soil in place. Crimes committed by young men during the period dropped by over half.

Rather than claiming that southern Europeans should work harder and longer on the lines of a Protestant Ethic, the National Recovery Administration set limits for working time and minimum wages per hour. Sixteen million workers were covered by these codes. Workers went onto an eight-hour day and a minimum wage of $1.25 was introduced. A board was set up to investigate and fine those employers who disregarded this.

Rather than the EU Commission's ritual claim of the need for 'structural reforms', implying reduction of trade union rights, the Wagner National Labour Relations Act of 1935 gave workers the right to form and join trade unions and obliged employers both to recognise them and to take part in collective bargaining. This combined both a social right and the aim of increasing wages to increase demand.

Rather than claiming the need to extend the age for retirement, as some governments in Europe have done since the onset of the Eurozone crisis, the New Deal Social Security Act of 1935 set up the first nationwide pension scheme. Workers and employers had to pay into a federal pension fund. Each state was also expected to work out a plan for unemployment insurance. The Act covered, and was to benefit, 35 million people.

Rather than claiming that combating poverty was up to EU member states themselves, and refusing to lend funds directly to them to do so, the Reconstruction Finance Corporation lent money to state and local governments to assist the poor. Rather than offering money to banks at 1 per cent, which they then lent out at six or seven times as much, the Reconstruction Finance Corporation also lent money to firms which were in debt and threatened with closure, and to others that wanted to invest but could not gain bank finance. Rather also than claiming that southern Europe should resolve its own financial crisis, the Tennessee Valley Development Act of 1933 and the Tennessee Valley Authority administering it included seven of the least developed American states in the deep south and was a regional, environmental and social programme which reinforced the involvement and development of local communities.

The New Deal and democracy

What the New Deal centrally did was repudiate the postwar case of Hayek (1944) that government planning is the road to serfdom. It also has tended to be overlooked that planning, rather than simply federal investment, was embodied in Roosevelt's statement of the case for a Tennessee Valley Authority. This was approved by Congress in May 1933, following a long period of pressure for the privatisation of government-owned properties at Muscle Shoals, Alabama. As Roosevelt put it:

It is clear that the Muscle Shoals development is but a small part of the potential public usefulness of the entire Tennessee River. Such use, if envisioned in its entirety, leads logically to national planning for a complete river watershed involving many States and the future lives and welfare of millions. It touches and gives life to all forms of human concerns ... It should be charged with the broadest duty of planning for the proper use, conservation, and development of the natural resources of the Tennessee River drainage basin and its adjoining territory for the general social and economic welfare of the Nation.

(Roosevelt, cit. Selznick 1949)

In citing this in his *TVA and the Grass Roots*, Selznick submitted that the TVA was many things, but most significantly a social instrument not only *within* a democracy but reinforcing it at local levels, including the engagement of local communities in their own future, such as in promoting and supporting cooperatives. He related this to countervailing what otherwise is denial of local empowerment by bureaucratic directorates and also presciently argued 'organisation' and 'method' are key words:

Wherever we turn in considering the implications of a program for democracy these terms are inevitably involved. No democratic program can be unconcerned about the objectives of a course of action, especially as they affect popular welfare. But the crucial question for democracy is not what to strive for, but by what means to strive. And the question of means is one of what to do now and what to do next and these are basic questions in politics. If the problem of means is vital it is also the most readily forgotten. 'Results', 'achievement' and 'success' are heady words. [But] they induce submission and ... also enfeeble the intellect.

(Selznick 1949: 8)

Selznick then extended this case in terms which are highly relevant to a European Union that has enlarged its market without deepening economic and social cohesion and risks a centralised bureaucracy as a response to the Eurozone crisis that could further deny the autonomy of elected governments. As he put it:

Centralization has been proceeding apace in all fields of human organization. Efficiency has been, in this view, a rigorous leveller, erasing the diversity of individual enterprise and local control in the interests of large hierarchized units. This process operates not in government alone but in many other fields as well, and always brings with it like and ambiguous consequences. In exchange for the benefits of order and coordination, initiative has been stifled and the power of decision indispensable element of democratic action lodged in far-off places, remote from the beneficial influences of local areas which become merely the objects of bureaucratic manipulation.

(Selznick 1949: 22)

In the case of the European Union, new member states which formerly were part of the Soviet bloc and therefore lacked liberty are now not free to undertake any economic, social or political initiative for higher levels of social employment and welfare that has not been sanctioned as legitimate by an unelected European Commission and a Stability Treaty that 'compels' them to reduce debt, avoid deficits and increase austerity.

Postscript

If Weber was wrong in equating the rise of capitalism with a Protestant Ethic, he was right in warning that bureaucracy could defeat democracy. Although posing it as an 'ideal type' in the sense of an archetype, this was not in the sense that he idealised it. Rather, he deplored it. He recognised that its pyramidic power structure was oligarchic rather than democratic, impenetrable to its clients and 'soulless' in its denial of individualism, lamenting: 'specialists without vision, sensualists without heart; this nullity that imagines that it has attained a level of civilization never before achieved' (Weber 1930: 182).

Weber claimed that 'the big question' was what alternative could 'keep a proportion of mankind free from this parcelling out of the soul, from this supreme mastery of the bureaucratic way of life' (Weber 1957: 182). In this regard, he was addressing what had been identified as a tendency to an 'iron law of oligarchy' in organisations, or what Weber himself called the 'iron cages' within bureaucracy, concluding pessimistically that they would 'defeat democracy' with political parties becoming hierarchical in order to function effectively, while ministers came and went and bureaucracies stayed. This is being confirmed in Europe now, less within political parties than within the bureaucracies of the European Union. An answer to it was offered at the time of the Giscard draft Constitution for Europe, but rejected by him, by allowing that majority decisions could enable some member states to adopt policies that they wished without these binding others.

At an international level, this would avoid the concern of both Rousseau and Mill that minorities could be permanently disenfranchised. It has been replicated in the case of 'enhanced majority voting' in the EU proposals for a Financial Transactions Tax, where two member states, including the UK, declined to adopt it. This has not gained resonance with electorates in convincing them that this could merit their voting for governments which otherwise are condemned to submit to supranationalism.

The enabling principle also has relevance to whether or not there can be a framework for global governance. One of the failures of the Keynes plan for such governance was that it would be supranational and impose penalties on surplus trade nations by compelling them to revalue their currencies, which was rejected by the US at the Bretton Woods conference. If adopted by the G20 of heads of state and government following the 2008 financial crisis, which so far has been as ineffective as the G20 of finance ministers after the Asian financial crisis in failing even to anticipate the next, this could enable a framework for global cooperation. All have a vested interest in recycling surpluses, which, in the case of social investments and those to protect the environment, is to their mutual rather than only their competitive advantage in generating both trade and welfare, and on which some of them could act not only in agenda setting for others, but also to their own advantage.

Bibliography

Abulafia, D. (1977) *The Two Italies: Economic Relations between the Kingdom of Sicily and the Northern Commune*, Cambridge: Cambridge University Press.
Amato, G., and Verhofstadt, G. (2011) 'A Plan to Save the Euro, and Curb the Speculators', *The Financial Times*, International Edition, 4 July.
Ambrosius, B. (1977) *Die Durchsetzung der Sozialen Marktwirtschaft in Westdeutschland 1945–1949*, Stuttgart: Dt. Verl.-Anst.
Argyris, C., and Schön, D.A. (1996) *Organisational Learning II*, Reading, MA: Addison-Wesley.
Becker, W. (1980) 'Die Entscheidung für eine neue Wirtschaftsordnung nach 1945. Christliche Werte in der Sozialen Marktwirtschaft Ludwig Erhards', in Roth, R.A., and Seifert, W. (eds.) *Die zweite deutsche Demokratie. Ursprünge, Probleme, Perspektiven*, Köln, Wien: Böhlau.
Bion, W.R. (1963) *Elements of Psycho-Analysis*, London: Heinemann.
Bourdieu, P. (1977) *Outline of a Theory of Action*, Cambridge: Cambridge University Press.
Bourdieu, P. (1984) *Homo Academicus*, Paris: Editions de Minuit.
Bourdieu, P. (1990) *The Logic of Practice*, Cambridge: Polity Press.
Brzezinski, Z. (1970) *Between Two Ages: America's Role in the Technetronic Era*, New York: Viking Press.
Cook, R. (2003) *Point of Departure*, London and New York: Simon & Schuster.
Crowell, E. (2006) *Weber's 'Protestant Ethic' and his Critics*. MA Thesis: The University of Texas at Arlington.
Crozier, M., Huntington, S.P., and Watanuki, J. (1975) *The Crisis of Democracy*, Report on the Governability of Democracies to the Trilateral Commission, New York: New York University Press.
Dinnerstein, D. (1978). *The Rocking of the Cradle and the Ruling of the World.* London: Souvenir Press.
Esping-Andersen, G., and Regini, M. (eds.) (2000) *Why Deregulate Labour Markets?* Oxford: Oxford University Press.
ETUC (2011) *Mobilising for Social Europe*, Athens: European Trade Union Confederation, 19 May.
EU (2012) *Treaty on Stability, Coordination and Governance*, Brussels, March.
Fanfani, A. (2009) *Catholicism, Protestantism, and Capitalism*, Rome: IHS Press.
Fischer, J. (2012) 'Fischer schlägt Alarm', *Süddeutsche Zeitung*, 4 June.
Freud, S. (1900) 'The Interpretation of Dreams', in *The Complete Psychological Works of Sigmund Freud*, London: Hogarth Press; New York: Basic Books.
Freud, S. (1912) 'The Dynamics of Transference', in *Collected Papers*, vol. II, London: Hogarth Press; New York: Basic Books.
Freud, S. (1915) 'The Unconscious', in *The Complete Psychological Works of Sigmund Freud*, London: Hogarth Press; New York: Basic Books.

Friedman, M. (1970) 'The Social Responsibility of the Firm is to Increase its Profits', *The New York Times Magazine*, 13 September.
Friedman, M. (1980) *Free to Choose*, New York: Harcourt Brace Jovanovitch.
GCEE (2011) German Federal Council of Economic Advisers, 9 November, Available: www.sachverstaendigenrat-wirtschaft.de/aktuellesjahrsgutachten.html.
Guérot, U. (2012) 'Reinventing Europe: Germany Debates Political Union', *European Foreign Policy Scorecard*, 5 September, Available: www.ecfr.eu/content/entry/commentary_the_euro_debate_in_germany_towards_political_union.
Harris, K. (1982) *Attlee*, London: Weidenfeld and Nicolson.
Hayek, F. von. (1944) *The Road to Serfdom*, Routledge, New York.
Hayek, F. von. (1950) 'Full Employment, Planning, and Inflation', in *Studies in Philosophy, Politics, and Economics*, Chicago: University of Chicago Press.
Hayek, F. von. (1976) *Law, Legislation, and Liberty: The Mirage of Social Justice*, Chicago: University of Chicago Press.
Holland, S. (1980) *UnCommon Market: Capital, Class and Power in the European Community*, Basingstoke: Macmillan.
Holland, S. (1993) *The European Imperative: Economic and Social Cohesion in the 1990s*, Nottingham: Spokesman.
Holland, S. (2003) *How to Decide on Europe – The Proposal of an Enabling Majority Voting Procedure for the European Constitution*, Available: www4.fe.uc.pt/ceue.
Holland, S. (2010) 'Financial Crises, Governance and Cohesion: Will Governments Ever Learn Up?', in Richardson, J. (ed.) *From Recession to Renewal: The Impact of Financial Crises on Public Services*, Bristol: Policy Press.
Howell, D.R., Baker, D., Glyn, A., and Schmitt, J. (2007) 'Are Protective Labour Market Institutions at the Root of Unemployment? A Critical View of the Evidence', *Capitalism and Society*, vol. 2, no. 1, pp. 1–71.
Hutton, W. (2002) *The World We're In*, London: Abacus.
Hutton, W. (2008) *The Writing on the Wall: China and the West in the 21st Century*, London: Abacus.
Jastrow, J. (1899) 'The Mind's Eye', *Popular Science Monthly*, vol. 54, pp. 299–312.
Kelly, J. (2005) 'Industrial Relations Approaches to the Employment Relationship' in Coyle, J., Shapiro, A-M., Shore, L.M., Taylor, S., and Tetrick, L.E. (eds.) *The Employment Relationship*, Oxford: Oxford University Press.
Keynes, J.M. (1919) *The Economic Consequences of the Peace*, London: Macmillan.
Keynes, J.M. (1936) *The General Theory of Money, Interest and Employment*, London: Macmillan.
Klein, M. (1932) *The Psycho-analysis of Children*, London: Hogarth Press.
Klein, M. (1952) *Developments in Psychoanalysis*, London: Hogarth.
Lindbeck, A., and Snower, D.J. (1988) *The Insider-Outsider Theory of Employment and Unemployment*, Cambridge, MA: MIT.
Lowney, C. (2003) *Heroic Leadership: Best Practice from a 450-Year-Old Company That Changed the World*, Chicago: Loyala Press.
Manchin, R. (2005) *After the Referenda*, Brussels: Gallup Europe (29 June).
Mill, John Stuart ([1861] 1993), *Considerations on Representative Government*, Chapter 7 *Of True and False Democracy; Representation of All and Representation of the Majority Only*, London: Dent-Orion.
Münchau, W. (2010) 'No Happy New Year for the Eurozone', *The Financial Times*, 9 January.

Münchau, W., and Atkins, R. (2004) 'Working Longer to Save Jobs: But Will It Help Europe Close the Productivity Gap?', *Financial Times*, 23 July.

Nietzsche, F. (1887) *The Genealogy of Morals*, translated by Golffing, Francis (1956), New York: Anchor Books.

Oliveira, T.C., and Holland S. (2012) 'On the Centrality of Human Value', *Journal of Economic Methodology*, vol. 19, no. 2, pp. 121–141.

Richards, B. (1989) *Images of Freud: Cultural Responses to Psychoanalysis*, London: Dent.

Rifkin, J. (2004) *The European Dream*, New York: Tarcher/Penguin.

Robertson, H.M. (1933) *Aspects of the Rise of Economic Individualism: A Criticism of Max Weber and his School*, Cambridge: Cambridge University Press.

Rosenfeld, H. (1950) 'Note on the Psychopathology of Confusional States in Chronic Schizophrenia', *International Journal of Psychoanalysis*, vol. 31, pp. 132–137.

Rousseau, J-J. (1762) *Du Contrat Social*, Paris: Garnier, 1960.

Schneider, M. (1975) *Neurosis and Civilization*, New York: Seabury Press.

Schopenhauer, A. (1818) *The World as Will and Representation*, 1st English translation (1883), London: Routledge and Kegan Paul.

Segal, H. (1950) 'Some Aspects of the Analysis of a Schizophrenic', *The International Journal of Psychoanalysis*, vol. 31, pp. 268–278.

Selznick, P. (1949) *The TVA and the Grass Roots*, Berkeley: University of California Press.

Sinn, H-W. (2003) 'The Laggard of Europe', *CES Ifo Forum*, Münich, no. 4, special issue 1.

Sklair, L. (2001) *The Transnational Capitalist Class*, Oxford: Blackwell.

Spaak (1956) *Report from the Delegation Heads to the Ministers of Foreign Affairs*, Brussels: Secretariat of the Intergovernmental Committee Created by the Messina Conference.

Spiegel (2011) 'Die Gezeichneten', 11 September.

Tawney, R.H. (1920) *The Acquisitive Society*, New York: Harcourt, Brace and Howe.

Tawney, R.H. (1926) *Religion and the Rise of Capitalism*, New York: Harcourt, Brace.

The Telegraph (2012) 'Standard & Poor's Cuts Ratings of Nine Eurozone Countries', 13 January.

Varoufakis, Y., and Holland, S. (2010). 'The Modest Proposal for Resolving the Eurozone Crisis', Available: http://yanisvaroufakis.eu/euro-crisis/modest-proposal/.

Varoufakis, Y., and Holland S. (2011) *A Modest Proposal for Overcoming the Eurozone Crisis*, Levy Economics Institute of Bard College, Policy Note 2011/3.

Viner, J. (1978) *Religious Thought and Economic Society*, Durham: Duke University Press.

Weber, M. (1905) *The Protestant Ethic and the Spirit of Capitalism*, republished in *The Protestant Ethic and Other Writings*, New York: Penguin, 2002.

Weber, M. (1930) 'The Theory of Social and Economic Organisation', in Parons, Talcott (ed.) *Wirtschaft und Germeinschaft*, London: William Hodge.

Weber, M. (1957) 'Some Consequences of Bureaucratization', in Coser, L., and Rosenberg, B. (eds.) *Sociological Theory*, New York: Macmillan.

Wittgenstein, L. (1953) *Philosophical Investigations*, Oxford: Blackwell.

13 Freedom, citizenship, culture and the changing role of the intellectual class
A European perspective

Steve Austen

Now that the Treaty of Lisbon, effective from December 2009, has come into force, a legal framework has been introduced that has unmistakably changed the relations between the member states and the European Union in favour of a transnational definition of citizenship. The Dutch parliament anticipated this move in 2008 by referring to the EU as a union of member states and citizens (Parliamentary Proceedings 2008–2009). Although this introduced dual citizenship, the instruments for promoting (European) citizenship have not been adapted to this new situation in any of the member states. The question of the role that the intellectual class can play in growing international public space has to be analysed.

It is some time since the European Union could be seen as a purely economic treaty community. The European market for commodities and services is a fact. The European Commission supervises compliance with the rules of play. The governments of the 28 member states, united in the European Council, provide the Union with an increasing number of tasks that are defined, published and implemented after approval by the European Parliament and in many cases after approval by the national parliaments too. This enables a continual improvement of the working of the European market and makes it more accessible to all markets and interested parties, including the European citizens and their informal and formal civic initiatives.

The role of the intellectual opinion leaders is undergoing a substantial change. Anyone who follows the quality international press repeatedly comes across the complaint by a famous writer, philosopher or academic that in Europe there is no intellectual community of opinion-makers to be found any more like the one that was so decisive for the post-war social debate. People then point out that, at least until recently, there was an apparent consensus on the ideal of edification that gave the cultural élite the moral authority to do everything that was in the interest of that ideal. So it is hardly surprising that, during the post-war years of reconstruction, in spite of the considerable and irreconcilable religious and ideological differences between the various ranks, classes and religious or ideological groups, there was virtually unanimous majority support for the largest and most important of the political projects: the banishment of war and the striving for peace for all the nations of the Western European continent.

For a long time, little was needed to be able to count on the implicit approval of the population of those countries. The common enemy behind the Iron Curtain made the energetic international policy of the respective governments necessary and unquestioned. Besides, the steady rise in the standard of living, a spin-off of the German economic miracle, favoured the idea of a more European orientation. The fact that the large-scale US financial development aid known as the Marshall Plan had created the conditions for that prosperity disappeared relatively quickly from the collective memory.[1] This was perfectly understandable for the residents of a continent who wanted to boost their self-awareness and belief in their own strength along with their regained freedom as soon as possible.

'The Netherlands can have its say again.' That is how the national pride in my native country could be summed up. Variations on this slogan could be found in every country of the 'free West'. As a result, the construction of national identity received an enormous boost. Dutch identity, for instance, certainly as it was to be propagated abroad, could not consist of anything other than tolerance, freedom of thought, forbearance and internationalism. For understandable reasons, the quality press and thus the opinion-makers were unaware that this package of national virtues was based more on the wishful thinking of the administrative and intellectual élites than on everyday reality. So ideal types of Dutch character and national virtues came in handy, all the more so because the very recent history had not given much cause for cheerfulness: it is simply hard to imagine how a people that until 1940 had been primarily interested in themselves and their mercantile activities were suddenly, five years later, to undergo a massive spiritual development that would change each and every one of those citizens into independent-thinking cosmopolitans. By now it is clear that the moral uniqueness and superiority of the Netherlands that was propagated for years by the official government bodies and others was above all a marketing concept (Austen 2004).

One of the rules of marketing is that such concepts are only successful as long as consumers believe them, and the product or service that is marketed does not differ too much from the 'brand'. This involves the implicit assumption that, probably all over the Western world, the role of the cultural and intellectual élite was considerably less effective than the protagonists themselves supposed. So what about the ideal of edification or what is left of it? After all, this is based on the assumption that the transfer of knowledge can raise society as a whole to a higher level. That presupposes an informed class that is willing and able to transfer that knowledge to others who are not yet in possession of it. Unlike what many people think, I suspect that the sharing of knowledge is in a pretty healthy state in the modern liberal democracies of Europe, at any rate appreciably better than in the years of the Cold War. The fall of the Berlin Wall has created scope for pluriformity not only in the former Socialist arena but also in the former West. It is obvious by now that offering scope for pluriformity can also have unwelcome side-effects, but I see that as part of the deal. How that is to be dealt with is an almost permanent object of debate among politicians, figures in authority, parents and teachers, social institutions and the public.

The enormous number of solid contributions to the opinion pages of the major European papers concerning individual freedom, sovereignty and identity is ample proof that the intellectual and administrative élite welcomes the opportunity to take an intensive part in the social debate. Its members do so no longer as representatives of some nomenclature, whether self-appointed or not, but as individuals, as active and responsible citizens. For some this is not enough and they publish essays, collections of articles or pamphlets, under their own imprint or that of a publisher, which are then discussed in various old and new media. However that may be, all those different insights, opinions and analyses appear on the internet and are commented on there by anyone who wants to do so. Talk programmes and discussion evenings follow, often leading to renewed interest, so that the cycle starts anew.

The vertical communication that determined the relations in the social debate to a large extent before the arrival of the internet has gone. The era of paternalism, including its enlightened form, is over, although it must be mentioned that in some of the new member states of the EU frenetic attempts are being made to return to pre-democratic forms of government interference. No matter how threatening this may be for the development of a flourishing civil society, it will presently become clear that this is a rear-guard action. Moral authority no longer belongs as a matter of course to a privileged élite, although it is by no means clear how authority is to be handled nowadays. It seems that generally applicable frameworks can no longer be taken for granted, that citizens themselves want to decide whether to conform to certain insights or forms of behaviour.

This by no means implies that the transfer of knowledge is a thing of the past. On the contrary, if you want, you can find all kinds of things that can adjust insights in the field of society, politics or ideology. A genuine proliferation of courses, study trips, lectures and information networks is the result. The participants are curious and are prepared to pay in order to obtain more insight. All the same, there is another, striking aspect of the disappearance of the chain of edification. The disappearance of gatherings of figures in authority who could command confidence, opinion-makers and religious and political authorities causes concern among the many who, for whatever reason, do not or cannot share in the individual quest for the enrichment of knowledge. It causes concern and a feeling of impotence and injustice among the many who like the world to be easy to grasp. This explains the rise of successful and unsuccessful rat-catchers. Alarmed citizens often long for reassuring concepts; the more familiar and recognisable a concept is, the more support its provider enjoys.

For the time being, it is irrelevant that these are often romanticised models from the past. As long as the desire of the insecure citizen is satisfied with fairy-tales whose happy ending is already known, support for the reintroduction of the old and trusted currency, the prohibition of dual citizenship or ending European cooperation will not decline in the near future.

To start with the last point: until recently, Europe was one of those typical élite projects, from the very first the result of a political paternalism that was dominant at the time. That did not make it any less visionary or revolutionary.

Certainly in political terms, it was evidence of a rather unusual international solidarity, however much that was based on Catholic ethical principles and harked back to idealised images of Europe under Charlemagne. It is to the credit of the French politician Robert Schuman that, partly thanks to his Franco-German background, he made the political spirit in both countries ripe for a Europe of the *Völker*, that is, citizens, as we would say today (Schuman 2010). The fact that the citizens themselves had no say in the matter was part of everyday political reality.

The predecessor of the present European Union, the European Coal and Steel Community, was a supranational organ, a High Authority. It was a body that exercised certain powers that were binding on the member states. This made it possible to achieve results and to bring objectives closer than the individual states would have been able to achieve on their own. The transfer of authority, which is regularly a subject of public concern in various European countries, is a part of meeting one's international obligations. The word 'obligations' says it all.

Strangely enough, the embedding of a country in an international system of reciprocal rights and obligations means a reinforcement of national sovereignty because that is now constantly scrutinised by all of the partners to the treaty and can be expressed on the basis of agreements made by all the parties. Seen in this light, the European Union is not a threat to the nation state, but a reinforcement of it.

In everyday life, modern citizens surrender their sovereignty on numerous occasions in order to maintain their identity better. Whether it is a matter of buying a ticket for the train, taking part in a marathon or going to the theatre, citizens part with some of their sovereignty in order to make use of the space that they share with other citizens who have made the same agreement with the transport company, the sports organiser or the entertainment provider. In short, sovereignty only gains significance in an interactive context in which common agreements, made on the basis of individual interests, determine the transfer of competences that make advantages accessible which would otherwise not be accessible. A citizen who is not prepared to surrender sovereignty is a purely theoretical phenomenon. Even somebody who has never made use of public transport will have to go outside and move in the traffic, which entails giving up sovereignty, otherwise this independent sovereign individual will soon be dead and buried.

All the same, the question of sovereignty remains a source of concern and confusion, and the opinion pages in the quality press are no exception. A good many writers assume that the political unification of Europe means by definition that this will lead to the United States of Europe, even though we know that a form of state of that kind could only be created if 28 governments were to sign the treaty. There is no need to have any illusions about the approval of such a proposal; it would have collapsed even before the voting took place. There is probably not a single member state that sees a federal Europe as a realistic option. So why are there the constant warnings and arguments for or against such a thing as a United States of Europe? Apparently supporters and opponents of this model cannot see any other possible outcome for the political process in which Europe is involved at the moment. In the opinion of these commentators, there are only two conceivable and mutually exclusive forms of state: the nation state (which can also have a federal character, such as the Federal Republic of Germany, Switzerland and Belgium) and the federal state.

It does not help, of course, if prominent members of the European Parliament call for the rapid transformation of the Union into a federation. Guy Verhofstadt and Daniel Cohn-Bendit are impatient and imagine that they are giving a positive impulse to the debate by seeing a political federation as the remedy for all ills in their latest book (Cohn-Bendit and Verhofstadt 2012). What neither of them wants to consider – and many of their supporters and critics are in agreement with them on this – is that the European Union may develop further as a political entity, but not at all in the direction of a federal state. The Union is already something entirely new that does not exist anywhere else in the world, and should be regarded as a work in progress to which all stakeholders contribute. The familiar forms of state such as the nation state, the federal state, the confederation and the political federation were once inventions too as the result of considerations of political power that prevailed at one time. However, in the case of these forms which were once innovative, it is true that, apart from a few exceptions, the population of these states had a negligible say, if they had any at all. That has changed. The decisions on the future of Europe are taken by democratically elected governments that require the approval of their democratically elected parliaments and the approval of the directly elected European Parliament.

The likelihood that 'old' forms will be chosen is thus so small that it can be discounted. Moreover, there is an important and striking facet to the process of political unification of Europe: it is taking place in complete openness. Every consultation is followed step-by-step by the media and released for immediate public discussion. Without the free press and the internet, the process of European unification would be considerably frustrated. As a result, more people than ever before in European history are sharing in thinking about their and our future. There is an enormous reservoir of mental resources and critical knowledge available that finds its way to the politicians and policy organs.

In an era in which innovation has risen to such prominence in every sphere of social life, should the formation of the state suddenly lag behind? The facts point in a different direction. The development that the EU has undergone since the setting up of the European Coal and Steel Community can already easily be compared with the successful social and industrial revolutions. We can state that the Union does not resemble any other existing form of state. It is not a nation state, it is not a federation or a confederation, it is something completely new that cannot be found anywhere else in the world. In the words of Van Rompuy, it is 'something original, something unique, and should be regarded as the largest area of democracy, freedom, prosperity and social justice in the world'.[2] It is a developing political entity that differs not only from familiar forms of the state, but also from familiar international organisations, be they supranational, intergovernmental or multilateral. The unique and specific character of the EU is expressed in the application of the concept of the democratic constitutional state to an international organisation, thereby providing a framework for the extension of the European citizenship that is known to all citizens. The framework of the democratic constitutional state they have been familiar with for a long time, or have been gradually getting to know since the fall of the Wall and joining the EU, now applies to the territory of the Union as a whole and is guaranteed by the Treaty of Lisbon.

As formulated in the Schuman plan (1950):

> Thousands of years ago in primitive tribes, the first human communities were formed beyond the family bond while based on it. Later villages were added and the city became more and more developed. Nobody claims that such an evolution runs against the role of the family. In the same way every supranational organisation that extends beyond the nation does not diminish or absorb it but confers on it a broader and higher field of action.
>
> (Schuman 2010)

So here we have a common framework that improves the functioning of the nation states, the member states of the Union. Without the Union, the member states separately would be in a worse position. The Union is a sort of insurance policy, a kind of extra security. The Union does not replace the member states, but strengthens and improves their survival as autonomous states. It is the added value that enables the member states to maintain and reinforce their economic, political and social sovereignty better in the escalating violence of globalisation. This however does not diminish the search for a national cultural identity.

European unification strengthens the demand for national cultural identity. Through the process of homogenisation of national policies in practically all domains of daily life, the only policy that remains in the hands of the member state is that of culture, as agreed to by the Treaty of Maastricht. In this way, the policy on culture offers the member states an excellent opportunity to distinguish themselves from other member states. All over Europe, policy on culture bore the marks of the nation state's need for representation that had been customary ever since the emergence of the nation state as such.

More and more member states came to regard domestic policy on culture as national policy. Culture, after all, was by now becoming the only way in which the member states could profile themselves. International cultural cooperation was increasingly confined to forms of national presentation outside the national borders.

It is this tendency that eventually turns against European unification, especially if this is to be understood as a cultural process. However, the Treaty of Maastricht does offer possibilities for Europe to come into action alongside the inviolable art and cultural policy of the member states. Section 4 of article 128 of the Treaty instructs the Commission to take account of the cultural component in every one of its measures to guarantee the cultural diversity of Europe.

This instruction, however, has never been seriously implemented. There is no instrument to monitor it, and the willingness of the member states to translate this section into serious content is so small as to be negligible, satisfied as they are with the possibility of being able to manifest themselves all over Europe as they choose through their national cultural policy. But there is more to it than that. As Angela Merkel does not fail to emphasise, economic cooperation has to be followed by political cooperation. That is neither a new idea, nor the particular vision of the Federal Chancellor; it is the consequence of the Treaty of Maastricht that has gone down in history as a major benchmark for ongoing political and economic cooperation in Europe. Maastricht witnessed not only the setting up of the European Union, but also the inclusion of the notion of the European citizen in the treaty.

As Hoeksma (2011) convincingly argues, with the approval of the Treaty of Lisbon, the political context in Europe has become clear and unambiguous in terms of the law of nations and the philosophy of law. Hoeksma speaks of a dual democracy. This has consequences for citizenship in the Union: a citizen of a member state has all the rights and obligations of national citizenship, but has in addition a unique relation of citizenship with the Union, which neither replaces nor infringes on that national citizenship. This national citizenship was for a long time accompanied by a national cultural component. The embedding of cultural policy in the process of fabricating a national cultural identity ensures that the relation between the state and its citizens acquires a (cultural) added value, which in turn did justify the spending of considerable sums of taxpayers' money on the arts.

This symbiosis is now in danger of coming to an end. The nation state is no longer the only supplier of possibilities of identification for the citizen. Rights, obligations and services are becoming increasingly valid and applicable in all the member states of the Union, and that includes citizens of the other 27 member states. This calls into question the role of artistic and intellectual activities as the provider of opportunities to identify with the nation and its culture. The fact that the latest austerity measures have been introduced to the national culture budget in many member states without much opposition from their citizens seems to indicate that by now the traditional bond between state, art institutions and public has been considerably diluted. Not only the relation with politics calls for revaluation, but the relation with civil society calls for serious attention too. All the same, I do not think we should be trying to return to the relations of the twentieth century.

The introduction of European citizenship makes clear that it is not threatening the respective domains of national cultural activities or forms of expression, on the contrary. I would like to call this citizenship dual citizenship of the European Union. It is not to be confused with dual citizenship of two nations, which enables a person to be a citizen of two different countries, with rights and obligations that are separate and independent of one another. That is not the case of dual citizenship of the Union: a Dutch citizen is at the same time a citizen of the Union, by which the rights and obligations of all the 28 member states of the Union apply in conformity with the provisions of the Treaty of Lisbon.

The significance of this European citizenship can hardly be overestimated. While the raison d'être of the Union in its initial years lay mainly in the prevention of war and the promotion of peace on the European continent, with the dying out of the last eye-witnesses to the madness of the Second World War, the anchoring of the peace objective of the EU has disappeared from collective memory, or at least ceased to be an overriding perspective for young Europeans. If you were born in peacetime, you do not miss the war.

Of course, considerable attention must be paid in the respective programmes for citizen education in all the member states to the political and intellectual genesis of Europe, if only to contrast the sometimes rather cumbersome and laborious path of the democratic decision-making process with the period before the war when there were no such intergovernmental and supranational democratic processes. An additional factor is that those member states who until 1990 were members of a different Union, the Union of Socialist Soviet Republics, had no experience at all with parliamentary democracy or had an idealised picture of life in the prosperous states of the West. The public space in the West, however, has undergone enormous changes since the collapse of the Soviet Union and the emergence of the European Union. The cultural component of European citizenship has to be defined.

The traditional national art institutions, the intellectual class as well as opinion leaders throughout Europe are confronted with a process in which the classical role that was a shared assumption in Europe from the Restoration on, namely to be connected in one way or another with the nation state's need for representation, is rapidly declining in significance. As providers of meanings, value orientations, and historical and social contexts, their role lies precisely in the performing of an intermediary role between different citizens and between civil society and the political class. Art institutions are by their very nature natural meeting places for gaining depth and orientation with respect to the principles of the value community that forms the basis of a democratic Europe. New alliances are necessary if that potential is to be exploited to the full.

Whether the term 'cultural citizenship' helps us any further is highly questionable. The term originated in the United States. The publications on the subject prove to be mainly concerned with so-called group rights, particularly the cultural rights of minorities. They have been articulated by bringing them together under the label of cultural citizenship.

Through the introduction of this concept, various conceptions of citizenship inevitably come into collision with one another.

The traditionalists point out that citizenship is an individual matter. After all, it is a question of a personal relation between the citizen and the state, a relation that is anchored in the constitution, which guarantees everyone's equality before the law. According to this view, the state ensures that civil rights in relations between citizens and between citizens and the state are guaranteed by setting up independent institutions that monitor compliance with the constitution.

The protagonists of cultural citizenship consider that collective rights must be recognised, such as for ethnic groups, but also for women, trans-genders, etc.

The influence of the latter concept on government policy in Europe has been and still is substantial. The notion of the multicultural society is grounded in sociological studies that take the group rights mentioned above, based on group identity, as their starting point. Although a vigorous debate has been conducted on the multicultural society, a fundamental, broad discussion of the concept of citizenship is not yet in sight.

It seems to me that introducing special cases of the notion of citizenship such as 'cultural citizenship' or 'new cultural citizenship' does not further the debate on citizenship. After all, we cannot rule out the possibility that those who devise these terms are arguing for special rights for certain groups of citizens, rights that other citizens will be denied. Moreover, it might mean that groups that fall under such definitions ought to accept different responsibilities for the public space, the general interest, the functioning of civil society and the democratic constitutional state. This is all part of the implicit suggestion that group identities, in so far as they exist, must lead to legislation per category, which erodes the principle that all citizens are equal before the law.

By now the question is no longer that of whether citizens are prepared to assume a share of the responsibility for how the public domain is organised, but rather: how can it be organised in such a way that political decision-making processes can be stimulated by it? Is there still a role for national cultural institutions, artists and intellectuals here, and if so, how is it to be understood?

The European Union resolutely breaks with a political practice in which the relations between the European states were determined by geopolitical and power relations. In their place, a network of fine-meshed interdependences is emerging, much too quickly for some, in every sphere of social life. The innovative aspect of this reality is that not only the governments but also the world of industry and commerce and the citizens are increasingly linked with one another in a transnational way, which inevitably and increasingly leads to a complex of shared responsibilities.

In an ever increasing mesh of national, regional and urban interdependencies in Europe, the early medieval citizen seems to be a good starting point for thinking about the meaning of European citizenship. The concept of citizen harks back to the Latin *civis*, a member of the *civitas*, a political community that is not necessarily tied to a particular territory.

Citizenship as it will gradually have to take shape in the EU will lead to a complex discussion that makes it difficult to make hasty decisions. That immediately explains the attraction of the European concept: how the future is shaped is partly up to us. This process makes the greatest demands on the cultural competencies of the Europeans. For many the idea of a dual citizenship is completely new and that is one of the reasons why it is vigorously rejected by large groups of voters in almost every member state. Nevertheless, these defensive phenomena are part of an inevitable cultural process that marks the transition from exclusively national to more European solutions. The success of this development can be illustrated by the most evident result of the European integration: the growing arena of peaceful relations between the member states.

For the first time in its history, the Von Clausewitz doctrine has had a serious consequence in the international political relations within the EU (Von Clausewitz 1832). War is no longer 'the continuation of politics by other means', but the internationalisation of the democratic forms governing mutual relations between states has bestowed new and promising possibilities on diplomacy.

War has not yet been completely banned, but it is no longer an option in the eyes of the governments and peoples of Europe. This innovation in politics and diplomacy, for the time being, only applies on EU territory. The EU treaty is by no means a military agreement, unlike NATO, nor is the EU based on reciprocal peace treaties between the member states. The absence of military conflicts in the Europe of the EU since 1946 is a historical novelty. Seen from this perspective, the award of the Nobel Peace Prize to the EU is not unimportant. On the contrary, it is quite possible that there will be no armed conflicts in Europe during the next 65 years, simply because politics itself has proven to be capable of transcending the borders of national politics without giving up the sovereignty of the nation state. The sovereignty of the nation states who are members of the European Union is strengthened by their membership, on condition that the respective member states satisfy elementary criteria of the democratic constitutional state. It is precisely through the incorporation of these principles in the provisions of the EU treaty that measures threatening the freedom of the press, religious and political opinions can be countered through the instruments available to the European Commission. Seen in this light, the participation of the democratic member states in a European space that guarantees civic liberties is an additional guarantee for the early pinpointing and detonation of political activities that are directed against the freedom of the individual and might thus end up by disturbing the peaceful coexistence of the member states of the Union.

For some member states, the prospect of a flourishing and thus uncontrollable civil society is an unwelcome idea. The notion that a democracy can be organised, run and further developed without consulting the citizens is still prevalent, especially in the new member states of the Union. In some cases, a parliamentary majority is used to curb civil rights 'democratically' – for example, by introducing legislation that limits freedom of expression, freedom of meeting or association, or the pluriformity of the press. However, they increasingly find the European Commission on their trail. By signing the Treaty of Lisbon, the member states have accepted the transfer of national sovereignty to the prerogatives of Brussels, such as the authority to maintain the democratic European value community as it is protected by the Treaty of Lisbon.

A relatively new phenomenon is that recent regulations, such as the joint measures taken in Brussels, directly affect the lives of all individual citizens in Europe. This is why some people appeal to their national governments with regard to effects that they feel to be detrimental. In reaction to this, in some cases we see governments bending over backwards to curry favour with the citizens – it may be for electoral reasons, for example – by suggesting that they regret the measures emanating from Brussels as well. There is an interesting tension in cases of this kind between citizens who call upon their government to correct measures dictated by Brussels, on the one hand, and citizens who appeal to Brussels to try to prevent their government from adopting measures that would curb civil rights, on the other. In such cases, in spite of the alleged scepticism about Europe, it is increasingly common for the citizens not to take everything that the national government considers to be in the national interest lying down. They know, after all, that they have the backing of the citizenship of the EU that has been laid down in the treaty regulations and accepted by their own government. It is thus logical for the public space in Europe to be increasingly full of initiatives from young European citizens who point to the value community that must form the core of every society at local, regional, national or international level.

The presence of anti-democratic currents is a part of an Open Society that is constantly developing. However, it is virtually impossible any more to keep movements by individuals and organisations, governments or interest groups who are opposed to the system of law out of the public eye. Individual contraventions of civic rights by state organs are immediately highlighted and, often via the internet, presented to the international community of citizens.

Many politicians and institutions have to get used to the idea that honest government has to be accompanied by a maximum of transparency. As a result, trivial argumentation or personal motives can be recognised at a very early stage, abuses can be combatted, and political corruption and conflict of interests become increasingly difficult. The EU can thus be seen to have added a chapter to the Von Clausewitz doctrine that could be called: the EU is the continuation of peace by other means. After all, the EU functions as a platform and supervisory body, so that an opportunity can be given to all 500 million citizens to give expression to the experience of individual liberty within an increasingly clear political and juridical framework. No other continent offers this in such a generous, clear and pioneering way as the territory of the European Union.

Seen in this light, after centuries of armed conflict, Europe has achieved a new state of existence for which the word 'peace' is inadequate. Certainly, in the early years of European cooperation the avoidance of war was the leading principle. As a result of this, that cooperation was in the first interest focused on the economic front. Whoever manages to subject the largest industrial conglomerates of France and Germany to the rules of a High Authority to be jointly established by them has replaced individual interest by shared interest. It is easy to understand that the shared interest makes it considerably more difficult to enter into hostilities, as long as it is backed up by the respective parliaments.

While at first it was logical for governments to consult with one another on harmonisation and decision-making, today citizens are demanding a say. The absence of the threat of war in the territory of the EU enabled steady work to continue on strengthening the community values to guarantee the strength and continuity of the Union. Paradoxically enough, it is precisely the Union that has enabled the transition from a community of nation states bound by a treaty to a system of guarantees for democratic values in all of the member states. The Union has made it possible for all citizens in the EU to voice their approval or disapproval of the further stages of the political development of Europe.

The governments of the member nation states not only increasingly realise that their voting behaviour in the European Council requires the approval of the national parliaments, but they also feel the need to take into account the voting behaviour in the directly elected European Parliament. Finally, in so far as the domestic policy of national governments deviates too much from what has been agreed in Brussels or in the Treaty of Lisbon, they will have to fear the corrective measures of the European Commission, the European Court of Justice or the European Court of Human Rights. Anyone who is properly aware of this will be able to see that the democratic content of the EU is not at all in a bad way, especially by comparison with the situation in some of the member states. Anyone, including the heads of state, who accuses the EU of not being democratic enough will thus have to realise that it is not uncommon for those who voice such criticisms to bear some responsibility for the democratic content that is the butt of their criticisms.

A recent example of this is the speech by David Cameron, the prime minister of the United Kingdom (Cameron 2013). At first sight, Cameron's criticism of the Union for lacking democratic principles seems strong. When it comes to the possibility of citizens electing or dismissing their own European government, the Union (still) has its weak spots. This, however, is not in the last instance due to the fact that Cameron's government and the preceding British governments have cherished the ideal of limiting the significance of the European Union to that of a free trade zone.

It is well known that free trade zones are by nature undemocratic. If Cameron is so concerned with the democratic principles of the EU, even if it were to be limited to his ideal of a community of states based on a treaty, he will be forced to recognise that there is no international trading union that functions as democratically as the EU at present (Hoeksma 2013). These and similar, in a certain sense, incongruous positions adopted by government leaders and politicians, local authorities and members of the prevailing administrative élite are no exception in the present discourse.

Members of the Dutch government and parliament also have no difficulty, no sooner than they have returned from Brussels, in using the national broadcasting channels to contradict or criticise the agreements that have been made there. Of course, this attitude undermines the further inevitable extension of the European Union and above all acceptance of the unification process by the citizens. Realisation that the Union offers additional guarantees, besides citizenship in the nation state for all who have a European residence permit, is not yet given enough emphasis in the national citizenship programmes. All the same, there are great opportunities for giving the experience of European citizenship a new and appealing content. The value of the European dimension will now have to be added to the respective citizenship programmes of the member states designed to provide information about the origins of the nation state and the democratic national institutions.

The idea that the Union will, to a greater or lesser extent, replace one's own nation state can be vigorously combatted. After all, they are both complementary. While originally it was enough to convince participants in citizenship education programmes of the necessity of the EU by referring to the absence of war, which was indeed the primary objective of the European Coal and Steel Community, the notion of freedom – which was still too closely associated with freedom from occupation and dictatorship – can be given a new content. That will also enable us to put an end to the complaints about the absence of a single European people, a European 'national' anthem, a shared European feeling, a European identity, and so on (Critchley 2013). These aspects of belonging are already there, particularly at the level of the nation states and the regions.

Although these notions are not always based on observable reality and are certainly not the result of democratic decision-making – quite the contrary – these ideas and rituals are desirable and necessary to contribute to the definition of the notion of freedom that is created precisely by the additional guarantees that European citizenship offers the citizen. Freedom in Europe means that every one of the 500 million citizens knows that they are linked with all the other Europeans, that they can develop their own personality as they choose without the interference of any political or social force, that they have freedom of movement in the widest sense of the word within the territory of the Union, and that outside it they can count on the protection of the national and European organs.

This individual freedom for European citizens has its limits, as applies to every activity that forms part of a treaty-based community. Investigating the possibilities that individual freedom within the public space of Europe offers has only just begun. It is to be hoped that the mantra of no war, peace and security can slowly but surely be replaced by a new content for the notion of peace that is now related more than ever to the experience of citizenship in a community that shares European values. Whenever it is a question of giving form to entirely new concepts, especially when the governments and citizens of 28 democratic member states must take part, it will call for a continuous process of trial and error and harmonisation. Perhaps the best comparison is with the procession to Echternach,[3] in which the pilgrims are obliged to take three steps forwards and two steps backwards – a good exercise in European progress. The intellectual and artistic contributions of young Europeans that are emerging everywhere are sufficient grounds for optimism.[4]

Notes

1 The European Recovery Programme (ERP), unofficially named after George Marshall, provided 16 European nations with administrative and technical assistance up to US$13 billion from 1948 to 1952.
2 Intervention by Herman Van Rompuy, President of the European Council, at the ceremony on the occasion of the entry into force of the Lisbon Treaty, Lisbon, 1 December 2009.
3 The hopping procession of Echternach (Luxembourg), inscribed in 2010 on the Representative List of the Intangible Cultural Heritage of Humanity.
4 To mention a few: the Dutch polemical writer Willem Schinkel, the Flemish-Polish

philosopher Alicia Gescinska, the Czech economist Tomas Sedlacek and the Dutch philosopher and newspaper editor Rob Wijnberg.

Bibliography

Austen, Steve (2004) *De Europese Culturele Ambitie*, December, The Hague: SMO.
Cameron, D. (2013) *Britain and Europe*, Speech delivered in London, 23 January.
Cohn-Bendit, D., and Verhofstadt, G. (2012) *For Europe!*, CreateSpace Independent Publishing Platform, September.
Critchley, S. (2013) Interview by M. Westerduin, Amsterdam: Volkskrant, 3 January.
Hoeksma, J. (2011) *The EU as a Democratic Polity in International Law*, The Hague: T.M.C. Asser Institute.
Hoeksma, J. (2013) 'Cameron miskent het belang van democratie', *Financieel Dagblad*, 28 January.
Parliamentary Proceedings. *Kamerstukken II 2008–2009*, 31 702, no. 3.
Schuman, Robert (2010) *Ten Propositions, For Europe*, Paris: Fondation Robert Schuman.
Von Clausewitz, C. (1832) *On War*, Berlin: Dümmlers Verlag.

Part V
The future of Europe
Navigating between national sovereignty and democratic cosmopolitanism

14 The EU and the quest for political union

Jaap Hoeksma

Introduction

In the first decade of the twenty-first century, a significant change has occurred in the debate about the end goal or *finalité politique* of the European Union (EU). At the start of the decade, a number of outstanding scholars reiterated the original dilemma that the EU had either to become a federal state or to establish itself as a union of states. The founder of the Department of Political Science at the University of Geneva, Dusan Sidjanski, began his study on the revival of federalism in Europe in 2001 with the almost Caesarian line that the EU is divided between two opposing tendencies that are developing at its heart: the community dynamic, which builds a union with a federal vocation, and intergovernmental cooperation in foreign and internal policies (Sidjanski 2001). A few years later, the Belgian political scientist Paul Magnette published a book entitled *What is the European Union?* in which he emphasised that, since the seventeenth century, legal theorists have repeated that only two forms of union between states are possible: either the confederation, born of an international treaty concluded between sovereign states, where all decisions are unanimously adopted by state representatives; or the federal state, established by a constitution, where the law voted on by a bicameral parliament applies directly to the citizens. *Tertium non datur.* There is no third way (Magnette 2005).

Over the last year, however, the debate about the future of the European Union has become dominated by the question as to whether or not the EU should evolve towards a political union and, if so, how deep this union should go. Although the suggestion has been outright rejected by a number of government leaders, notably by the British Prime Minister Cameron in his Europe speech of 23 January 2013, the German Chancellor Merkel and President of the European Council Van Rompuy are utilising the discussions about the strengthening of the EMU to argue that the creation of a political union is the best way forward for the EU. The insistence of these prominent European politicians on the use of this term raises a number of fundamental questions, two of which will be addressed in this essay: (1) Is it conceivable for the EU to develop towards a political union? (2) If so, what are the consequences for political science and the theory of international relations?

The Westphalian system of international relations

The term political union is being introduced in order to signify something different from both a state and a union of states. The EU is not a state as it is composed of 28 sovereign states. It is neither a union of states since it also consists of citizens. The term political union is therefore meant to denote a new phenomenon of international law, which can no longer be described in terms of the prevailing theory, known as the Westphalian system of international relations.

The importance of this system that emerged as a result of the 1648 Peace of Westphalia, and has formed the dominant paradigm for political thought ever since, can hardly be overestimated. It lays the foundation for the United Nations and lies at the heart of the present practice of distributing international justice. One of the most essential hallmarks of the Westphalian system consists of its approach to the concept of sovereignty. This concept has an internal and an external aspect. The internal dimension of the Westphalian concept of sovereignty implies that states do not have to recognise a higher authority as they had done under the feudal system. The external dimension connotes that states deal with each as equals and that they refrain from interfering in each other's affairs. Since the nineteenth century, the main domestic consequence of this system has become that democracy and the rule of law are necessarily confined to a state. The most important implication for the financial domain, which has developed over the centuries, is that currencies are exclusively related to states as well. Debts incurred by sovereign states are therefore referred to as 'sovereign debts' (Padoa-Schioppa 2010). As to the relation with the outer world, the system allows for conflicts between states to be settled by the use of force. The conduct of war forms an integral part of the Westphalian system. Notably, the violation of national sovereignty constitutes a legitimate reason for war. Even the granting of asylum by a state to refugees from another state may be regarded by the latter as an unfriendly act, justifying military reprisal.[1]

In his essay On Perpetual Peace of 1796, the German philosopher Immanuel Kant severely criticised the European states for their eagerness to indulge in war (Kant 1796). He compared their behaviour to that of the so-called *sauvages* in America and concluded that the latter were in many respects much nobler than the former. Determined to contribute to the prevention of future wars, Kant investigated the possibilities for states to co-exist in a peaceful manner. He identified two options: states wishing to avoid war could either form a 'federation of free states' or merge into a universal state. As Kant feared that a world republic might lead to a universal dictatorship, he preferred the concept of a society of nations.

A revolutionary breakthrough

Kant is generally regarded as the intellectual father of the United Nations, which was established in the aftermath of World War II. The absolute sovereignty of states, which had resulted in absolute atrocities, was restrained by the UN

Charter and by the 1948 Universal Declaration of Human Rights. Over the decades, the sovereignty of states has been further limited in favour of the protection of individuals by such measures as the prohibition of the act of genocide, the prevention of forcible return of refugees, the foundation of the International Criminal Court and the gradual introduction of the principle of the responsibility to protect (R2P) in the first years of the twenty-first century.

The Council of Europe, founded in 1949, curbed the sovereignty of its member states in a similar, although more stringent, manner as the UN. The primary tasks of the Council of Europe as an intergovernmental organisation are to promote cooperation between European governments and to enhance democracy and respect for human rights at the national level (Petaux 2009).

Neither the UN nor the Council of Europe questions the concept of sovereignty as such. In this respect, the six member states of the European Coal and Steel Community (ECSC), which entered into force in 1952, chose a principally different path. Driven by their determination to prevent the renewed outbreak of war, they decided to transfer the exercise of parts of their sovereignty to a higher organisation, which they created for this purpose. Both from a practical and a theoretical point of view, the new approach had huge consequences. For the first time since 1648, states voluntarily accepted the existence of a higher authority and of a higher community, within which they would be bound by decisions that could even be taken against their own will. Although they originally did so in a limited field and for a limited period of time, the prudent Dutch author Jos Kapteyn described the practice of the ECSC in 1974 as a revolutionary breakthrough of the classic pattern of international organisation (Kapteyn and Ver-Loren van Themaat 1974, Kapteyn et al. 2008).

The decision to start the process of European integration with the introduction of common control over coal and steel was of course not an arbitrary choice. By the middle of the twentieth century, coal and steel were indispensable for the conduct of war. By establishing joint control over these commodities, a renewed outbreak of war between the archrivals France and Germany had not only become unthinkable, but also practically impossible. Simultaneously, a common market was created in which these products could be traded freely between companies and individuals residing in the participating states. In view of its apparent success, the scope of the European experiment with shared sovereignty was soon to be broadened to the whole of the economy.

In the preamble to the Treaty of Rome, the six founding states of the EU expressed their determination to lay the foundations for an ever closer union between the peoples of Europe. It is commonplace to argue that this formula forms a carefully crafted compromise between the advocates of a federal Europe and the proponents of a 'Europe des Patries'. From the present perspective, however, it may be noted that the language of the preamble does not fit in the semantic field of the Westphalian system of international relations. It is, therefore, also feasible to suggest that the often repeated phrase 'ever closer union between the peoples of Europe' points towards a future beyond the Westphalian limits of statehood and international organisation.

Beyond a union of states

The decision to provide the three distinctive European communities, i.e. the European Economic Community, Euratom and the ECSC, with one institutional structure, which was implemented through the 1965 Merger Treaty (Kapteyn *et al.* 2008), may be regarded as a turning point in the early history of the EU. Although it had no immediate effect on the daily lives of the citizens of the member states, it caused a shift in focus from the negative impulse of the prevention of war to the positive determination to construct a common future. By deleting the limitation in time, which had been characteristic for the ECSC, the six member states signalled their intention to lay the foundations for not only an ever closer, but also an ever-lasting union.

This impact of the Merger Treaty was underpinned by the case law of the European Court of Justice, in which it was established that 'the European Economic Community constitutes a new legal order of international law, in which the citizens of the member states are called upon to cooperate' (Case C-26/62, Van Gend & Loos v. Netherlands Inland Revenue Administration, 5 February 1963). Shortly afterwards, the Court also put beyond doubt that the law of the Community has direct effect and, in case of conflict, takes precedence over that of its member states (Case C-6/64, Flaminio Costa v. ENEL, 15 July 1964). At the time of the entry into force of the Merger Treaty, the Communities were already developing in the direction of a distinct entity with one single market and a common legal order.

The contours of the emerging new polity were further shaped by two declarations of the Heads of State or Government. In the Declaration on European Identity, endorsed in 1973, they emphasised the democratic character of its, by now, nine member states and described the European Communities as 'a single entity' (EC 1973). In the Declaration on Democracy of 1978, they went on to express their determination to defend the principles of representative democracy, the rule of law, social justice and respect for human rights on the level of the member states, adding that the forthcoming elections of the European Parliament formed 'a clear expression of the common democratic ideals of the peoples of the member states' (EC 1978).

From a theoretical point of view, the reinforcement of the principle of Qualified Majority Voting (QMV) in a number of fields through the 1986 Single European Act implied that the European Communities could no longer be regarded as a mere union of states (for an opposing conclusion, see Forsyth 1981). This conclusion can be drawn on the basis of the following considerations: the concept of a union of states is not compatible with a common legal order; while unions of states may have parliamentary assemblies, they do not dispose of directly elected parliaments; the right to veto forms a quintessential quality of unions of states.

To put this development in its historical context, it may be recalled that the fall of the Berlin wall, which was to drastically change the political landscape of Europe, coincided with the evolution of the EC beyond a Westphalian union of states.

The state that failed

Hardly any other treaty in modern history has been so complex and multi-faceted as the 1992 Treaty on European Union (TEU). Concluded by 12 member states, it sought to place the process of European cooperation on a new footing. One of the most contested elements of the TEU consisted of the introduction of EU citizenship. According to Article 8 of the Treaty, each national of a member state is also a citizen of the European Union. Consequently, EU citizenship can only be obtained by acquiring the nationality of a member state.

Critics of the treaty dismissed the new status as an empty shell, since the rights granted to EU citizens were not much more than those they already enjoyed under the provisions of the single market (Jessurun d' Oliveira 1995). From a federalist point of view, however, the decision of the member states to introduce EU citizenship, entailing the right to consular protection abroad as well as the right to vote where you live in European and local elections, meant a further step away from the end goal of a union of states. According to the Westphalian paradigm, an international organisation has no citizens. It is merely composed of states. Against this background, federalists argued that the introduction of EU citizenship in itself could not be regarded but as a step towards the creation of a European state. Intuitively, the Danish voters took the same approach, albeit from a different angle. They rejected the Maastricht Treaty in a referendum out of fear that the proposed EU citizenship would replace their national status and that, consequently, their country would cease to exist. The European Council succeeded in allaying this fear by adopting a conclusion in December 1992, in which it emphasised that EU citizenship is merely additional to and shall in no way replace the national citizenship of the member states (EC 1992).

It seems at least remarkable that the same course of events should have repeated itself during the debate about the so-called Constitution for Europe. By presenting a new treaty on European Union as a Constitution for Europe, the European Council brought the discourse on Europe again into the semantic field of states. As Magnette explicated already, constitutions are associated with federal states, in which the law voted on by a bicameral parliament applies directly to the citizens. By using the language of states in the debate about the EU, the European Council gave the impression that the Union would eventually become a federal state, regardless of the views and wishes of the citizens. Once more, the citizens – this time from France and the Netherlands – reacted intuitively by voting against the proposed Constitution for Europe. In doing so, they effectively prevented the EU from developing into a federal state.

The Lisbon Treaty

After it had been established beyond doubt that the European Union is neither a state nor a union of states, the EU has not ceased to exist. Instead, the Lisbon Treaty has constructed the EU as a new phenomenon of statehood and international law beyond the Westphalian system of international relations. The task of lawyers is to study texts. The question must therefore be addressed as to which provisions of the new treaty that has come to replace the ill-fated constitution allow for the conclusion that the EU has outgrown the Westphalian system of international relations. As a preliminary remark, it should be mentioned that the drafters of the Lisbon Treaty deliberately dropped the term 'constitution' in favour of the notion of treaties. Actually, the Lisbon Treaty codified the basic texts in two treaties, i.e. the Treaty on European Union (TEU) and the Treaty on the Functioning of the European Union (TFEU). It may therefore be concluded that the EU is firmly based in international law.

Article 1 of the TEU confirms this presumption by clarifying that the EU owes its existence to the member states. It codifies the principle that the member states confer competences to the Union. As a consequence, Article 4 of the TEU puts beyond doubt that the Union has to respect the essential state functions of member states as well as their national identities, inherent in their fundamental structures, political and constitutional, inclusive of regional and local self-government. In effect, these provisions serve to ensure that the EU will not be turned into a federal state. Article 50 of the TEU corroborates this conclusion by granting each member state the right to unilaterally withdraw from the Union.

The second sentence of Article 1 of the TEU introduces the peoples and citizens in the Treaty. The term 'ever closer union among the peoples of Europe', which originally appeared in the Treaty of Rome, paves the way for including the citizens in the very construction of the EU. Title II TEU, comprising Articles 9–12, repeats the provision that every national of a member state shall be a citizen of the Union and explicates that the functioning of the Union shall be founded on representative democracy, thereby enabling the citizens to participate in the democratic life of the Union. Finally, Article 6 of the TEU stipulates that EU citizens shall enjoy the rights, freedoms and principles set out in the Charter of Fundamental Rights of the EU, which shall have the same legal value as the treaties.

This provisional overview of the Lisbon Treaty allows for the conclusion that the EU can no longer be described in terms of the traditional categories of state and union of states, but rather constitutes a new phenomenon of international law.[2] This finding is confirmed by the fact that Article 12 of the TEU explicitly attributes an active role to the national parliaments of the member states in the governance of the Union.[3]

The Kantian dilemma of statehood and international law

With the benefit of hindsight, it gradually becomes possible to discern that both sides of the debate about the end goal or *finalité politique* of the EU have been caught in a predicament that may be described as the Kantian dilemma of statehood and international law. As indicated above, Kant saw two options for states wishing to cooperate in order to avoid war. In his view, they could either merge into a federal state or form an association of states. In the first case, sovereignty would be entrusted to the new state; in the second case, it would remain with the cooperating states. The Westphalian system of international relations does indeed not allow for a third option: within the confines of this paradigm, shared sovereignty is a *contradictio in terminis*. However, the emergence of the EU demonstrates that it is feasible for states to transfer the exercise of sovereignty without losing statehood. In fact, all member states of the EU are internationally recognised states, while the Lisbon Treaty also grants international legal personality to the EU per se. Moreover, each EU member state is also a member of the United Nations, whereas the EU enjoys special status with the UN. Finally, the member states of the EU continue to treat each other as sovereign states, notably by maintaining embassies, ambassadors and diplomatic staff on each other's territories.

A second revolutionary breakthrough

Twenty years after the entry into force of the Maastricht Treaty, the implications of the TEU are starting to come to the fore. The pooling of the exercise of sovereignty in a growing number of fields, as put into practice by the member states of the European Communities, led to the paradoxical situation that they seemed to be willing to sacrifice democratic accountability for the sake of European integration. While the EC had already started in the 1970s to emphasise the democratic character of its member states, the EU turned the existence of a properly functioning democracy, including stable institutions, into a precondition for the accession of new members. The Copenhagen Criteria, as they were called after the Danish capital where they had been approved in 1993, were necessitated by the growing number of candidate states, which had regained independence after the collapse of the Soviet Union. Increasingly presenting itself as a union of democratic states, the EU was forced to consider its own democratic credentials. This process was enhanced by the criticism of academic organisations, such as the Commission Meijers, which argued that the EU threatened to undermine the national democracies of its member states and that the Union faced an unprecedented democratic deficit. With reference to an aphorism of the Marx brothers, it was often suggested that the EU did not meet the criteria for accession to the Union.

The conceptual problem confronting the Union in this respect was that the notions of democracy and international organisation were thought to be irreconcilable. According to the prevailing Westphalian system of international relations, a confederal union of states could by definition neither have citizens nor be democratic. For the governments of the day, however, these theoretical ramifications were not yet apparent. Caught in the dilemma between state and union of states, they described the EU as *a constructio sui generis* and tacitly agreed to accept the *paradox of the finalité politique*, which implied that progress in the field of European integration could only be made if and as long as the end goal of the EU remained unspoken.

In the absence of a blueprint for the development of the EU, the members of the European Council had to chart a path forward into unknown territory.

Twenty years on, it may be suggested that the TEU has laid the foundation for a second revolutionary breakthrough in the classic pattern of international relations. While the purpose of the first breakthrough was to experiment with the transfer of the exercise of sovereignty to a higher authority in order to avoid the renewed outbreak of war, the goal of the second was to establish democratic control over the exercise of sovereignty which had been transferred by the member states to the EU. Whereas the former effort resulted in the creation of a new legal order of international law, the latter was to lead to the emergence of a new type of polity beyond the confines of the Westphalian paradigm of international relations (see, e.g. Curtin 1997, van Gerven 2009, Telò 2009).

EU citizenship

From this perspective, the overriding reason for introducing EU citizenship is that citizens form the foundation of any democracy. By providing the EU with citizens, the Heads of State or Government assembled in the European Council crossed the line between international organisation and transnational democracy. From a conceptual point of view, it may be noted that the Council found a remarkably innovative way of achieving this result. The citizenship of the EU is not a direct but rather a coupled or additional citizenship. To put it in general terms: the citizenship of an international organisation has been made conditional to that of member states. Consequently, the Council could easily allay the fears of the Danish electorate that their national status would cease to exist. It may therefore be suggested that the EU has developed a new model of relations between citizens and international organisations. On a small scale, it could be imagined that the citizens of Belgium, the Netherlands and Luxembourg would also become Benelux-citizens, if any purpose would thereby be served. In a broader context, however, it could also be conceived that the citizens of the member states of the United Nations might become UN citizens as well. Although the latter suggestion may not seem realistic for the time being, its conceptual possibility has been put beyond doubt.[4]

EU citizenship is two-sided: on the one hand, EU citizens form a constitutive element of the construction of the Union as a political entity (Eijsbouts 2011); on the other hand, citizens enjoy the rights and obligations conferred on them by the treaties and notably by the Charter of Fundamental Rights of the EU and by the European Convention for the Protection of Human Rights and Fundamental Freedoms, to which the EU is to accede (Article 6, paragraph 2, TEU). EU citizens' rights are no longer confined to the economic rights of the internal market, but also include civic and political rights, such as the right to vote and to be elected, the right to diplomatic protection and the right to family life. In hindsight, it is striking to note that this double-sided approach to citizenship may already be discerned in the famous Van Gend & Loos case of 1963. Looking ahead, the EU Court should be credited for clarifying the concept of EU citizenship by pointing out in 2001 that 'citizenship of the Union is destined to be the primary status of nationals of the member states' (Case C-184/99, Rudy

Grzelczyk v. Centre public d'aide sociale d'Ottignies-Louvain-la-Neuve, 20 September 2001). The dynamic character of this concept is illustrated by the subsequent case law of the Court and it may still take quite some time before its full potential is realised.

Finally, the present construction of the EU also allows for the inclusion of an element of direct democracy in the functioning of the Union. While Article 10, paragraph 3, of the TEU stipulates that every citizen shall have the right to participate in the political life of the Union, Article 11, paragraph 4, foresees the introduction of the European Citizens' Initiative (ECI), which has been heralded by its advocates as 'the first element of transnational, participatory and digital democracy in history' (Citizens' Initiative 2012), but it is still too early to pass judgment on the effectiveness of the new instrument.

The euro

In the Westphalian approach, the euro is a currency without a state (Hoeksma 2011). The concept of absolute and undivided sovereignty of states implied for the financial markets that each currency ought to be backed by a state. In this line of thought, states are the only institutions strong and stable enough to guarantee the credibility of currencies, notably by their exclusive right to raise taxes. In the Westphalian system of international relations, states and financial markets have become inextricably intertwined. This state of affairs is symbolised by the term 'sovereign debt', which is used in order to describe the debts owed by a state.

For advocates of the traditional system, the euro as the common currency of the member states of the Economic and Monetary Union (EMU) embodies an unfeasible concept and was from the outset doomed to fail. The course of events triggered by the collapse of Lehman Brothers in 2008 seemed to prove them right. As a result of towering sovereign-debt burdens in a number of member states, the implosion of the euro appeared to be a matter of time. In their analysis, the EU had either to become a federal state in order to save the euro or to abandon the project of a common currency altogether.

In a post-Westphalian concept of international relations, however, it is perfectly possible to regard the EU and the member states of the EMU as the joint sovereign behind the euro. In fact, the construction of the European Central Bank offers a fine example of the way in which sovereignty is shared between the member states and the Union. The ECB's mandate is to take care of monetary and financial stability in the euro zone as a whole. While the ECB is an institution of the EU, which has its legal basis in the Lisbon Treaty (Article 13 TEU), its shares are held by the participating national central banks. Consequently, the national central banks of the 17 member states of the EMU are the joint owners of a fully fledged EU institution!

Complicated as this may seem, the structure can be elucidated by looking at the principles underlying the sharing of profits and losses. The Statute of the ECB specifies that the monetary income is divided among the participating national central banks according to a certain capital key. As this key is based on gross domestic product and population, it is highly comparable to the attribution of votes in the Council of Ministers or the number of members in the European Parliament. In line with this key, the profits and losses of the ECB, for example, from the liquidity assistance to banks or the programme of buying sovereign bonds, are divided among the participating national central banks and thus among the member states of the EMU.[5]

The conclusion of treaties in a democratic polity

It would be euphemistic to state that the global financial crisis triggered by the downfall of Lehman Brothers may be regarded as a blessing in disguise for the EMU inasmuch as it exposed the inherent weaknesses of its construction. During the array of consultations and meetings arranged to protect and save the common currency, however, the question has emerged whether member states of the EU are free to conclude international agreements between themselves outside the framework of the EU on subjects within the competences of the Union. Can they strengthen or even change the existing treaties by adopting subsequent treaties among themselves without proper involvement of the EU institutions? Put in a broader context, the question which has arisen is whether the entry into force of the Lisbon Treaty has consequences for the conclusion of treaties on issues under the competence of the EU.

The provisions of the Lisbon Treaty are quite unambiguous. If member states intend to *change* the existing EU treaties, they have to follow the procedures laid down in Article 48 of the Treaty on European Union (TEU). Should they desire to *strengthen* the treaties, they may resort to the provisions on enhanced cooperation, contained in Article 20 of the TEU and Articles 326–334 of the Treaty on the Functioning of the European Union (TFEU). Despite this clear wording, the Heads of State or Government of 25 member states gathered on 2 March 2012 in Brussels in order to sign an international treaty among themselves.[6]

The purpose of the Treaty on Stability, Coordination and Governance in the Economic and Monetary Union, which went into force on 1 January 2013, is to strengthen the EMU. Each of the measures provided for in the treaty, also known as the 'fiscal compact', aims to re-establish the confidence of financial markets in the common currency and in the underlying legal structure. The intuitive impression that these objectives are clearly within the scope of the EU treaties is confirmed by the contracting parties inasmuch as they express the intention to incorporate the content of the fiscal compact into the existing EU treaties as soon as possible and at the latest within five years. It may be suggested therefore that, despite the political difficulties of the day, the European Council should have had recourse to the revision procedures contained in the Lisbon Treaty and should have enabled both the European Commission and the European Parliament to play their role in the endeavour. All the more so as the so-called 'Six Pack', which also aimed at strengthening economic governance and entered into force on 13 December 2011, had been prepared in accordance with existing EU procedures.

In conclusion, it may be submitted that the European Council has chosen the wrong venue for signing the fiscal compact. By placing their signatures under this agreement in the compound of the European Council, the Heads of State or Government involved gave the impression that they were acting in their capacity as members of a European institution, while they actually signed a separate intergovernmental treaty. More importantly, they should have realised that the Lisbon Treaty signifies the evolution of the EU from a union of states to a transnational polity of states and citizens. Consequently, they ought to have acknowledged that treaties concluded in or alongside the framework of the EU should not only meet established standards of international law, but also enjoy democratic legitimacy.

Conclusion

The gist of this article is to argue that the process of European integration is characterised by two revolutionary breakthroughs in the classic pattern of international organisation. The first one, achieved by the ECSC, consisted of the transfer of the exercise of sovereignty to a higher authority. This experiment laid the basis for the EEC and Euratom as well as for the 'single entity', which came into being as a result of the 1965 Merger Treaty.

The second breakthrough has been forged by the effort to establish democratic control over the jointly exercised sovereignty. Whereas the European Communities basically remained a union of democratic states, the EU also aspires to be a democracy in its own right. This breakthrough has been realised in a number of steps. It started with the introduction in 1979 of direct elections to the European Parliament and was taken explicitly forward with the introduction of EU citizenship by the Maastricht Treaty. The 1997 Amsterdam Treaty continued by including 'democracy' in the core values of the EU proper. The Lisbon Treaty enhances this evolution by codifying the democratic principles on which the functioning of the EU is based, thereby simultaneously increasing the powers of the European Parliament (Bogdandy 2012).

At this juncture it may be concluded that the differences between the UN, the Council of Europe and other international organisations, on the one hand, and the EU, on the other hand, have become clear and evident. While the states, members of an intergovernmental organisation, may or may not constitute formal democracies of their own, the organisation as such is by definition not democratic. The administration of international organisations is exclusively governed by the rules of diplomacy. The evidence concerning the EU gathered in this essay, however, allows for the conclusion that the Lisbon Treaty constructs the EU as a democracy without turning the Union into a state. The hallmark par excellence of the EU is that the Union applies essential principles of democracy and the rule of law to an international organisation. Consequently, the European Union may be described in post-Westphalian terms as a union of democratic states based on the rule of law, which also aspires to constitute a law-based democracy of its own.

The current debate in the European Council

This conclusion sheds fresh light on the debate, conducted in the European Council, as to whether the EU should develop towards a political union. The fact that the Heads of State or Government have initiated this discussion should be welcomed as it implies that they have moved beyond the perennial dilemma of state or union of states. The question presently under discussion, by the greatest possible majority of the European Council, is therefore not whether the EU has to become a political union, but rather how deep this political union should go. Questions like these cannot be answered with mathematical precision. The boundaries, within which solutions must be found, are drawn in the EU treaties, on the one hand, and in national constitutions, on the other hand.[7]

Article 1 of the TEU, in combination with Article 4, lay down the principle that member states confer competences on the Union without allowing the Union to undermine the national identity of its member states. In other words, member states transfer the exercise of sovereignty to the EU only in so far as the achievement of their common objectives requires. Applying this principle to the current debate about the strengthening of the common currency, the quintessential question is how much exercise of power should be transferred by the member states to the Union in order to achieve the goal of maintaining the euro. Although the elaboration and implementation of this concept forms a challenge of unprecedented magnitude, the approach in itself epitomises the distinctive character of the EU.

In Chapter V of the report *Towards a Genuine EMU*, the President of the European Council invokes the principle that democratic control and accountability should occur at the level at which the decisions are taken (European Council 2012). In order to be convincing, this presumption should be elaborated and explained. The purpose of this essay is to provide the theoretical framework for the functioning of the EMU as part of a democratic structure. By formulating its views on the preconditions for democratic legitimacy in a more transparent manner, the European Council may well enhance its efforts to strengthen the EMU. In doing so, the Council will simultaneously further the democratic character of the EU as a whole.

Reinventing Europe

At the close of this essay, it has become possible to present clear and unequivocal answers to the two fundamental questions raised in the introduction. As the analysis of the provisions of the Lisbon Treaty shows, it is entirely feasible for the EU to develop into a political union. There are even solid reasons to suggest that the EU already constitutes a political union ever since its foundation. The text of the Lisbon Treaty corroborates this suggestion as Article 10, paragraph 3, of the TEU explicitly grants citizens the right to participate in the political life of the

Union, while the fourth paragraph stipulates that political parties at the European level contribute to forming European political awareness.

The most important theoretical implication of the emergence of the EU is that the Union has outgrown the Westphalian system of international relations. Consequently, the EU embodies a third category besides the existing pair of states and unions of states. The EU has established itself as a union of states and citizens that is based upon the transfer of the exercise of sovereignty and is coupled with citizenship. The combination of these two characteristics creates the conditions under which an international organisation may evolve into a transnational democracy. While various forms of relations between states and citizens, on the one hand, and international organisations and citizens, on the other hand, may be qualified as political unions, the construction of the European Union allows for the more accurate description of the EU as a union of states and citizens.

From a conceptual point of view, the developments since the entry into force of the Maastricht Treaty may be summarised in the conclusion that the EU has not contented itself with forming a Kantian association of states, but rather endeavours to function as a representative democracy of its own. This goal, however, may be achieved only if the EU succeeds in overcoming its democratic deficit. The main challenge for Europe's present and future leaders is to enable the EU to further evolve from a formal into a living democracy of states and citizens. It has taken the EU over 50 years to develop a new model of governance beyond the Westphalian system of international relations. The coming decades will have to prove whether the EU has indeed reinvented Europe in a stable and lasting manner.

Notes

1 Hence the expression in the preamble to the 1951 UN Refugee Convention of the wish that 'States will do everything within their power to prevent this problem from becoming a cause of tension between States'.
2 The view that the European Communities formed a new phenomenon in international law was suggested already by Pescatore (1974).
3 This is further regulated in Protocol (no. 1) on the role of National Parliaments in the European Union.
4 This conclusion may strengthen the line of thought developed by the German philosopher Jürgen Habermas (2011) in his plea for a future world government.
5 I am highly indebted to Dirk Schoenmaker, Dean of the Duisenberg School of Finance, for sharing his views on the construction of the ECB with me.
6 The two non-participating EU member states are the Czech Republic and the United Kingdom.
7 In Germany, for example, by Articles 23, paragraph 1.3 juncto Article 79, paragraph 3 of the Constitution.

Bibliography

Bogdandy, A. von. (2012) 'The European Lesson for International Democracy: The Significance of Articles 9–12 EU Treaty for International Organizations', *EJIL*, vol. 23, no. 2, pp. 315–334.

Citizens' Initiative (2012) 'After The First Six Months – State of the Art of ECI', 1 November, Available: www.citizens-initiative.eu.

Curtin, D.M. (1997) *Postnational Democracy. The European Union in Search of a Political Philosophy*, The Hague: Kluwer Law International.

EC (1973) *EC Bulletin 12*–1973.

EC (1978) *EC Bulletin 3*–1978.

EC (1992) *EC Bulletin 12*–1992.

Eijsbouts, T.W. (2011) *Onze primaire hoedanigheid*, Inaugural lecture, Leiden.

European Council (2012) *Report towards a Genuine Economic and Monetary Union*, 5 December.

Forsyth, M. (1981) *Unions of States*, Leicester: Leicester University Press.

Habermas, J. (2011) *Zur Verfassung Europas*, Berlin: Springer.

Hoeksma, J.A. (2011) 'The EU as a Democratic Polity in International Law', *CLEER Working Papers* no. 2.

Hoeksma, J.A., and Schoenmaker, D. (2011) 'The Sovereign Behind the Euro', in *A Polity called EU; Essays on the Exercise of Sovereignty in the European Union and the Euro Area*, Nijmegen: Wolf Legal Publishers.

Instituut Clingendael (2008) *Nederland, de EU en het Verdrag van Lissabon*, Den Haag: Instituut Clingendael.

Jessurun d' Oliveira, H.U. (1995) 'Union Citizenship: A Pie in the Sky?', in Rosas, A., and Antolo, E. (eds.) *A Citizens' Europe*, London: Sage.

Kant, I. (1796/1939) *Perceptual Peace: A Philosophical Proposal*, London: Peace Book Company.

Kapteyn, P.J.G., and VerLoren van Themaat, P. (1974) *Inleiding tot het recht van de Europese Gemeenschapen*, 2nd edition, Deventer: Kluwer.

Kapteyn, P.J.G., McDonnell, A., Mortelmans, K., and Timmermans, C.W.A. (2008). *The Law of the European Union and the European Communities*, Alphen aan den Rijn, the Netherlands: Kluwer Law International.

Magnette, P. (2005) *What is the European Union? Nature and Prospects*, London: Macmillan.

Padoa-Schioppa, Tommaso. (2010). 'Markets and Governments Before, During and After the 2007–20xx Crisis', Per Jacobsson Lecture, Bank for International Settlements, Basel, Available: www.bis.org/events/agm2010/sp100627.htm.

Pescatore, P. (1974) *The Law of Integration. Emergence of a New Phenomenon in International Relations, based on the experience of the European Communities*, Leiden: Sijthoff.

Petaux, J. (2009) *Democracy and Human Rights for Europe, The Council of Europe's Contribution*, Strasbourg: Council of Europe.

Rosas, A., and Antolo, E. (eds.) (1995) *A Citizens' Europe*, London: Sage.

Sidjanski, Dusan (2001) *The Federal Approach to the European Union*, Paris: Notre Europe.

Telò, M. (ed.) (2009) *The European Union and Global* Governance, Oxon, New York: Routledge/GARNET.

van Gerven, Walter (2009) 'The EU Should Develop into a Political Entity with a High Degree of Democratic Legitimacy', in Wouters, J., Verhey, L., and Kiiver, Ph. (eds.) *European Constitutionalism beyond Lisbon*, Antwerp: Intersentia.

15 Europe between two worlds

Elemér Hankiss

The crisis – an equation with many variables

Europe is desperately struggling with crisis, trying with all its might to put out the fire first here, later there, and when success seems within reach, the flames flare up once again. There are many causes for this relative helplessness. Understandably, the European Union focuses mostly on the *economic and political* reasons which originally triggered the crisis and are responsible for its prolongation. This is what its mandate and its institutional system are destined for. These efforts have not been particularly successful to date. One reason for this might be that economics and politics are only part of the overall system of society and, consequently, mastering economic and political problems does not in itself eradicate the crisis.

The crisis is multi-dimensional, both in Europe and elsewhere – an equation with many variables, where besides economic factors social, cultural, psychological, behavioural and even spiritual aspects play important roles. Formulas and equations consisting merely of economic and political variables will necessarily collapse and prove unsolvable. Fortunately, however, the situation is not as bad as it sounds, since modern economics does attempt to grasp economic phenomena in their full complexity.

The fact that economic processes are deeply embedded in the tissue of social existence is something we have known through the works of Max Weber, Mihály Polányi, Amitai Etzioni and others. Over the past half a century, a whole line of new disciplines has unfolded in order to explore these connections. It is enough to think of recent achievements in fields such as theoretical and crisis economics, social economics, behavioural economics, cultural economics, welfare economics, identity economics, game theory, rational choice theory, quality of life studies, GNP–Gross National Happiness Index, or research into human capital. Today the conviction is growing ever stronger that we must go 'beyond the GDP approach' even in political circles.

There is, however, a further factor which may play a crucial part in the analysis and interpretation of the crisis but receives relatively little attention in discussions today. This factor is *history*, more accurately, the possibility that our current crisis may not be a singular, one-off occurrence but a late stage in the prolonged radical transformation of European/Western civilisation which has been underway for a longer period. It is this aspect of the crisis I will examine below.

Crisis and history

We need to be cautious in using the concept of 'crisis'. The threat of a crisis of Western civilisation has surfaced repeatedly for almost a century.

Ontological crisis

There are some excellent thinkers who instead of a crisis of Western civilisation talk about the crisis of human existence in general; in other words they believe that crisis is an original and ongoing human condition.

Theories of decline

Some authors describe the history of mankind, in contrast to utopias of progress, as a process of decline, a transition from a former 'golden age' to the 'iron age' of the present which is supposed to represent the end of history. Herod, Ovid, the prophet Daniel, St. Augustine, Rousseau, Freud, Camus and others are often mentioned in the context of such a view of history.[1]

The experience of decline and crisis grew particularly pronounced in the twentieth century with the emergence of post-modernism – or at least the view that, although there is clearly some development in certain areas (health, science, freedom, rights), this growth also has dangerous, destructive and unforeseen consequences. The famous German philosopher Karl Löwith (1967) goes so far as to state that all attempts that aim to present history as a line of progress driven by God to ultimate victory are blasphemous. He writes about the 'terrible history' of humanity.

The sense or experience of decline is particularly pronounced in Western and, within that, in European civilisation. This, to use a contemporary turn of phrase, is a serious competitive disadvantage as opposed to the dynamic experience of growth determining the up-and-coming economies of our time.

Macro-historians

Other thinkers who see the world in large-scale processes of world history, such as Polibios, Danilevsky, Spengler, Toynbee or Sorokin, claim that civilisations run along cyclical courses: they emerge, unfold, reach completion, then begin to decline and eventually disperse, disappear or become immersed in a subsequent civilisation. Most of these authors claim that European/Western civilisation is now past its apex; indeed, it might already be in an advanced stage of decline (Borkenau 1981, Polányi 1994, Voegelin 2000).

'Axial' periods?

There are also philosophers, historians and social scientists that see the history of humanity, and within that, of Western civilisation, not as progress or decline, but as a radical breach, a great transformation or change.

Not least among them is Karl Jaspers (1949, 1953), who, leaning on Max Weber's work, has applied the term 'axial period' to the stupendous shift between 800 and 200 BC in which early civilisations built on a magical world view became transformed into ancient civilisations built on monotheism, reason and the central role of man. This was the period of great religious founders and thinkers such as Homer, Parmenides, Heracleitos, Archimedes, Socrates, Plato, Euripides, the prophets Elias, Esau and Jeremiah, Buddha, Lao-tse, Confucius, Zoroaster; a period when the cosmos opened up, man was awakened to the universe and its transcendence and began to look for his place in the cosmos and for meaning in general. Jaspers' theory was later carried forward by Eisenstadt (1986, 2006), and Bellah and Hans (2012), as well as others.

The question emerges, however, whether the axial period described by Jaspers was indeed the only truly radical turn in our history. In other words, have there not been other comparably great changes in the history of our civilisation?[2]

Many of the historians of Western civilisation believe that a similarly grandiose transformation of the social sphere, of culture, mentality and behaviour took place on the verge between traditional Western civilisation and the Modern Age, starting with the Renaissance and the Enlightenment. Karen Armstrong (2006) and Yves Lambert (1999) expressly talk about a *second axial period* in this context.

A third 'axial period'?

There are a number of signs which show that, owing to an acceleration in historical processes, a new and great historical transformation began around the middle of the nineteenth century. Historians, philosophers, theologians and social scientists (and even some natural scientists) describe this change, and try to make sense of it, as a transition between modernity and post-modernism; the modern age and the post-modern age. Over the past decades, there has been enough literature published on this transition to fill a library (Bauman 2007, Featherstone 1995, Foucault 1986, Gellner 1992, Harvey 1989, Hassan 1988, Hofstede 2001, Inglehart 2010, Jameson 1991, Lyotard 1984).

If such a transition really has begun and is taking place, it is hard to define the time boundary between the two periods. Modern civilisation and the supposed post-modernist period fit into each other in a 'meshed-like' fashion.[3] What we mean by this is that several traits of post-modernism had already appeared in the modernist period, while a number of elements of modernism live on in the post-modern era. This last characteristic has induced several researchers to speak of the last fifty years not as a transition but as a continuity or a belated unfolding of modernism.

One thought-provoking example, Baudelaire's famous *and* notorious book *Les fleurs du mal*, first appeared a century and a half ago, in 1857. This was a time when modernism was unfolding with a new-found dynamism in bourgeois society, the belief in development and the economic and scientific revolution. Nevertheless, scholars claim that the first flashes of post-modernist sensibility and the post-modernist existential experience may be detected in these poems and the prolonged wave of decadence in the arts which followed. The sheer magnitude, the almost dramatic character, of this shift certainly justifies analysing the last 50–100 years, with certain reservations, as the unfolding of a new axial period. An age when the economic-social-cultural structure of the world has been in radical transformation, and the interpretation of the universe, life, man's position, role and existence have also transformed.

If this is the case, if we are indeed living in the age of such a grand transformation of civilisations, this kind of historical process is the only framework in which the current crisis and, within that, the crisis of Europe can be interpreted with any hope. In order to assist with this project, I outline below a few symptoms and elements of this great transformation. I only mention in passing the economic, political and social changes which are widely known and analysed today – my focus is on the changes which are taking pace in individual and societal consciousness, in behaviour and the dominant world view of people.

Modernism and post-modernism

Let me start with a simple table (Table 15.1) where I pair opposing concepts to characterise the changes which took place *in the world* and *in the understanding*

Table 15.1 Historical turning points

1990	2013
World order	World chaos?
American empire	New empires?
Pax Americana	Bellum Americanum?
Global balance	Toppled?
Dominance of the West	West losing ground, emergence of a multi-centred world, appearance of new power centres
Global peace	Global conflict?
Safety	Spread of terrorism
Economic growth	Economic crisis?
Possibility of unlimited growth	Unsustainable growth
Age of affluence	Seventy-seven years of famine
Free world	The developed world 'locking up'?
Triumph of democracy	Malfunctions of democracy?
Internationalism	Strengthening of new nationalisms
Tolerance	Strengthening of fundamentalisms
The world becoming more fair and just	The world becoming less fair and just?
An indifferent world	An increase/decline(?) in solidarity?
The poor are silent	The poor in rebellion?

of the world around the turn of the millennium. I believe that the significance of these changes is clear.

The question is what all of this means for Europe. Are we ever to come out of the crisis if we do not take into consideration the way in which the great empires of the world have been re-structured: Global balance has been shaken and the West is losing ground. Major new conflicts are emerging along new fault-lines. Global threats are turning against our freedom. Democracy is malfunctioning, nationalist and fundamentalist trends are on the increase and glaring injustices are inscribed in our social structure?

Let us go further. Can we expect to master the current crisis unless we take heed of the massive change which has taken place in our *behavioural culture* over the past century? In order to illustrate this transformation, I offer another simple table (Table 15.2) to juxtapose the basic rules of human behaviour which characterised the world of our parents/grandparents and those which inform our world today.

These two cultures of behaviour are not only different – they are sharply opposed. One contains more responsibility, the other more freedom. One emphasises solidarity, the other responsibility for the full unfolding of the personality. One speaks more about constancy, the other about change. One demands more consideration, the other more initiative.

Which behaviour culture is better suited to promote and enable the emergence of a new European society?

The situation is made more complicated by the fact that at present these two behaviour cultures mingle in the lives of all of us. This uncertainty can partly hinder our personal evolution, but it is also conceivable that some sort of synthesis of these two orders of behaviour will serve in future as the basis for a new set of rules for social life. It may be argued that this is not a problem for the EU or Brussels to solve, but it is certainly an important dilemma faced by European men and women.

I shall offer one single example to illustrate the situation. Let us explore the opposition 'you are a sinner'–'you are innocent'. Judeo-Christian culture has struggled with the idea of sin and a sense of guilt for millennia. Its cult of guilt had a positive social role, but it also narrowed down and paralysed the lives of

Table 15.2 Changing rules of behaviour

Traditional/modern	Post-modern
Love thy neighbour!	Love yourself!
Sacrifice yourself!	Fulfil yourself!
Be modest!	Be successful!
Accept your place!	Find your place in the world!
Obey!	Be free!
Save!	Consume!
You are a sinner	You are innocent
Take care!	Take a risk!

millions. The struggle to break free from a universal sense of guilt began during the Renaissance and then the Enlightenment and since Nietzsche has turned into a veritable march of triumph. Today's consumer society blares forth the belief about man's grandeur and original innocence around the clock. In the world of advertising, for instance, the worst sin conceivable is if, say, a cup of coffee is spilt and soils the tablecloth or a white blouse. But even this is not a final or mortal sin, since the fabric soon re-emerges in its innocent snowy white glory from the glittering mass of bubbles of the washing machine, which shines with an almost transcendent halo. In this civilisation, the disturbance is not sin itself but a sense of guilt. As the American cartoon figure Zizzy put, 'Recently I have been feeling guilty about feeling guilty.' Torments of guilt are as damaging to the life of society and the individual as is a sense of innocence verging on the psychopathological. Not to mention the fact that both can hinder finding ways out of crisis.

Below are more examples of the pairings of concepts employed by experts to describe the transition from modernity to post-modernism (Table 15.3).

The question emerges once more which of these two attitudes is better suited to guide Europe out of the crisis – faith in the triumphant progress of history or the post-modernist attitude which seeks a path amidst different possible histories. Is it the almost arrogant self-assurance of Western man that leads out of the present crisis the belief that he and only he has access to ultimate truth, or is it the sceptical and even self-questioning reflexivity and pluralism of post-modern man? Here again, there seems to be a need for some kind of balance to emerge or to be brought about.

The age of uncertainty

A further sign which hints that we are undergoing a major historical shift is that, in this age of transition, half way between a disintegrating old world and a nascent new order, man seems overcome by a sense of uncertainty which is growing ever more dominant and disquieting. This process is mostly present in the Western world and, within that, in Europe, but it is also there in different forms and to varying extents in other societies. As far as I know, the concept and the phrase 'the age of uncertainty' first appeared in the title of a book by John K. Galbraith published in 1977. In response, a multitude of books were written

Table 15.3 The transition from modernity to post-modernity

Modernism	Post-modernism
Linear view of history; progress	Histories
Rationalism	Reflexivity
Order, predictability	Uncertainty
Universalism	Pluralism
One single 'truth'	Assumptions, 'arguments'
Integrated, essential 'self'	Deconstructed self, 'no-self'

using the concept by historians and intellectual historians (Hobsbawm 1995, Bauman 2007), theologians and philosophers (Byrne 2001, Berger 2010), social scientists (Faulkner *et al.* 2009, Hess 2011), strategy researchers (Gritzalis *et al.* 2003), media researchers, art historians, economists (McGrath and MacMillan 2000), and many others. The 1990s particularly were a time of heightened experience of social, economic, political and, not least of all, ontological uncertainty.

Ulrich Beck (1992, 1999) talks about the emergence of a 'society of risk', Donald H. Rumsfeld about a world 'defined by surprise and uncertainty', the famous French author on public affairs Richard Cohen about 'history becoming chaotic', George Soros about 'the crisis of global capitalism', while Stanley Hoffmann about a 'global jungle' and Alain Greenspan about 'a chaotic period'.

Spiritual crisis

A further symptom of a historical shift might be that several outstanding thinkers, philosophers and writers of the twentieth century talk about a profound spiritual crisis. Partly in the wake of Kierkegaard, Unamuno wrote about 'the agony of Christianity' as far back as 1921, and Ortega y Gasset in 1931 about 'the rebellion of the masses', Jaspers in 1932 about 'the disintegration of all spirituality' and 'ultimately the crisis of human existence', Paul Valéry in 1924 about 'the dismantling of human personality', T.S Eliot (1934) referred to his own time as 'an age of troubled faiths and atrophied beliefs' and talked about 'a materialist civilisation which is like a living corpse', while Horkheimer (1947) writes about 'an eclipse of reason'.

The sense of crisis spread further in the second half of the century. Camus (1971) talked about 'losing transcendence', Husserl (1970) about 'the crisis of European thinking', Peter Berger and Thomas Luckmann (1995) about 'the crisis of reason', Joseph Campbell (1968) about 'the universal tragedy of man' and 'fairy tales of happiness', Marcuse (1964) about 'one dimensional man', Jan Patocka (1985) about 'the crisis of intellect' and 'the spiritual crisis of mankind', Terry Eagleton (2007) about 'the eclipse' of reason and meaningfulness, Zbigniew Brzezinski (1990) about 'the gnawing of philosophical anxiety', Kolakowski (1991) puts the modernist period 'in the docks' for the accused Jacques Monod (1971) writes about 'the poverty of the modern soul' and its 'despair', while Bertrand Russell (1929) declares that man must 'step through the gate of darkness' (Hankiss 1999, 2001).

'Bubbles'

In an age of great historical transformations, a profound intellectual/spiritual crisis may also appear when the symbolic sphere around a given human community becomes dispersed. What do we mean by that?

For as far back as we can think, humans have surrounded themselves not only with the walls and bastions of their caves and cities, with institutions, legal systems, habits and customs, weapons and tools, but also with a protective sphere of symbols: myths and religions, beliefs and knowledge and the magical beauty of works of art; in other words, their civilisation. Inside this 'bubble' of civilisation, they could feel safe and free and could believe that their lives had meaning and significance (Cassirer 1944, Scheler 1961, Durand 1969, Gehlen 1988, Borkenau 1981, Berger and Luckman 1980).

Civilisations, however, are transient structures and sooner or later lose their capacity to protect their community and to offer responses to the everyday questions of life and the ultimate questions of human existence. And when a protective envelope like that collapses or is dispersed, the human community in question is left alone in a dark, senseless universe. To a varying extent, they experience Pascal's horror. Contemporary humanity is in a particularly difficult situation.

The trap of globalisation

We are born with soft skulls, but newborns are soon surrounded by safety. First comes the warm bubble of the cradle, the soft fabric of cushions and curtains. Then the world begins to open wide – the house, the garden, the neighbourhood provide the new bubble which provides safety and offers interpretations of the world. Later the circle of friends, the school, village and town, the country and eventually the entire globe emerge and stretch their protective bubble around the young and developing human being.

What gives us the real sense of shock and crisis today is the sudden expansion of our world. The fact that, unexpectedly detached from the bonds of his own original society, contemporary man is expected to scan a far wider range in which to find the answers to the common questions of everyday life, as well as to the ultimate questions of existence and death. As the interpretative frame broadens, the truths, values and guiding principles of former times become inflated and lose their glow and strength. Billions of people suffer today, to varying extents, from the fact that the 'globe' is not yet able to interpret the world, life or the universe for them; nor is it able to offer a chance of a rich and meaningful life. The same applies, to a varying extent and in different forms, to societies living in relative affluence or in poverty. Europe is also victim to the same malaise.

Secularisation

A further factor which causes contemporary man to become increasingly lonely is the progress of the secular, which has been on the advance for hundreds of years. Traditional civilisation used to surround man in a far more tender and cushioned way with its world of magic, beliefs, myths; it was richer in values, answers and important illusions than the cold, rigid, secularised word of modern rationality.

Scientific revolution

Despite all of its grand achievements, even the scientific revolution causes difficulty. The reason for this is that, as the myths, beliefs and misconceptions which were once used to interpret the world are now becoming dispersed, so the world itself becomes more dreary, empty and meaningless for the contemporary. As Nobel laureate physicist Steven Weinberg (1977: 154) wrote: 'The more we understand of the universe, the more meaningless and pointless it seems to become.'

Regarding cosmology, in the past, even the sky itself surrounded man with a protective sphere. The image of the cosmos was at all times interrelated with human life/destiny. But this connection has become increasingly detached over the past decades and in Europe the dissociation has been particularly sharp and powerful. The magical cosmos of early tribal societies was filled with spirits, souls and demons, both benevolent and malevolent, which could be pretty well managed through magic and ceremonies. The situation was similar regarding the mythical cosmos of the Greeks and other early civilisations. Plato's universe and human life in general were ruled by the same eternal 'ideas' or 'forms'. In the cosmos of Judaism, Christianity and Islam, that of traditional European civilisation, man, and humanity, played a central, meaningful and significant role.

The Copernican revolution shook this once secure position. People have been and still are unable to make much of this new image of the world for everyday use. Even in the age of Einstein, Hoyle, Penrose and Hawking, our everyday view of the world is Ptolemaic. Our experience is that the Sun orbits around the Earth, it rises in the morning, creeps up to the sky and reaches its apex at midday, then slowly descends and finally sets beyond the horizon. There have been attempts to 'humanise' the new cosmos. Newton and Kant, for instance, detected profound harmonies between the laws of the cosmos and of human life. They were impressed by the bright stars in the sky above and both made efforts to explain that this cosmic harmony could also be translated into the practice of human life. If only, they claim, man lived according to the moral law, his life could be as perfect and harmonious as the orbits of the celestial bodies with their geometric precision.

How can we relate, however, to Einstein's space-time as the new frame of human life? Where, in which nook or corner of this space-time can we find our own place? Where can we find a guiding principle to serve as a compass in our lives; what does E say about a source for the meaning of life in the universe? Matters only got worse as the 'quantum universe', i.e. the universe of quantum physics, became known – a discipline quite amazing in its scientific achievements. Humanity is no longer protected by the starry sky above. Swept away by the 'big bang', lost in the chaos of electrons, neutrons, quarks, bosons, leptons, strings and superstrings, what has man to hold on to? Where and how can s/he find the purpose and meaning of her/his life and existence?

And what has all this to do with the crisis and its solution? Apparently, we have gone a long way from the problems of Europe (and the world) struggling with crisis. I believe, however, that this is only apparent because the sense of uncertainty and insecurity which has flooded Europe is the uncertainty not only of making a living but also of human existence. This is not only a crisis of European economy and politics, but also of human lives and human existence. If millions, ten millions and hundred millions of people lose certainty, if they lose their faith in their own past and future, if they fail to find their place in the world and the universe, if they lose their faith in the meaningfulness of human existence, then the whole dynamism of their lives may be broken.

Indeed, the dynamism of European society may be broken. A society where people are overcome with a sense of uncertainty, contingency or even meaninglessness of their lives stands a poor chance of finding its way out of the crisis by successfully solving its economic and social problems. The question, of course, is what European society can do in order to overcome the age of uncertainty and hesitation so it can be at least as successful in a world of post-modernism as it was in the centuries of modernism.

Notes

1 By contrast, the history of mankind is described as progress by Democritos, Protagoras, Epicure, Bacon, Turgot, Kant, Schelling, Hegel, Comte, Spencer, Marx, Thomas H. Huxley and, generally, most philosophers of history in the modernist period.
2 In the models of historians, who describe history as a cyclical process, the point where the development of a civilisation suddenly tips over into decline can also be seen as a major breach, an 'axial period'. Marx, on the other hand, sees profound changes in the succession of slavery, feudal and capitalist society.
3 This is also how traditional Western civilisation and subsequent modernity fit together.

Bibliography

Armstrong, Karen (2006) *The Great Transformation: The Beginning of Our Religious Traditions*, 1st edition, New York: Knopf.
Baudelaire, C. (1857) *Les fleurs du mal*, Paris: Poulet-Malassis et De Broise.
Bauman, Zygmunt (2007) *Liquid Times: Living in an Age of Uncertainty*, Cambridge: Polity Press.
Beck, Ulrich (1992) *Risk Society. Towards a New Modernity*, London: Sage.
Beck, Ulrich (1999) *World Risk Society*, Maldern: MA: Polity Press.
Bellah, Robert N., and Joas, Hans (eds.) (2012) *The Axial Age and Its Consequence*, Cambridge, MA: Belknap Press.
Berger, Peter L. (2010) *Between Relativism and Fundamentalism: Religious Resources for a Middle Position*, Grand Rapids, MI: W.B. Eerdmans.
Berger, Peter L., and Luckmann, Thomas (1980) *The Social Construction of Reality: A Treatise in the Sociology of Knowledge*, New York: Irvington Publishers.
Berger, Peter L., and Luckmann, Thomas (1995) *Modernity, Pluralism and the Crisis of Meaning*, Gütersloh: Bertlelsmann.
Borkenau, Franz (1981) *End and Beginning: On the Generation of Cultures and the Origins of the West*, New York: Columbia University Press.
Brzezinski, Zbigniew (1990) *Post-Victory Blues*. Lecture, Academy of World Inquiry, School of Foreign Service, Georgetown University, Washington, 25 October.

Byrne, James M. (2001) *God: Thoughts in an Age of Uncertainty*, London: Continuum.
Campbell, Joseph (1968) *The Hero with a Thousand Faces*, Princeton, NJ: Princeton University Press.
Camus, Albert (1971) *The Rebel*, New York: Knopf.
Cassirer, Ernst (1944) *An Essay on Man. An Introduction to the Philosophy of Human Culture*, New Haven: Yale University Press.
Durand, Gilbert (1969) *Les structures anthropologiques de l'imaginaire*, Grenoble: Dunod.
Eagleton, Terry (2007) *The Meaning of Life*, Oxford: Oxford University Press.
Eisenstadt, S.N. (ed.) (1986) *The Origins and Diversity of Axial Age Civilizations*, Albany: State University of New York Press.
Eisenstadt, S.N. (ed.) (2006) *The Great Revolutions and the Civilizations of Modernity*, Leiden: Brill.
Eliot, T.S. (1934) *After Strange Gods*, London: Faber and Faber.
Faulkner, Robert, Shell, Susan, and Schneider, Thomas E. (eds.) (2009) *America at Risk: Threats to Liberal Self-Government in an Age of Uncertainty*, Ann Arbor: University of Michigan Press.
Featherstone, Mike (1991) *Consumer Culture and Postmodernism*, London: Sage.
Featherstone, Mike (1995) *Undoing Culture: Globalization, Postmodernism and Identity*, London: Sage.
Featherstone, Mike, Lash, Scott, and Robertson, Roland (eds.) (1995) *Global Modernities*, London: Sage.
Foucault, Michel (1986) 'Of Other Spaces', *Diacritics*, vol. 16 (Spring), pp. 22–27.
Galbraith, John Kenneth (1977) *The Age of Uncertainty*, London: BBC and Deutsch.
Gehlen, Arnold (1988) *Man: His Nature and Place in the Universe*, New York: Columbia University Press.
Gellner, Ernest (1992) *Postmodernism, Reason and Religion*, London: Routledge.
Giddens, Anthony (1990) *The Consequences of Modernity*, Oxford: Polity Press.
Gritzalis, Dimitris, De Capitani di Vimercati, S., Samarati, P., and Katsikas, S. (ed.) (2003) *Security and Privacy in the Age of Uncertainty: 18th International Conference on Information Security, May 26–28, 2003, Athens, Greece*, Boston: Kluwer.
Halik, Tomas (2012) *Night of the Confessor: Christian Faith in an Age of Uncertainty*, Turner, Gerald (trans.), New York: Image Books.
Hamvas, Béla (1983) *Világválság* [World Crisis], Budapest: Magvető.
Hankiss, Elemer (ed.) (1999) *Europe After 1989: A Culture in Crisis?* Washington: Georgetown University, School of Foreign Affairs.
Hankiss, Elemer (2001) *Fears and Symbols. An Introduction to the Study of Western Civilization*, Budapest: Central European University Press.
Harvey, David R. (1989) *The Condition of Postmodernity. An Enquiry into the Origins of Cultural Change*, Oxford: Blackwell.
Hassan, Ihab (1988) *The Postmodern Turn: Essays in Postmodern Theory and Culture*, Columbus: Ohio State University Press.
Heinberg, Richard (2011) *The End of Growth. Adapting to Our New Economic Reality*, Gabriola Island, BC: New Society.
Hess, David J. (2011) 'Bourdieu and Social Studies: Towards Reflexive Sociology', *Minerva*, vol. 49, no. 3 (January), pp. 333–348.
Hess, Stephen, and Northrop, Sandy (2011) *American Political Cartoons: The Evolution of a National Identity, 1754–2010*, New Brunswick, NJ: Transaction Publishers.
Hobsbawm, Eric (1995) *Age of Extremes. The Short Twentieth Century, 1914–1991*, London: Michael Joseph.

Hofstede, Geert H. (2001) *Culture's Consequences: Comparing Values, Behaviors, Institutions, and Organizations across Nations*, Thousand Oaks, CA: Sage.
Horkheimer, Max (1947) *Eclipse of Reason*, New York: Oxford University Press.
Huntington, Samuel (1997) *The Clash of Civilizations and the Remaking of World Order*, New York: Norton.
Husserl, Edmund (1970) *The Crisis of European Sciences and Transcendental Phenomenology. An Introduction to Phenomenological Philosophy*, Carr, David (trans.), Evanston: Northwestern University Press.
Inglehart, Ronald (*et al.*) (2010) *Changing Human Beliefs and Values, 1981–2007: A Cross-Cultural Sourcebook Based on the World Values Surveys and European Values Studies*, Mexico, DF: Siglo Veintiuno Editores.
Jameson, Frederic (1991) *Postmodernism, or the Cultural Logic of Late Capitalism*, Durham, NC: Duke University Press.
Jaspers, Carl (1949) *Vom Ursprung und Ziel der Geschichte*, Zürich: Artemis-Verlag.
Jaspers, Carl (1953) *The Origin and Goal of History*, Bullock, Michael (trans.), London: Routledge.
Kolakowski, Leszek (1991) *Die Moderne auf der Anklagebank*, Zürich: Menessa Verlag.
Lambert, Yves (1999) 'Religion and Modernity as a New Axial Age: Secularization or New Religious Forms?', *Sociology of Religion*, vol. 60, no. 3, pp. 303–333.
Lane, Christopher (2011) *The Age of Doubt: Tracing the Roots of Our Religious Uncertainty*, New Haven, CT: Yale University Press.
Löwith, Karl (1967) *Weltgeschichte und Heilsgeschehen. Die theologischen Voraussetzungen der Geschichtsphilosophie*, 5. Aufl. Stuttgart: Kohlhammer.
Lyotard Jean-Francois (1984) *The Postmodern Condition: A Report on Knowledge*, Bennington, Geoff, and Massumi, Brian (trans.), Minneapolis: University of Minnesota Press.
Marcuse, Herbert (1964) *One-Dimensional Man: Studies in the Ideology of Advanced Industrial Society*, Boston: Beacon Press.
McGrath, Rita Gunther, and MacMillan, Ian (2000) *The Entrepreneurial Mindset: Strategies for Continuously Creating Opportunity in an Age of Uncertainty*, Boston, MA: Harvard Business School Press.
Monod, Jacques (1971) *Chance and Necessity*, New York: Alfred A. Knopf, Inc.
Niebuhr, Reinhold (1943) *The Nature and Destiny of Man. A Christian Interpretation*, vols. 1–2, New York: Scribner.
Ortega y Gasset, José (1957) *The Revolt of the Masses*, Carey, J.R. (trans.), New York: Norton.
Patocka, Jan (1985) *La crise du sens*, Brussels: Ousia.
Polányi, Karl (1944) *The Great Transformation*, New York: Farrar and Rinehart.
Russell, Bertrand (1929) *Marriage and Morals*, London: George Allen & Unwin.
Scheler, Max (1961) *Man's Place in Nature*, Boston: Beacon Press.
Unamuno y Jugo, Miguel de (1921) *The Agony of Christianity*, Loving, Pierre (trans.), New York: Payson & Clark.
Valéry, Paul (1924) 'La crise de l'esprit', in *Oeuvres 1–2*, Édition établie et annotée par Jean Hytier, Paris: Gallimard.
Voegelin, Eric (2000) *Order and History*, vols. 1–5, Columbia: University of Missouri Press.
Weinberg, Steven (1977) *The First Three Minutes: A Modern View of the Origin of the Universe*, New York: Basic Books.

16 The post-Euromaidan future for Europe

Ferenc Miszlivetz

Recent and dramatic events in Ukraine support the assumption that the fundamental crisis of democracy we face cannot be defined and confined by the boundaries of the nation state and national politics. Accordingly, the nation state cannot be considered the exclusive unit of analysis or framework for civic participation any longer. Furthermore, national governments prove to be increasingly less capable of delivering on their promises to their national constituencies, and do not have the capacity to defend, protect or support their societies vis-à-vis robust and uncontrolled global markets, environmental catastrophes, legal and illegal migration or organized international crime. As a consequence, people feel less and less safe in the world.

There is, therefore, much need for what is called regional and global governance. The weakness and ineffectiveness of international and global organizations is well known. The EU was seen as a model and solution for regional governance up until it, too, came under pressure from severe, multilevel and interdependent crises. Instead of creating new frames and enabling institutions, including civil societies at the regional and transnational level, the EU, by its very nature an elite-driven project, has undermined and emptied out national democracies at least since the outbreak of the financial crisis. Paradoxically, it has remained a magnet for outsiders, especially in its southern and eastern peripheries where people identify a better, more dignified life with 'Europe', as Ukraine's second revolution within a decade has proven. Ukrainians were protesting, marching and dying for three months against their corrupt, tyrannical and ineffective post-Soviet state, seeing in 'Europe' the antipode of their past and an alternative to their present and future.

Dying for Europe. What Europe?

The Tragedy of Central Europe, Milan Kundera's famous essay written in 1984, starts with an unforgettable scene. Seconds before the Russian tanks started firing artillery at the building of the Radio, the head of the Hungarian News Agency turned to the world public opinion with the dramatic words: 'We are going to die for Hungary and for Europe.' Kundera suggests that 'to die for one's country and for Europe' is a phrase that could not be thought in Moscow: 'It is precisely the phrase that could be thought in Budapest or Warsaw.' To the great surprise of the educated West, more than half a century after the Hungarian revolutions (which were seen and interpreted as insane or at the best heroic and romantic but hopeless), young Ukrainians were ready to sacrifice their lives under EU banners in order to drag their country away from the nightmare of post-Soviet tyranny and to embark on a path they identify as 'European'.

This is occurring at exactly the moment when the EU itself faces a severe, complex and unprecedented set of intertwining crises that has compelled leaders to express deep concern about the future of the European construction and integration. In moments of European despair, lack of self-confidence and defeatist forecasts preparations are being made for the upcoming European Parliamentary elections. During the last three months of their second post-Soviet revolution in ten years, Ukrainians proved to be better (at least more convinced and dedicated) 'Europeans' than EU citizens themselves. The blue EU flag with golden stars for the first time in its history became a symbol of heroic self-sacrifice for freedom and human dignity. Euromaidan – the square of Ukrainian independence – has witnessed its inauguration in human blood for a life worth living that can be summarized in one word: Europe.

This concise metaphor contains a complex meaning that reaches far beyond the geographic or legal scope of a supranational set of institutions and regulations, rights and duties guaranteed by confusing treaties and monitored by a faraway, unaccountable bureaucracy. As one of the demonstrators interviewed at Maidan explained: 'I don't want to go there. I want to build Europe here.' What is the secret of these six simple letters? Why does the name of a Phoenetian queen from ancient Greece still have such a mesmerizing effect on those who want desperately to change their lives for the better? Why is it that the vast majority of the 'deeply divided' Ukrainian society of 45 million expressed their pro-European sentiments at the time of Julia Tymoshenko's release from prison?

'Ukraine is Europe', declares a proud poster on the Euromaidan. 'Ukraine will always belong to Moscow', declares Vaclav Klaus, a former president of the Czech Republic, one of the most Euroskeptic politicians of the former Soviet bloc countries. These two, mutually exclusive statements together provide the complexity of the post-1989 semi-continent whose borders to the east are rather blurred and difficult to define not so much in geographical but rather in political, social and cultural terms. On the one hand, there are the proud material and post-material cosmopolitan aspirations and a thirst for dignity and well-being; on the other, we see the old post-colonial Eurocentric exclusivity and hierarchical mindset at work. The first combines the national and local with the cosmopolitan; the second excludes them in the name of an obsolete, hardly existing, less and less imaginable cultural-geographic unit. Two mutually exclusive worldviews and aspirations are colliding within the apparently benign and easy-to-catch concept. The first one is stretching the borders, the second is desperately trying to close and seal them. These two forces – mindsets, belief systems, aspirations – are together shaping the future of Europe embodied as political parties, open or hidden social networks, populist or racist movements or exclusive elite clubs.

The robust and unexpected outburst of Ukraine's pro-Europe, pro-dignity revolution has significantly stirred up the apathetic and inward-looking European political spectrum – forcing politicians and institutions such as the Commission and the European Parliament to speak out and even act in the name of democracy and European solidarity. It is as if Europe's heart has begun to beat faster and her long-hidden soul has begun to take corporal shape.

The pro-Europe revolution of Ukraine is not the first wake-up call that has come from the margins. European peripheries have been in motion for decades: first the classic then the velvet revolutions reshaped and reframed the path of European integration by undermining the bipolar logic of the Cold War system resulting in a series of unintended consequences, unfulfilled expectations and paradoxes without solutions. After a short decade of promising, but at the end unsuccessful rapprochement between Russia and the EU, Ukraine has found itself in a sandwiched position. The Orange Revolution of 2004 was a clear answer to Russia's attempt at regaining power over its former Soviet republic. After the bravado of the eastern enlargement the same year, the EU neglected its new eastern neighbor and proved to be unable to provide adequate structured legal, financial and political assistance for pro-democratic forces.

The weaknesses of the enlarged European Union unfolded further after the outbreak of the global financial and debt crisis. Instead of mitigating negative consequences and offering shelter to the weaker economies among its member states, due to the lack of a common economic policy, the southern periphery of the Eurozone remained exposed to debt accumulation and its unbearable social consequences. Old stereotypes about cultural differences between the North and South surfaced, adding further rifts to the stubbornly surviving East–West divide; the lack of de facto cross-border solidarity for appropriate crisis management was revealed.

As a consequence of indetermination, the lack of 'politique finalité' and consequently clear strategic goals combined with policy implications, democracy is on the retreat in the EU at the national level instead of being built and institutionalized transnationally. After the collapse of the constitutional process, extreme and populist political parties and movements were on the rise. Inward-looking political actors and discourses started to dominate public life. A strange version of European neo-nationalism has been on the rise. Nobody talks anymore about Europe as the leader of the twenty-first century. The European dream was taken off the agenda of international seminars. From the often emphasized imagined position of a global leader, the EU shrank into a rather insignificant regional power category. It seemed to be in its weakest form when Putin started to gamble on Ukraine, holding it back from signing an associated partner's status in November 2013. From a Russian geopolitical angle, it seemed like a perfect moment to win a geopolitical game and strengthen the position of Russia on the road towards the dominating Euro-Asia power. Indeed, the timing looked perfect, the calculation well thought over – except for one simple factor: the determination, aspiration and willpower of Ukrainian civil society was missing from the picture. This negligence is a clear legacy of the Cold War and proof of the survival of the 'great power' chessboard logic: big players of power games, leaders of ex-superpowers are still unable and unwilling to calculate with the courage, perseverance, solidarity and the networking capacity of concerned civil society. Social and human values, aspirations for a dignified life and better life chances are unimportant factors for this mindset.

Deeper integration or collapse

After a period of denial, some European politicians became rather outspoken about the complex and increasingly political and socio-psychological nature of crisis. On 15 June 2012, a group of foreign ministers from Austria, Belgium, Denmark, Italy, Germany, Luxemburg, the Netherlands, Portugal and Spain issued a report with the telling title 'The Time for a Debate on the Future of Europe is Now'. Their analysis can be seen as an attempt at self-reflection and redefinition of European potential global role:

> In this era of globalization, the distribution of power in the world is shifting. New political and economic global players are gaining more influence. In dealing with these new powerhouses, we Europeans will only be able to uphold our values and pursue our interests effectively if we pool our strengths much more both internally and in dealings with the outside world.... We face the historic task of enabling Europe to become a global player.
> (Foreign Ministers' Group on the Future of Europe 2012)

The Future of Europe Group interprets the crisis as a wake-up call, and that a clear definition of future goals will help to solve immediate challenges: 'We need to provide a sense of direction and of Europe's purpose before it is too late. *What we are ultimately talking about is making the European Union and the Euro irreversible.*' The report recognizes that global transformation has arrived at a critical stage and started to produce formidable social, economic, ecological, security and consequently political consequences.

If the EU wants to be a global player, it also needs new enabling institutions legitimizing these aspirations. For the protection of external borders and other security reasons, a European Border Police and maybe even a European Army seem to be necessary. In the medium run, a European visa should replace national visas. On the institutional level, the EU needs fundamental reforms in order to make decision making fast and efficient and to increase its cohesion and capacity for action as well as better coordination between its institutions. All of these fundamental reforms need stronger democratic legitimacy which includes the improvement of democratic visibility. The direct election of the Commission President will be a step towards this goal.

The new wake-up call coming from eastern neighborhoods gave all of those suggestions to radical reforms an utmost actuality and urgency. Radoslaw Sikorski, Polish Foreign Minister, a leading member of the 'Future of Europe Group' of 11 foreign ministers used heavy words when arguing in favor of change of

EU institutions: 'If we are not willing to risk a partial dismantling of the EU, then the choice becomes as stark as can be in the lives of federations: deeper integration or collapse.'

The 'ever closer union' and the return of the nation state: towards a German Europe?

Against all the odds and perils of the multiple crises of the EU, the debate about the original mission of European integration seems to be gaining new momentum. Vicky Pryce raised the question about the meaning of an often cited sentence from the preamble of the Treaty of Rome that became an emptied out EU slogan: creating an 'ever closer Union among the peoples of Europe'. The question today applies to the quality of the integration processes of the entire continent and even beyond. Using the catch phrase of an 'ever closer union among the peoples of Europe' today opens up the Pandora's box of contradicting interpretations and unending debates and mutual misunderstandings thanks to the opaqueness of the project. Given this lack of clarity, one cannot identify clear cut methods and means to achieve it.

Although the dispute goes back to the very beginning of the integration process, it gained new impetus after the robust, fundamental but most importantly unexpected transformations triggered by the fall of the Berlin Wall and the collapse of communist dictatorships and authoritarian regimes in East Central Europe and the Soviet Union. More importantly, the very concept and scope of Europe was crying for re-interpretation after the demolition of the Iron Curtain. Political thinking, fantasy (or rather the lack of it) and, as a consequence, strategies for action were heavily embedded in and determined by the simplifying bipolar logic of the Cold War at the time of the Rome Treaty and the aftermath of the 1956 Revolution in Hungary. This seemingly 'iron' – and for many eternal – paradigm has fallen to pieces and has been fading away from politically correct European discourse since the outbreak of the velvet revolutions.

The velvet revolutions, a massive emergence of cross-border civil society networking and solidarity, heralded a new epoch both globally and more eminently in Europe and the former Soviet Union. As the first wake-up call, 1989/1991 started a completely new epoch in the history of European integration. From the late 1950s to the mid-1980s, the founding fathers had to deal with far less complexity and diversity in the integration process, which gave them, as well as analysts, the impression that integration can rely endlessly upon endogenous factors and energies. But in the new epoch of post-1989/1991 eastern enlargement, deepening and extending integration meant facing and dealing with growing uncertainties and unintended results. Beneath the shiny surface of the ambitious and grandiose single market, unpredictable and uncontrollable social and political actors and movements started to emerge, carving out their own stakes under the new rising sun of Brussels.

The time for cheering about a common European home did not last very long: the optimistic dialectics of 'unity in diversity' became an ambiguous aspiration for both old and new Europeans and has led to a clear message of the double 'no' in 2005. The elite-driven Big Bang eastern enlargement and constitutional convent opened the door for skepticism, ambiguity, decreasing trust in EU institutions and a shrinking solidarity among the peoples of Europe. The recent eruption of the global crises hit an institutionally mistrusted, financially imbalanced, socially polarized and politically disintegrating European Union. The citizens of the first transnational organization with citizenship do not feel united and the twentieth anniversary of European citizenship in 2013 passed almost completely unnoticed by the larger public. The grandiose language of Europeanization with its optimistic slogans became self-mockery or empty talk at best.

A clear re-emergence of national discourse and identity politics paralleled the fading of Euro-optimism. The revival of the nation state is a natural result of the failures of the post-1989 integration process that includes the lack of understanding of cataclysmic and complex changes, the missed opportunity to become a new, responsible and respected global leader, the incapability to install democracy on the supranational level and creating a real frame for identification for European citizens. The EU seen from this re-emerging national perspective remained a non-democracy superimposing rules, legal regulations and economic and financial policies upon full-fledged democracies.

After the permissive consensus of the 1960s and 1970s, the process and methods of integration were silently broken. Bilateralism took the momentum and a new/old hierarchy of European member (nation) states became more virulent and obvious. The politically modest, militarily reserved, but economically increasingly mightier Germany started to act as *primus inter pares* and unilaterally decided the fate of other countries. Instead of a European *demos* with a unique constitution and unprecedented shared sovereignty, as Ulrich Beck coined recently, a 'German Europe' started to assert itself.

The mirage of the nation state as an old/new savior of 'peoples' hides deep divisions: ethnic, cultural and linguistic cleavages that originated at its very inception and that were often created by external forces. In other words, the boundaries of 'nations', 'societies' and 'states' almost never coincide. As the examples of contemporary Scotland vs Great Britain, Catalonia vs Spain, 'Padania' vs Italy and especially Sicily, Transylvania vs Romania, or Belgium itself, the hard core of 'Europe' together with its peripheries demonstrate crystal clear that the 'modern European nation state', an artefact of eighteenth to twentieth century European history and capitalist development, could never be the magic bullet or an exclusive solution that offered the socio-psychological comfort of belonging vis-à-vis uncontrollable market forces and other negative consequences of globalization. Without any democratically institutionalized transnational regulatory mechanisms and decision-making processes they would rather be the source of further problems – if not an unstoppable chain of conflicts and chaos – than socially acceptable solutions and a base for social, political and economic sustainability.

German Europe vs new citizenship

Ulrich Beck in his recent book paints a frightening picture of 'German Europe' based on German euro-nationalism and a new German hysteria called stability guaranteed by austerity policy. Beck promotes a bottom-up Europe: a 'Europe of the citizen'. He is right in general terms that Europe could be reinvigorated if ordinary Europeans acted on their own behalf. The question is, how do we get there? Everyday European citizens of different regions in the North and South, East and West are either ignorant about each other or, if they are not, they feel mostly alien, envious, frustrated and threatened by 'others'.

In better cases, citizens from peripheries are eager to find jobs as *Gastarbeiter* in core countries and if they succeed they adjust as much as possible to stay there. Interested primarily in survival, they are far from becoming engaged in rebuilding Europe from the bottom up; and they are the luckier groups of losers of the fake or weak social integration. The others, the unemployed millions or those who live in permanent existential fear, outrage and anxiety, are not going to attend seminars and workshops about creating the new European citizen – they are rather the anti-citizens of Europe.

The ideological foundation of a German Europe is that of the modern European nation state and its international framework, the Westphahlian system. This system contains all of the inherent contradictions and tensions which remain subtle and manageable during relatively stable periods, but become a primary source of nationalistic fervor, populist and extremist movements, scapegoating and mutual exclusion in times of severe and prolonged crises. Our time is such a turbulent period and the EU, whose original function was to offer a new model vis-à-vis the chaos of the Westphalian system, is itself in chaos. Instead of offering common solutions and joint multilateral efforts to mitigate severe financial, economic and social pain, its strongest member states reintroduced bilateral negotiations and agreements with third partners in order to secure their national energy supply while criticizing smaller member states if they try to follow their example. Instead of burden sharing, the EU under German leadership introduced methods of punishment called 'austerity measures'. So we should not really be amazed about the escalation of scapegoating, mutual accusations, exclusion and national inwardlookingness.

The entire construction and mission of the EU envisioned and targeted the creation of a new sort of democratic polity, a set of transnational institutions, regulations and citizens' rights, in order to mitigate, manage and finally articulate these traditional social-cultural and political tensions within its expanding boundaries. What might be surprising and what was revealed by the past years of the crisis was how weak and socially empty and insensitive these institutions and regulations are, and how little de facto solidarity remains among European citizens belonging to economically and culturally different regions in times of real hardship and severe existential troubles.

Citizenship, social contract and the true political authority

European construction can be continued if Europe finds a new method and is able to step out from the double trap of neo-liberal economic policies and right wing populism. Debating, deliberating and identifying the new European public good might conclude in a new politics of de facto solidarity. But this has to be seen clearly: the social contract upon which democratic decision making is built is broken or seriously damaged in most member states of the EU. At the same time, it does not exist on the EU level. To recover Europe from the present social, political and economic turmoil, new social contracts are needed on all levels of governance. For this to happen, a broad consensus is needed within and among European societies about the European project. Amidst the present apathy, skepticism, frustration and inward-looking tendencies, the chances for such a broad social and political agreement are slim in the short run. But for exactly the same reasons, the politicization of the European public space is inevitable. In the vortex of the downward spiral, alternatives are popping up. Europe arrived at its political moment and has to pull together its energies and act after the second wake-up call. It can no longer be disguised that, alongside national democracies, the left has emptied out as well. Its mainstream being entrapped in neo-liberalism, it lacks a credible agenda. If it falls back to the old state-socialist, distributive paradigm, its revival will not last very long. If it opens up towards other progressive groups and new initiatives – including those social movements or subterranean networks who deliberately chose to stay outside the 'system' – it will enhance the chances for renewal and getting rid of old hierarchical and vertical power structures as well as obsolete dogmas and attitudes towards society and social change. In a sense, the global crisis and especially the crisis of Europe demands new visions and thus offers a great chance for progressive forces to come out of their trenches and deadlocks.

This alternative is not yet given and it will not occur as a natural side effect of the crisis. It needs political will, conscious intellectual efforts, courage and imagination, which presuppose self-reflection. New coalition building would have a significant impact on public discourse and political culture. It could prove the willingness of different old and new, post-modern, post-national players to take responsibility in a social sense and on a social scale both on national and on supranational levels. In the spirit of the founding fathers like Spinelli and Spaak, a broader coalition of democratic post-nationalist political forces is inevitable as it is evident from recent calls and memorandums of the European Movement and other pro-European organizations. The lingering questions of this New European Political Movement is if, when and how these different fragments, isolated parties, marginalized, self-entrenched, subterranean networks can emerge and create a political platform in the sense of a European People's Assembly.

There are no clear answers to these questions. There are no guarantees that this will happen at all and, if it happens, that it will be successful. Grasping a political moment also means taking risks; creating long-lasting and effective new coalitions requires self-limitation and getting rid of the narcissism and self-justification of political fragments, social movements and charismatic individuals. As many analysts of the deepening crisis and downward spiral of integration suggest, democracy itself needs renewal or rather rebirth. As an outcome of the present global and European turmoil, the processes of fundamental social, political and economic transformations will accelerate. At the end of this robust transformation, we might have more, but possibly also less, democracy. A European renewal of regional transnational democratization would certainly push the pendulum of global democratization.

Building efficient and long-lasting institutions, marked by a high level of public trust, needs special methods which correspond to the logic of a given historic period's techno-economic paradigm and legal-political regulations, and needs to be adjustable both to the conditions of the international system and that of the expectations of stakeholder participants. Looking at the not-so-short history of the European integration, one can observe that its first period ended with 1989. The collapse of the bipolar logic of the political and military world system and a transformation process began, which concluded in 2004/2005 with Big Bang eastern enlargement and, symbolically enough, immediately after that the collapse of the process of European constitutionalization by the double 'no' votes in Holland and France. During the third – rather short – period, the process of integration or rather construction has reached a critical point where its previously and partly hidden contradictions and weaknesses – first of all, the exhaustion of the community method – have become clear.

The crisis of the EU developed from a fiscal debt crisis to the crisis of the Eurozone and soon thereafter into a complex social and political crisis whose end and consequences are not yet foreseeable. The global financial and economic crisis hit the EU in a moment of rapidly increasing diversification, disorientation and regional disparities when its polarizing single market was not counterbalanced and coupled with common or coordinated economic policies. Neither was it extended by de facto solidarity from its center towards its periphery. Lacking legitimate and accountable supranational governance, good leadership and crisis management capabilities, the EU has embarked on a self-destructive phase.

Any further attempt and coordinated aspiration to continue the European construction will depend on the capability of European democracies and social economic and political actors to reach a new consensus about the European public good, redefining the scope, the speed and the method of integration. The European construction has arrived at a turning point. Europe is a complex system that requires the identification of new ways and methods, complex thinking, understanding and analysis. Oversimplified, one-sided and superficial 'solutions', such as further austerity measures, treaty amendments or introducing new fiscal policies in themselves, without taking into account side effects and interdependencies, will not be able to serve as real therapies but might instead further exacerbate and speed up the already dangerously fast downward spiral.

Two assumptions need to be taken seriously: (1) There is nothing 'natural' about the European construction; neither markets nor individual nation states are able to provide automatic solutions; (2) the EU does not exist and evolve in a vacuum; the golden times of nested integration are over. The new paradigm – or 'development model', in Delors' words – requires the understanding of increased interdependence and the acceptance of the growing uncertainties of our age. Alternatives can be worked out and legitimated by the major players and stakeholders of the European project only in open social debates and deliberations.

Transgressing national boundaries, as many social movements or waves of migrants do, or demanding similar rights and conditions of well-being, security and human dignity with neighboring countries (as is the case in Ukraine), signal the unrestrained momentum for the regionalization and globalization of democracy and participation. These new orientations, demands and aspirations need institutional and instrumental responses, legitimation and recognition on the part of major players at all levels. Reality is always far ahead of existing rules, legal regulations and the bureaucratic imagination during periods of fundamental transformation. This time the new, emerging realities in the EU's southern and eastern neighborhoods serve as severe provocations for a thorough rethinking of visions, policies and achievements in order to be able to act and react efficiently and in time.

A new consensus needs to be brokered through the confrontation and management of positive, concrete examples. The crisis of Ukraine can serve as such a progressive case if all of the major players (protestors and their opponents, political representatives, the EU, Russia and the US) understand their interdependent responsibilities to set up new rules and frames. What is clear and unique in this immediate and striking case is a new configuration and potential synergy for local, national, regional and global needs and aspirations for governance and civic participation.

Bibliography

Barber, Benjamin (2003) *Fear's Empire; War, Terrorism and Democracy*, New York: W.W. Norton.
Bauman, Zygmunt (2004) *Europe, an Unfinished Adventure*, Cambridge: Polity Press.
Beck, Ulrich (2013) *German Europe*, Cambridge: Polity Press.
Dempsey, Judy (2014) *What Ukraine's Crisis means for Europe*, February 17, Available: http://carnegieeurope.eu/strategiceurope.
Foreign Ministers' Group on the Future of Europe (2012) *The Time for a Debate on the Future of Europe is Now*, June 15, Available: http://euobserver.com/media/src/3f1d57b5e556a953646816f85eec29ab.pdf.
Habermas, Jürgen (2011) 'Europe's Post-democratic Era', *The Guardian*, November 10.
Habermas, Jürgen (2012) *The Crisis of the European Union*, Cambridge: Polity Press.
Hughes, Kirsty (2011) 'EU Democracy in Crisis', *OpenDemocracy*, January 16.
Jones, E. (2011) 'No Four Leaves Cover for Europe', *ALDE Europe*, December.
Kundera, M. (1984) 'The Tragedy of Central Europe', *New York Review of Books*, vol. 31, no. 7, pp. 33–38.
Kurlantzik, Joshua (2013) *Democracy in Retreat. The Revolt of the Middle Class and the Worldwide Decline of Representative Government*, New Haven and London: Yale University Press.

Laqueur, W. (2012) *After the Fall. The End of the European Dream and the Decline of a Continent*, New York: Macmillan.
Lyne, Sir Roderic (2014) *Ukraine Crisis Highlights a Critical Gap in European Security*, February 28, Available: www.chathamhouse.org.
Miszlivetz, Ferenc (2012) 'The Multiple Crisis of Europe', *Délkelet-Európa – Southeast Europe International Relations Quarterly*, vol. 3, no. 1, pp. 1–7.
Monnet, Jean (1978) *Memoirs*, New York: Doubleday.
Overholt, W. (2012) 'The Price for German Leadership', *International Economy*, Winter.
Palmer, John (2012) 'EU Voters May Finally Be Given Some Real Choices', *Open Democracy*, 22 March.
Rifkin, Jeremy (2004) *The European Dream*, New York: Jenny P. Tarcher/Penguin.
Rogoff, Kenneth (2011) 'The End of Europe', *Time Magazine*, August.
Schmidt, V. (2006) *Democracy in Europe*, Oxford: Oxford University Press.
Schmitter, Philippe C. (2000) *How to Democratize the EU and Why Bother?* London, New York: Rowmen and Littlefield.

Index

Page numbers in *italics* denote tables, those in **bold** denote figures.

Ackerman, Bruce 36–7, 38–9, 43
Amato, Giuliano 48
Anderson, Christopher J. 95
anti-politics 12–13
Armstrong, Karen 239
art institutions 214
Art of Not Being Governed, The (Scott) 13–14
Artner, Annamaria xvii, 139–51
asset stripping 14
Austen, Steve xvii, 207–20
austerity policies 48, 49, 61, 73, 80, 152–9, 192, 213; German influence on 168–9; Greece 153
Austria 37, 48

bailouts 44–5, 46, 84; Greece 79, 85; no bailout rule 126, 131
Bakhtin, Mikhail 9, 10
balance of payments 74
balance of trade 143–4, **144**
Bank Union 133
banks: creation of a banking resolution authority 79; European Banking Authority (EBA) 79, 87; European Central Bank (ECB) 77, 81–2, 87, 116, 131, 231–2; relationship between sovereign debt crisis and bank industry crisis 78; weakness of European banking system 80
Banning, L. 40
Barnier, Michel 196
Barroso, Jose Manuel 36, 38, 45
Baudelaire, C. 240
Bauman, Zygmunt 170, 174
Beard, Charles 40
Beck, Ulrich 169, 243, 255

Bellamy, R. 38
Bennhold, Katrin 167
Berger, Peter 243
Berlin, Isaiah 13, 16
Berlusconi, Silvio 153–4, 157, 197
Bersani, Pierluigi 157
Bestor, A. 37
Between Two Ages: America's Role in the Technetronic Era (Brzezinski) 195
Bianchini, Stefano xvii, 160–78
'Blueprint for a deep and genuine economic and monetary union' (EC) 46–7
Bohle, Dorothee 102
bond, meaning of term 191–2
Böröcz, József xvii, 19–34
borrowing, as credit 190–2
Bosnia-Herzegovena 173
Boundary Commission (UK) 199–200
Bowley, Graham 167
Bretton Woods system 42, 58, 116, 127
Brzezinski, Zbigniew 195, 243
budget constraints 82–4, 88–9

Cameron, David 48, 218, 223
Campbell, Joseph 243
Camus, Albert 243
Canache, Damarys 95
capitalism 183; behaviour of 14; gestalt perception of 193; globalized finance capitalism 184; market-generated autonomous capital 14–15; and the protestant ethic 193–5; unregulated capitalism 62
Castiglione, D. 38, 48
Central Europe 2, 16, 99, 111n11, 121, 129, 253

Centre for Economic Policy Research, Bocconi University 168
Centre for European Studies 166–7
Charter on Fundamental Rights 39, 228, 230
Chicago school 165
China 11, 23, 25, 199
citizenship: citizens' appeals against national government or EU measures 216–17; citizenship education programmes 218–19; cultural citizenship 214–15; European citizenship 213–14, 219, 227, 230–1; individual nature of 214; transnational definition 207; weakening of equality 15
civil rights 216–17
Cohen, Richard 243
Cohn-Bendit, Daniel 36, 211
Coinage Act (US) 41
Collapse (Diamond) 56
collective rights 214–15
common currency *see* monetary union
Commonwealth of Independent States 30
communism 12–13, 14; collapse of 15, 16, 253
competitiveness 148–9
constituencies 199–200
Constitution for Europe 189, 190, 196–7, 227
constitutional moments 35–52; defining the role of the nation (New Deal) 43–5; definition and characteristics 37–9; federalism as a step towards a genuine economic and political union 45–8; US constitutional moments compared with EU 39–43; view of EU legal framework as a developing constitution 39
Copenhagen criteria 229
corruption 103, 156
cosmos 245
Council of Europe 225, 234
'Crazy Vision of Europe, A' (article) 36
'creative response of human ingenuity' 56
'Crisis of Democracy, The' (report) 195
Croatia 171, 172
cross-border financial transactions 77
Crowell, E. 194
Csaba, László 102, 120
Csepeli, György 97
culture 212–13; cultural citizenship 214–15; interculturality 173–4
currency 118; control of money supply 120; currency board 120; exchange rate stabilisation 119

Darvas, Zsolt 102
debt: association with guilt 190–2; increase due to 2008 crisis 123, 145–6, 148, **148**; public and private debt trends 100–2, **100, 101,** 102; relationship between institutional trust and indebtedness in Eastern and Central Europe 99–100, **99**; sovereign debt 49, 54, 59–60, 73, 74, 77–8, 77–9, 78, 84–5, 122, 123–4, 224, 231
Declaration on Democracy 1978 226
Delors, Jacques 157
Delpa, J. 85–6
democracy 7, 13, 48, 233–4, 251, 257; Constitution for Europe 196–7; crisis of European democracy 185–7; dual democracy 213; formal and effective democracy 199–200; and global financial crisis 59–60; hard and soft power 195–6; lessons from the New Deal 199–203; and subterranean politics 62–4; theories of Mill and Rousseau 197–8
Democracy Index (Economist) 155
democratic dissatisfaction 93–114; distrust and the dominance of short-term policies in Hungary 103, **104**; early phase of Hungarian transition 104–6; governance without trust in Hungary 107–8; institutional trust and indebtedness in Eastern and Central Europe 99–100, **99**; institutional trust and indebtedness in the European Union 98–102; measuring political support 94–5; political consequence of distrust in Hungary 108–9; public and private debt trends 100–2, **100, 101, 102**; public trust and decision-making 95–8; satisfaction with democracy and fiscal balance 98–9, **99**; trust and satisfaction in the EU 2004–2011 **94**
denial 192
Denmark 156, 171
devaluation 122, 127, 141
Diamond, Jared 56
Die Zeit 36
Dinnerstein, D. 192
Douglas, Mary 10
Douthat, Ross 58, 59
Draghi, Mario 158

Eagleton, Terry 243
Eastern Europe 1, 2, 19, 25, 97, 99, 175, 185, 199

Easton, David 94
economic nationalism 167–9
Economist 35, 172
Einstein, Albert 245
elections 186
Eliot, T.S. 243
Elliott, Larry 58
Emerson, M. 127
Enlightenment 10, 15
environmental awareness 157
epistemological crises 7–8; characteristics of epistemological closure 8–9; liberal universalism 11–12
euro 36, 174, 182, 231–2; future of 133–4; stability of 121–2; *see also* European financial crisis; monetary union
Euro Plus Pact 130
Euro-sceptic parties 48
Eurobonds 79, 85–6, 89–90, 186
Euromaidan 249–59
Europe 2020 (growth plan) 89, 128
'Europe in the World: Crises and Responses: Navigating Europe's Future' (conference) 2
European Banking Authority (EBA) 79, 87
European Central Bank (ECB) 77, 81–2, 87, 116, 131, 231–2
European Citizens' Initiative (ECI) 231
European Coal and Steel Community 39, 210, 225, 226
European Commission, power over fiscal policy 83–4
European Convention for the Protection of Human Rights and Fundamental Freedoms 230
European Court of Justice 39, 83, 226
European Dream, The (Rifkin) 189
European financial crisis 1, 35, 44–5, 60–2, 76–80, 115–35, 183–5; balance of trade 143–4, **144**, **145**, **146**; balance of payments 145, **147**; blame and responsibility for 55–6; causes and diagnoses 61, 124–9; changes in member states' budgets 123; comparison with Yugoslav crisis 164–9; consolidation 58–9; contrasts between the New Deal and European responses to the 2008–2009 crisis 200; convertibility of national currencies 118; critical views of 58; decline of the gold standard 116; deterioration in competitiveness 148–9; devaluation 122, 127; disciplinary power of the markets 125; dysfunctional pattern of thinking 54–5; elimination of the possibility for exchange rate intervention 126–7; EMU as a cause 124–5; as an epistemological crisis 7–18; external balance 142; global financial crisis and democracy 59–60; ideological responses to 56–7; income balance 144, **147**; increasing development gap 149, **149**, **150**; increasing diversity of EU 128–9; indebtedness 123, 145–6, 148, **148**; inflation 116, 117, 118, 121–2, 142; irresponsible behaviour of national governments 125–6, 128, 133; lack of confidence in global economy 53, **54**; liquidity 116, 118; managing the crisis with post-Yugoslav instability 169–76; monetarism 116, 117–18; monetary framework of integration 118–20; multidimensional nature of 237–8; need for an independent central bank 126; need for changes in status and competences of the ECB 131; need for economic stimulation to be connected to structural modernisation 132–3; need for greater fiscal federalism 133–4; need for more efficient control of national budgets and better coordination of policies 130–1; need for new institutions and funds 131; and openness 8–9, 10; questions concerning the future of the Euro 133–4; reliability of state and market in organising Western democracy 7; role and importance of development and structural policies 128; share of trade of member countries 121; single market 121; solutions and perspectives 129–34; speculation 129; splitting, denial and projective identification 192; stabilisation policies and stability 116, 118, 131–2; stability of the Euro 121–2; sustainable growth based on competitiveness 117
European Financial Stability Facility (EFSF) 46, 131
European Financial Stability Mechanism (EFSM) 84, 89
European integration 26; already planned enlargements 27–8; closer union with US, effect of 28–30, **29**, 30–2; EU as a supra-state public authority 20; fusion of EU with Commonwealth of Independent States 30, **31**; global dominance and the geopolitics of alternative futures 24–6;

global economic weight 21–4, *21*, **22**, 25–6; monetary framework of integration 118–20; network-based strategy of distributed enforcement 19–20; no-further-enlargement strategy, implications of 26, **27**; reorganization of global governance after colonialism 20
European Left 155–7
European Redemption Fund (ERF) 86
European Social Model 187, 190
European Stability Mechanism (ESM) 37, 38, 45, 84–5, 89, 131
European Union (EU): absence of military conflicts since 1945 216, 217; closer union with US, effect of 28–30, **29**, 30–2; comparison with US 36; competing dynamics of neonationalism and integration 175–6; decision-making and democracy 60–1; and the democratic constitutional state framework 212; as a developing political entity 211–12; development of economic nationalism 167–9; economic inequalities of member states 25; effect of Ukraine crisis 250–2; enlargements 23, 24, 26, 27–8; European citizenship 213–14, 219, 227, 230–1; financial liberalization and market deregulation 183–4; freedom, notion of 219; fusion with Commonwealth of Independent States 30, **31**; global dominance and the geopolitics of alternative futures 24–6; global economic weight 21–4, *21*, **22**, 25–6; institutional separation of problem-solving and redistribution 49; lack of public discussion on change 64–5; limited absorption capacity 166–7, 171; as a model for regional governance 249; national concerns about citizens' freedom of movement 167, 170; need for a new method of European construction 255; need for deeper integration 252–3; no-further-enlargement strategy, implications of 26, **27**; question of finality 24; retreat of democracy 251; revival of the nation state 254, 255; secessionist discourse 48; shrinking solidarity 253–4; subterranean politics 62–4; as a supra-state public authority 20; view of legal framework as a developing constitution 39
evil 15–17
Exchange Rate Mechanism (ERM) 119

faith 56
Fanfani, Amintore 194
fascist, modern use of term 11
federalism 45–8, 74–5, 223; fiscal federalism 46–7, 80–1; fiscal federalism and centralization/decentralization 86–90; principles for a European model of fiscal federalism 81–6; United States of Europe concept 210–11
Federalist Papers, The 40
Felcsúti, Peter 132
Feldstein, M. 77
Fernandes, S. 85
Financial Integration in Europe (ECB) 77
Financial Times 36, 49
Finland 175
Fiscal Compact 60–1, 83, 88, 232–3
fiscal disunion 73–92, 87; autonomy of monetary policy from fiscal policy 81–2, 87; creation of a banking resolution authority 79; creation of Eurobonds 79, 85–6, 89–90; European financial crisis 76–80; federalism and centralization/decentralization 86–90; financial integration in the Eurozone 77–8; hard budget constraints 82–4, 88–9; interregional payments and international payments, risks of 74–6; limited transfer union 84–6, 89–90; national waste of European resources 88; principles for a European model of fiscal federalism 81–6; redemption fund proposal 86; relationship between sovereign debt crisis and bank industry crisis 78; weakness of European banking system 80
fiscal federalism 46–7, 80–1, 133–4; autonomy of monetary policy from fiscal policy 81–2, 87; and centralization/decentralization 86–90; hard budget constraints 82–4, 88–9; limited transfer union 84–6, 89–90; principles for a European model 81–6; redemption fund proposal 86
Fischer, Joschka 24, 35, 45, 48, 193
Foreign Ministers Group on the Future of Europe 252
France 46, 80, 158, 171
Frank, Thomas 56
free trade zones 218
freedom, notion of 219
Fukuyama, Francis 16

Gabriel, Sigmar 193

Galbraith, John K. 242
Gamson, William A. 94–5
Geary-Khamis Purchasing Power Parity 21
Genealogy of Morals (Nietzsche) 191
German Council of Economic Experts 86
Germany 35, 37, 46; bailouts 84; breach of stability pact's ceiling 126; criticism of response to European financial crisis 193; economic importance 80; *Grosse Koalition* 152; hegemony 48–9, 152–3, 189, 255; influence on EU austerity policies 168–9; perception of Greek bailouts 156; reluctance of Germany to support new Greek government 168; trade surplus 144, **146**, 155
gestalt psychology 190–1, 193
Gilding, Paul 55–6
Global Confidence Index survey 53, **54**
global economic weight 21–4, *21*, **22**, 25–6; already planned enlargements, effect of 27–8; closer union between EU and US, effect of 28–30, **29**, 30–2; fusion of EU with Commonwealth of Independent States 30, **31**; no-further-enlargement strategy, implications of 26, **27**
global integration 115
globalization 1, 167, 244; and democracy 59–60; and state erosion 13–14
gold standard 116, 127
'Goodbye, Federal Europe?' (article) 35
Grauwe, P. de 82
Greece 37, 38, 48, 133; austerity policies 153; bailouts 58–9, 79, 85; debts 46, 79; reluctance of Germany to support new government 168
Greenspan, Alan 57–8, 243
Grillo, Beppe 157–8
Győrffy, Dóra xvii, 93–114

Habermas, J. 63, 80
Hamilton, Alexander 40, 41, 81
Hankiss, Elemér xvii–xviii, 237–48
Hayek, F.A. 57
Hilbers, Paul 102
history of mankind 237–8; age of uncertainty 242–6; axial periods 239; behavioural culture 241–2, *241*; 'bubbles' of civilisation 243–4; decline of mankind 238; globalization 244; historical turning points 240–1, *240*; macro-historians 238; scientific revolution 245–6; secularisation 244; spiritual crisis 243; transition from modernity to post-modernism 239–42, *242*
Hoeksma, Jaap xviii, 213, 223–36
Hoffmann, Stanley 243
Holland, Stuart xviii, 189–206
Holocaust 11, 16
Holton, Robert 55, 57, 59
Homer-Dixon, Thomas 56
homogeneity 174, 212
Horioka, C. 77
Horkheimer, Max 243
Huhne, C. 127
Hungary 37, 100, 133; distrust and the dominance of short-term policies 103, **104**; early phase of transition 104–6; governance without trust 107–8; low employment rate 107–8; political consequence of distrust 108–9
Hurd, Ian 97
Husserl, Edmund 243
Hutton, Will 199

identities: collective identities 10–11, 16–17; Dutch identity 208; national cultural identity 212, 213; transformation 174–5
income balance 144, **147**
inflation 116, 117, 118, 121–2, 142, **143**
Inman, R.P. 47
insurance 87
interculturality 173–4
interest rates 85
International Herald Tribune 167
Internet 63
Ireland 133, 143, 197
Italy 37, 48; austerity policies 153–4; elections 2013 157; populism 158

Japan 25
Jaspers, Karl 239, 243
Jensen, Jody xviii, 1–3, 53–69
Judah, Tim 172

Kant, Immanuel 224, 228–9, 245
Kapteyn, Jos 225
Keynes, J.M. 197
Klein, Melanie 192
knowledge 208, 209
Kolakowski, Leszek 243
Kosovo 172
Kostyleva, Valentina 102
Kundera, Milan 249–50

Lambert, Yves 239

Lamy, Pascal 53
Latvia 102
Les fleurs du mal (Baudelaire) 240
Letta, Enrico 158
liberal consensus 8–9, 10, 13; and antipolitics 12–13; collective identities 10–11; enclave culture 10; liberal universalism 11–12, 16; 'politically correct' language 9; racism 9–10; redistributive injustice 17; return of evil 15–17; and state erosion 13–14; unreality 11
limited transfer union 84–6, 89–90
Lindbeck, Assar 195
liquidity 116
Lisbon Treaty 38, 43, 78–9, 81, 84, 166, 197, 213, 216, 227–8, 232, 233, 234–5
London School of Economics 62
Löwith, Karl 238
Luckmann, Thomas 243

Maastricht treaty *see* Treaty on the European Union 1992 (Maastricht treaty)
Macedonia 172
macro-historians 238
Maddison, Angus 21–4, 28–9
Magnette, Paul 223, 227
Mandelson, Peter 58
Manifest for Europe (Cohn-Bendit and Verhofstadt) 36
Marcuse, Herbert 243
markets 8, 55, 57, 59–60, 116, 120, 125, 140–1, 165
Marshall Plan 30, 208
Marx, Karl 15
McDougal Report 88–9
Menasse, Robert 65
Menéndez, A.J. 45
Merger Treaty 1965 226
Merkel, Angela 35, 36, 152, 153, 159, 168, 170, 189, 191, 213, 223
Mill, John Stuart 197–8
minimum wages 201
Miszlivetz, Ferenc xviii, 1–3, 249–59
modernism 239–42
monetarism 116
monetary union 35, 36, 41–2; as a cause of Euro crisis 124–5; opposition to 47–8; United States (US) 41; weaknesses 46; *see also* fiscal disunion
Monod, Jacques 243
monology 9, 10; moral monoism 16
Montani, Guido xviii, 73–92

Monti, Mario 154
Monti Report 79
moral legislation 11–12
Multiannual Financial Framework 2014–2020 86
Mundell, R.A. 36

nationalism 160, 173–4, 182; economic nationalism 167–9; neonationalism 174–5
neoliberalism 57, 60, 61, 165–6, 186
neonationalism 174–5
Netherlands 208, 218
'New Agreement for Promotion of European Recovery' 132
New Deal 43–5, 153; and democracy 199–203
New European Political Movement 257
New York Times 58
Newton, Isaac 245
Nicolaïdis, K. 48
Nietzsche, F. 191
North Atlantic Free Trade Agreement 28–9
Notre Europe 86

Oates, W.E. 45
Occupy! movements 1, 61
Offe, Claus 96
Ohnsorge-Szabó, László 107
'On Perpetual Peace' (Kant) 224
On Representative Government (Mill) 198
One Market Under God (Thomas) 56
optimum currency areas (OCA) 36, 74, 128, 140–1
Orbán, Viktor 108–9
Ortega y Gasset, José 243

Padoa-Schioppa, T. 121
Palánkai, Tibor xviii, 115–35
Patocka, Jan 243
Pelkmans, J. 127
Pianta, Mario 60, 61, 62, 64
Pickett, Kate 155
Polanyi, Karl 57
political support 94–5
political union 223; beyond a union of states 226; conclusion of treaties 232–3; Copenhagen criteria 229; current debate in the European Council 234; democratic control over the exercise of sovereignty 230, 233; EU citizenship 230–1; euro 231–2; failure of the EU as a state 227; limits on sovereignty 224–5; Lisbon Treaty 227–8; shared

political union *continued*
  sovereignty 228–9; Treaty on the European Union 1992 (Maastricht treaty) 227, 228; Westphalian system of international relations 224, 255
'politically correct' language 9
PolKorr 9, 12
populism 11, 12, 17, 158, 186
post-modernism 238, 239–42
power 195–6
production cycles 139–40
projective identification 192
protest 1, 61–2; subterranean politics 62–4
protestant ethic concept 193–5
Pryce, Vicky 253

qualified majority voting 196–7, 226
quantum physics 245

Rachman, G. 49
racism 9–10, 160, 170–1, 174, 175
Rampini, Federico xix, 152–9
rapture 56
rationality 7, 14, 15
Reaganomics 165
redemption bonds 191
Reform Treaty 35
religion 11, 173, 193–5
Religion and the Rise of Capitalism (Tawney) 193–4
Report on Public Credit to Congress (Hamilton) 41
retirement age 201
Richards, B. 192
Riekmann, Sonja Puntscher xviii, 35–52
Rifkin, Jeremy 189, 195
Robertson, H.M. 194
Romania 100
Rome, Treaty of 190, 225
Romhányi, Balázs 107
Roosevelt, F.D. 202
Rousseau, Denise M. 96
Rousseau, J.-J. 197–8
Rubinfield, D. 47
Rubio, E. 85
rule compliance 97
Rumsfeld, Donald H. 243
Russell, Bertrand 243
Russia 251–2

Sarkozy, Nicolas 153, 171
Scandinavia 155
Scharpf, F.W. 35, 36, 48, 49
Schengen treaty 170, 171, 174

Schmitter, Philippe C. xix, 65, 181–8
Schneider, M. 192
Schöpflin, György xix, 7–18
Schroeder, Gerhard 155–6
schuld 191, 193
Schuman, Robert 210, 212
scientific revolution 245–6
Scitovsky, Tibor 74–6
Scott, James C. 13–14
secularisation 244
Selznick, P. 202
Sen, Amartya 64–5
Serbia 172
Sidjanski, Dusan 223
Sikorski, Radoslaw 252–3
Singapore 25
Sinn, Hans-Werner 195
Snower, Denis 195
social responsibility 57
Soros, George 243
South Korea 25
sovereign debt *see* debt
sovereignty 14, 160, 167, 173–4, 175, 210, 216; democratic control of 230, 233; limits on 224–5; shared sovereignty 228–9; Westphalian concept of 224
Spaak Report 190
speculation 129
splitting 192
stability 116
Stability and Growth Pact 38, 46, 78, 83, 98, 130, 189
Stability, Coordination and Governance, Treaty on 83
Standard & Poors 190
state, the 13–15; erosion by globalization 13–14; market-generated autonomous capital 14–15
subterranean politics 62–4
Sunstein, C.R. 43
sustainable growth 117, 157
swarm intelligence 63
Sweden 155, 156

Tawney, Richard 193–4
taxation 14, 156, 184
Tennessee Valley Authority
Thatcher, Margaret 198
Thatcherism 165
'Time for a Debate on the Future of Europe is Now, The' (Foreign Ministers' Group on the Future of Europe) 252
"Towards a Genuine Economic and Monetary Union" (Van Rompuy) 82

Towards a Genuine EMU (report) 234
trade unions 128, 186, 195, 201
trading 57
Tragedy of Central Europe, The (Kundera) 249–50
Treaty on Stability, Coordination and Governance in the Economic and Monetary Union (Fiscal Compact) 38, 60–1, 83, 88, 232–3
Treaty on the European Union 1992 (Maastricht treaty) 35, 39, 73, 81, 212–13, 227, 228, 231, 232, 234
Treaty on the Functioning of the European Union (TFEU) 38, 46, 228, 232
True Finns 175
trust 38, 56, 93–4, **94**; definition 96; distinction between particular and general trust 96; distrust and the dominance of short-term policies in Hungary 103, **104**; early phase of Hungarian transition 104–6; governance without trust in Hungary 107–8; institutional trust and indebtedness in the European Union 98–102; measuring political support 94–5; political consequence of distrust in Hungary 108–9; relationship with decision-making 95–8; rule compliance 97
TVA and the Grass Roots (Selznick) 202
'two pack' resolution (13 June 2012) 83–4

Ukraine 53, 249, 250–2, 258
Unamuno y Jugo, Miguel de 243
unipolar movement 10
United Kingdom (UK) 37, 199–200
United Nations 224–5
United States of Europe concept 210–11
United States (US): bailouts 44–5; block grants 44; closer union with EU, effect of 28–30, **29**, 30–2; common currency 141–2; comparison with EU 36; constitutional moments 39–43; Court-Packing Plan 43; creation of a financial system 41, 78; federal government 40; financial crises 41; fiscal powers for Congress 40; interest rates 85; as a model of fiscal federalism 80–1; monetary union 41; New Deal era 43–5, 153, 199–203; public discourse on Europe 154; secession of 11 states 1860–1861 42–3
universalism 10, 11; bounded universalism 17; collective identities as an impediment to 16–17; liberal universalism 11–12, 16

unreality 11
Uslaner, Eric 96
USSR 22, **22**, 23, **27**, **29**, 31, 214

Valéry, Paul 243
van der Pijl, Kees 31
Van Rompuy, Herman 211, 223
velvet revolutions 253
Verhofstadt, Guy 36, 211
Véron, N. 80
Viner, Jacob 194
Von Clausewitz, C. 216, 217
von Weizsäcker, J. 85–6
voting 186, 198, 218; proportional representation 198, 199; qualified majority voting 196–7, 226; transferable vote 199

Wagner, Alexander F. 95
Walker, N. 39
war 216, 224, 225
Washington consensus 165
We the People! Transformations (Ackerman) 38–9
Weber, Max 193–5, 203, 239
Weinberg, Steven 245
Westphalian logic 24
Westphalian system of international relations 224, 255
What is the European Union? (Magnette) 223
Wheare, K.C. 73, 87
Whittington, K.E. 37–8, 44
Wilkinson, Richard 155
working time 201
World Bank 55
World Economic Forum Summit, Dubai 53
Wydra, Doris xix, 35–52

xenophobia 160, 167, 170–1, 174, 175

Yugoslavia 16; comparison with EU financial crisis 164–9; influence of religions on nationalist arguments 173; international relations in the post-Yugoslav space 172–3; notion of 'Yugosphere' 172; post-Yugoslav political elites' support for EU accession 172; self-management 165
Yugoslav crisis 1980–1987 161–4

eBooks
from Taylor & Francis

Helping you to choose the right eBooks for your Library

Add to your library's digital collection today with Taylor & Francis eBooks. We have over 45,000 eBooks in the Humanities, Social Sciences, Behavioural Sciences, Built Environment and Law, from leading imprints, including Routledge, Focal Press and Psychology Press.

Choose from a range of subject packages or create your own!

Benefits for you
- Free MARC records
- COUNTER-compliant usage statistics
- Flexible purchase and pricing options
- 70% approx of our eBooks are now DRM-free.

Benefits for your user
- Off-site, anytime access via Athens or referring URL
- Print or copy pages or chapters
- Full content search
- Bookmark, highlight and annotate text
- Access to thousands of pages of quality research at the click of a button.

ORDER YOUR FREE INSTITUTIONAL TRIAL TODAY

Free Trials Available

We offer free trials to qualifying academic, corporate and government customers.

eCollections

Choose from 20 different subject eCollections, including:

- Asian Studies
- Economics
- Health Studies
- Law
- Middle East Studies

eFocus

We have 16 cutting-edge interdisciplinary collections, including:

- Development Studies
- The Environment
- Islam
- Korea
- Urban Studies

For more information, pricing enquiries or to order a free trial, please contact your local sales team:

UK/Rest of World: **online.sales@tandf.co.uk**
USA/Canada/Latin America: **e-reference@taylorandfrancis.com**
East/Southeast Asia: **martin.jack@tandf.com.sg**
India: **journalsales@tandfindia.com**

www.tandfebooks.com